Status of Peasants and Monks in British India

Status of Peasants and Monks in British India

Suraj Vashishisth

CYBER TECH PUBLICATIONS
4264/3, Ansari Road, Daryaganj, New Delhi-110002 (India)
Ph.: 011-23244078, 011-43559448 Fax: 011-23280028
E-Mail: cyberpublicationsdelhi@yahoo.com
Website: www.cybertechpublications.com

STATUS OF PEASANTS AND MONKS IN BRITISH INDIA

Suraj Vashishth

First Edition 2010

Published by : Asian Offset Printers

G.S. Rawat for **Cyber Tech Publications**
4264/3, Ansari Road, Daryaganj, New Delhi-110002 (India)
Ph.: 011-23244078, 011-43559448 Fax: 011-23280028
E-Mail: cyberpublicationsdelhi@yahoo.com
Website: www.cybertechpublications.com

Preface

According to strict social science definitions, colonial India was a peasant society. By far the vast majority of the population of the subcontinent lived in villages, and well over half the working population was engaged directly in agriculture. These villages were not isolated communities: the urban population was small by comparison but substantial, and urban magnates maintained important social, economic, and political ties to the countryside to secure the steady stream of agricultural goods that sustained city life. The state was organized into territorial provinces that transcended lines of caste and clan and whose complex bureaucratic dimensions reflected the agrarian revenue potential. Clear cultural, social, economic, and political distinctions could be and were made between town and country. Most importantly, the typical unit of production was the family household, which may or may not have owned the land upon which it worked but, regardless, directed its combined labor to the cultivation of crops.

A Monk is a person who practices religious asceticism, the conditioning of mind and body in favor of the spirit, and does so living either alone or with any number of like-minded people, whilst always maintaining some degree of physical separation from those not sharing the same purpose. A peasant is an agricultural worker who subsists by working a small plot of ground. There were free and unfree peasants. Free peasants could leave the manor as they wished. Unfree peasants had to buy their way out of the manor by paying their lord. During the British period the Monks and Peasants faced hard times. The book is an outcome of serious efforts on part of the author to walk into the existing conditions of Peasants and Monks during British Period. The book also lightens the policies followed by the Britishers towards them. It is a landmark work by the author in the respected field. Worth reading by students, teachers, researchers and scholars

— *Author*

CONTENTS

1

Introduction and History

According to strict social science definitions, colonial India was a peasant society. By far the vast majority of the population of the subcontinent lived in villages, and well over half the working population was engaged directly in agriculture. These villages were not isolated communities: the urban population was small by comparison but substantial, and urban magnates maintained important social, economic, and political ties to the countryside to secure the steady stream of agricultural goods that sustained city life.

The state was organized into territorial provinces that transcended lines of caste and clan and whose complex bureaucratic dimensions reflected the agrarian revenue potential. Clear cultural, social, economic, and political distinctions could be and were made between town and country. Most importantly, the typical unit of production was the family household, which may or may not have owned the land upon which it worked but, regardless, directed its combined labor to the cultivation of crops. Colonial India also had a history of significant religious variety.

Indeed, few visitors to the subcontinent over the last twenty-five centuries-from Alexander to al-Biruni to Attenborough-have failed to make note of this fact. Fewer still have failed to remark upon the vast numbers of holy men who wander the subcontinent, reside in its villages, towns, and cities (often near shrines) and throng its sacred places. These holy men, known generically as sadhus (Hindu) and fakirs (Muslim), can be described as monks inasmuch as they belong to one of many

Indian monastic traditions of social detachment and spiritual discipline. As in the European tradition, however, monasticism in India encompasses a wide variety of religious experience. While frequent pilgrimage, alms, and tests of physical endurance are and have long been important aspects of the lives of many Indian monks, Indian monasticism cannot be reduced to itinerancy, begging, and asceticism. Many monks are and have long been devoted to careful study and spiritual contemplation, conducted entirely within the walls of a sanctuary in an attempt to create a paradise on earth. Still others were expert in the arts and science of warfare.

Though the institutionalized forms of charity-such as the creation of hospitals-common to western monasticism have not been nearly so prominent in India, many Indian monks were respected as able healers, and service (seva) remains a central ideal of most Indian religious traditions. Indeed, the ritual removal of Indian monks from "worldly" concerns has long presaged (and was preparatory to) their active engagement in the world, whether conducted from a religious center or as part of an itinerant or soldiering life-style.

Finally, Indian monks come from all sections of society, including the peasantry, though the degree to which monastic orders recruited from the ranks of the low-born in rural society (whether peasants or artisans) varied. However, at least one major monastic community-the Ramanandis, who look to Ramanand of fourteenth-century Banaras for religious inspiration-has long been dedicated to the recruitment of novices (both male and, to a lesser degree, female) from the entire social spectrum. Understanding how this Ramanandi recruitment philosophy has worked in historical practice, particularly during the colonial era, is one of the aims of this book.

Indian peasants and monks did not live in social and religious isolation, from the world or from each other. Indeed, the lives of peasants and monks in colonial India were (and are) intricately intertwined: monks depended on peasants for agrarian labor, material sustenance, and monastic recruitment; peasants looked to monks for spiritual guidance, religious knowledge, and ideological leadership. Both expressed increasing concern in the colonial era with questions of religious identity and social status, in part because those questions had immediate and long-range political and economic ramifications. Peasants and monks addressed those questions by advocating both attacks on and manipulations of social hierarchy, that is, caste.

The story of those attacks and manipulations, and their implications for colonial India, make up a large part of the history described in this book. However, this history also includes significant religious and cultural change, which should not be ignored. Furthermore, the world that peasants and monks lived in, and assisted in creating, came to occupy a central place in the history of colonial and nationalist India. That world is with us still, nearly a half-century since independence from British rule, and, it can be argued, contributes to the ongoing crisis of religion and the state in north India.

This book, then, is a history of the ways in which religion intersected with dramatic political and social change in colonial India. It will come as no surprise to social historians that religion has been drawn upon to express material complaint in times of rural social, political, and economic stress; a corollary, in modern south Asia at least, is that monks have readily assumed the burdens of peasant advocacy.

But, despite the importance of radical monks who led rural rebellions, most of the social history that has described them does not explain the role of religion, or the exceptionally religious, in peasant society; rather, it merely comments upon the fact. This is as true for colonial India as it is for late antique Rome.

Peter Brown has observed that social historians of the late Roman empire have "tended to stress the spectacular occasions on which the holy man intervened to lighten the lot of the humble and oppressed: his open-handed charity, his courageous action as the spokesman of popular grievances-these have been held sufficient to explain the role of the holy man." But, Brown adds, such a view sees too little of the life of the holy man....Dramatic interventions of holy men in the high politics of the Empire were long remembered. But they illustrate the prestige that the holy man had already gained, they do not explain it. They were rather like the cashing of a big cheque on a reputation; and, like all forms of power in late Roman society, this reputation was built up by hard, unobtrusive (and so, for us, partly obscure) work among those who needed constant and unspectacular ministrations.

Certainly there are plenty of cases of peasant grievance expressed in religious language in Indian history; likewise there is no shortage of peasant movements led by holy men. Indeed, some of those grievances and movements find their way into this book.

But I would be telling only half the story were I to confine myself to such matters, because the long process of change that allowed monks to lead peasant movements in Gangetic India under colonial rule was as much ideological, cultural, and religious as it was material, economic, and social. The history of peasants and monks in the nineteenth and twentieth centuries in India includes the growth and transformation of a conscious "Hindu" historical discourse, which itself was the result of a prolonged process of religious institutionalization. That history is also the story of the coming of age of the "middle peasant"-the tenant farmer and small proprietor, clinging tenaciously to the margin of property-however one chooses to describe his politics and understand his fate.

A main purpose of this work, consequently, is to explore directly and in depth the religion that aids in defining the world of the Gangetic peasantry in colonial India. This involves broadening the working definitions of religion beyond the personal and private to include much of what is normatively considered political, social, and economic; it also involves understanding peasants in terms not only of what they do-i.e., their labor, behavior, riots, and occasional rebellions-but also of what they believe and think and say and write. I hope that by so doing we gain a better sense of the mental worlds that produced and gave meaning to action in colonial north India, whether that action was violent or gentle, religious, social, economic or political. This recourse to culture and, ultimately, religion should not be seen as an abandonment of social history as such, but as a recognition that while social history has enabled us to ask important questions, it has not provided the tools with which to craft satisfactory answers.

RELIGION AND POLITICS

India has long been represented as a place of timeless peasants and ageless monks, and not just by an intellectual elite that is today labeled "Orientalist." To the British administrator, the peasant represented an India that was noble, honest, and good. The monk, by contrast, represented an Orient that was mysterious, unpredictable, and dangerous. In ideological terms, this was a necessary juxtaposition: the colonial official, steeped in both utilitarian philosophies of rule and romantic notions of benevolent despotism, saw himself as the protector of the common man-the peasant-against the extortions of idle, urban elites and the corruptions of corrosive superstition. Thus the picture of the hardy peasant and his negative imprint manifest in the nefarious monk were central to the strategic-and for the most part unconscious-posturings of British colonial officials on the right side of history.

But the image of India as peasant and monk writ large was not confined to European imaginations: Mohandas K. Gandhi's political technique played on British idealizations of the peasantry and monasticism and of India generally. From the nationalist perspective, the ability of the Indian National Congress to control the peasants and monks of India was of less importance than the British perception that Congress possessed the ability to do so. And Gandhi, who represented both humble peasant and simple monk, seemed to speak for India's masses, whether or not he could control them.

The peasant-monk ethos defined Gandhi's very existence: his simple garb, his spare meals, his ashram (sanctuary), his celibacy, his daily routine of meditation and constructive work, his nonviolence-all evoked ideals of religious asceticism and rural simplicity. This ethos, and the relentless dedication to truth (satyagraha) that sustained it, afforded Gandhi substantial moral influence, for a time, among peasants and monks as mahatma, great soul. Gandhi as mahatma was both more and less than an imagined miracle worker, a figment of rural imaginations run rampant. Because Gandhi seemed able to speak to India's monks, the British were soon convinced that he could speak for India's peasants.

This conviction emerges with crystal clarity in the official reaction to the fact that hundreds of monks attended the 1920 Indian National Congress meeting in Nagpur, anxious to see and hear the man who was bringing mass politics to the national level and to involve themselves in his-and in many ways their own-political idiom. An observer dispatched to report on the Nagpur proceedings to the government noted in his account that "an association of the most powerful sadhus called Nagas [soldier monks] had been formed at Nagpur" and that "a meeting of over a hundred of these sadhus had been held in the Congress Camp and they had decided to undertake non-cooperation propaganda."

Great significance was attached to this act, since it was maintained that these "sadhus visited most of the villages and towns and the masses had a high regard for them, and thought a great deal of their instructions and preachings. When these Nagas took up non-cooperation, the scheme would spread like wild fire among the masses of India and eventually Government would be unable to control 33 crores of people and would have to give Swaraj." The official report also noted that Gandhi personally thanked the sadhus for their support and urged them to "visit the vicinities of cantonments and military stations and explain to the native soldiers the advisability of giving up their employments"-thus recalling the fears of sepoy disloyalty that still resonated after the rebellion of 1857. After the Nagpur Congress, the intelligence branch of government would become increasingly concerned with the activity of "political sadhus."

Colonial and nationalist idealizations of peasants and monks were reductive, one-dimensional, and misleading: most peasants and monks in British India were not immediately concerned with the national implications of colonial rule, let alone nationalist politics-despite Bankim Chandra Chattopadhyay's (1838-1894) late nineteenth-century fictional representations of patriotic sadhus sprung organically from the soil of Bengal and ranged against oppressive, foreign rule; despite Gandhi's desire to attract the participation of peasants and monks in a mass-based nationalism; and despite Nehru's efforts to lecture peasants on the meaning of Bharat Mata-mother India-in the 1930s. But peasants and monks were not unconcerned with politics and their place in an Indian nation. Rather, their politics were locally defined, their concept of nation (as country) deeply embedded in Indian social and cultural history. Though their brief engagement in the nationalist politics of India drew them for the first time into the narrow beam of the historian's searchlight, it was not the first time peasants and monks had combined to bring about social and ideological change.

The peasants and monks who populate the history of Gangetic India were historiographically complex, because they could think and speak for themselves; indeed, their thoughts and opinions are the basis of this study. Peasants and monks in British India acted and spoke in ways that seemed strangely out of character for people normally (and normatively) engaged in agricultural labor and the disciplined pursuit of spiritual truth. Completely independent of nationalism, many peasants of Gangetic India in the late nineteenth and early twentieth centuries began to voice loud objections to the servile status that society and the state ascribed to those who worked the soil. It gradually became clear that many of those peasants thought of themselves not as cosmically created servants (shudra) devoid of any history, but as the descendants of divine warrior clans (kshatriya) firmly rooted in the Indian past. The dimensions of those assertions, the discourses drawn upon to articulate them, and the elite reaction to them reveal a wealth of information not only about peasant culture but of popular ideological change during the colonial era.

Monks, likewise, had strong opinions that informed and were informed by the goings-on in Gangetic society. They were willing and able (indeed expected) to leave behind the secure confines of the monastery, the contemplation of sacred texts and images, and the cycles of ritual and worship, to engage themselves in society's all-too-temporal concerns. Prior to 1800, such engagement included soldiering, trade, banking, protecting pilgrimage sites and religious endowments, and enlisting as mercenaries in the armies of regional states. But it also included living in villages amongst peasants, artisans, and laborers, and ministering to their daily religious needs.

After 1800 and the colonial monopolization of armed force, involvement in society's concerns meant, increasingly, attending to the vexed question of status and hierarchy, which seemed to have gained political urgency under British rule. Many monks in the nineteenth and twentieth centuries, consequently, dedicated themselves to aggressive (and even, at times, egalitarian) social reform, which included the amelioration of the stigma of physical labor and the inculcation of a just moral order. And because monks confronted these issues in society, the issues eventually confronted them inside the confines of the monastery. The question of social status would consume the energies of numerous monks and peasants during much of the twentieth century; the discourses and ideologies brought to bear to deal with that question are the main concerns of this study.

A history of religious and social change runs up against numerous obstacles in India, not the least of which is the historiography produced by "communalism." It has become by now a truism that colonial officials were quick to ascribe religious identity, particularly Hindu and Muslim "communal" identity, as the motivating force behind all precolonial conflict, in part as a way of justifying their own presence as representatives of a stabilizing, secular force. What is less obvious is the extent to which the tentacles of colonial understanding have gripped Indian historical consciousness and the degree to which nationalist (and much postnationalist) historiography bears their circular scars.

This wounded historiography contributes in no small way to the recent political impasse over a fully razed mosque and a partly raised temple in north India. Unfortunately, coming to terms with this fact has often meant the historiographical withdrawal from any discussion of religion as a stimulus to historical change, either directly, as belief and ideology, or indirectly, as the discursive and institutional bases of social reform.

Applied to the day-to-day practicalities of imperial rule, the colonial fixation on an India-past and present-alllegedly rife with religious violence inspired colonial officials to distrust the very nature and content of Indian monasticism. This distrust was, in part, inspired by the at times vigorous (if unorganized) resistance offered by unruly bands of armed monks as the English East India Company subdued the huge province of Bengal.

Nevertheless, the colonial willingness to see evil and corruption in the figure of the Indian monk was remarkable for its longevity and imaginative creativity. An early example of this can be seen in the writings of Colonel William Henry Sleeman (1788-1856), who is generally credited with the suppression of thagi (banditry, thought to have been ritually inspired) in the 1830s. Sleeman held that most Indian holy men were merely bandits, criminals, and rogues in disguise:

> *Three-fourths of these religious mendicants, whether Hindoos or Muhammadans, rob and steal, and a very great portion of them murder their victims before they rob them....There is hardly any species of crime that is not throughout India perpetrated by men in the disguise of these religious mendicants; and almost all such mendicants are really men in disguise; for Hindoos of any caste can become Bairagis and Gosains; and Muhammadans of any grade can become Fakirs.*

Sleeman also alleged that monks were guilty of spreading seditious rumors and recommended the compulsory registration of all such individuals according to a strict Vagrant Act.

The colonial distrust of religion in the context of peasants (and soldiers) was also evident in the rumors that circulated throughout the empire over the outbreak of the 1857 rebellion. Two such rumors were of particular interest and were repeated by none other than Benjamin Disraeli in a speech to Parliament: namely, that the bloody events of that year were in part coordinated by religiously symbolic acts such as the mysterious passing of a chapati (thin wheat bread cooked over fire) from village to village and, in what was thought to strike an even deeper chord, the circulation of a lotus flower from sepoy to sepoy through entire regimental units.

Three decades later, in the 1890s, the often strident efforts of local sadhus to generate popular support in the countryside for a growing movement to prohibit the slaughter of cows in Uttar Pradesh and Bihar aroused great consternation among provincial officials-a consternation not unrelated to the widespread apprehension that the rebellion of 1857 had been sparked by the use of cow (and pig) fat in the cartridges of the new Enfield rifle.

That sadhus generally were seen as a potential source of criminal mischief by officials of the Raj is evident in the publication in 1913 of a police handbook in Urdu that described the various religious orders and, in detailed line-drawings, examples of representative figures-down to the distinctive sandalwood-paste sect marks. Sadhus would soon be considered a fount of outright sedition with the emergence of a newer form of resistance to colonial rule: mass nationalism. The colonial distrust of monks can be perceived not only in the early disdain for the Mahatma's political style, but also in the official attitude toward monks in north India who gravitated toward Gandhi in the early 1920s.

Such monks were derided in the police fact sheets as "political sadhus," about whom almost no information was provided about monastic affiliations. Indeed, if a common feature can be discerned in the tone of the police reports on "political sadhus," it is the official attempt to dispute and discredit the religious credentials of the individuals under scrutiny.

For example the police report depicted Swami Biswanand, who would become a prominent labor leader in the coal fields of south Bihar, as a person of "very bad moral character," who was "absolutely inconsistent," and whose "word or actions can never be relied on." Another, Pursotam Das, was portrayed as "a man of low character, [who] frequents prostitutes' houses," and was said to have been "turned out of the Chatubhuj Asthan [monastery] by the Mahanth [head] for misconduct." A third,

Raghubar Saran Kuer, was cited for preaching "race hatred in a violent manner" and for abusing the police in filthy language; his allegedly weak religious loyalties could be seen in his willingness to shed his "sanyasi dress" and don the clothing of "a national volunteer," i.e., Gandhian homespun cotton.

On first glance, then, the typical "political sadhu" of colonial India seems rather an unsavory fellow. However, the official record of the integrity and character of subjects under police scrutiny cannot be relied upon. It was only to be expected that police and intelligence officials would editorialize negatively about the morals, behavior, and sincerity of religious commitment of individuals opposed to colonial rule. Failure to do so would have risked the loss of important ideological ground to the agitators, and even the possibility of appearing politically unsound oneself.

Whatever the "true" moral character of sadhus, their political actions were a function of religious and philosophical commitment and not a reflection of any alleged personal failings. It is equally probable that their political behavior informed their religious outlook. As such, the "political sadhu" represented an important example of the ties that bound religious community, or sampraday, to society. Colonial administrators may not have appreciated the subtleties and importance of sampraday; they certainly feared, however, the power of sampraday loyalties to challenge even British imperial authority, and they strove therefore to dismiss the sampraday dimension of what they characterized as a political sadhu "problem."

Despite colonial fears of the political sadhu and Gandhi's own efforts to include sadhus in noncooperation as a symbolic challenge to the British, the colonial disdain for monasticism was to a large degree mirrored in nationalist circles. At the level of province and locality, the monastic orders would have been seen as a throwback to a premodern age, the sectarian complexities of which tended to undercut claims to Hindu political solidarity. Such claims were voiced with increasing stridency throughout the north after 1890, and in increasing proximity to Congress, by such organizations as the Arya Samaj, the Sanatana Dharma Sabha, and the Hindu Mahasabha. Those sadhus willing to subordinate their sampraday loyalties to these new religio-political formations or, alternatively, to the philosophical (and nonviolent) dictates of Gandhi, would have remained within the ambit of nationalist politics, whether defined as secular or Hindu.

Without question, many would have been driven away-though measuring such patterns of political involvement is difficult in the extreme.

However, one revealing case is that of the peasant leader Swami Sahajanand Saraswati, who was drawn into nationalist politics in 1920-1921 by the force of Gandhi's personality, but who would break publicly with Gandhi in the mid-1920s on the basis of his (Sahajanand's) vision of the obligation of the monk to serve the needs of the oppressed peasant. Sahajanand Saraswati's commitment to peasant welfare derived in large part from a conscious dedication to Vaishnava ideals of equality and social reform-notwithstanding the fact that he himself emerged out of a long tradition of Shaiva monasticism that competed vigorously with Vaishnava (and particularly Ramanandi) monasticism for the allegiances of peasant society.

In any event, Congress distaste and colonial disdain for sadhus would soon have historiographical consequences, as official documents and nationalist records emerged after Independence as the main sources for writing Indian political history, the only legitimate subjects of which were seen to be Congress, communalism, and colonialism. In that framework, the only significant figure accorded any kind of creative religious status was Gandhi himself; all other manifestations of socially engaged religion would be read backward from the dramatic events of 1946-1947 (and, later, 6 December 1992) as part and parcel of the communalism that would divide the subcontinent along lines Hindu and Muslim.

The work of a number of social historians of provincial politics would remedy to some degree the linear understanding of nationalist history by emphasizing the importance of local contingencies in the evolutionary dynamics of political institution-building. However, insofar as those provincial histories were predicated upon understanding the local dynamics of nationalism, the eyes of these historians were still trained upon those individuals and institutions who articulated the new, totalizing religious sentiments.

In the past decade, a group of scholars referred to as the "subaltern collective" has criticized as "elitist" not only historical approaches that adopt colonial and nationalist agendas as thematic points of departure, but the heavy use of colonial and nationalist documentation (and the unconscious adoption of the mentalities therein). This criticism, though grounded in the conviction that the actions of peasants and workers-"subalterns"-should be understood as part of a failed history of national fulfillment, can also be leveled from the perspective of religion. For members of the subaltern collective, the poverty of this "elitist" historiography is

demonstrated beyond doubt by its failure to understand and assess the mass articulation of this nationalism except, negatively, as a law and order problem, and positively, if at all, either as a response to the charisma of certain elite leaders or in the currently more fashionable terms of vertical mobilization by the manipulation of factions.

The involvement of the Indian people in vast numbers . .. in nationalist activities and ideas is thus represented as a diversion from a supposedly 'real' political process, that is, the grinding away of the wheels of the state apparatus and of elite institutions geared to it, or it is simply credited, as an act of ideological appropriation, to the influence and initiative of the elite themselves.

This powerful critique has had the potential to galvanize much historical writing by bringing historians closer to the voices and actions of ordinary people as they grappled with the changes overtaking their lives. An excellent case in point is the subaltern consideration of Baba Ramchandra, a man who would have been disparaged as a "political sadhu" by the government but who was in fact the central instigator of peasant dissent in Awadh between 1919 and 1922. In revisiting this important moment of agrarian radicalism, the historian Gyanendra Pandey contrasts the peasant world of Awadh to the conception of the peasant held by Gandhian nationalists and by the colonial state, and demonstrates thereby the conflicting aims of Indian nationalism and peasant rebellion.

Baba Ramchandra is introduced as "a Maharashtrian of uncertain antecedents who had been an indentured laborer in Fiji and then a sadhu (religious mendicant) propagating the Hindu scriptures in Jaunpur, Sultanpur and Pratapgarh, before he turned to the task of organizing Kisan Sabhas [peasant associations]."

As a peasant leader, he evoked the moral world of the god-king Ramchandra of epic Ayodhya to combat expropriative landlord tyranny. That moral world was described in Tulsidas' Ramcharitmanas, "a favourite religious epic of the Hindus in northern India and especially beloved of people in this region"; its immediacy in the agrarian environment was reflected in the increased currency of such religiously charged phrases as "Sita Ram," "Jai Ram," and "Jai Shankar" as both egalitarian forms of address and as rallying calls for peasants gearing up for political action.

Hidden in the shadows of the subaltern consideration of Baba Ramchandra are the social and religious institutions that underpinned the agrarian radicalism of Awadh. Such institutions provided an autonomous peasant and monastic culture organized to work for progressive change, whether in the context of economic crisis, political mobilization, social reform, or spiritual awakening.

It was because of their ties to peasant society through important religious communities that Baba Ramchandra and other sadhus (Sahajanand Saraswati for example) could engage in peasant politics so effectively. In the nineteenth and twentieth-century Gangetic north, many sadhus were committed to a powerful critique of hierarchy that came to constitute a major principle behind social and ideological change.

The most important, but by no means the only, proponent of such change in Gangetic north India was the Ramanandi sampraday. Ramanandi social commentary gained institutional momentum over the centuries, but was extremely influential by the early 1800s, as peasant society gravitated toward its progressive and assimilative rhetoric. Baba Ramchandra was very much part of that Ramanandi, Vaishnava ethos, a fact that contributed substantially to his immediate and positive reception by landless and land poor peasants in the countryside.

The links between monks and peasants before the twentieth century were best represented by the individuals and establishments that made up the Ramanandi sampraday. By the turn of the twentieth century, new ideological movements began to emerge from within peasant society itself, spearheaded by populist scholars who asserted genealogical descent in the royal kshatriya (warrior) lineages of Ram and Krishna, Vishnu's *avatars* (earthly forms).

Baba Ramchandra's recollections of the peasant dissent in Awadh, not to mention his own recruitment into the peasant movement, place great emphasis on the organizational framework of peasant-kshatriya identity campaigns that were already in place. It should be emphasized that without such a framework peasant activism would have been far less successful and may even have failed to attract the attention of Congress leaders and the colonial state, not to mention later generations of historians.

More recently, the work of Sandria Freitag on community and communalism in the Gangetic north has also focused on the trajectories of popular action in the context of the emergent Indian nation but has distinguished itself from subaltern scholarship by closer attention to the autonomy of cultural and religious change, particularly as expressed in collective action and the symbolic language of crowd violence.

For Freitag, religion provided the institutional base for "public arena" activities, such as festivals, in which increasingly wide community identities were expressed with greater political urgency as the colonial era drew to a close. Her stress on popular action (and riots in particular) rather than ideas has the effect of deemphasizing religious ideology as a causal factor in a history that seeks to explain something with massive ideological ramifications, namely, Hindu versus Muslim communalism.

This effect is both necessary and intended: Freitag notes at the outset that while we have access to the symbolic language expressed through collective action over time, we cannot know the thoughts of individual rioters as they go about their business. Hence it would be fruitless to speculate on the ideologies that motivated rioters or whether something so finite and discernible as ideology was at work.

More importantly, the focus on action in the frame of the public arena provides sufficient evidence to argue that communalism (and, ultimately, Partition) was an unintended consequence of shortsighted colonial strategies combined with nationalist political culture, rather than the political fruition of "age-old" animosities expressed in "insensate violence," as the colonial mythology would have it.

Beneath and within the actions of crowds accommodating themselves to the logistical needs of the colonially malformed and increasingly communalized public arena, however, were significant religious ideologies that were neither Hindu nor Muslim in the political sense. Acknowledging this fact affords greater historical and cultural depth to the history examined by Freitag.

For example, after 1900 the colonial state became increasingly concerned with the Ram Lila festival, which reenacted annually the life of the god-king Ramchandra in towns and villages throughout the Gangetic north. Official consternation derived from politically motivated innovations in the festival, such as the inclusion of famous rebels from 1857 and well-known extremists (e.g., the Rani of Jhansi on horseback with a British soldier transfixed on her spear, and Lala Lajpat Rai, the fiery Arya Samajist Congressman from the Punjab) in the festival tableaux and processions.

As the annual occasion for the celebration of the life of Ramchandra, the Ram Lila was central in the ritual calendar of all Ramanandis. In Ramnagar (across the Ganga from Banaras), the feasting of hundreds of Ramanandi sadhus during the festival afforded substantial political legitimacy to the Maharaja of Banaras, who sponsored the annual performance at considerable expense.

The Ramnagar Ram Lila would grow into a thirty-one-day affair and would be performed in an elaborate-and permanent-reproduction of Ayodhya housed within the palace grounds. But whether in Ramnagar or in villages and towns throughout the north, the Ram Lila took on an added importance for peasants claiming (after 1900) a lineal descent from the kshatriya house of Ramchandra, because it represented an annual opportunity to imbibe the grandeur and glory of their most famous progenitor.

Hence, to fully appreciate the historical significance of the Ram Lila, it must be understood in the context of Ramanandi monasticism and peasant-kshatriya identity.

Together they point to a Vaishnava religiosity on the rise in precolonial and colonial India beneath the rubric of Hinduism that would seek to overtake such religiosity in the twentieth century. Like Hinduism, Vaishnavism was grounded in a long process of institutionalization in festival, pilgrimage, temple construction, monasticism, and mythology.

What is more, this institutionalization depended on the creative tensions between political power and religious authority in the precolonial period, prior to the nineteenth-century withdrawal of the state from the popular spectacle that became such a crucial public arena.

Given the degree to which religion obtruded into the political process in colonial India, studies of political action predicated on religious institutions can and should be complemented by inquiries into the political meanings of religion.

The injection of the cultural into social history has moved us carefully in this direction, but neither the sporadic irruptions of subaltern rebellion nor the long-term patterns of crowd violence, however eloquent, can speak adequately to the full import of religious ideology in social history.

Admittedly, this poses a problem for historians of India, because any study of religion as a motive force in political and social change can be misconstrued as an argument for the fundamentally religious basis of Indian politics.

It also poses a problem for many social historians of peasant society, who tread softly when it comes to assessing religion in terms of meaning, since religious consciousness tends to cut across the class lines that make social-historical analysis so meaningful. Notwithstanding these risks, this foray into the religious world of the peasant is especially called for, if for no other reason, because the peasant world was, in large part, religious. Were we to obscure that fact in our historical representation of peasant society, we would be depriving peasants-about whom so much has been written as agents of their own history-of the historical voice they know best. And we would be depriving ourselves, as historians, of important insights not only regarding peasant history but into the ways ordinary people came to terms with the decline of colonial rule and the rise of an Indian nation.

2

Most Prominent Sages

Sectarian traditions associated with precolonial Vaishnava and Shaiva soldiering and, more particularly, colonial sources describing monasticism in the nineteenth century confirm that the history of monasticism reflected social and ideological change in north Indian society. Likewise Ramanandi hagiography, read carefully, can reveal a great deal about popular ideological change in the Gangetic north, both within and without monastic life. This was true in the fourteenth century, when Ramanand is believed to have uttered the words quoted above; it continued to be true in the early 1600s, when Nabhadas listed in the Bhaktamal ("the garland of devotees") the five brahman men, the two women, the kshatriya prince, the weaver, the cobbler, the peasant, and the barber who represented the first generation of Ramanand's disciples.

However, of fundamental importance to present-day Ramanandi identities are the first four decades of the twentieth century-and in particular the years 1918-1921, when "radical" Ramanandis decided to reject any institutional monastic connection between Ramanand and Ramanuja, the twelfth-century theologian of south India who had long been regarded as the originator of Vaishnava bhakti and, hence, a prominent figure in Ramanandi tradition.

Needless to say, the Ramanandi conception of Ramanand would undergo fundamental, and controversial, change as a result of this decision. This chapter examines the ideological debates in the early twentieth century that occasioned this new vision of Ramanand, and the social and historiographical causes and consequences of those debates. The object is to bring the social and ideological dimensions of twentieth-century Ramanandi egalitarianism into better focus.

On the margin of Ramanandi history there has existed an ongoing European and American historiography of Indian religious belief, which has occasionally, though unevenly, touched on Ramanand and Ramanandis.

Though this historiography has not yet altered in any substantial way the trajectories of ideological change in Gangetic society, it has on occasion come into sharp focus in the eyes of monks and lay devotees. This point was reinforced for me recently (18 October 1994) in Jaipur: while we were discussing the role of the Galta pith (religious center) in the history of Vaishnava soldiering in the eighteenth century, the Galta mahant's eldest son and heir apparent to the mahantship, Avadesh Kumar Mishra, suddenly produced copies of two articles, Peter van der Veer's "Taming the Ascetic" and Richard Burghart's "Founding of the Ramanandi Sect."

The pages were worn and the margins full of handwritten commentary. We proceeded to discuss the contents of both articles for over an hour; Burghart's piece was of particular interest to Avadesh Kumar Mishra, since (as we shall see in the pages below) it contains arguments that implicitly favor the Ramanuji side (favored by Galta) of a debate that began in 1918 and continues to influence the structure of the Ramanandi sampraday.

It is appropriate, then, to begin this chapter on the historiographical margin, by way of introducing the interpretive dilemmas occasioned by the study of Ramanand and Ramanandis, for academics as well as monks.

RAMANAND OBSCURED

Notwithstanding the importance of the Ramanandi sampraday as the largest Vaishnava monastic order in north India (and perhaps the largest monastic community, Shaiva or Vaishnava, in India), Ramanand and Ramanandis have gradually receded from the pages of historical scholarship on

India. One reason is an increasing scholarly interest in the sant tradition, since about 1400 an important literary-cum-religious movement in north India that until recently was regarded as the heir to Ramanand's broadly articulated bhakti-sadhna message of "disciplined love for god." Indeed, it can be argued that the increasing interest in sant studies has pushed Ramanand and Ramanandis into the background. Guru Nanak is included among the sants, as are several figures claimed by Ramanandis as members of Ramanand's original circle of disciples, most notably Ravidas and Kabir.

Sants are bound to each other in the clarity of scholarly hindsight by a disdain for brahmanical knowledge and ritual, an outspoken disregard for idols and images, and a dedication to egalitarian poetic verse-all of which lends to the study of sant literature a distinctly counter-elitist, folk-culture appeal.

In addition, many scholars have been drawn to the uncompromising criticism of caste hierarchy common to sant rhetoric, not to mention the "low-caste" origins of most sant practicioners. Also a factor is the chronological implausibility of Ramanand's life when viewed from the perspective of his main sant disciples. Charlotte Vaudeville, a pioneer in the field of sant literary and historical scholarship, calculated that Ramanand "would have had to live more than 118 years in order to be the real Guru of all the twelve disciples" attributed to him. The consensus among sant scholars today is that later sant traditions created a guru-disciple link with Ramanand in order to afford the sant poets greater social and political respectability.

However, the relative paucity of scholarship on Ramanand must also stem from the mixed social and political message sent by his life, as it is remembered. As both a Sanskrit-educated brahman and a Vaishnava-bhakti visionary, Ramanand is believed by many to have occupied an important and neglected space between two competing "Hinduisms": one composed of sophisticated pandits, the other of radical poets. For Indologists reared on the basic structural oppositions of caste hierarchy, the difficult question is, can one life occupy both ends of the spectrum? So little of a reliable nature is known about Ramanand that the question cannot be answered with certainty.

The multiple and seemingly contradictory meanings of this important life, in addition to the relative lack of "hard" biographical data regarding it, have inspired one scholar to cast doubt on Ramanand's authorship of the famous verse discounting caste and to argue that Ramanand did not intend at all for a community, or sampraday, to gather around him and his message.

Indeed it would require little in the way of argumentation to suggest further that Ramanand never even existed but was conjured up by monks at a much later date to satisfy a drive for brahmanical respectability within the order. With the thorny problem of Ramanand out of the way, it would be much easier to understand Indian social and cultural history as an ideological struggle ranged above an uncompromising caste divide. But Ramanand, shadowy and mystifying though he may be, has been kept alive by the force of Ramanandi tradition, although that tradition itself has undergone dramatic change.

Ramanand tends to be eclipsed in particular by Kabir and Ravidas, two figures who from the Ramanandi point of view were among Ramanand's inner circle of disciples and whose ideologically potent verse, therefore, finds frequent expression in Ramanandi tradition.

Kabir and Ravidas flourished in the fifteenth and early sixteenth centuries and are remembered for the steadfast challenge they posed to the very idea of varna and jati as systems of human classification. Based on the rhetorical structure of his verse, Kabir appears to have hurled his invective from a self-imposed perch well beyond the social system; Ravidas, by contrast, spoke from deep within society, focusing on his own lowly status as a cobbler to better apprehend and articulate the injustices of varna.

Kabir questioned the very foundations upon which varna and jati rested, entreating the learned brahman to "look in your heart for knowledge. Tell me where untouchability came from, since you believe in it."

He assaulted the sensibilities, interspersing direct insults with stark depictions of the blunt corporeality of human existence and thereby entering into an immediate and passionate dialogue with the listener. Kabir's object was to lay bare human conceits, which he did by aiming sharply worded barbs at the brahman pandits who thronged the steps leading down to the Ganga in Banaras or at lecturing qazis (scholars of sharia, or Islamic law), comfortably ensconced among legal tomes. Though Ravidas did not utilize invective and shock tactics to make his point, he nonetheless urged his listeners, in a passage reminiscent of Ramanand's couplet, to "ask not about caste,....What is there in clan or caste? Brahmin, Kshatriya, Vaishya, and Shudra, all belong to the same caste." He insisted, "A family that has a true follower of the Lord is neither high caste nor low caste, lordly or poor."

The followers of Kabir and Ravidas who do not consider themselves Ramanandis have used varying strategies to pursue their goal of a more equal and just society. For example, there is the wide discrepancy between the original message of Kabir and the methods of his present-day devotees, noted by David Lorenzen: "The songs of Kabir himself display such a militant iconoclasm that it is quite consistent to assume that he meant to break with both Islam and Hinduism and establish an independent religious tradition. His followers, however, seem to have soon brought their sect into the orbit of non-caste Hinduism."

By "non-caste Hinduism" Lorenzen means to evoke a religious strategy that accepts "many of the behavioral forms or structures of caste Hinduism while at the same time infusing them with an ideological content that is in direct opposition to basic socioreligious values characteristic of caste Hinduism." While Kabir's present-day followers ultimately embrace varna, then, they manipulate it to suit the social needs of their own shudra and untouchable constituents. The full historical irony of this doctrinal-behavioral strategy was particularly evident in Patna during the 1987 all-India conference of the Kabirpanth. Notwithstanding the strident anti-varna pronouncements of modern-day Kabirpanthis, this conference was held under the auspices of the national headquarters of the Yadava Mahasabha, the political heir to the Yadav-kshatriya movement of the pre-1947 era and currently a major caste organization deeply involved in state and national politics.

But while the followers of Kabir seemed to have moderated his radical anti-establishment message, a process of radicalization seems to have occurred among followers of Ravidas. The modern Chamar (untouchable leatherworker) followers of that sant have developed a clear social agenda and are in no way reluctant to seek reform openly. A Chamar leader of Lucknow struck a militant pose by reinterpreting Ravidas as among those who "demolished the philosophical fort of the Brahman's culture by denouncing unequivocally the distinctions of caste, sect, sex, and special privileges, and by downgrading sacrificial rituals, temples, and bibliolatry."

Similarly, today's Chamars of Shri Govardhanpur, on the southernmost edge of Banaras, "have no intention of accepting their lot as if it were decreed by fate or religion" and have been working since 1967 to erect a large Ravi Dasi temple in the hope that "their four-story edifice will rival temples in other sectors of the city and become a familiar part of the pilgrims' circuit."

Though it is a much larger, wealthier, more powerful, and socially more mainstream monastic community, attitudes in the Ramanandi sampraday bear striking similarity to the modern ideologies espoused by the Ravidasi and Kabirpanthi communities, no doubt because of the importance of both Ravidas and Kabir to Ramanandi tradition.

Indeed, the disagreements that would come to divide the sampraday after 1918 indicate that many Ramanandis believed that Ramanand-presaging Kabir-had intended all along to destroy the edifice of caste through concentrated polemic and vitriolic attack; others depicted Ramanand-like Ravidas-as a saint who rose above the injustices of caste and sought its atrophy through disuse. Ranged against them, however, was a strong subgroup of Ramanandis who felt that there was a place for both religious and social hierarchy within the sampraday-that some sadhus, by virtue of their sectarian pedigree, were "purer" and worthy of greater respect than others, and that some sadhus, by virtue of their caste background prior to entering the sampraday, were deserving of better treatment in the monastic community.

THE LIFE AND STYLE

Ramanand is today held by Ramanandis to have been an avatar of Ramchandra, the god-king of epic Ayodhya, returned to earth to rescue Hinduism from the corrupting effects of human divisiveness. The institutional centrality of Ramanand has long been reflected in the guru parampara (preceptor lineage) that connects every Ramanandi through an unbroken succession of gurus with Ramanand himself and, eventually, Ramchandra. The details and meanings of Ramanand's life, which were the subject of heated controversy in 1918-1921, emerge from commentaries on the Bhaktamal, a verse compendium describing important devotees authored by Nabhadas, himself a Ramanandi, in the early seventeenth century.

The beginning of the twentieth century did not mark the first time Ramanandi memory was hauled up for inspection, and a review of an earlier controversy confirms that efforts to manipulate the institutional memory of Ramanand reflects changing attitudes toward caste in the sampraday. According to orthodox Ramanandi tradition, an important gathering of Vaishnavas took place in the Galta region of Jaipur in the early 1700s, the ostensible purpose of which was to organize a defense against attacks by Shaiva gosains. The less-heralded agenda was the elevation of Ramanand to a level equal to that of Ramanuja, the twelfth-century Tamil theologian long considered the founder of Vaishnava bhakti, in north Indian Vaishnavism, and the delimitation of thirty-six legitimate "gateways" through which a Ramanandi could claim a guru-disciple link to Ramanuja. Those thirty-six gateways descended only through the twice-born (i.e., brahman, kshatriya, and vaishya) male disciples of Ramanand and excluded his shudra, untouchable, and female disciples.

Though the latter (including, importantly, Kabir and Ravidas) were still considered followers of Ramanand, they "lost their role as a transmitter or preceptor of the tradition"; their disciples, in turn, who may have considered themselves Ramanandis, "now found themselves outside the Ramanandi sect." Nevertheless, "other genealogies indicate that male and female Hindus of servant [shudra] and untouchable birth were still being admitted into the Ramanandi sect"-and, hence, that the corporeal fact of being shudra, untouchable, or female was not what offended Ramanandis in the early 1700s, but the staunch anticaste ideology articulated by those "tainted" members of Ramanand's inner circle.

Thus while prior to Galta Ramanandis may have denied outright the relevance of caste (not to mention gender) distinctions, after Galta they moved toward an ambiguous ideological position: they chose to "recognise the category of caste but adopt an entirely neutral attitude toward it with reference to their sectarian recruitment."

In addition to ushering in what was the first major ideological transformation in the Ramanandi sampraday, the Galta meeting also represented the historical context for the composition of the first major addition to the Bhaktamal, entitled Bhaktirasbodhinitika and authored by Priyadas in 1712. Priyadas would add 634 verses to the extant 214-verse Bhaktamal, and his work would be included with almost all subsequent commentaries. His substantive contribution was to append the miraculous legends that have become commonplace today concerning many important figures in Nabhadas's Bhaktamal, including Tulsidas, Mirabai, Kabir, Ravidas, and, of course, Ramanand. This process of hagiographical accretion continued into the nineteenth and twentieth centuries, particularly after 1918 when a group of sadhus from Ayodhya would take up, once again, the question of Ramanand's relationship to Ramanuja.

In the nineteenth century, however, a major change would take place in the way Ramanandis (indeed, all Indians) communicated religious tradition, which in itself may have contributed to (and certainly shaped the logistics of) the unfolding of the 1918-1921 controversy. This change was manifest in the printing press, which was gradually popularized throughout north India in the latter half of the nineteenth century.

The result of this popularization, I would argue, was an increasing doctrinal self-consciousness among literate Ramanandis, and a hagiographical text as central as the Bhaktamal would not be immune to such a process. The rendering of the verse and commentary of the Bhaktamal into a form accessible to early twentieth-century Vaishnavas would have been a task that required constant oral exposition. In the major Vaishnava establishments throughout the Gangetic region, Ramanandi scholars were thus constantly engaged in exegesis of the Bhaktamal as a matter of experiencing and expressing faith, guiding lay Vaishnavas and young Ramanandis, and articulating a universal moral code. The relatively autonomous nature of those establishments had meant (prior to the arrival of printing presses) that local exegeses of the Bhaktamal hagiography could conflict and still not threaten the overall ideological integrity of the sampraday.

By the nineteenth century, however, with the spread of presses throughout the Gangetic north, this was increasingly no longer the case. A widely known commentary of the Bhaktamal was a Persian manuscript by Tulsiram, entitled Bhaktamalpradipan (Bhaktamal illuminations). Tulsiram was a highly esteemed rasik Ramanandi scholar of Ambala, a sizable town north of Delhi in what is now the state of Haryana. Two important Hindi translations of Tulsiram's commentary were published in 1867, marking in all likelihood the first time this text had been rendered in multiple copies by a printing press. One translation, by Hari Baksh Ray, was produced fairly close to Tulsiram's home in the town of Solma.

The other translation (with minor additions), done by Pratap Sinha of Muzaffarpur District in north Bihar and entitled Bhaktakalpadrum (or, the tree of devotees), was so popular that by 1874 a third edition had been issued by the respected Naval Kishore Press of Lucknow; by 1952 a twelfth edition was published by its offspring, the Tejkumar Press.

The next major Bhaktamal commentary to emerge, entitled Shri Bhaktamal: Tika, Tilak, aur Namavali Sahit and authored by Sitaramsharan Bhagvan Prasad (a nephew of Tulsiram) in 1903, would be reissued several times. The cumulative effect of the appearance in print of multiple Bhaktamal editions must have been dramatic-not because of any partisanship Bhagvan Prasad, Tulsiram, or any other scholar-devotees may have evinced on the issue of Ramanand's identity, but because the representations and interpretations of Ramanand's life could now not only confront one another in print but, inevitably, would encounter the variety of local, unpublished interpretation.

Of the three published Bhaktamal commentaries just noted, the most recent-Bhagvan Prasad's-would increasingly be regarded as the most authoritative. Bhagvan Prasad was a well-known Ramanandi scholar-devotee and a resident of Kanak Bhavan in Ayodhya, an influential rasik establishment. He was also deeply engaged in the British-Indian intellectual exchange of the late nineteenth and early twentieth centuries, and his treatment of the life of Ramanand reflected this intellectual milieu, right down to his textual critique of nineteenth-century British scholarship. Bhagvan Prasad's account relied for the most part on earlier versions of the Bhaktamal, including especially another Persian-language version by Tapasviram entitled Ramuze Mihovafa. Tapasviram (1815-1885) was Bhagvan Prasad's father and Tulsiram's brother.

Hence, Bhagvan Prasad was in all likelihood regarded as the scion of north India's first family of Bhaktamal exegesis. In addition to drawing on his family's expertise, however, Bhagvan Prasad cited a Hindi document entitled Shri Ramanand Yashavali [The eminent renown of Ramanand], which was said to be based on a portion of the Agastyasamhita that detailed events said to be destined to occur in the future-thereby lending the account an unimpeachable Sanskrit, Vaishnava authority. It is likely that the details of Ramanand's life as depicted in Bhagvan Prasad's commentary (given below) derived primarily from this latter source, since his version conforms in all particulars to that given in a Hindi translation of the Agastyasamhita by one Ram Narayan Das in 1904, rendered in English by R. G. Bhandarkar in Vaishnavism, Saivism, and Minor Religious Systems in 1913.

What emerged as a result of Bhagvan Prasad's exegetical labors was a critical examination of the fundamentals of Ramanandi tradition, an account of a life of unparalleled importance that tried to reconcile a variety of proto-doctrinal opinions through exhaustive scholarship. Was Bhagvan Prasad conscious of the cultural and historical import of his work? Certainly he understood its significance as a document of sampraday record.

It is for this reason that he began the text with what he called Shri Vaishnava Namavali, a list of 108 prominent Vaishnavas throughout the central Gangetic region. The Namavali is more than just a list, however, for it supplements names, dates, and places with a confirmation of each individual's contribution to the sampraday. It represented a way of commemorating the breadth of Ramanandi achievement, both geographically and intellectually; it also allowed Bhagvan Prasad to express his own personal religious roots within the Ramanandi universe.

Bhagvan Prasad's account of the life of Ramanand spans approximately eighteen pages. It begins with the list of twenty-two gurus, starting with Ramanuja, who is referred to here only as "shri 108 swami," and ending with Ramanand, whose name is preceded by the phrase, "ananta shri bhagvan," or eternal God. This represented what would have been the generally agreed upon (if not official) spiritual lineage of Ramanand and therefore was a crucial element of Ramanandi guru parampara in the early twentieth century. Ramanand's immediate guru was Raghavanand, who, in addition to being accorded the honorific "shri 108," is given the suffix acharya, or virtuous leader.

The reader is told that prior to meeting Ramanand, Raghavanand (whose name, like Ramanand's, can be translated as "bliss in God") gathered about him a multitude of devotees and traveled the length and breadth of India, finally settling in Kashi (Varanasi), where he became a well-known teacher and "initiated people from all four varna [brahman, kshatriya, vaishya, shudra] and four ashrami [student, householder, retiree, and ascetic] as fervent devotees of Ram." This phrase is significant because Raghavanand's varna-blind guru style emerges as a precursor to Ramanand's own, for which the latter is so famed. Bhagvan Prasad then goes on to remark that Ramchandra became manifest as a disciple to Raghavanand in the avatar form of Ramanand. "In this manner," he continued, "the glory of the auspicious path of Shri 108 Ramanuja spread and continues to spread like nectar all over earth."

The next five-and-a-half pages focus on the great significance of Ramchandra's decision to descend to earth in the body of Ramanand, the description of which repeatedly employs the metaphor of a "bridge spanning the ocean of the world of mundane existence"; to the twelve main disciples of Ramanand, plus an additional two, Galabanand and Yoganand; and to a chart that lists the deities that took up residence in each of the bodies of these disciples.

Five further pages trace Ramanand's birth and childhood, and, most importantly, the circumstances of his discipleship to Raghavanand, which led ultimately to the creation of the Ramanandi sampraday as a distinct body of devotees. Bhagvan Prasad encapsulates the essentials of that account as follows:

Ramanand (originally Ramadatta) was born into a respectable kanyakubja brahman household in Prayag in 1300. He began schooling at the age of four and proved to be such a promising student that by the time he was eight there was nothing more the scholars of Prayag could teach him. At the age of twelve he took up residence in Kashi, where he became the student of an dandi sanyasi and lived according to smarta doctrine. He one day encountered Raghavanand in Kashi, who immediately foresaw his destiny and prophesied that young Ramadatta's body was on the verge of expiration, and therefore urged him to take refuge in Hari (Vishnu). Ramadatta referred the details of Raghavanand's outburst to his dandi sanyasi guru, who confirmed the prophecy but could offer no remedy.

The sanyasi therefore urged Ramadatta to save himself ["protect your body"] by taking refuge with the great seer [i.e., Raghavanand]. The youth went to Raghavanand, prostrated before him, and said, "hé great master, consider this body and soul an offering and protect it in this world and the next." Having performed the initiatory mantras and bestowed the name Ramanand upon him, Raghavanand then instructed his new disciple in the techniques of controlled breathing [pranayama] and deep meditation, so that when death [kal] came to spirit Ramanand away, he appeared already corpse-like. Ramanand eventually emerged from this death-like trance chanting the "shri mantra" and immediately became absorbed in serving his new guru.

At this juncture, Bhagvan Prasad remarked that Ramanand's yogic abilities were only to be expected, inasmuch as "he is himself in reality the avatar of the great master [i.e., Ramchandra]; in any event [he continues], this is all a big lila [sport] and therefore proper." Bhagvan Prasad's comment here seems gauged to forestall the criticism that an avatar of god should not have to suffer such human frailties as mortality and waste meditative effort in cosmic subterfuge. Bhagvan Prasad then took special pains to point out the circular elegance of Ramanand, the very image of god, going about his menial duties as a disciple to Raghavanand, who is depicted in the same breath as both guru and devotee of Ramanand.

The author picks up the thread of Ramanand's life at a later date: "Ramanand then undertook a series of long pilgrimages that led him all over the subcontinent. Upon returning to Kashi, Ramanand approached Raghavanand to perform the appropriate ritual guru darshan [literally, viewing] of reunion. Ramanand's codisciples meanwhile had been demanding that Raghavanand punish Ramanand for having not paid close enough attention to commensal restrictions while away on pilgrimage." Raghavanand perforce ordered Ramanand to "go forth and propagate your own sampraday."

One or two points need to be emphasized here. First, Bhagvan Prasad's edition of the Bhaktamal should be understood not simply as a scholarly tour-de-force and a concrete example of deep faith, but as a commemoration, indeed celebration, of the Ramanandi sampraday. At the heart of that commemoration lay the divine figure of Ramchandra as lived through the avatar Ramanand. This important life is thus retold as lila, cosmic sport, an expository mode that allows the narrator to reconcile Ramanand's godliness with the all-too-human predicaments in which he finds himself.

Indeed, such predicaments are an essential part of lila, because they allow the audience to elicit human meaning from the behavior of gods on earth; were gods to refrain from becoming mortal and engaging in human activity, with mortal circumstances, lila would lose the inner logic that fuels it-hence the epic, heart-wrenching tale of Ramchandra exiled from Ayodhya and beset by the forces of evil. Ramanand is thus presented not only as a disciple in a religious community that descends from Ramanuja, but is portrayed as a humble student in performance of guru-seva (service).

The crucial moment of the lila, of course, occurs when Ramanand is expelled from the discipleship of Raghavanand and the guru-brotherhood of his codisciples, an event that then enables him to complete the drama by creating the Ramanandi sampraday. Nothing in this account would have appeared problematic to Bhagvan Prasad, who in 1908 traced his own guru parampara back through forty-two generations of discipleship to Ramchandra of Ayodhya; in this parampara, Ramanuja was tenth in descent and Ramanand thirtieth. It would, however, prove offensive to a younger generation of Ramanandis a decade later.

OTHER RAMANANDIS

Varying conceptions of Ramanandi parampara (tradition) both prior and subsequent to Bhagvan Prasad's Bhaktamal commentary in the first decade of the twentieth century suggest that ambiguity on the question of Ramanand's life tended to be the rule rather than the exception, a fact that enabled Ramanand to be all things to all Ramanandis. That this was no longer the case by 1918 is evidenced by the rancorous dispute that erupted over a new Ramanandi ideological orthodoxy that conceived of Ramanand as entirely independent of Ramanuja. The versions of Ramanand's life that I present in brief below have in common a Ramanand that hails not from

Prayag, the heartland of the Gangetic north, but from the peninsular south. First among these is a highly rudimentary biographical sequence that had been dictated to Francis Buchanan in the early nineteenth century during his tour of South Bihar. This version, as told by Jagannath Das, a Ramanandi of wide renown in Bihar and a main informant of Buchanan regarding Ramanandis, described Ramanand as a Dravira, or south Indian, brahman and disciple of Vedant Acharya, a Ramanuji and also a southerner. Though Jagannath Das understood Ramanand as fundamentally important to his own religious identity, Ramanand was nevertheless an intermediate link in a religious tradition that began with Ramanuja five or six guru-generations earlier.

Over a century after Buchanan's tour a different version of Ramanand's life appeared in the Journal of the Royal Asiatic Society, authored by the well-known missionary and Indologist, J. N. Farquhar. Farquhar began his 1920 consideration of the life of Ramanand by acknowledging his good fortune at having the opportunity to attend the kumbh mela, India's largest pilgrimage festival, at Allahabad (Prayag) in 1918, where he met with many Ramanandis, including no doubt some younger sadhus who would soon lead the call for a new, more stringent Ramanandi tradition.

Based on encounters with Ramanandis at the Prayag kumbh, Farquhar theorized that Ramanand was a south Indian who migrated northward around 1430, took up residence in Kashi, and flourished there until about 1470. Notwithstanding this southern connection, which he would eventually abandon in any case, Farquhar contended that Ramanand was completely unconnected to Ramanuja or any Ramanuji gurus, but acknowledged that he nevertheless borrowed liberally from the qualified monism of Ramanuja; only in later generations would Ramanandis and Ramanujis begin to associate with each other because of the proximity of their philosophical doctrines.

By 1920, of course, the question of Ramanand had already erupted into a full-blown controversy within the Ramanandi community itself, and the issue of the Journal of the Royal Asiatic Society, which no doubt was as closely read in Allahabad,

Banaras, and Patna as in London, was sure to spark many responses. That of Rai Bahadur Lala Sita Ram is of particular importance, because of an extensive correspondence he carried on with the eminent linguist and Indologist Sir George Grierson from about 1904 until the mid 1930s. Sita Ram was a retired magistrate and deputy collector of Uttar Pradesh who became associated with Allahabad University and eventually authored the definitive, Vaishnava history of Ayodhya.

In a letter sent to Grierson at the end of June 1920, Sita Ram expressed his strong objections to several points in Farquhar's essay and offered a number of corrections to it, arguing in no uncertain terms that Ramanand was originally a guru in the Ramanuji tradition who later branched off to develop his own teachings of boundless love that refused to countenance the narrow-mindedness of caste and ritual. Interestingly, however, Sita Ram raised no objection to Farquhar's original contention that Ramanand was a brahman from the south. Grierson received this particular correspondence two years after his essay on "Ramanandi, Ramawat" for the Encyclopaedia of Religion and Ethics. Nevertheless, the imprint of Sita Ram's Ramanandi views on the social implications of Ramanand's bhakti tenacity, along with Bhagvan Prasad's Bhaktamal-derived narrative of Ramanand's life, emerge clearly in Grierson's article.

The representations of Ramanand by Grierson and Sita Ram on the one hand and by Farquhar on the other reflect the determination of each party to offer a complete and static view of a Ramanandi sampraday that was in reality experiencing the throes of dramatic change. Grierson and Sita Ram's Ramanand was a disenchanted Ramanuji who tried to span the caste divisions of fourteenth-century Gangetic society with a message of love and equality.

Farquhar's Ramanand, by contrast, was completely independent of the Ramanujis; Farquhar even argued, based both on his experience with Ramanandis and on his perception of the orthodoxy of a number of prominent "medieval" disciples, that "there is no evidence that [Ramanand] modified the social rules of caste in the slightest."

In retrospect, Farquhar's presentation of the historical question of Ramanand reflects his attempt to reconcile the many different (and often conflicting) opinions he must have encountered during his discussions with Ramanandi sadhus at the 1918 kumbh. Grierson, by contrast, left India in the mid 1890s; his presentation of Ramanand's life, therefore, reflects his connections with an older generation of Ramanandi scholars in closer contact with colonial officialdom, such as Lala Sita Ram and Sitaramsharan Bhagvan Prasad, the Bhaktamal exegete.

These local variations on the theme of Ramanand's life were no doubt supplemented by numerous others through the course of the nineteenth century, versions that differed not only in relatively minor details but on the overarching question of Ramanuja. The variety and fluidity of parampara in the pre-1918 phase serves to highlight again the most salient organizational feature of the sampraday, namely, the many-centered nature of Ramanandi authority. A product of the constantly shifting fortunes of powerful monasteries in local settings, this diffuse populism meant that the only opportunity for reconciliation of ideological differences (and perhaps the only occasion that required any reconciliation) in the sampraday occurred approximately once every three years on the occasion of the kumbh mela (held by turns in Nasik, Ujjain, Allahabad, or Haridwar)-and then only among those sadhus who chose to attend.

THE RISE OF RADICAL RAMANANDIS

The quest for power and influence in the Ramanandi sampraday took place on the ground of the past, and those best able to negotiate that ground ultimately dictated the immediate social and political dimensions of the monastic community. The major transformation in the institutional memory of the sampraday occurred between 1918 and 1921: an extended moment, focused on Ayodhya in what is now eastern Uttar Pradesh, but concluded at the Ujjain kumbh in what is now western Madhya Pradesh. The events of 1918-1921 extended thus to the southwesternmost edge of the Hindi-speaking north, to Malwa, the Vindhya Range, and the headwaters of the Chambal River-a region that represents for many the border between south and north India. The location of Ujjain was geoculturally appropriate for the denouement of the crisis, given the implications of the debate for southern influences in the Ramanandi sampraday. While the object in the early 1700s in Galta was to elevate the status of Ramanand vis-à-vis Ramanuja while restricting the entry of radical anti-varna sentiment into the sampraday, the motive in 1918-1921 seems to have been to loosen that social stricture by making Ramanand altogether supreme and eliminating all mention of Ramanuja.

Though Ramanand's divine status was practically assumed by Ramanandis at the turn of the century (at least, judging by Bhagvan Prasad's Bhaktamal commentary), by 1918 a group of Ramanandis rejected vehemently the possibility that Ramanand was a member of someone else's (i.e., Ramanuja's) sampraday and insisted instead that he single-handedly founded the order. At stake, it was argued, was Ramanand's position as the unequivocal proponent of Vaishnava bhakti (love for god) in the north, an issue that naturally would have some bearing on his status as the originator of the sampraday that took his name. However, while many conceded that Ramanand was an important link in the descent of Shri Vaishnava belief, they held Ramanuja to be the original earthly fount of knowledge and devotion.

Conversely, the radical Ramanandi element could stomach no presentation of Ramanand that compromised in any way his complete and total control over his own destiny and the destiny of his religious community. I favor the term "radical" to describe these sadhus because they chose to elevate a core article of faith to force a reconstituted Ramanandi memory. The radical position demanded either allegiance or refutation: a Vaishnava was either a Ramanuji or a Ramanandi. Those who chose to retain the Ramanuja link-regardless of their opinion regarding Ramanand's divinity-found themselves accused of opposing the avatar status of Ramanand and were labeled (and stigmatized) accordingly. After 1921 both sides would seek the moral high ground by claiming the appellation "Shri Vaishnava."

Much of the resentment on the part of this new radical element stemmed from the association of Ramanuja and Ramanuji-oriented Vaishnavas with elitist attitudes and commensal practices. For instance, Shivnandan Sahay (Bhagvan Prasad's first biographer) noted in 1908 that among the many differences between Ramanujis and Ramanandis, the former "only allow initiation to brahmans and kshatriyas." In fact, such attitudes were not new.

As noted earlier in the discussion of the Galta conference in the early 1700s, there had been a long-standing desire among elements within the order to limit (or at least control the ideological effects of) the entry of low-status individuals. We noted in the previous chapter as well the presence of elitist pockets in the Ramanandi sampraday in the early nineteenth century: Buchanan had observed in 1812 that though the terms Ramanandi and Ramawat were "applicable to either Brahman or Sudra, and in general both live together and are called Avadhut . . . , some Brahmans affect superior purity, will not eat with the Sudras, and are called Acharyas." (By 1918 the term acharya, which refers to a person of virtuous conduct, would come to be associated with Ramanuji elements in the sampraday; by contrast, das, which means servant or slave, was symbolic of one's Ramanandi status.)

Finally, it may be noted that the perceived elitism of Ramanuji circles in the north was generally consistent with the historian Burton Stein's conclusions (albeit for an earlier period) regarding the marked "Brahman-dominated Hindu orthodoxy" of south Indian Shri Vaishnava institutions, especially at Tirupati and Srirangam, which prohibited the infiltration of shudras.

While social and religious elitism was not a new phenomenon in the sampraday, the emergence of a widespread and coordinated opposition to that elitism was. In retrospect, one early indication that a major shift in attitudes was in the air may have been evident in the 1911 census returns for religious sect in Uttar Pradesh. The first response of a sizable number of Vaishnavas, when asked their sect (i.e., Vaishnava or Shaiva) by census officials in 1911, responded that they were

"Ramanandis." Given the subsequent conflict, it is likely that this response was provoked by increasing resentment felt by Ramanandis in their relations with elitist acharya elements in the order.

The catalyst for the conflict was provided in 1918 by a visit to Ayodhya by the head of the Shri Vaishnava Totadri math in south India. Particularly galling to many Ramanandis was the fact that the Anantacharya (eternal leader) from the south refused to prostrate before Sita and Ramchandra images in two major Ramanandi temples, refused to accept prasad (a ritual offering of food or drink), and in general "behaved like a strict Brahman who thought the Ramanandis an inferior community."

These angry recollections stand in sharp contrast to those of Swami Dharnidharacharya, a rising young Bihari intellectual of Ayodhya who drew close to the visitor from the south during his brief visit in 1918. Dharnidharacharya, looking back in the 1930s, was so impressed with the philosophical and moral discourses by the Anantacharya held regularly in Kanak Bhavan that, as he put it, "my heart was cleansed and I realized that there would be no better opportunity to become his disciple." When he became the chela (disciple) of the Anantacharya, he was given the name "Dharnidhar Ramanujadas," or Dharnidhar, slave of Ramanuja.

This choice of names could not have failed to irritate those radical Ramanandis who had begun associating the elitist elements in the sampraday with the figure of the south Indian theologian, Ramanujacharya. However, the use of "das" as a suffix suggests as well that the Ramanuji-Ramanandi battle lines were not firmly marked out at that time (1918), and that many Ramanandis accepted a servile position with respect to the acharyas in the order.

The radical Ramanandi opinion that began to solidify after 1918-much to the dismay of Dharnidharacharya and similar figures-was characterized by its proponents as svatantra (sovereign or free) and held essentially that Ramanand had originated a religious tradition wholly independent of any connection with Ramanuja and the Shri Vaishnavas of the south. Central to the propagation of this view was another young Ramanandi sadhu, one Bhagavad Das (later Bhagavadacharya), who had become a disciple of a prominent rasik guru in Ayodhya in 1919. To redress the many injustices and insults that he felt were being heaped upon Ramanandis by Ramanujis in the sampraday, Bhagavadacharya formed two committees: the "Shri Ramanandi Vaishnava Mahamandal," a "supra-council" that directed the svatantra movement, and the Puratatvanusandhayini Samiti, charged with identifying and studying historical documents associated with Ramanand.

Both were devoted, ultimately, to purging the sampraday of Ramanuji elements. Bhagavadacharya was soon challenged to a debate, which took place in the Hanumangarhi, the main naga fortress of Ayodhya. After it became apparent that no one had the rhetorical skills to defeat Bhagavadacharya, his guru and reportedly the most powerful intellect in Ayodhya, Mahant Swami Rammanoharprasadacharya of Bara Asthan (big place), was persuaded to oppose him in debate. According to recent Ramanandi recountings of these events, it was felt that since there was no one in Ayodhya who possessed the courage to face Rammanoharprasadacharya, the Ramanuji side would emerge victorious. In the end, and contrary to all expectations, the young disciple won the day.

The Ayodhya debate, which occured in 1919 or 1920, did not in any way signal the end of the matter. Indeed, according to Ramanandis it only created the need for the more august "historical" debate at the 1921 Ujjain kumbh. The specific question to be addressed was whether the sacred books of the south Indian Shri Vaishnavas offended Ramchandra; implicit to the debate was whether Ramanuja was regarded by Ramanand as a monastic predecessor. The Ramanuji side was defended by Swami Ramprapann Ramanujadas of the Totadri math; Bhagavadacharya argued on behalf of the radical Ramanandi position.

The jury took little time in deciding in favor of Bhagavadacharya and stating that henceforth the Ramanandi sampraday was to be independent of Ramanujacharya and south Indian Shri Vaishnavas. The new guru parampara placed Ramanand twenty-second in descent from Ramchandra and included no mention whatsoever of Ramanuja. Crucial to the Ujjain victory was the discovery of a fifteenth-century guru parampara that made no mention of Ramanuja; this parampara was said to have been authored by Agradevacharya, a grand-disciple of Ramanand, and was uncovered by the aforementioned research committee (Puratatvanusandhayini Samiti).

Even the conclusion reached at Ujjain did not completely resolve the dispute, and those Ramanandis who are today thought of as Ramanujis continue to reject the validity of the 1921 Ujjain debate. Among their objections are the charges that the fifteenth-century guru parampara was forged by Bhagavadacharya, and that the juries for both the Ayodhya and Ujjain debates were strategically loaded with prominent naga mahants and others sympathetic to the radical postition. Indeed, it would take years of writing and propagandizing before Bhagavadacharya's position would be regarded as "orthodox" by Ramanandis themselves. In a 1924 contribution to a major Hindi-language journal of Banaras, one Shyamsundardas continued to insist that the "thread of descent [in the Ramanandi sampraday] began with Ramanuja."

Three years later Bhagavadacharya would publish his first major work, ShrimadRamanand-Digvijayah (The World-Conquest of Ramanand), a four-hundred-page treatise in Sanskrit and Hindi on the life of Ramanand, thus correcting the hagiographic "deficiencies" of Ramanandi tradition. In the introduction to that work, Bhagavadacharya rearticulated his position on Ramanuja, focusing in particular on the narrative of Ramanand's life found in the Bhaktamal: "The intention with which Nabha-ji composed his poetic verse is a point of great dispute. There is no harm in suggesting that Nabha-ji's intent was to show that Shri Ramanandacharya used the very same philosophical system that Shri Swami Ramanujacharya had used to propagate religious ideas....However, it would constitute a great error to suggest that he intended to depict Shri Ramanand Swami-ji as a disciple of the sampraday and tradition of Shri Ramanuja Swami-ji."

In the same year (1927), another debate would be held in Vrindaban; according to a recollection of these events by one late twentieth-century admirer of Bhagavadacharya, the Ramanujis were said to have behaved so disrespectfully that, henceforth, they would no longer be considered part of the fourfold division of Vaishnavas (known as the chatuh-sampraday) and would no longer be allowed to share ground with Vaishnavas at the major festivals. The extent to which the radical position came to dominate Ramanandi attitudes throughout the north is reflected in the fact that Ramanujis failed to take part in the ceremonial procession of the monastic orders at the 1932 kumbh held in Ujjain.

Many scholars continued to assert into the 1930s, however, that Ramanand was not the sole, independent originator of the sampraday. In the early 1930s, Kalyan (Benediction), a widely distributed monthly magazine published in Gorakhpur, brought out a special number on the lives of famous yogis and swamis, entitled Yogank. This issue described Ramanand as a follower of Ramanuja who had been excommunicated for careless commensal behavior while on pilgrimage. Avadh Kishor Das, a supporter of the radical position and the editor of a 1935-1936 collection of essays on Ramanand and the Ramanandi sampraday, responded by attacking the editors of Kalyan:

We have nothing whatsoever in common with the Ramanuji sampraday. We disagree with them on every point. Ramanand a follower of a sampraday which we do not even accept as legitimate? How many hearts burn with this statement? But it does not end there. This enemy of the Ramanandi sampraday has launched a heavy attack....

The editor and author of Kalyan should realize that jagat-guru [lord-of-the-world] Shri Ramanandcharya-ji was never a follower of the Ramanuji sampraday but was rather according to the eternal proof of the shrutis [revealed wisdom] and shastras [legal texts] the leader of the Shri sampraday, which later became known by his name. No one excommunicated him and he was not any common devotee, but was the leader of countless devotees and the avatar of lord Shri Ram.

Avadh Kishor Das concluded by exhorting Ramanandis to confront those responsible in Gorakhpur and demand an explanation and an apology.

Eventually the views of the radical faction came to dominate the Ramanandi sampraday. Ramanandis became those who adhered to the svatantra, or independent, position and refused all links with the Ramanuja heritage, while those who retained those links were known as Ramanujis. Since guru parampara represented a fundamental element of Ramanandi identity, the dispute was certain to affect everyone in the sampraday.

Even Sitaramsharan Bhagvan Prasad, who by all indications endeavored to remain aloof from Ayodhya politics and left little in the way of comment on the radical interpretation of Ramanand's life, seems to have been touched by the controversy.

In 1908, a decade prior to the eruption of the dispute, Bhagvan Prasad's guru parampara had placed Ramanuja tenth and Ramanand twentieth in descent from Ramchandra. Bhagvan Prasad passed away in 1932, over a decade after the Ujjain decision. In a 1940s memoir written by one of his admirers and dedicated to explicating the subtleties of Bhagvan Prasad's teachings, a guru parampara is given that is said to have been taken from the pages of Bhagvan Prasad's 1928-1929 diary. This guru parampara makes no mention whatsoever of Ramanuja. Likewise, in subsequent editions of Bhagvan Prasad's commentary on the Bhaktamal, a guru parampara of Ramanand is given that places Ramanand twenty-second in descent from Ramchandra, again omitting mention of Ramanuja.

There remain, however, pockets of Ramanuji strength throughout north India. Vaishnava centers today dominated by Ramanujis include the Janaki-asthan in Sitamarhi, north Bihar (said to be the exact location where Sita was discovered emerging from the furrow left by her father's plowing), and the Galta Pith on the outskirts of Jaipur. Indeed, even Ayodhya continued to harbor many sadhus who chose not to accept the parampara advanced by Bhagavadacharya. Among them was Dharnidharacharya, who returned in 1924 despite bitter memories of Ayodhya as the center of the movement to repudiate Ramanujacharya. Indeed, as far as he was concerned (writing in the 1930s), a final decision was never reached regarding the official guru parampara.

Bhagavadacharya himself would rise, in the 1970s, to the very pinnacle of Vaishnava monastic authority as a result of his lifelong efforts. His was a circuitous route to the top, however, and along the way he would alienate many within and beyond Ayodhya, including his own guru, Mahant Rammanoharprasad, whom he defeated in debate. Even though his ShrimadRamanand-Digvijayah was published in 1927, and despite the fact that his radical position was gaining increasing acceptance among Ramanandis through the 1920s and 1930s, it would appear that Bhagavadacharya was regarded as something of a revolutionary for many years. Indeed, in 1929 Swami Raghuvaracharya of Bara Asthan (the math in Ayodhya that Bhagavadacharya had joined in 1919 and had been obliged to leave after defeating his guru in debate soon thereafter) authored a commentary on the Anandabhashya (Discourses on Bliss), which was purported to be the specific teachings of Ramanand; this text would remain unchallenged through the 1930s and 1940s as the authoritative statement of Ramanandi doctrine.

Following the tumultuous 1920s, Bhagavadacharya would retire to a cave at Mount Abu and begin formulating his scholarly campaign; he would eventually shift his base of operations to the city of Ahmedabad in Gujarat and begin writing in earnest. In 1955 Bhagavadacharya publicly took issue with the way Ramanandi doctrine was being taught, denounced Raghuvaracharya's Anandabhashya commentary as completely devoid of any connection to Ramanand's true teachings, challenged all comers to a debate on the veracity of the sources for that text, and promised to produce a document of his own. His opponents remained (according to him) silent, so in 1958 he published ShriJanakikripabhashyasya (The Discourses of Shri Janaki, or Sita).

In 1963 Bhagavadacharya authored yet another treatise, entitled ShriRamanandabhashyam (The Discourses of Ramanand), which created considerable consternation among major sampraday figures in Ayodhya and Banaras. In 1967 his first major work, ShrimadRamanand-Digvijayah, was reissued (as ShriRamanand-Digvijayah) by the Adhyapika

Shrichandandevi Press, Ahmedabad, signaling the consolidation of his position as India's preeminent Ramanandi intellect.

By the late 1960s Bhagavadacharya was approaching his hundredth year and presumably had outlived most if not all of his opponents from the 1920s; indeed, his very longevity may have contributed to his ascent in sampraday politics by the 1970s.

More important, however, were his organizational and literary energies, which during the 1940s, 1950s, and 1960s were manifest in social reform efforts to eradicate untouchability, in his authorship of more than forty articles and books in both Sanskrit and Hindi on Ramanandi doctrine, and in his editorship of a journal, Tatvadarshi (Reflections on the Supreme Spirit).

In 1971 his centenary was celebrated with great fanfare in Ahmedabad. Judging by the hundreds of luminaries in attendance, Bhagavadacharya had attained great stature both within and outside the Ramanandi sampraday-particularly in Gujarat state politics and in the all-India associational politics of the Bharat Sadhu Samaj (or Indian Sadhu Society).

Finally in 1977, at the Prayag kumbh, a wide array of sampraday leaders would declare him the first jagadguru-Ramanandacharya (universal leader [wearing the mantle of] Ramanandacharya) since Ramanand himself, and the twenty-third in descent from Ramchandra, in gratitude for his lifelong service to the sampraday. Not only would this mark the pinnacle of Bhagavadacharya's career, the granting of such an honor to the firebrand of the 1920s would signal that the radical Ramanandi view had achieved wide acceptance in Vaishnava circles by the 1970s.

In a variety of ways, then, the concerns expressed in Ayodhya in 1918-1921, which continue to ripple through north India today, mirrored those of the early eighteenth century in Galta. The important difference, however, is that in the early twentieth century the side generally perceived to have predominated-the radical Ramanandi faction-favored a radicalization of the meaning of Ramanand's life with respect to Ramanuja and varna.

By articulating a guru parampara free of any mention of Ramanuja, radical monks were in effect rejecting the very notion of social superiority which, in their view, fueled the Ramanuji "acharya" avowals of religious exclusivity. Given the details of Ramanand's contested life and the core Ramanuji assertion that Ramanand was expelled from the society of monks for careless eating practices while on pilgrimage, an opinion after 1918 on the question of Ramanuja as a spiritual antecedent of Ramanand could only be articulated with reference to caste and commensality.

While this question is taken up in greater detail below ("Caste and the New Ramanandi Order"), it should be noted that van der Veer has argued (rightly) that caste was not the only consideration in an individual's decision to support either the Ramanuji or the Ramanandi position. Van der Veer cites as evidence the fact that "even abbots of Kurmi and Barhi [cultivator and carpenter] castes chose to become Ramanuji." While I agree generally with van der Veer's position, I disagree with two assumptions that are implicit in his observation. T

he first is that the low ascriptive status of Kurmis and Barhais was self-evident (to observers and to the subjects themselves) and remained unchanged through the twentieth century. While this assumption was shared by the brahmanical and colonial elite in the early twentieth century and appears commonplace in the discourse of backward classes of the late twentieth century, it was probably not an assumption shared by many Kurmis and Barhais themselves in the 1920s.

For Kurmis, Barhais, and others, caste in the first half of the century was very much in the eye of the beholder, and many in those communities held themselves to be of high-caste status and were actively promoting programs of varna reidentification in an effort to claim for themselves a noble, kshatriya past. And, I would argue, whether they considered themselves high caste in the 1920s depended very much on whether they conceived of varna merely as a social idea to be manipulated or as a fundamental, essential, and all-encompassing mold from which there was no escape-in a word, as caste.

Van der Veer's second assumption, which emerges out of the first, is that given a low ascriptive status, Kurmis and Barhais should have supported Bhagavadacharya's radical position, thus demonstrating a disdain for caste hierarchy. While quite plausible at first glance, this assertion should raise a logical query: if in fact Kurmis and Barhais indeed believed themselves to be of low status, how could they possibly evince a disdain for caste in the first place? The answer, of course, is that while they were no doubt aware of the many assertions that they were socially inferior, they did not necessarily consider themselves to be of low status. Rather, the overt Kurmi and Barhai support for the Ramanuji position should be read as a conscious expression of their own perceptions of themselves as high status, which would be consistent with peasant attitudes toward caste and status that were coalescing outside the sampraday.

And again, a belief in one's high status requires a commitment to the very idea of hierarchy. Varna, jati, and caste are slippery concepts under the best of circumstances. This is in part because the very idea of status had long been a matter of contention in north India. Crucial to my understanding of caste is the examination from within of all casual assertions of ascriptive status, including caste. I would argue that the success of the radical Ramanandi faction in the Gangetic region after the 1920s (and particularly by the 1970s) signifies that caste no longer represented an all-encompassing, unquestioned social code for a critical mass of Vaishnava sadhus. Discerning what such ideological shifts may have meant for "ordinary people" outside the sampraday.

NEW HAGIOGRAPHY

The altered mythology of Ramanand's life imposed by the radical sentiment entailed the evolution of a new and more socially and religiously aggressive Ramanandi history. In the early 1930s a group of influential Ramanandis, tacitly supported by Bhagavadacharya, formed the Ramanandi Literature Publication Committee whose goal was the publication and propagation of Ramanandi books. The founding members of the committee included Sitaramiya Mathuradas, who had played a leading role in the 1918 committee that investigated the tradition of the Ramanandi community; Ramballabhasharan, a leading rasik of Ayodhya; and Bhagvandas, a prominent mahant of a naga akhara in Ayodhya.

The committee provided an important forum for the articulation of the wider social and religious concerns of Ramanandi history, conceived almost entirely in terms of two broad historical themes: caste elitism and the coming of Islam to India. Ramanandi concern with caste elitism focused on the restrictive recruitment practices of the major historical rival to Vaishnava monasticism, the Dasnami organization said to have been established by Shankaracharya in the beginning of the ninth century. The Ramanandi history of Islam in the subcontinent depicted Ramanand as the champion of a Hinduism that had been weakened by internecine struggle with Dasnamis and therefore vulnerable to violent Muslim persecution.

Much like their perception of Ramanuja's Shri Vaishnava practices, radical Ramanandis understood brahman elitism to be the defining feature of the Dasnami order. Bhagavadacharya described the exclusivity of Shankaracharya's Dasnamis as the religious and social antithesis of core Ramanandi teachings:

Having overcome Buddhism, Swami Shankaracharya-ji established his own monastic society. But in this he was not entirely successful. His insipid monism was incapable of drawing any followers. It was also heretical and mean-spirited. His path was only open to the brahman jati; it was difficult for others to enter. As a result, brahmans [given their small numbers] could not enlarge this community, and others were not given the opportunity to try. Ramanand understood the precise nature of this dilemma. He was well-acquainted with the consequences of parochialism. From its very inception the sampraday was egalitarian. Swami Shri Ramanand was not at all reluctant to place its egalitarianism before the world. The result was that one huge community was formed, and this was the equivalent of a holy boon for the spread of religion.

Ramanandi hindsight in the twentieth century decried the Vaishnava-Shaiva rivalry as "Hindu versus Hindu" conflict. In order to endow the narrative of this internecine strife with dramatic force, the new Ramanandi historiography relied on a depiction of Muslims as unidimensional villains bent on the destruction of a divided Hindu society. In the words of Sitaramiya Mathuradas, Shaivas stood by opportunistically "while Vaishnavas were butchered by Muslims." Bemoaning the caste-mindedness that was thought to have fed rival monastic antipathies and Hindu decline vis-à-vis Islam in this period, another author wrote, "This was not a time to bicker about jati differences, this was a time to 'worship god and be part of god.'" The egalitarian presciptions of radical Ramanandis in the 1930s relied, then, on a new Ramanandi view of the past rife with distinctly anti-Muslim rhetorical tones.

It should be noted that Ramanandis in early twentieth-century Ayodhya struck this ardently anti-Muslim pose despite the fact that much of the land with which the various orders within the sampraday enriched themselves was given to the Ayodhya monasteries by Shuja ud-Daula (the Nawab of Awadh) in the late eighteenth century. Judging from Buchanan's description, written in the second decade of the nineteenth century, an antagonism toward things and people Islamic at that time could not have been further from the minds of Ramanandis: "The Ramanandis or Ramawats [of Gorakhpur district] have very numerous establishments, and a great deal of land free of revenue, the greater part of which I am told, they obtained from Suja ud Doulah, to whom they contrived to render themselves very agreeable. They are indeed skilful courtiers. Most of the lands were therefore granted to the convents of Ayodhya, near where this prince resided." Nevertheless, the radical Ramanandi view in the twentieth century broke with its eighteenth-century antecedents and held that fourteenth-century north Indian Hindu society had been embroiled in internecine squabbles and had suffered the relentless persecution of Muslim tyranny.

A vision of Muslim persecution in the past did not mean, however, that the Ramanandi sampraday had no room for some Muslims in the present. The radical vision articulated by Bhagavadacharya included the careful reiteration that the "first generation" of Ramanand's followers emerged from virtually all sections of society-especially, in the person of Kabir, Muslim society. Ramanand's first circle of disciples represented an ideal model for coexistence in the present, but on Ramanandi terms: Bhagavadacharya laid great stress on the assertion that "Vaishnava religion is not reserved for only one certain jati and only one lineage; rather, any jati, any lineage, any class, and any person can find a place in its huge domain."

And not only was Kabir the quintessential example of devotion and diversity in this paradigmatic vision of society, along with the other disciples he was thought to have been a manifestation of Vaishnava divinity: "Much as the community of gods took the form of monkeys and aided Ramchandra when he was an avatar, many liberated souls took earthly form in the age of avatar Ramanand.

Narad, Bhisham, Bali and others became brahmans, kshatriyas, vaishyas, shudras, Muslims, etc. and carried out fully the wishes of Ramanand." In much the same way that the radical Ramanandi vision deemed varna insignificant in matters of belief, Islam too was conceived as but a minor impediment to participation in a community driven by Ramanandi love. If "thousands of brahmans, kshatriyas, vaishyas, shudras, and untouchables fell in love with the beauty of Vaishnavism," why exclude Muslims? Indeed, according to Bhagavadacharya, Ramanand invited such a diverse range of devotees to be his own disciples precisely so he could "through them cleanse Bharat [India] all at once in the unremitting current of the Ganga." The exact dimensions of the "cleansing" process were left to the discretion and imagination of the reader.

CASTE AND THE NEW RAMANANDI ORDER

Bhagavadacharya's strident reiteration of Ramanand's fourteenth-century liberalism signified the reemergence of the view that caste status could constitute neither an obstacle nor an asset to full participation in the sampraday. The experiences of other Ramanandis of the late nineteenth and early twentieth centuries confirm this general disdain for commensal restrictions according to caste, but at the same time reflect a fundamental equivocation on the issue of varna differentiation. Perhaps no individual better reflects the Ramanandi disdain for caste than Bhagvan Prasad, the Bhaktamal exegete who ranked among the top intellectuals of Ayodhya at the turn of the century.

Bhagvan Prasad was born in 1840 into a family of scholarly, well-to-do Kayasths, already noted for their long-standing contributions to Ramanandi literature. Much of his childhood was spent in Mubarakpur, a prestigious Kayasth enclave near the town of Chapra in Saran District. In Mubarakpur a local Ramanandi named Shivcharan Bhagat-a Koiri (vegetable gardener) "whose knowledge of Persian was so great people addressed him as munshi (scribe)"-had an early influence on Bhagvan Prasad's religious education.

In 1858, one year after his marriage, Bhagvan Prasad became a disciple of Swami Ramcharandas, of Parsa village, Chapra District, who bestowed upon him the name Sitaramsharan, a typically rasik title that connotes taking refuge (sharan) in the conjoined deity of Sita and Ramchandra. In 1863 Bhagvan Prasad became a subinspector of schools, and his subsequent employment in this line took him all over Bihar.

It was not until 1881, however, that Bhagvan Prasad was introduced to the famous rasik of Bhagalpur, Shri Ramcharandas Hanskala, and was granted the title Rupkala, which may be translated as "manifest beauty." Bhagvan Prasad never had children, and between the years 1885 and 1895 his mother, father, and wife all passed away; left with no immediate family ties to Bihar, Bhagvan Prasad, like his father and uncle before him, retired to a contemplative life in Ayodhya.

In addition to earning a broad reputation as a rasik poet and Ramanandi scholar, Bhagvan Prasad gained a certain notoriety during his government service as one who was only too willing to flout the norms of public decency. While in Patna as Deputy Inspector of Schools, as biographer Shivnandan Sahay noted with reluctant admiration, Bhagvan Prasad frequently "attended to the personal religious needs of his palanquin-bearing Kahar, his servants, and his shoe-repairman as Vaishnavas, one and the same." Bhagvan Prasad's blatant disregard for caste in the pursuit of the Ramanandi ideal of religious devotion aroused the consternation of many of his peers, who complained that ministrations to people of shudra and untouchable status would only result in a depletion of the economic and social services provided by those segments of society. In particular, respectable people were greatly put out by what appeared to them a presumption of dignity on the part of lowly shudras.

According to Sahay, many of them raised objections to Bhagvan Prasad's ministrations to mere laborers-in this case Kahars-on the grounds that the latter would develop ideas about proper and improper work and eventually refuse to perform the back-breaking task of palanquin-bearing. While the fears of respectable society may have been real, it is also extremely likely that Bhagvan Prasad's close religious interaction with shudras and untouchables evoked a more visceral response, quite apart from any impending scarcity of laboring Kahars.

Even Sahay himself felt obliged to apologize for his subject's behavior, explaining that "as far as I understand, his idea was that by ministering to these people they would be more attentive to the salubrity of their meals and would thereby not be faced with any obstacles en route to salvation."

Bhagvan Prasad's ministrations reflected his own personal interpretation of the social mandate implicit in the religious message of Ramanand. However, Ramanandi ambivalence toward caste emerged in discussions about the prescribed stages of a sadhu's entry into the sampraday. In his biography of Bhagvan Prasad, Sahay expressed the view that originally anyone (including untouchables) could have become Ramanandi sadhus, but that by his time (the early 1900s), "Ramanandis bring disciples from only those jatis from whom water can be taken."

For those designated shudra by the elite, this phrase, "from whom water can be taken," was a common enough euphemism for a person of "pure shudra" status, with whom restricted physical contact could be made. From the elite perspective, such physical contact would have occurred in the course of consuming goods and services common in everyday life; the designation "pure shudra" implied a substantial body of "impure"-hence untouchable-people with whom physical contact was both unnecessary and improper.

Buchanan, in the early nineteenth century, had included in the term "pure shudra" the well-known designations of Kayasth, Koiri, Kurmi, Kahar, Goala, Dhanuk (archers, cultivators, palanquin bearers), Halwai (sweets vendor), Mali (flower gardener), Barai (cultivator and vendor of betel-leaf), Sonar (goldsmith), Kandu (grain parcher), and Gareri (blanket weavers and shepherds).

By the late nineteenth century Kayasths had begun organizing a movement to reject their ascribed shudra status in favor of a kshatriya one; by the early twentieth century, many others-particularly Kurmis, Koiris, Kahars, and Goalas-followed the Kayasth lead (although each utilized distinct arguments) and defined for themselves similar kshatriya identities. All these reform movements, however, had in common serious attempts at the redefinition of physical labor in terms that reflected the newfound desire for respectability. Shivnandan Sahay's observation that "Ramanandis bring disciples from only those jatis from whom water can be taken" reflects a subtle but important equivocation on the issue of caste, an equivocation that spelled the difference between those who were able to join the ranks of Ramanandi sadhus and those who could only benefit from the teachings of Ramanand and Ramanandis.

Furthermore, the fact that an initiate had gained entry into the sampraday did not necessarily mean he was guaranteed equal treatment irrespective of varna status. According to Lala Sita Ram, author of an important Vaishnava history of Ayodhya, numerous exceptions were made for high-caste novitiates of a major naga akhara (the Hanuman Garhi in Ayodhya). Those exceptions included a waiver of the thirteen-year age limit for initiation as well as freedom from having to perform "any lowly tasks," i.e., having to prepare meals, clear and clean dishes, carry wood, and draw water from the well. It is worthwhile noting, in this context, that present-day Ramanandis claim that prior to 1921 all Ramanandis had to perform these lowly tasks for the acharyas among them-who were exempted from such work and whom the Ramanandis would label "Ramanuji" after 1921-and that this was one of the main reasons that Bhagavadacharya strove to repudiate all connections with the south Indian Ramanujacharya. And despite the apparent victory of Bhagavadacharya and the rise to orthodox status of his views, in areas where Ramanujis remain strong Vaishnava sadhus are fully cognizant of and responsive to caste distinctions. According to Burghart, who worked primarily in Janakpur in Nepal's eastern terai,

> [The sadhus] claim that one's mind and body are formed of one's caste, and since the soul dwells within one's mind and body until death, caste rules of commensality must be observed within the sect. For this reason Ramanandis of male Twice-born body do not accept 'imperfect' (kacca) food or initiation from Ramanandis of Once-born [shudra] body. Even the Ramanandi Renouncers and Great Renouncers . . . who dress in bark, roam in itinerant monasteries and smear ashes on their body observe caste rules of commensality amongst themselves.

While Lala Sita Ram candidly accepted the fact of such caste distinctions in the process of training monks, he nevertheless defended what he saw to be the progressive attitude of the Ramanandi sampraday in the early twentieth century. For instance, he noted in his correspondence with Sir George Grierson that "a visit to any of the akharas of Ramanandi bairagis will convince that Sudras of all classes are as freely admitted and invested with the sacred thread as the twice born."

Investiture with the sacred thread conferred, by definition, elite "twice-born" status and was theoretically reserved for vaishyas, kshatriyas, and brahmans. By performing this ceremony on behalf of shudras, the Ramanandi sampraday (or some in the sampraday) effectively undermined the hierarchy implicit to caste through the adroit application of varna ideology. The practice of sacred thread investiture in Ramanandi akharas should ultimately be understood in the context of the kshatriya identity movements of the early twentieth century, inasmuch as it encapsulates in a single ritual the entire thrust of the kshatriya campaigns. Lala Sita Ram's assertion of Ramanandi progressivism in this regard would suggest that the sampraday was involved, at least tangentially, in the process of varna reidentification.

It should be added that the willingness to countenance varna distinctions in monastic recruitment and training and the recognition of the varna systemics implicit to sacred thread investiture as a strategy for shudra social advancement are both entirely consistent with the essentially Ramanuji position expressed by Sita Ram in his reaction to Farquhar's 1920 presentation of Ramanand.

Hence the Ramanandi sampraday in the early twentieth century did not (and still does not, if we accept the arguments of Burghart and van der Veer) constitute a monolith of opinion on the relevance of caste rank in monastic life.

That a debate was emerging at this time in the sampraday, with varna and status as the central issues, is clear; it is also clear that the debate was closely linked both chronologically and thematically with the divisiveness over guru parampara in 1918-1921.

Hence the position taken by Shyamsundar Das in 1924, who (like Sita Ram) has already been cited for his Ramanuji stand with respect to Ramanand's guru antecedents: in the pages of north India's most respected Hindi-language periodical, the Nagaripracharani Patrika, Shyamsundar Das disputed the contention that "Ramanand broke completely with the strictures of varnashramdharm [living according to the dictates of varna and one's stage of life]" even though "there is no doubt that in choosing his disciples he gave no thought to considerations of jati."

Questions of caste propriety were inescapably linked to the issue of guru parampara, inasmuch as the choice of one's disciples (or, conversely, one's guru) represented the most concrete expression of social ideology.

By the 1930s three discernible factions appear to have emerged around the issue of caste status in the sampraday. Again, disagreement revolved around whether an individual-in this context a shudra individual-retained his varna status after becoming a Ramanandi monk.

The egalitarian view, favored by a group led by Bhagavadacharya, held that "amongst sadhus there is no varna system at all" and that "someone of shudra origins can be considered just as pure upon becoming a Vaishnava ascetic as a Vaishnava from a brahman family."

In opposition stood Swami Raghuvaracharya (the author of Anandabhashya, theologically dismissed by Bhagavadacharya in later years) and his adherents, who maintained that "the varna system does in fact exist amongst sadhus and upon becoming a Vaishnava ascetic a brahman remains a brahman and a shudra remains a shudra," and thus "the two could never eat together."

A third view, maintained by "Udasin" scholars of Ayodhya, occupied the middle ground between the two opposing factions by arguing that though "the shudra Vaishnava who exhibits all the qualities of a good Vaishnava can be considered pure in all respects . . . , this [purity] is only ornamental; in reality, he is not the same as everyone else."

Because of the multiplicity of authoritative voices in the sampraday, the question of varna would prove to be difficult to resolve. Bhagavadacharya would himself take up the cause of untouchables after his move to Ahmedabad. Apprehensive of the potential divisiveness of the controversy, particularly given the increasing influence of monks like Bhagavadacharya, one Ramanandi urged "all the scholars of the sampraday [to] convene and issue a judgment." Whether such a meeting ever took place is not known, though it is clear that the conflicting attitudes continued to thrive.

CONCLUSION

The belief in a glorious past in which persecutions by both Muslims and Dasnamis were overcome, the devotion to the central figure of Ramanand (and through him Ramchandra) unfettered by an association with the south Indian brahman Ramanuja, and the dedication to an egalitarian social order that invited the participation of elite, shudra, and untouchable alike-these constituted the core reference points for a radical Ramanandi after 1921. The following poem by Ramavatar Yadav, entitled "Yatindra-stav" (Hymn to a Great Sadhu) and featured prominently in a 1935-1936 publication honoring the reinvigorated conception of Ramanand, brought these three elements together to glorify the living past of the sampraday:

> *Though Hindu jati was lost in a fog of ignorance, you shined a light on the right path.*
>
> *Though we endured many blows at every step, you nourished us with great support and wisdom.*
>
> *Though some fled the battleground of their fate, you injected vitality back into their veins.*
>
> *You cleansed the holy ground once again, and showed the world the one-ness of Vishnu.*
>
> *Who could have exposed the fallacy of high and low if such a sadhu had not entered the world?*
>
> *Who else could have inspired the notion that no one is impure amid the tranquility of God's realm?*
>
> *Who else could have drawn so many across the ocean of existence in the sparkling moment of Ram-mantra?*
>
> *Who else could have inspired Kabir and Ravidas to liberate the oppressed with but a bit of verse?*
>
> *Who else could have comforted the fallen souls who flocked to them beneath a shower of resplendent love?*
>
> *Who else could have banished the evil notion that "he who can be cut and wounded must not be Hindu?"*
>
> *Who else could have shown such valor destroying the monolith of sin and expelling narrow-mindedness?*
>
> *Surrounded by enemies everywhere, who would have preserved the name "Hindu" had such a sadhu not arrived?*

In their reconstructed hagiography radical Ramanandis viewed Ramanand, like Ram himself, as the savior of Hindu India. Ayodhya, as north India's center of Ram worship and, hence, the main geographic focus of Ramanandi devotional attentions, could only grow in stature along with Bhagavadacharya during the twentieth century-and, not coincidentally, at the expense of older centers, such as Galta, dominated by Ramanujis.

And as Bhagavadacharya's stature grew, so did the new Ramanandi emphasis on a history of Muslim tyranny as both a catalyst and a backdrop for Hindu decline prior to the arrival of Ramanand. In retrospect, then, some of the factors that would combine to render Ayodhya a political flash point in the late twentieth century were already coming into place after 1918. As we shall see in the following chapters, Ayodhya would be reinforced as a central place in the popular imagination of north Indians through other, nonmonastic means.

From the mid-nineteenth century onward, the increasing use of print by Ramanandis would create new strains in the sampraday, simply by bringing into focus the varying versions of tradition extant in the community of monks.

Hence, print technology would help to intensify the transformation of long-held hagiographical differences into full-fledged ideological battles. That such battles were fought prior to the arrival of the printing press-though perhaps with less frequency-seems clear from the decisions taken at Galta in the early eighteenth century. Because many important monastic centers tended to be far apart and off the beaten track, rendering long-distance communication difficult, such periodic meetings were crucial to the resolution of sampraday conflicts.

The kumbh mela would answer this need in the eighteenth and nineteenth centuries, by serving as a periodic-but not too frequent-forum for settling internal as well as intersectarian disputes and for making major sampraday announcements. As a medium for the articulation of sectarian views, however, the kumbh would be supplemented and, increasingly after 1921, superceded by the printed word. Bhagavadacharya's investiture as jagadguru-Ramanandacharya in 1977 at the Prayag kumbh itself, an honor that capped a five-decade torrent of publications, is the strongest example of this new monastic reality.

The existence of the office of jagadguru Ramanandacharya after the 1970s should not be taken, however, as an indication that a supreme monastic authority can now quash doctrinal dissent in the sampraday.

To the contrary, the creation of the position has resulted since the death of Bhagavadacharya (in 1981 by most accounts) in multiple claims to the title, most of which recognize Bhagavadacharya as the first jagadguru-Ramanandacharya since Ramanand himself.

Hence, despite the dominance of radical Ramanandi views, the sampraday still does not constitute an ecclesiastical monolith with one group of religious leaders dictating religious opinion for the rank and file to follow. The sampraday remains, fundamentally, a populist organization, the monastic systemics of which depend on the recognition, respect, and support individual gurus and swamis receive in villages, towns, and cities throughout north India.

An important consequence of this institutional flexibility is that multiple views on guru parampara and caste can continue to coexist in the twentieth century, without necessarily threatening the overarching integrity of the sampraday.

Indeed, the fact that there existed a mediating, "Udasin" view on the issue of caste in the sampraday in the 1930s is of great significance here, suggesting that the contending factions in the sampraday were not involved in a damaging, two-party conflict.

Indeed, it is possible to argue that this represented the institutionalization of ambiguity on the question of caste, which in turn has allowed the sampraday to contain a broad array of social ideologies through much of the twentieth century and, thereby, to continue to broaden its appeal in north Indian society.

To what extent did the campaigns for peasant-kshatriya status outside the sampraday, discussed in the following chapters, contribute to or inform the varna debate among Ramanandis, and vice versa?

Given the intricacy of monastic networks in peasant society and the nineteenth and twentieth-century interests of monks in social reform, there should be no doubt that the two worlds spoke to each other in myriad ways.

However, as has been noted in the conclusion to the previous chapter, a new feature of religious and social discourse in peasant society in the early twentieth century was the initiative taken by local intellectuals beyond the arena of monastic sampraday.

In other words, the relationship between peasants and monks, and the popular conception of religion in day-to-day affairs, was undergoing change in the early twentieth century. Discerning that change and its social, political, and economic implications is a task for the following chapters.

3

Britain and British India

British India was not simply a place but an amalgam of ideas, politics, and people both British and Indian. The extended exchange of meaning that occurred between Britain and India, the most visible result of which may well be the idea of caste, figures prominently in the emergence of peasant-kshatriya identity and also (though perhaps in a more subtle manner) in the history of Ramanandi monasticism. Hence it is appropriate to describe at the outset the political-cultural dimensions of the colonial world and the ways in which that world touched the lives of peasants and monks in Gangetic India. The cultural and intellectual exchange between Indians and Britons in colonial India was predicated on an imbalance of power; notwithstanding the ugly face of imperialism (and perhaps because of it), this exchange shaped the very dimensions of colonial culture and turned (to borrow the phraseology of the psychologist Ashis Nandy) India and Britain into intimate enemies. The British empire in India depended upon the effective organization, maintenance, and exercise of force, material as well as ideological. For Nandy, however, more important than any military ordnance was the idea of imperial power, embodied in colonial India by the notion of martial valor.

The central implication of that important idea in the psychology of imperial rule was the rise and eventual dominance of a muscular, hyper-masculine ethos in imperial India. Hence, "many nineteenth-century Indian movements of social, religious and political reform . . . tried to make Kshatriyahood the 'true' interface between the rulers and the ruled as a new, nearly exclusive indicator of authentic Indianness." It has been suggested in response to Nandy that the search for a martial Indianness only occurred in a narrow "zone of contact," a zone restricted to the urban world of bureaucracy, scholarship, and nationalism and peopled with the "self-conscious Indians" who were "the elite, the articulate, the Westernized."

Accordingly, we should seek to know more about the other Indian "'out there,' in the villages far from the Western experience, who is not consciously embattled by the West, not torn about his Indianness, who carries on being his Indian 'self' without a sense of the historical problematic in which he is unwittingly situated."

The peasants of British India were the villagers who lived "far from the Western experience." However, the history of kshatriya reform, which spoke directly to the question of status in a distinctly colonial society, suggests that they were in fact not so greatly removed from the "zone of contact." Torn less about their "Indianness" than their British-Indianness, they were at least as concerned with questions of self and identity as their "westernized, intellectual" compatriots, particularly those in the elite nationalist movement.

The aggressive articulation of kshatriya identity in the early twentieth century is evidence of the extent of their involvement in the colonial culture; the desire to appropriate a kshatriya ideal extended deep into peasant society, to productive cultivators on the margin of land-control and status in the Gangetic countryside.

Further, what people "out there" wrote, discussed, and believed was based on a sense of the past that relied on myth, legend, and lineage, not to mention British examinations and recapitulations of that myth, legend, and lineage. However, the articulation of peasant-kshatriya identity differed in significant ways from the kshatriyahood of the colonial elite in that the latter usually combined martial status with landed power, imperial certification, and brahmanical patronage. Peasant kshatriyahood, by contrast, lacked all these assets, but drew on Vaishnava identities and discourses nurtured in part by institutional connections to Vaishnava-particularly Ramanandi-monasticism. And, though that monasticism existed in religious centers located far (ideologically if not geographically) from the western experience, it too spilled over on occasion into the "zone of contact."

It has been argued that the popular concern with identity and status was part of, and perhaps a response to, processes of ideological change centered on the notion of caste in British-Indian society-particularly in proximity to the census office.

Certainly the thoughts, words, and deeds of peasants and monks in the colonial era confirm that caste was a subject of great interest to all, in large part because the ideology of inequality and status (and, by implication, equality and identity) implicit to caste enabled individuals, communities, and the state to facilitate, moderate, or obliterate social change.

And certainly the caste we have come to know in the late twentieth century is in part (some would say in large part) the product of a colonial discourse: British imperial anthropology manifest by the late nineteenth century in a pervasive British-Indian census bureaucracy, which inadvertently reified brahmanical hierarchy-or an ideology of inequality articulated by brahmans who resided atop that hierarchy-as part of a process of colonization writ cultural.

But while the empire can be held accountable for many evils, one suspects that the full burden of caste injustices cannot be laid squarely on its shoulders.

Status and social rank-and the peasant, monastic, and colonial fixation on status and social rank-should be understood as part of a much older, though perhaps more socially restricted, Indic discourse of varna. Scholars have disagreed widely on the degree to which varna represents an integrated, all-encompassing model of and for Indian social relations; few, however, contest the precolonial existence of the discrete religious, political, and economic roles of priest (brahman), warrior (kshatriya), merchant (vaishya), and servant (shudra) that make up varna.

That varna was conceived by brahmans in the distant past as an implicitly hierarchical division of labor is confirmed by the unimpeachable antiquity of the myth of the primordial man, from whose head and mouth sprang brahmans, torso and arms kshatriyas, loins and thighs vaishyas, and legs and feet shudras.

These ideas did not require a European colonial state to ensure their ideological longevity; they did require, however, certain enforced inequalities (including gender inequalities) in post-Vedic, precolonial Indian society-a detailed consideration of which is, fortunately, beyond the scope of this study.

While we can presume that, historically, most brahmans and perhaps many kshatriyas and vaishyas subscribed to the hierarchy implicit in varna, we cannot know the extent to which that subscription was shared by shudras. The historiography of ancient and medieval India suggests that shudras did not necessarily care for the servile status ascribed to them.

The principle of social hierarchy, and the fundamental human inequalities that it implied, would have been even more repellent to a substantial portion of the population relegated to a social realm beyond and therefore below the four varna and existing by definition on the periphery of society. Members of this group of perennial outsiders, bound in economic, political, and social servitude to varna society in intricate and myriad ways, have been known generally by a variety of names.

They have been derided as dasyu (barbarian), dasa (slave), paraiyan (pariah), and untouchable; they have been patronized as harijan (as Gandhi's children of god) and scheduled (as names on a government list); and they have asserted themselves as untouchable, achhut (untouched) and, more recently, dalit (oppressed). For historians seeking to understand the history of this underclass prior to the twentieth century, however, its voices are difficult to discern.

Untouchable, shudra, vaishya, kshatriya, and brahman are large, unwieldy categories. Rendering them socially and economically practicable are a plethora of occupational groupings, known generally as jati, that developed over time in Indian society and inclusion in which was thought to be predicated on birth. The thousands of extant jati identities are theoretically locatable within the fourfold varna hierarchy or, without, as untouchables. To the extent the Indic social order was value-laden and led to axioms of physical, moral, and intellectual superiority and inferiority, varna (and the untouchability it implies) represents an interesting analogue to the western notion of race.

However, varna and race have differed not only according to strict definitions, but insofar as they evolved in distinctly different geographic, material, and human environments.

As is well known, those environments suddenly overlapped with the arrival of the Portuguese near the turn of the sixteenth century, the result of which was the hermeneutic of caste. Caste, and the racial hierarchy that it came to evoke for many Indians and Britons alike, is an important hybrid (and historically locatable) idea that permeates much of the colonial past and the people who lived it.

The colonial understanding of India, increasingly centered on caste, relied on a corps of elite officials who sought to understand and compartmentalize the complexity of religious, cultural, and social life and who presented their amassed data in gazetteers, census reports, surveys, and other encyclopedic compendia.

Typical north Indian examples of such men are Francis Buchanan (later known as Francis Hamilton, 1762-1829), James Tod (1782-1835), Henry Miers Elliot (1808-1853), W. W. Hunter (1840-1900), William Crooke (1848-1923), H. H. Risley (1851-1911), George Grierson (1851-1941), and L. S. S. O'Malley (1874-1941). They and others like them worked either for the English East India Company or for the Government of British India.

Their role was to study, interpret, and report on Indian society; their research was based on translation, linguistic analysis, philological speculation, statistical surveys, textual study, ethnography, anthropometry, and observation; and their understanding was heavily colored by their cultural predispositions, administrative functions, and political roles.

The volumes they produced immediately entered the public domain and, as politically vital information, became authoritative ethnographic, cultural, and historical texts for Europeans and Indians alike.

In short, Indian meaning-of obvious importance to the successful functioning of government-was collected, analyzed, and reproduced in standardized form by the ruling power. This bringing of Indian meaning to political authority was not only necessary for administration, but also served to politically revalidate that body of knowledge.

It is not entirely surprising, therefore, that peasant ideologues looked to this official literature in the twentieth century to buttress their kshatriya identities.

Insofar as the official literature often drew on elite Indian sources, especially with respect to caste, this process should also be seen as an official certification of a brahmanical discourse of hierarchy. Great caution must be utilized, therefore, when drawing upon this literature in the context of kshatriya reform, to ascertain whether hierarchy was in fact being popularized or whether it was being manipulated and thereby subverted.

Another reason to exercise caution with the official literature-inspired in part by the publication of Edward Said's Orientalism-is the fact that the information therein is colored by the colonial predispositions of its British authors.

It is true that all interpretation falls victim at some point to cultural and psychological subjectivism; as Nandy points out in his effort to comprehend the salient psycho-cultural dimensions of colonialism, "The West has not merely produced modern colonialism, it informs most interpretations of colonialism. It colours even this interpretation of interpretation." Like Nandy, we should endeavor to focus upon our own interpretive dilemma and put it to good analytical use, thus making our work all the more meaningful.

By identifying the cultural-and, with Nandy, the psychological-subjectivity of British interpretation in the nineteenth and early twentieth centuries, we can speculate about the nature of British-Indian society during the colonial period. A bulwark of colonial power was the colonial elite's conception of Indian society, especially the idea of caste. Caste was the ideological linchpin of colonial authority, a language of race spoken by the powerful and understood by the powerless, and therefore central to the colonial Indian world.

But, as the historian Nicholas Dirks has cautioned, "The assumption that the colonial state could manipulate and invent Indian tradition at will, creating a new form of caste and reconstituting the social, and that a study of its own writings and discourse is sufficient to argue such a case, is clearly inadequate and largely wrong."

All the arguments of the cultural hegemony of the colonial state notwithstanding, what is presented in British understanding reflected a form of Indian social, cultural, and religious reality. Historians can and should learn not only from the reflected reality, but from the mode of reflection itself. Going one step further, it can be argued that one cannot be utilized to the exclusion of the other.

As a reflection of reality, caste and the body of orientalist literature upon which it relied represents one side of an emergent British-Indian dialogue, a dialogue that developed dialectically into a cultural system all its own: partly British, partly Indian, wholly British-Indian.

The other side of that dialogue-grounded in a popular discourse that was all-too-infrequently perceived by colonial officials, not to mention postcolonial scholars who rely overly on colonial commentary-is the understanding and reshaping of social relations by peasants and monks in colonial north India.

The way these peasants and monks came to terms with varna, jati, race, and caste thus forms the central problem of this study. Peasants and monks were particularly well poised to examine these concepts in the context of political action and religious identity in the colonial period.

The former were regarded as of low status (i.e., shudra), ostensibly because of their engagement in agricultural labor. Yet their position of relative social inferiority was offset by their significant demographic strength, their centrally productive role in society, and the opportunities for economic advancement that confronted them in the nineteenth century. Buoyed by these material strengths, peasants in Gangetic India began to reject the shudra definitions ascribed to them by the social elite.

Likewise, monks did not stand aloof from the worldly concerns of status and hierarchy but remained intensely devoted to a commentary and, more often than not, a critique of that world. The many ways peasants and monks conceived of social relations constituted not only important and overlapping arenas of cultural change during the colonial period, but informed the conception of race and caste after independence from British rule in 1947.

What emerges then is that "Hindu" ideas have impinged in important ways on social and political change in Indian history. This should not appear surprising, inasmuch as the term Hindu has long communicated social and political meaning. Persians, Greeks, and Arabs first used variations of the term Hindush as a geographic designator to describe the territory to the east of the Indus (ancient Shindu) River; "Hindu" later came to be used by Turkish, Persian, and finally European (and especially British) observers as a religious signifier describing someone who followed a system of beliefs (today collectively termed "Hinduism") distinct from the then more familiar Islam.

In fact, as the etymological development of this term would indicate, Indian religion may have been too complex and discrepant to be described adequately under the single rubric, as a Hindu-ism.

A systematic Hinduism did of course emerge in recent centuries, influenced in part by European attempts to understand Indian religion according to European paradigms, in part by a nationalist movement that sought to draw on noncontradictory religious meanings, and in part by religious reformers who sought to reconcile regional religious contradictions so as to participate in the emerging Indian political discourse of nation and race. Underneath the rubric of that emergent, "modern" Hinduism existed a divisible multiplicity of overlapping religious systems.

In the Gangetic north this included, by the eighteenth century, expanding monastic institutions of Vaishnava belief centered on bhakti, or love for God. Vaishnava bhakti, or the conception of Vishnu and his avatars as deserving of complete devotion, is the religious ground upon which much of the ideological change described in this study takes place. The following pages are an attempt to reinvest those terms with social and political meaning and in the process instill in social and political history a sense of cultural change.

INDIAN SADHUS AND SHUDRAS

Sadhus and Shudras in North India, ca. 1700-1900

This chapter has three related objectives. First, it introduces and situates Shaiva and Vaishnava monasticism and related religious movements in the late eighteenth and early nineteenth-century Gangetic north, particularly in the context of expanding colonial rule. Second, it seeks to understand Indian monasticism not as timeless and static (which is how sadhus often represent the religious worlds to which they belong), but as historically measurable, comprising competing social institutions organized around distinct religious and ideological principles and responsive to continually changing political circumstances and economic pressures. Third, and most importantly, I argue in this chapter that north Indian Vaishnava monastic circles contained strong reformist mentalities evident in the relationships between Ramanandi monks and people of low status, particularly in comparison to the competing religious perspectives in the central Gangetic region of Bihar and eastern Uttar Pradesh.

These reformist mentalities can be seen as well in traditions relating to both Shaiva and Vaishnava monastic soldiering in the precolonial era, with which this chapter begins; however, the main discussion is focused on the nineteenth century and relies primarily, but not exclusively, on surveys, censuses, and scholarship produced by the colonial desire to possess greater knowledge about Indian society. The subject of Vaishnava reformist mentalities as a basis for ideological change is pursued in the following chapter, which is a more detailed consideration of Ramanandi views on religion, caste, and inequality in the early twentieth century.

Subaltern Sadhus

Besides affording an intriguing view of popular ideological change, the history of Indian monasticism is an excellent index of the changing political culture of north India during the transition to colonial rule. Prior to 1800, gosains and bairagis (Shaiva and Vaishnava monks, respectively) exercised broad political and economic influence as merchants, bankers, and, most importantly, soldiers.

Powerful mahants (abbots) speculated in real estate and engaged in extensive moneylending activities in order to diversify monastic endowments in urban centers throughout the north, thus facilitating links between the increasingly regional political economies of the late Mughal era. Indeed, Christopher Bayly has suggested that gosains in particular "came the nearest of any Indian business community to the emerging bourgeoisie that European theorists from Sleeman to Marx wished to see." Gosains were so well entrenched in Asian commerce that Warren Hastings saw fit to avail the English East India Company of their good offices in what was ultimately a failed bid to acquire trade relations with Tibet and China in the late 1700s.

Gosains and bairagis were able to engage successfully in trade and finance during the eighteenth century because they not only possessed excellent commercial intelligence and political connections but had access to a sufficient degree of independent armed force to back their profit-making ventures. In fact, the unsettled conditions of the middle of the century can be seen in retrospect to have benefited the monastic armies, since in addition to protecting monastic endowments, sectarian shrines, pilgrimage routes, and commercial interests, gosain and bairagi regiments were increasingly incorporated in the armies of the major regional powers. Hence, despite the early commonality of commercial interests between the new English trader-rulers and the well-placed gosain and bairagi merchants, it was inevitable that in the rich province of Bengal armed monks and

Company soldiers would come into conflict. When it did occur, that conflict took the form of a prolonged series of skirmishes in Bengal and Bihar over four decades (1760s to 1800), usually referred to as the "sanyasi and fakir rebellion."

At one level, this rebellion seems to have stemmed from purely materialist motives, namely, from the excessive revenue burdens introduced by the Company on monastic and nonmonastic landlords alike and from the tendency of Company officials to side with landlords in disputes with powerful gosain moneylenders.

More important, however, was the fact that sadhus were accustomed to bearing arms while on pilgrimage routes through Bengal and in some cases possessed the right to levy contributions from villages along those routes; in addition, many sadhus sought military service with landlords and petty rajas in the region. Company officials, for their part, were increasingly opposed to such practices and sought to discourage the armed bands of sanyasis and fakirs from operating in the province. One early encounter, recorded by the noted Company surveyor James Rennell who at the time (1766) was mapping territory just south of the Himalayan foothill kingdom of Bhutan, bears testimony to the martial potential of armed monks and the resentment of armed sadhus at the new impositions being placed on them by the Company state. Rennell happened upon a skirmish in progress between Company troops and a force of seven hundred such sadhus; the wounds he received included a saber gash that "cut through my right Shoulder Bone, and laid me open for nearly a foot down the Back, cutting through and wounding some of my Ribs, . . . a cut on the left Elbow, which took off the muscular part of the breadth of a Hand, a Stab in the Arm, and a large cut on the head."

The Company prevailed in that particular confrontation, but over three decades would pass before the akharas (monastic armies) would be disarmed in Bengal or, at the very least, driven beyond Company-controlled territories. This prolonged confrontation between Company soldiers and armed sadhus is generally understood in terms of the Company desire to establish itself as militarily supreme in the province of Bengal. Rarely, if ever, are the ideological implications of the conflict examined by social historians, and the term "rebellion," considered a political overstatement given the nature of the conflict, seems now to have been discarded.

However, the phenomenon of armed monasticism certainly posed more than simply a "law and order" challenge for newly ascendant Company officials. Armed sadhus were the very antithesis of the world the company-state was endeavoring to create in the eighteenth and nineteenth centuries, namely, a settled peasant society that would render forth vast agrarian revenues on a regular basis with as little resistance as possible. The modern state in India could not countenance recalcitrant sadhus wandering about the countryside armed, dangerous, often naked, and claiming to represent an alternate locus of authority.

The Company needed a modern sadhu: a priestly monk unconcerned with worldly power and given over completely to religious contemplation and prayer. Hence Warren Hastings's proclamation of 21 January 1773 banishing "all Biraugies and Sunnasses [bairagis and sanyasis, or armed Vaishnava and Shaiva monks] who are travellers strangers and passengers in this country" from the provinces of Bengal and Bihar, save "such of the cast of Rammanundar and Goraak [Ramanand and Gorakhnath] who have for a long time been settled and receive a maintenance in land money . . . from the Government or the Zemindars of the province, [and] likewise such Sunasses as are allowed charity ground for executing religious offices." In other words, those sadhus who were "neither vagrants nor plunderers but fixed inhabitants," who "quietly employ themselves in their religious function," could, in Hastings's view, be tolerated.

Armed monasticism holds more than just military and political-cultural interest, however. There are indications that the rise of Vaishnava and Shaiva monastic soldiering afforded, or in some way reflected, increased entry of people of low social status, particularly those deemed shudra by the twice-born elite, into the major monastic orders in Gangetic north India. In this sense, the history of the armed akharas is not unlike that of the Sikhs in the Punjab, the arming of whom, according to W. H. McLeod, was occasioned by the prolonged infusion of Jat peasants into the Nanakpanthi community. By the eighteenth century the profusion of Jat Sikhs cemented in demographic fact the professed egalitarianism that had long been a powerful ideological component of Guru Nanak's teaching. Hence for McLeod, Sikh hagiography (which speaks of a unilateral decision on the part of Guru Govind Singh to militarize the Nanakpanth in 1699) masks slow processes of social and demographic transformation.

Similarly, it is possible to perceive the social dimensions of militarization by looking within Shaiva and Vaishnava monastic traditions regarding the decision to take up arms. For example, a widely accepted Dasnami legend recorded by J. N. Farquhar in the early twentieth century held that Shaiva monks took up arms during the reign (and with the approval) of the Mughal emperor Akbar (r. 1556-1605) to defend brahman sanyasis against the persecutions of Muslim fakirs. While the motivational elements of this tradition can be challenged on the basis of both historical and historiographical evidence, it is perhaps more significant that Farquhar also related his general impression that the arming of Shaivas relied on the heavy recruitment of shudras into the elite ranks of the Dasnami order.

Whether shudras were indeed actively recruited as soldier Dasnamis, or whether the assertion of past military recruitment became a convenient way of explaining the increasing number of shudras in the order, the fact remains that today certain segments of orthodox, high-caste Dasnamis avoid commensal relations with warrior monks because of the latter's supposedly low origins.

One can see stronger suggestions of the involvement of shudras (and, indeed, others of low and marginal status such as women and untouchables) in traditions relating to Vaishnava monastic soldiering. One important Vaishnava narrative holds that the arming of bairagis was the product of a conscious decision made in 1713 by leaders of the four main Vaishnava sampraday-often referred to collectively as the chatuh-sampraday, namely, the orders organized around the teachings of Vishnuswami, Madhvacharya, Nimbarkacharya, and Ramanujacharya (in which Ramanandis were included).

According to this tradition, the major Vaishnava mahants met at Galta, a temple complex and monastic center very near Jaipur, and decided to resort to arms to defend against increasing attacks by Shaiva monks. Significantly, the Galta meeting in 1713 also marked the emergence of Ramanandis (those who look to Swami Ramanand for inspiration) as the dominant force not only among the followers of Ramanujacharya's teachings, but among Vaishnavas in north India generally.

The Galta tradition provides an interesting twist, however: it was also decided in 1713 to declare the untouchable, shudra, and female members of Ramanand's original fourteenth-century coterie of disciples as "illegitimate" transmitters of tradition; in other words, untouchables, shudras, and women would continue to be admitted as Ramanandi novitiates, but henceforth they would have to link themselves to the Ramanandi past via one of the original male, twice-born (in this case, either brahman or kshatriya) disciples of Ramanand.

While on the one hand this decision may have reflected the rise of caste mores amongst Vaishnavas, I prefer to interpret it as a move by socially conservative Vaishnavas to limit the ideological effects of what may have been a heavy influx of non-twice-born Ramanandis.

According to a related and specifically Ramanandi tradition recorded by the anthropologist Peter van der Veer in Ayodhya in the 1980s, loosely organized bands of armed bairagis wandered about north India long before 1700 and were given formal military hierarchy by one Swami Balanand in the eighteenth century. Today the Balanand math (temple-cum-monastery) in Jaipur continues to claim credit for the formalization of the armed Vaishnava akharas.

Though elements of the Galta and Balanand traditions appear contradictory (the reasons for which become clearer in the following chapter), they both point to the importance of Ramanandis, and particularly Ramanandis in the Jaipur region, in the formation of soldiering orders among Vaishnavas. That a Vaishnava call to arms should have been associated with the increased influence of Ramanandis is not surprising, since the social liberalism that is associated with Ramanand would have facilitated the process of military recruitment by opening monastic ranks to the lowly.

This point is underlined in Ayodhya itself, where a banner emblazoned with Swami Ramanand's famous admonition against inequality-"Ask not of caste and the like, if you love God you belong to God"-decorates the entrance to the Hanuman Garhi, the main headquarters of Vaishnava soldier monasticism in north India.

Records housed in the Kapad Dwara (warehouse of valuables) of the Jaipur state provide independent corroboration of Vaishnava arms and of attempts to limit the entry of the low-born into the Ramanandi sampraday in the Jaipur region after 1700. In the 1720s and until his death in 1743, Maharaja Jai Singh II evinced a strong interest in religious affairs, particularly religious affairs having to do with the Vaishnava institutions in his realm. And, not unlike Warren Hastings a half century later, Jai Singh II apparently looked askance at the phenomenon of armed monasticism and sought to discourage it.

To this end, he solicited and received four separate bond agreements containing pledges from prominent Vaishnava mahants, nine of whom identify themselves clearly as "Ramanandi," to give up the practice of keeping arms and to boycott or otherwise punish those who continued to do so. From separate correspondences it is evident that the Maharaja also solicited opinions from Bengali Vaishnavas regarding the rights of shudras and other low classes, and obtained pledges from Ramanandi mahants and other Vaishnavas not only to maintain strict caste rules in commensal relations but to no longer accept shudra and antyaj (low-born) disciples.

The fact that Jai Singh II's efforts to impose orthodox behavior on Vaishnava monks involved the demilitarization of the armed akharas in tandem with the barring of low-born novitiates suggests that arms and low status were connected not just in the Maharaja's vision of a neo-orthodox Vaishnavism but in the social-historical reality of Ramanandi monasticism.

Hence, though questions and ambiguities remain, both Vaishnava and Shaiva monastic traditions evince links between soldiering and low status. What requires further elucidation are questions regarding functionality and causation: namely, did the need for an armed defense on the part of the monastic orders compel a relaxation of social restrictions in order to spur recruitment? Or, conversely, was the arming of monks the result of the influx of peasants (as with pastoralist-cum-peasant Jats in the Sikh case) and others of low or marginal status into monastic communities, and if so why was militarism the result of that influx? (This is a question that needs greater elaboration with respect to Sikhs as well.)

A third possibility that must be considered and that, by implication, obscures any functional relationship between militarization and social change is that the history of monastic soldiering has been used in the more recent past by conservative, high-caste elements in the orders to explain (by way of apologizing for) the contemporary presence therein of shudras, untouchables, and women.

An important related question concerns the organizational status of the military akharas in the nonmilitary sections of the religious orders with which they were associated. The tenuous relationships that today exist between "orthodox" (and generally high-caste) Vaishnava and Shaiva monks, on the one hand, and their respective military akharas, on the other, suggest that sectarian traditions regarding the sudden mobilization of the latter in defense of the former may well have masked more prolonged-if contentious-processes of social openness within the orders as a whole. Indeed, the fact that the military akharas survived the monopolization of arms by the East India Company in the late eighteenth and early nineteenth centuries and continue to thrive as important sections of both Shaiva and Vaishnava monasticism in the late twentieth century suggests that their significance to the religious life of north India was (and is) more social than military.

Whatever the answers to these questions, more research is necessary to know the exact fate of the monastic armies after the passing of the eighteenth century. Certainly, despite the loss of an explicit military function, the trappings of military culture implicit to armed monasticism remained for the most part intact under British rule. The soldier sadhu would become domesticated as a conventional monastic type (as naga) and would complement other forms of monasticism organized around scholarship, devotion and worship, itinerancy, or some combination thereof. Given the apparent survival of the culture (if not the function) of military monasticism, it seems likely that members of the wealthy akharas were able to fall back on the substantial endowments, mostly in the form of land, acquired during the turbulent eighteenth century when their military and financial services were in demand.

It is also possible that the many thousands of soldier monks supported by the frequent warfare of the eighteenth century simply melted back into the peasant countryside after the supremacy of British-Indian arms had been established in the early nineteenth century. Such an eventuality would be difficult to document; nevertheless, this was the argument of W. G. Orr-whose main evidence was the nineteenth-century proverb that "the man who smears his body with ashes [i.e., the naga sadhu] can wash it clean again, but the man who has his ears pierced (that is, becomes a Yogi) is a Yogi all his days."

SADHUS AND THE SOCIAL ORDER

As is clear from the foregoing, any detailed discussion of the social and political dimensions of north Indian monasticism prior to the nineteenth century is fraught with historiographic pitfalls stemming from the general lack of strong documentary evidence with which to confirm or refute religious tradition. This situation changes as we enter the nineteenth century: Company officials sought to gain a more sophisticated social, political, and economic understanding of the society over which they had acquired administrative, judicial, and revenue-collecting powers, and consequently they amassed a wealth of detail regarding the religious dimensions of north Indian life.

The history of this acquisition of knowledge about India is well known and need not be repeated here, save to note that the knowledge acquired took a variety of forms. On one extreme was scholarship focused on the literary splendor of ancient India, grounded in Sanskrit philology and brahmanical tradition and best symbolized by the translations of classical texts by such luminaries as Sir William Jones and H. T. Colebrooke. On the other extreme were the likes of James Tod and Francis Buchanan, who combined an interest in traditional Indian historiographies (and particularly kshatriya, or royal, genealogies) with a facility for recording in voluminous detail the political, social, religious, and economic life of specific regions.

Buchanan is of particular importance here, because his accounts of Bihar and eastern Uttar Pradesh include frequent and detailed reference to religious belief, popular modes of worship and religious instruction, and the regional structure of monastic organizations. Such descriptions appear in these accounts in three discrete forms: first, Buchanan's "topographical" sections, which describe each subdistrict jurisdiction, include an assessment of the relative strength and appeal of monastic gurus; second, his descriptions of each caste usually contain reference to its religious customs and attitudes; and third, the same section on caste concludes with a general discussion of the "sages and sects" of the district, organized according to monastic perspective. The value of such a three-tiered approach is that it affords a textured and multidimensional picture of the monastic and religious life of the Gangetic core.

Perhaps the most immediately revealing feature of Buchanan's Bihar accounts, from the monastic perspective, is what they omit: armed monks. Buchanan made only one brief reference to military monasticism, and that only to explain its absence. Noting that many Ramanandi nagas continued to find service "in the armies of the Rajas beyond the Yamuna" (beyond direct British control in what is now Rajasthan, southern Uttar Pradesh, and Madhya Pradesh), Buchanan observed that the few who remained in south Bihar "have been obliged to abandon arms and predatory habits, and for some time their bands have not ventured to traverse the country." Buchanan's village-based sages are closer to the normative image of the nonthreatening monk implicit in Warren Hastings's 1773 proclamation barring itinerant, armed sadhus from passing through in the province of Bengal. A similar portrait would be painted by Horace Hayman Wilson, the eminent Sanskritist of the mid-nineteenth century, who observed that "the tenants of these maths, particularly the Vaishnavas, are most commonly of a quiet inoffensive character, and the Mahants especially are men of talents and respectability, although they possess, occasionally, a little of that self-importance, which the conceit of superior sanctity is apt to inspire."

In retrospect, it can be argued that with the gradual removal of armed monks from territories controlled by the Company in the late eighteenth and nineteenth centuries, north Indian monasticism turned inward, away from worldly martial pursuits and toward more aesthetic, devotional, and literary accomplishments. In the Vaishnava context, this would have meant a greater emphasis on rasik-oriented bhakti, or "devotional aestheticism," which had a constituted powerful strand of both Ram and Krishna worship since the sixteenth century.

The rasik tradition emphasizes heightened emotion, the careful perception of sensory experience, and in the Ramanandi context, a focus on Sita as a means of access to Ram; consequently, many "rasiks," as the practitioners of this mode of religious devotion were known, adopted the persona of a handmaid to Sita. As we shall see in the next chapter, many of the main players in the politics of the Ramanandi sampraday in Ayodhya and throughout the Gangetic north were associated with the rasik tradition.

Whatever the particular mode of asceticism, the majority of the sadhus in Buchanan's accounts wielded a great deal of popular influence as village gurus-a role that combined the duties of teacher, counselor, spiritual guide, and pious exemplar. Hence it would not be inappropriate to understand them as "guideposts for the common person's society and its changing moral character" and the religious arena they inhabited as a "locus for raising social issues and for initiating and influencing change within Indian society." In addition, these village gurus represented the point of contact between rural peasants and the monastic networks that crisscrossed the subcontinent. Buchanan's work took him through much of deltaic and upper Bengal and the Gangetic core, including regions that became known by 1901 as the Bihar districts of Purnea, Bhagalpur, Monghyr, Patna, Gaya, and Shahabad, and the Uttar Pradesh districts of Basti and Gorakhpur. While all his accounts are of immense social-historical value, three of them-Bihar and Patna (1811-1812), Shahabad (1813), and Gorakhpur (1813)-possess enough religious and social detail to afford an intriguing statistical snapshot of the demography of monasticism and its popular appeal in the early nineteenth century.

Each account begins with a "topography" of the district, organized according to administrative precinct, or thana. Bihar and Patna (conforming roughly to the 1901 Gaya and Patna Districts, respectively) contained a total of seventeen thanas of widely varying size and population; Shahabad ten; and Gorakhpur twenty-eight (two of which were completely deserted and most of which were relatively sparsely populated).

Buchanan's treatment of each begins with a one-paragraph description of the geographical setting and basic demographic and physical dimensions, then turns to a brief mention of the thana's administrative, police, and juridical personnel. This is followed by a much more detailed statement of the institutional strengths and local authority and appeal of each religious perspective in the thana. Rather than percentages, he employed the Indian anna standard of sixteenths; occasionally he would utilize eighths, twelfths, twenty-fourths, and thirty-seconds when greater simplicity could be employed or greater accuracy was called for.

The following, rather lengthy excerpt from Shahabad District's "Dumraong" (variant of Dumraon) thana is typical in many ways of Buchanan's descriptive method:

This jurisdiction, although very large and populous, is so compact, and the native officers of police are so centrically [sic] situated, that little inconvenience is felt from these circumstances. The police of a small portion adjacent to Vagsar [var. Buxar, Baksar], at the N.-W. corner of the division, is under the inspection of the military officer commanding that fortress. This is the only division in the district which enjoys the advantage of a court for the trial of small debts, without applying in the first instance to the judge.

The commissioner for this court is also the hereditary Kazi, who resides at Kazipur 3 miles N. from Dumraong, the residence of the police officers, and near one side of his jurisdiction, both circumstances attended with considerable inconvenience. The Kazi [judge] confines himself entirely to the deciding of causes [cases?], and attestation of deeds, and appoints deputies to perform all religious ceremonies. Here is also a hereditary Mufti, a description of officer, with which I have not previously met. No Pirzada [Sufi shaikh] resides, and those who become Murids [followers], employ vagrants.

Of the Hindus 4/16 are unworthy to the notice of any sage:

4/16 are of the sect of Sakti; 2/16 adhere to Siva. Of these 6/16 five belong to the Brahmans, and one to the Dasanami Sannyasis. Most of the Brahmans reside [i.e., they do not visit periodically from other thanas], and Ritu Raj Misra, a Sakadwipi, who lives at Vagsar, and is the family priest of the Bhojpur Rajas, has very extensive authority and influence. He is a man of considerable learning, and affects very austere manners, to which last circumstance is probably owing much of his authority, although those who receive sacred instruction from his mouth, are mostly if not entirely of the sects of Saiva or Sakti, he is of the sect of Vishnu; and it is alleged, that the form of prayer, which he gives, is addressed to some form of this deity, which is indeed quite the same to his followers, as they do not understand a word of it. Perhaps however this may be a story invented by some of those, who are envious of his success. As the form of prayer is a profound secret, the truth could not easily be discovered. The Dasanamis have 2 maths, and about 20 smaller houses here called Mathiyas. At the 2 maths there reside about 15 men, who have relinquished the world; some of the inferior houses are occupied by persons, who indulge in the pleasures of matrimony.

3/16 of the Hindus adhere to the sect of Nanak. There are 4 meetings, all belonging to Jagdishpur [a town in central Shahabad], and the men, who preside, abstain from wedlock.

Two of these places have the title of (Gadis) thrones. 2/16 of the Hindus adhere to Vishnu, and follow chiefly the Ramawats, but some are disciples of Madhava, and some of Nima; no one, however with whom I met, could tell the number of houses, that belonged to each. There is one Akhara at Dumraong and 40 at Vagsar, all occupied by persons entirely dedicated to God. There are also 50 houses occupied by married persons, who instruct the canaille, and are called Vaishnavas. All were originally Sudras.

1/16 of the Hindus follow the new routes to heaven: the Kavir Pangth has 10 Gurus, who occupy Mathiyas, some of them married, some single; while there are 20 persons, that adhere to the doctrine of Siva Narayan.

The remainder of Buchanan's discussion in this particular thana (as with most other thanas) is focused on the quality of the soil, the types of irrigation, the number of houses of various kinds and their manner of construction, local fortifications, the main places of worship, the major festivals, local history and legend, and any interesting archeological or antiquarian remains in the vicinity.

A few points that emerge in the above excerpt merit special emphasis, inasmuch as they relate to broader patterns in Buchanan's accounts. First, in each thana Buchanan noted the proportion of the population (usually between one-eighth and one-fourth, but occasionally as high as one-half) considered by his informants (of whom more later) to be "unworthy" of religious instruction. He nevertheless included in most of his topographical descriptions the relatively small proportions dedicated to such reformist sects as the Kabirpanthis and Sivanarayanis, both of which were aggressively egalitarian and, indeed, anti-brahmanical and hence tended to attract followers from a wide social spectrum, including untouchables and "unclean" shudras.

Taken together, these facts suggest that while Buchanan's religious description did not altogether ignore the religious views and practices of people deemed extremely low-status, he nevertheless dealt mostly with what may have been considered acceptable and demographically important, if not respectable, religious points of view; again, this would reflect the middle and upper-caste views of the people from whom he gleaned his data, not to mention the Bengali pandits who assisted him in his surveys and who in any case looked askance at much of Bihari culture.

In any event, the lengthy discussions that usually followed Buchanan's religious tabulations include local village deities whose worship was often conducted by the socially and culturally marginalized lower classes; these were the kinds of people, and the kind of religious traditions, excluded in the systematic numerical descriptions that began each section.

The second point that requires emphasis is slightly more complex. Buchanan's description of the sectarian dimensions in Gangetic Bihar and eastern Uttar Pradesh took two complementary forms. On the one hand, Buchanan conceived of three main divisions of Hindu religion: Shaiva-Shakta, Vaishnava, and panthi (the more recent "routes to heaven" espoused by Kabir, Nanak, and the like).

On the other hand, within these large (and often overlapping) divisions were religious communities organized around the institutional ties of gurus, which usually took monastic form. Dasnami sanyasis represented the main Shaiva monastic group; Ramanandis (often referred to as Ramawats) the main Vaishnava monastic group.

The main panthi community that emerges in Buchanan's accounts was the Nanakpanth, associated with the teachings of Guru Nanak, which was particularly influential in south Bihar. Other, much less prominent (at least, in the Gangetic core regions described by Buchanan) religious perspectives that possessed varying degrees of monastic manifestations were represented by the (Shaiva) Kanphat yogi community, which looked to the teachings of the fifteenth-century Gorakhnath (on account of which they are frequently referred to as Gorakhnathi and Gorakhpanthi); the (Vaishnava) Radhaballabhi sampraday, centered on the worship of Krishna as Radha's lover; the ("reformist") Kabirpanth, and the more recent (also "reformist") Shivanarayani (centered in nearby Ghazipur District in what is now Uttar Pradesh) and Daryadasi communities (centered in Shahabad District). At the risk of an overly long aside, it should be noted that there is a tendency to be overly schematic when describing the sectarian dimensions of monasticism. Such a tendency should be carefully qualified if not avoided outright. It is best to understand Vaishnava, Shaiva, and Shakta as terms that refer to distinct yet overlapping, and evolving, systems of religious meaning with broad popular appeal that have been drawn upon in varying degrees by thinkers over the past millennium. Two extremely important figures were Shankaracharya and Ramanujacharya, each of whom is remembered to have identified in complex metaphysical and epistemological discourses the most efficacious way of perceiving divine truth(s). They themselves have long been associated with or, perhaps more precisely, been thought of as founders of major monastic communities with distinct sectarian (Shaiva as opposed to Vaishnava) dimensions.

However, while Shankaracharya's status as the founder of the Dasnami order has remained unquestioned by Dasnami sanyasis, Ramanujacharya's status as a formative figure in the Ramanandi sampraday has been a matter of major contention, particularly in this century-a contention best symbolized by the very name that has come to be associated (even as early as the eighteenth century) with the monastic community that for many years viewed Ramanujacharya with great reverence. The examination of the history of this contentious moment in the Ramanandi sampraday, and of the socially radical understanding of the life of the fourteenth-century Ramanand that was re-crystallizing at this time, is the central object of the next chapter. What is important to recognize here is the manner in which individual monks were able to endow the doctrinal tenets and social philosophies of their orders with wider Indic meanings.

Another important and more recent figure in the religious history of the subcontinent is, of course, Guru Nanak, whose perception of an ineffable god became the spiritual fount for Sikhism. However, interpretations of Nanak's teachings varied, and as a result the Nanakpanthis observed by Buchanan in early nineteenth-century Bihar should not be confused with the khalsa Sikhs of the Punjab, though the communities were closely related. Buchanan himself noted that the followers of Nanak were divided into two groups: "the Khalesah sect founded by Govinda [i.e., Guru Govind Singh], and confined in great measure to the west of India," and "the Kholesah or original Sikhs who prevail in Behar."

In other words, most Nanakpanthis in Bihar remained aloof from the khalsa-fication of the sampraday. Today, the Nanakpanthis described by Buchanan would be referred to as "Udasin" and see themselves as the caretakers of universal truths articulated by Guru Nanak, particularly as mediated through Nanak's eldest son, the exceptionally long-lived Shri Chand (1494-1629).

Upon the death of Nanak, the mantle of leadership in the Nanakpanth passed not to Shri Chand but to one of Nanak's favored disciples, who became known as Guru Angad, thus beginning the succession of ten gurus that would end with Govind Singh. According to modern histories based on prevailing khalsa Sikh hagiography, Shri Chand and his followers were expelled in the sixteenth century from the Sikh community. According to Udasin tradition, by contrast, the links between the Shri Chand and his followers, on the one hand, and the Sikh gurus and their adherents, on the other, remained strong well into the seventeenth century. For example, Udasins have long maintained that the sixth guru, Hargovind Singh, placed his son Gurditta under the personal and spiritual care of Shri Chand, who by this time was nearing the end of his long life. Indeed, not only is Gurditta himself remembered as an important Udasin guru, four of his disciples are said to have founded the principal Udasin subsects.

The history of the gradual bifurcation of Nanakpanthis into what Buchanan called the Khalesah versus Kholesah divisions, or what today would be called Sikh versus Udasin, is closely linked to the changing demography of Sikhism in the Punjab and the rise of a khalsa military culture in the seventeenth and eighteenth centuries-in contrast to developments in the Gangetic north, where the rise of a military ethos in religious communities occurred primarily among

Vaishnavas and Shaivas. That division was further hardened by the British recruitment of Sikhs into the Indian army, the rise of the Singh Sabha in and beyond the Punjab, and the emergence of Akali politics surrounding the status of Sikh shrines (controlled before 1925 by Udasins) in the nineteenth and twentieth centuries.

Buchanan's tabulations of monastic groupings within either the Shaiva-Shakta or Vaishnava rubric are further complicated by the fact that he tended to draw a distinction between monastic gurus and brahman gurus. This practice probably reflected the fact that many of his local monastic informants themselves drew such a distinction; it may also have reflected the socioreligious predilections of the Bengali pandits who assisted him in his data gathering. Despite these factors, however, it is likely that in the case of Vaishnavas, brahman gurus such as the influential Pandit Ritu Raj Misra, mentioned in the extract cited above, were affiliated with Ramanandi teachings-though the exact nature of that affiliation remains unclear.

The Ramanandi connections of Vaishnava brahmans emerge in a later passage describing monastic establishments in Buxar (which was, Buchanan noted, the main Ramanandi center in Shahabad District). Buchanan observed that in Buxar "the convents of the Brahmans, who have adopted this [the Ramanandi] order, as usual are confounded with those occupied by Sudras, nor have I been able to distinguish the number of each"; in a characteristic aside, he added that "my Bengalese assistants[,] confounding them [Bihari Vaishnavas] with the Vaishnavas of their own country, hold them in the utmost contempt."

In contrast to the Vaishnava credentials of most brahman gurus in Shahabad, Buchanan observed that "most of the Pandits, who act as Gurus in [Bihar and Patna] districts, worship Sakti as their favourite, and are Tantriks." As he proceeded northwest from Shahabad into Gorakhpur District and closer to Ayodhya, which by this time was firmly established as a major Ramanandi monastic and pilgrimage center, Buchanan recorded increasing numbers of brahmans serving as Vaishnava gurus.

Buchanan's observations respecting the religious appeal of gurus may be represented in tabular form. Table 1 below shows the population ratios (shown here as percentages) claimed as adherents by the main monastic communities and brahmans out of those persons said to "receive religious instruction" in the three most detailed of Buchanan's accounts-Bihar and Patna (two separate districts), Shahabad, and Gorakhpur. "Guru patronage" figures are shown for Brahmans, Dasnamis, Ramanandis, and Nanakshahis (from considerations of space, the less prominent religious perspectives, such as Kabirpanthi and Radhaballabhi, are not included). The column to the far right under the heading "RRI/Hindus" shows the total percentage of Hindus who, according to Buchanan, "received religious instruction" from gurus; the four columns to the left show percentages of that total number of Hindus who received religious instruction.

Guru Patronage in the Gangetic Core, 1811-1813 (percent)

	Brahman	Dasnami	Ramanandi	Nanakshahi	RRI/Hindus
Patna	14	30	8	39	53
Bihar	14	40	9	37	62
Shahabad	37	23	16	20	76
Gorakhpur	64	11	20	1	85

Source: Buchanan, Bihar and Patna, 1811-1812; 1:57-262, and 2:723, table 4 (population); Shahabad, 1812-1812, 51-151; "An Account of the Northern Part of the District of Gorakhpur, 1812," 139-345. The population figures used to calculate the above percentages for Shahabad and Gorakhpur rely on the tables provided in Martin, The History, Antiquities, Topography, and Statistics of Eastern India, vol. 1 (Behar and Shahabad), Shahabad Appendix, 44; and vol. 2 (Bhagalpoor, Goruckpoor, and Dinajpoor), Goruckpoor Appendix, 9, respectively.

Two points should be kept in mind when reading Table 1. First, and most important, higher percentages of brahman gurus in Shahabad and, more especially, Gorakhpur Districts were Vaishnava in their religious outlook, and though it is difficult to quantify, many of them would have had ties to the Ramanandi sampraday, particularly as Buchanan moved closer to Ayodhya on the western edge of Gorakhpur. This means that the percentage of guru patronage for Ramanandis is much higher in those districts than shown in the table. Second, the gradual rise in the strength of Ramanandis (particularly if we understand increasing numbers of brahman gurus to be Ramanandi) as Buchanan traveled west from Patna and Bihar to Shahabad and thence to Gorakhpur was, in all likelihood, directly related to the gradual rise in the percentages of Hindus who "received religious instruction."

The reason for this is the liberal social philosophy of the Ramanandi sampraday, which would have attracted many low-status groups into the institutional and ideological ambit of Vaishnava belief.

Indeed, Buchanan's remarks on religious practice in the Gangetic core, together with comments by other observers through the nineteenth century, indicate that Vaishnava gurus (and Ramanandis in particular) pursued a far more aggressive program of social and religious reform in comparison with their Dasnami and Nanakpanthi counterparts.

Consequently, Vaishnava bairagis were drawn from the entire varna spectrum and included not only brahmans but many shudras. I have already related Buchanan's observations respecting the profusion of both brahman and shudra Ramanandi gurus in Buxar, the Vaishnava center of Shahabad District. In Patna, Buchanan remarked that while some Vaishnava gurus are brahman, "most are Sudras." And even in Purnea District near the border of Bengal, where most of the Vaishnava gurus tended to follow the teachings of the Bengali saint Chaitanya, Buchanan noted that "the Ramanandi Brahmans and Vairagi Sudras are usually confounded together, and the name Ramayit [var. Ramawat] is given to both."

Equally important was the fact that Ramanandis, according to Buchanan's accounts, encouraged their lay followers to adhere to a rigid moral code and a strict daily regimen. Describing Vaishnavas as "everywhere the most strict," Buchanan noted that "some few of them here [Bihar and Patna] will neither pray nor even show common civility to any god but those of his own sect." The emphasis on a pure life applied as well to daily diet: "All the Hindus, Brahman or Sudra, of the sect of Vishnu [i.e., Ramanandis or their adherents], are remarkably strict in eating, reject altogether rice cleaned by boiling, all parched grains, and animal food"; by contrast, Buchanan observed that "all the Sudras, except those of the sect of Vishnu, drink avowedly."

Adherence to rigorous Vaishnava mores under the tutelage of Ramanandis, even for untouchables, thus afforded a substantial aura of self-respect. Again, Buchanan: "men of impure or vile tribes, who wish to be thought better than their neighbors, and who abstain from meat, fish, and spirituous liquors, are called Bhakats [devotees] . . . and at the recommendation of the Vairagis [var. bairagi], who are their gurus, have given up an indulgence of their appetites." Not only were Ramanandis eager to attract followers into the sampraday irrespective of status, especially those derided as "vile" and "impure," but they were ready to encourage a pure lifestyle as a way of undermining the caste discrimination that stigmatized low-status populations.

For Buchanan this picture of purposeful, upright Ramanandi behavior stood in stark contrast to the conduct of the Dasnamis and Nanakshahis. Adherents of the former were "so careless or ignorant that they never have taken the trouble to inquire from their instructor whether the secret prayer is addressed to Siva or Sakti, and they do not understand a word of it." He added in a later passage, while Dasnamis "affect a life of mortification, . . . they are accused of being in private very indulgent to their sensual appetites." Further, he mentioned no special dietary restrictions prescribed by Dasnamis that might have enhanced both the self-image and the social respectability of the lower status groups among their followers. Perhaps more revealing was Buchanan's observation that while Dasnami gurus benefited from the patronage of numerous shudras as lay followers, "Sudras are not admitted into the order."

Buchanan recorded similar criticisms with respect to Nanakpanthis. Based on his extensive discussions with Mahant Govinda Das, a leading Nanakpanthi of Bihar, Buchanan observed that "the Fakirs [Govinda Das's own term] of the Kholasah sect of Sikhs [i.e., Nanakpanthis or Udasins] admit into their own order only Brahmans, Kshatriyas and Vaisyas; but among their followers they admit all Hindus, who are not vile; and they entirely exclude all Mlechchhas , such as Muhammedans or Christians." On the level of theological and devotional commitment evinced by Nanakpanthis, he observed:

> The assemblies at the Sanggats [meetings] are quite irregular, and depend entirely upon the accidental offerings, that are made. Even at Rekabganj [in Patna City], by far the greatest place of [Nanakshahi] worship in these countries, there are not now four daily assemblies; but it is said, that formerly these meetings were regular, and when no offering was made by any of the laymen, the Mahanta defrayed the expense; but Govinda Das considers this as unnecessary, and no meeting takes place, but when some person makes an offering.

Buchanan also noted that inclusion in the Nanakpanthi community as lay followers did not necessarily involve an abandonment of prior religious practices and convictions: devotees "follow exactly the same customs that they did before their admission" and "observe the same rules of caste, employ the same Brahmans as Purohits [ritual officiants] in every ceremony, and in all cases of danger worship exactly the same gods." However, while Govinda Das asserted that "Vishnu, Brahma and Siva are gods [and that] he occasionally makes them offerings," he claimed to do so "merely in compliance with the custom of the country." By contrast, in personal spiritual instruction Govinda Das acknowledged "only one supreme God (Parameswara)" who "ought to be the only object of worship," to the exclusion of the secondary Hindu deities listed above. These latter admissions by Govind Das would seem to imply a conscious recognition on his part of the divergence that had developed between the normative dictates of religion set out by Guru Nanak in the sixteenth century and Nanakpanth religious practice extant in the early nineteenth century.

Though he did not remark upon it, Buchanan's descriptions of Dasnamis and Nanakpanthis reveal interesting similarities, particularly with respect to social exclusivity in matters of monastic recruitment and a general impression of laxity in religious observances. Today there is little question of the strong affinity between Dasnamis and Nanakpanthis (or Udasins). Ghurye noted in the 1950s that "the philosophy of the Udasi ascetics is the same monistic Vedanta as that of the Dasanamis," and that "whenever there is any quarrel with the Vaishnava ascetics, they [Udasins] are always to be found on the side of the Saiva sadhus." The anthropologists Baidyanath Saraswati and Surajit Sinha recorded in Banaras in the 1960s an Udasin tradition that the first person to take initiation from Shri Chand was Bhakta Giri, a Dasnami sanyasi of Bodh Gaya. And Udasins assert that not only was Shri Chand an avatar of Shiva, but that Shri Chand and Guru Nanak only articulated Udasin truths that had existed since time began.

Though measuring sectarian prosperity and decline is exceptionally difficult, it would appear that the proximity to Shaivism and the rise of khalsa politics conspired to diminish the institutional fortunes of the Nanakpanthi community in Bihar by the end of the nineteenth century. Such a conclusion is at least suggested by the meager returns for Nanakshahis of any kind, particularly as compared to Ramanandi bairagis and Dasnami sanyasis, in the census figures for the years 1891 and 1901 in the Bihar districts of Patna, Gaya, and Shahabad (roughly congruent with Buchanan's Patna, Bihar, and Shahabad districts).

In retrospect, Nanakpanthis in Bihar may be understood to have experienced what Richard Eaton has described as a process of "accretion": Udasins in Bihar, by gradually approximating Shaiva beliefs and practices, came to be regarded (and, indeed, regarded themselves) as Hindu by the early twentieth century.

This process would have been spurred as well by khalsa Sikh reforms emanating from the Punjab after the middle of the nineteenth century, which were designed to purge from Sikhism "corrupt" Hindu practices, establish for Sikhs a distinct, non-Hindu religious identity, and bolster khalsa Sikh institutional fortunes in the twentieth century at the expense of Udasins.

Perhaps not unlike khalsa Sikhs in the Punjab, Ramanandis in the early nineteenth century were exceptional for their unwavering, aggressive moral posture in the Gangetic core districts surveyed by Buchanan. This was coupled with, and possibly contributed to, the improving material fortunes of the sampraday in the central Gangetic region during the eighteenth and nineteenth centuries, the evidence for which exists in the history of the major pilgrimage centers of Banaras and Ayodhya. In their anthropological survey of Banaras carried out in the 1960s and '70s, Baidyanath Saraswati and Surajit Sinha discovered that the two most prolific monastic communities were the Dasnami and the Ramanandi.

That Dasnamis predominated in Banaras is not at all surprising given that the city, as Kashi, was long regarded as Shiva's place, but the rise to prominence of Ramanandis there is a fact worthy of note. Even more remarkable is that, according to Saraswati and Sinha, of the forty Ramanandi institutions in Banaras, two were claimed to have been founded by Ramanand himself in the fifteenth century, while the remaining thirty-eight were founded between 1700 and 1968 (with over half founded after 1900). Likewise, in his own very different anthropological exploration, van der Veer observes that "there can be no doubt about the fact that Ayodhya became an important pilgrimage centre only in the eighteenth century," and that Ramanandis rose to dominate the religious topography of the town at the expense of an established Dasnami presence and with the patronage of Awadhi nawabs headquartered in Lucknow.

Hence, the eighteenth and nineteenth centuries should be seen as a time of expansion for Ramanandi monasticism vis-á-vis the competing religious orders, and not merely in terms of enlarged monastic endowments but numbers of lay and ascetic adherents as well. This trend did not escape the notice of observers, both Indian and European. H. H. Wilson noted in the late 1820s that

> the ascetic and mendicant followers of Ramanand, known indiscriminately as Ramanandis or Ramawats, are by far the most numerous class of sectaries in Gangetic India: in Bengal

they are comparatively few: beyond this province, as far as to Allahabad [i.e., in what is now Bihar and eastern Uttar Pradesh], although perhaps the most numerous, they yield in influence and wealth to the Saiva branches, especially to the Atits [Dasnamis]: hence [i.e., west of Allahabad], however, they predominate, and either by themselves, or their kindred divisions, almost engross the whole of the country along the Ganges and Jamna: in the district of Agra, they alone constitute seven-tenths of the ascetic population.

The Ramanandis have very numerous votaries, but they are chiefly from the poorer and inferior classes, with the exception of the Rajaputs and military Brahmans, amongst whom the poetical works of Sur Das and Tulasi Das maintain the pre-eminence of Rama and his Bhakts [devotees].

One large agricultural community of Bihar that increasingly patronized Vaishnava monks, according to Herbert Hope Risley, the celebrated ethnologist-anthropometrist of the late nineteenth century, were Kurmi peasants. This is a remarkable transformation, given Buchanan's observation eighty years earlier that the vast majority of Kurmis in Bihar looked to Dasnami sanyasis for religious guidance.

An important observation made at the end of the nineteenth century by Jogendra Nath Bhattacharya, president of the College of Pandits in Nadia (in Bengal), helps to put these changes in religious-historical perspective: "the Vaishnavas are very fast extending the sphere of their influence, and many of the Tantrics [Shaivas and Shaktas] are now espousing Vaishnava tenets in order to have the advantage of enlisting among their followers the low classes that are becoming rich under British rule." That such a process was already under way in the early nineteenth century is suggested by Buchanan's surprised observation that Vaishnava images were installed in a prominent Dasnami math in northern Gorakhpur and were receiving the undivided attention of the gosains there.

These religious transformations may help explain, in turn, the terminological ambiguities that plague any historical discussion of monasticism in the Gangetic north. Perhaps the best example of such ambiguity is the term gosain itself, which even in the early nineteenth century had begun to lose its specific Shaiva and Dasnami connotations in the Gangetic core of Bihar and eastern Uttar Pradesh to become a general term denoting sadhus.

Prior to 1800, "gosain" in the Gangetic core referred primarily to Dasnami nagas. This continued to be the case in the vicinity of Patna as late as 1810, during Buchanan's visit: describing the mutual enmity felt by monks in the various orders in Patna and Bihar (later Gaya) Districts, he remarked that "the title Gosaing, which the Brahmins of the sect of Vishnu adopt in Bengal, is considered by the followers of Ramananda as highly disgraceful, and as appropriate to the Dasnami-Sannyasis, their most bitter enemies."

However, upon heading west from Patna and crossing the Son river, which separated Shahabad from Patna and Bihar (later Gaya) Districts, Buchanan found that the usage of the term gosain began to alter: in the town of Ara, less than ten miles west of the Son, the principal Ramanandi referred to himself as Gosaing. As Buchanan moved further west into Gorakhpur, he observed that "here the term Guru is not very commonly used, and that Gosaing is applied as synonymous, and is applied to the sages of all castes and sects."

By the close of the nineteenth century, Risley found that the term in Bihar also applied to house-holder Vaishnavas, in addition to being employed as a synonym for bairagi. By 1910 the term gosain had become fully applicable to both Shaivas and Vaishnavas, even in Patna and Gaya Districts. Hence, local subdistrict officers conducting village-by-village surveys in Bihar were describing thakurbaris, or Vaishnava temples, erected or inhabited by gosains. However, the term "gosain" also continued to refer to Shaiva monks throughout Gangetic south Bihar, as illustrated by the existence of "a pucca Shivalay [brick-built Shiva temple] built by Gosain Bisun Puri 30 years ago at the cost of about Rs. 2000/-."

Conversely, there were no references to bairagis having constructed Shaiva temples or tending to Shaiva images in the village notes of Patna, Gaya, and Shahabad Districts; furthermore, the term "bairagi" continued throughout the nineteenth century (and continues today) to refer specifically to Vaishnava sadhus.

Given the increased applicability of the term "gosain" and the general impression among nineteenth-century observers of the spread and dominance of Ramanandis in the Gangetic north, it seems likely that as non-Vaishnava sadhus increasingly adopted Vaishnava tenets or melted into Ramanandi institutions, the terms that had heretofore described those sadhus began to be lose their specific sectarian associations. An additional factor that has already been noted was that in the eighteenth century Ramanandis had gained control of major monastic centers in the Gangetic north, such as Ayodhya; consequently, much of the terminology and religious practices associated with those places would have been absorbed by the Vaishnava newcomers.

These explanations, if correct, would imply that the terminological shift would have already begun by the early nineteenth century in regions considered Vaishnava strongholds, and indeed, Buchanan's observation (noted above) on the loose applicability of the term "gosain" in Gorakhpur and, to a lesser extent, Shahabad Districts seems to bear this out. This explanation is further supported by a consideration of the term atit (literally, detached) which, in the early nineteenth century, referred specifically to the less orthodox ranks of Dasnamis who made up the vast majority of Shaiva sanyasis in the north. Atits, according to Wilson, were not nearly so strict in their ascetic practices as dandi (orthodox) sanyasis, and consequently could engage in business transactions, own property, and officiate as temple priests; many atits, then, would have been far more susceptible to popular religious attitudes than their dandi counterparts.

By the late nineteenth century, Risley observed that the term applied both to Vaishnava sadhus and to "degraded" Shaiva sanyasis, which for Risley meant those who had "succumbed to the temptations of the flesh"; meanwhile, William Crooke, who directed the census in Uttar Pradesh, argued that a distinction needed to be drawn between householder (or married, gharbari) and sanyasi atits, and that while the latter were generally regarded as Shaiva, they were addressed with the Vaishnava invocation, "Namo Narayanaya," or "bow to Narayana." By the mid twentieth century, "atit" (like gosain) had ceased to have a specific Shaiva connotation.

An unfortunate consequence of this growing terminological imprecision is that it renders useless from the ascetic perspective much of the strictly quantitative data generated by the colonial censuses of the late 1800s and early 1900s. This is because far more individuals in Patna District referred to themselves in the 1891 census as gosain (3,438) and atit (1,218) than as bairagi (546) or sanyasi (621); likewise a decade later, in the 1901 and 1911 censuses for Patna District, there were many more gosains than atits, bairagis, and sanyasis combined. Shahabad District, by contrast, showed large returns (around 7,000) for atits in all three censuses, on average nearly three times that of all other sadhus combined.

In addition, the population figures referring to one or another ascetic identity were highly aberrant over the three censuses in Bengal province (which included Bihar), rendering any interpretation virtually impossible. Indeed, so pronounced were the aberrations in the first large-scale British-Indian census in 1872 that census officials decided to omit the returns for the relative numbers of "various religious sects" in the province of Bengal. The situation had not improved even by the 1911 census, the director of which noted that "it was decided not to attempt to obtain a record of Hindu sects, previous experience having shewn that the results are so inaccurate or incomplete as to be of little or no statistical value."

The interpretive problems were particularly pronounced in Bihar, and one source of confusion for census officials there may well have been the general terminological fluidity noted above, which in all likelihood enabled sadhus to refer to themselves in a variety of ways depending on the phrasing of census inquiries regarding identity. Another factor that would have further complicated the task of interpreting the aggregate data was the very size and diversity of the province of Bengal, which until 1912 included the culturally distinct regions of Bihar, Bengal, and Orissa. Though those regions possessed a shared religious vocabulary, that vocabulary did not necessarily refer to comparable religious phenomena.

The situation was less complex to the west, in Uttar Pradesh, which was not only more homogeneous culturally but, especially in the western plain between Banaras and Agra, predominantly Vaishnava. However, as we shall see in the next chapter, by the early twentieth century the Vaishnava ascendancy over sectarian rivals was of less significance than internal distinctions among Vaishnavas themselves, particularly among Ramanandis.

RELIGION AND SOCIAL CHANGE

For the historian, religion cannot not be understood independently of status and the social order, however these are expressed. Thus far I have concentrated on the social dimensions of monastic sampraday in the Gangetic core as revealed in Vaishnava and Shaiva soldiering prior to the nineteenth century, in the religious networks described by Buchanan in the early nineteenth century, and in random observations up to 1900. My primary aim here has been to describe the presence of a Vaishnava reform-mindedness in the Gangetic north, rooted in the greater social openness and broader socioreligious vision evident in the Ramanandi sampraday as compared with the other major monastic communities. My discussion reflects approaches to social relations either implicit in religious tradition (particularly with regard to monastic soldiering) or, more particularly, explicit in the opinions articulated by gurus, particularly in Buchanan's accounts.

Hence, thus far, the discussion reflects the views of sadhus. By contrast, it is much more difficult to discern for this period-even in Buchanan's rich prose-the opinions that low-status people (whether shudra or untouchable) may have held on issues of status, religious identity, and monastic recruitment. Sadhus were often self-conscious social actors, accustomed to offering guidance based on their worldviews and to having their opinions solicited and registered with care.

By contrast, the opinions of shudras and untouchables (whether cultivators, artisans, or laborers) were generally unsolicited, and as a result their voices were not heard-at least, not until the early twentieth century when, abruptly, many erstwhile shudras emerged as able social activists and vociferous articulators of kshatriya (and decidedly non-shudra) status.

However, it is important to note here a key element of those chapters so as to place the present discussion in broader perspective. The success of kshatriya reform movements depended on the ability of popular intellectuals (who, in most cases, were not sadhus) to initiate new kinds of religious discussions as a basis for social change. Kshatriya reform did, at times, benefit from the intellectual contributions of individual sadhus and, more frequently, from the authoritative opinions of prominent swamis recorded in regional publications. However, it did not depend upon the leadership of monks or even the active complicity of monastic institutions.

The fact that peasant and artisan intellectuals could initiate a religious discourse to advance a specific social agenda meant that religion for them (the intellectuals, if not all peasants and artisans) had become, at some fundamental level, a more private affair, and that the sadhu either as holy man or as guru and counselor was no longer as crucial a component of popular religious life. This should not, I would argue, be taken to signify the decline of monasticism in north Indian peasant life as such. However, the increasing "laicization of religion" should be understood as one among several challenges facing Indian monasticism, particularly after the middle of the twentieth century.

4

Practices Under British Rule

Richard Wellesley was not quite 38 years old when he became governor-general at Calcutta in May 1798. He believed in British imperialism and thought that John Shore had been a weak governor. Because of the European war he exaggerated the threat of the French in India. In June he learned that the French governor Malartic of Mauritius was raising volunteers to fight for Tipu Sultan against the English.

Only a hundred recruits joined him, but Wellesley used it as an excuse to bully Tipu. His brother Arthur Wellesley advised him to be patient and let Tipu explain. Richard Wellesley goaded Madras into preparing for war and got Nizam 'Ali to dismiss his French officers and support the British East India Company. In February 1799 the combined army of the Company had 40,000 men with more than 100,000 camp followers. Tipu had only about 37,000 men and used his mobility and a scorched-earth strategy. After being defeated on March 27 by Company commander George Harris, Tipu retreated to Seringapatam. General Baird, who had suffered 44 months imprisonment in a Seringapatam dungeon, wanted revenge and led the attack that stormed and plundered the Mysore capital.

Tipu was killed, and Arthur Wellesley had to use flogging and hanging to restore order. More than half of the two million pounds of booty was claimed by the officers as prize money, Harris getting £143,000. Richard Wellesley was offered £100,000, which he declined.

Governor-General Wellesley had 14,000 European troops but declared 31,000 were needed. The Company reluctantly agreed to 21,000, but the number only reached about 18,000. Wellesley installed a five-year-old Hindu prince in the small traditional kingdom of Mysore. By a treaty in 1800 Nizam 'Ali gave up the Mysore territories he had gained in both wars to the Company for protection and an end to his paying an annual subsidy. His many troops were disbanded and caused local disorders for several years.

The Company gained control of Tanjore when the raja Serfogi they had installed accepted a £40,000 annual pension in October 1799. Five months later Wellesley ordered the Company to take over the port of Surat as its nawab was given a pension. Wellesley believed that the English could govern better. After Muhammad 'Ali's son Umdat-ul-Umara died, the regents for his son rejected a pension agreement. So Wellesley offered one to Umdut-ul-Umara's nephew, and the Company took over the Karnatak in July 1801. The Directors approved the new treaty because they believed the family of Muhammad 'Ali had forfeited its previous treaty rights by treasonable correspondence with Tipu.

More complicated machinations were used in regard to Awadh (Oudh). Vazir 'Ali resented having to live in Calcutta, escaped, and with several thousand armed men killed the Benares resident Cherry and other Englishmen in 1799. After Zaman Shah invaded from Afghanistan to Lahore again in the fall of 1798, Bombay governor Duncan and Wellesley sent envoys with gifts to urge the Persian shah to destabilize Afghanistan and oppose the French. In 1800 Zaman Shah was imprisoned and blinded by his half-brother Shah Mahmud. In 1799 Awadh's Sa'adat 'Ali had written to Wellesley that he would abdicate; but when he learned he could not choose his successor, he changed his mind. Wellesley ordered more troops into Awadh and told the Nawab he would have to pay for them. Sa'adat 'Ali objected that this violated the treaty; but in February 1800 he agreed to pay the Company and disband his own forces.

The next year Wellesley demanded that the Awadh nawab cede at least half his territory to the Company, and the threat of force made him agree in November 1801. The ceded land of Rohilkhand and the Lower Doab bordering Bihar was most fertile. Sa'adat 'Ali was required to "act in conformity to the counsel of the officers of the Honourable Company." Wellesley named his brother Henry as president of the board of commissioners and lieutenant-governor of Awadh. This military and administrative control by the Company in exchange for subsidies in the name of a defensive alliance was called the "subsidiary alliance system."

In 1799 Richard Wellesley decreed that no newspaper could be published unless it had been previously inspected by the Government's Secretary, and the penalty for failure was deportation. He founded the College of Fort William in Calcutta to educate civil servants. The uninformed Directors objected, but they were overruled by Robert Stewart (Viscount Castlereagh) on the Board of Control. In 1806 the Directors established Haileyburg College in England and reduced Fort William College to teaching Indian languages to Bengali civilians. Wellesley believed in free trade and arranged for 3,000 tons of shipping for private British traders so that they could compete with foreign merchants. Believing that the British could provide superior government, Wellesley made plans to improve drainage and roads in Calcutta and proposed experimental agriculture at Barrackpur. He encouraged missionaries, and the Bible was translated into Indian languages. He prohibited the sacrifice of children at Saugor Point by the Hughli River and tried to reduce the number of Hindu widows burned in sati.

Tukoji Holkar died in August 1797, and his sons fought over Malwa. Jaswant Rao Holkar emerged as regent and defended the Holkar House against the Maratha empire of Daulat Rao Sindia, who had 40,000 disciplined men under the French general Perron in his northern armies. The latter had Nana Fadnavis arrested on the last day of 1797, and Daulat's father-in-law Sarza Rao Ghatge terrorized Puna for three months to raise money. Nana was released in July 1798. That month the Company made a treaty with the Peshwa, who agreed to exclude the French from his army and pay the force from Bombay. This secret treaty was renewed annually three times. Meanwhile Lakhwa Dada led the war of Mahadji's widows against the tyranny of Daulat Rao Sindia that lasted four years. Young Peshwa Baji Rao II defeated the Kolhapur raja in 1799. Nana Fadnavis died in March 1800, and Daulat Rao became the Peshwa's chief minister. The civil war in Daulat's family ended when Lakhwa Dada and the widows were driven out of Seondha in May 1801.

Jaswant Rao Holkar captured Ujjain in July 1801; he was defeated by Sarza Rao Ghatge in October but continued to fight by invading the Deccan. In 1802 opium addict Anand Rao Gaikwar asked the British for military aid against his brother Malhar Rao Gaikwar and his Arab mercenaries. Bombay governor Jonathan Duncan sent 2,000 men with Major Walker, who arranged a subsidiary treaty that ceded territory to the Company, defeating Malhar Rao and disbanding the Arab soldiers. After Jaswant Rao forced Peshwa Baji Rao to flee Puna, the Peshwa turned to the English and on the last day of 1802 signed the treaty of Bassein granting him 6,000 troops in exchange for 2,600,000 rupees annual revenue. Castlereagh criticized this treaty for allying with weak Puna instead of letting the divided Marathas settle their own conflicts. He objected to a clause that forced the Peshwa to accept British arbitration in his disputes with others. Some historians have considered the Bassein treaty the end of Maratha independence and the beginning of the Company's empire of India.

In February 1803 Jaswant Rao left Puna with a small garrison and plundered his way toward Hyderabad and Ahmadnagar. The civil war and drought caused a famine in central India. In May the British entered Puna and restored the Peshwa. Daulat Rao Sindia refused to agree to the Bassein treaty and organized a Maratha coalition with Raghuji Bhonsle II, Gosain Himmat Bahadur, and Gani Beg of Bundelkhand. However, Jaswant Rao Holkar made demands and declined to join. In this war Wellesley limited officers' baggage to what could be packed on animals. Arthur Wellesley gathered an army in the Deccan and captured Ahmadnagar in August 1803, and the next month he defeated the combined forces of Sindia and Raghuji at Assaye, killing 1,200 but suffering 1,600 casualties. In the north Commander-in-Chief Gerard Lake took the fortress of Asirgarh, and Sindia asked for a truce. Arthur Wellesley's army was doubled by the forces of Stevenson, and Berar without Sindia's cavalry was defeated with heavy casualties. French officers surrendered and evacuated the fort at Delhi. At Laswari the Marathas fought so courageously that Wellesley took their survivors into the Company's service. Sindia accepted a subsidiary force and defensive alliance, losing Agra, Delhi, and Gujarat, while Raghuji gave up Orissa and other territory on the east coast.

In April 1804 Governor-General Richard Wellesley declared war on Jaswant Rao Holkar. General Lake wanted help from Sindia; but the Governor-General refused to recognize Sindia's claim to the fortress at Gwalior even though his brother Arthur Wellesley told him he was wrong. Lake sent Col. William Monson to block Holkar's return to Hindustan; but the zealous Monson went too far and lost half his men and all his guns during his retreat from Holkar's cavalry in the August rain. The Bharatpur raja had been given some of Sindia's territory for providing Lake with 5,000 cavalry, but now he went over to Holkar's side. Holkar invaded Hindustan, occupied Muttra, and besieged Delhi in October. Lake surprised his forces at Farrukhabad in November, inflicting 3,000 casualties on the Marathas while the British only had two killed and 26 wounded.

They took Fort Dig the next month, and after a siege the Jats of Bharatpur agreed to a treaty in April 1805. The raja was allowed to keep Bharatpur; but he had to pay an indemnity of two miliion rupees, and he could not employ Europeans without the Company's permission. The raja had paid Amir Khan to attack Lake's supplies and raid Rohilkhand; Lake defeated and dispersed the bandits with his cavalry, though Amir Khan joined Holkar.

Richard Wellesley was recalled in July 1805 and replaced by Charles Cornwallis, who reported that William Pitt had commented that Wellesley "had acted most imprudently and illegally." The war increased the Company's debt from £17 million in 1797 to £31.5 million in 1805. Wellesley was also criticized for issuing orders autocratically without consulting his Council. Before Cornwallis could reverse the subsidiary treaties, he died at Ghazipur in October 1805. Senior councilor George Barlow became acting governor-general and concluded a treaty with Daulat Rao Sindia the next month. Lake chased Jaswant Rao as far as Amritsar, where the Sikh Ranjit Singh declined to join his cause against the English. Jaswant Rao Holkar accepted a treaty in December 1805 that let him keep his territory in the Deccan. Barlow also left the Rajput and small states west of the Jumna River to the depredations of Sindia, Holkar, and Amir Khan; Lake was so upset that he resigned in protest. To save money Barlow greatly reduced the number of forces and disbanded the recruited Marathas, cutting the annual deficit in half to one million pounds.

Madras commander John Cradock required sepoys to shave their beards, banned caste marks on the face, and made them wear hats usually worn by Christian converts. Hindus and Muslims were greatly offended, and Cradock was willing to rescind his order; but Governor William Bentinck and the Council insisted on the new turban they had approved. On July 10, 1806 at 3 a.m. sepoys attacked the Europeans, shooting dead about a hundred and wounding many more. Col. Robert Gillespie brought dragoons and killed more than 300 mutineers, imprisoning the others. A few were tried and executed, and most of the others were discharged; three regiments were disbanded. Cradock and Bentinck were recalled.

Gilbert Elliot, Earl of Minto, arrived as governor-general in July 1807. After the French invaded Portugal, the British occupied Goa. Learning that Napoleon had made a treaty with the Russians, Minto sent John Malcolm to Persia, Mountstuart Elphinstone to Kabul, and Charles Metcalfe to Lahore to try to negotiate alliances. Malcolm never reached Teheran, where the French already had influence. In Afghanistan, Shah Shuja, brother of the deposed and blinded Shah Zaman, had overthrown Shah Mahmud about five years before; he agreed to an alliance against the French, but he himself was soon overthrown and fled to Ranjit Singh and then to Ludhiana, where the British gave him refuge. Metcalfe tried to persuade Ranjit Singh to give up his recent conquests in the Sutlej and Jamuna regions. An army led by David Ochterlony persuaded Ranjit Singh to agree to a treaty in 1809 that allowed him to retain them but limited the number of his troops. Minto feared an alliance of Muslim aristocrats and sent Col. Barry Close against Amir Khan, who withdrew from Berar. In 1810 Minto sent a force that captured the islands of Mauritius and Bourbon from the French. With little warfare in India during his six years Lord Minto improved the finances of the Company.

In 1813 the Earl of Moira (known as Lord Hastings after 1817) became governor-general and commander-in-chief. The Company's charter was renewed for another twenty years in 1813, and for the first time the Parliament declared Crown sovereignty over its possessions and ended its monopoly on Indian trade. Europeans still could not reside in the Company's territories without a license and could be deported. Parliament also encouraged missionaries to provide moral education and authorized a bishop. The Charter Act of 1813 provided £10,000 to advance the study of Sanskrit, Persian, and Arabic, but the money was not spent until ten years later. The Company now had a surplus, and Lord Hastings invested in road construction and irrigation. Awadh nawab Sa'adat 'Ali died in 1814 and left a huge surplus. When Major Baillie recognized the oldest son Ghazi-ud-din instead of the favored second son, the latter retired on a pension in Benares. Lord Hastings visited Lucknow and accepted a loan of ten million rupees (£1,250,000) from Ghazi-ud-din that helped finance the Gurkha war. Later Baillie demanded a similar loan, which was paid for by Terai territory taken from the Gurkhas. The defeat of Napoleon by Arthur Wellesley (Wellington) in 1815 allowed the British to end their policy of neutrality in India.

Jaswant Rao Holkar secretly assassinated his brother Kasi Rao and nephew Khande Rao, as the stress of his defeats caused him to go insane in 1807. For four mad years until he died in 1811 his state was in anarchy. Then his favorite mistress Tulsi Bai gained power, while his minister Amir Khan led the plundering Pathans of central India. Raghuji Bhonsle II did not accept a subsidiary alliance, and his Berar was also in disorder because of the lawless Pindaris and the Pathans. In 1809 he forced Amir Khan to retreat to Nagpur; but his attempt with

Daulat Rao Sindia to capture Bhopal in 1813 was defeated by Nawab Vazir Muhammad the next year. Raghuji died in 1816. Because his son Parsoji Bhonsle was blind, paralytic, and ill, his cousin Appa Sahib acted as regent. When Raghuji's widow Baka Bai challenged him, Appa Sahib made a subsidiary alliance treaty in May 1816. When Parsoji died the next year, Appa Sahib became gadi and met with the ministers of the Peshwa and Sindia.

The marauding Pindaris were a loose collection of brigands with no religious or national unity, and they had been ravaging Malwa, Marwar, Mewar, and other Rajput states. Company territory had been attacked in Mirzapur and South Bihar in 1812 and the northern Sarkars in 1816. These incursions into Company territory weakened the Council's resolve against armed intervention; but Board of Control president George Canning was still vetoing the extermination of the Pindaris because of the risk of a general war. In Rohilkhand in 1816 Muslims rioted after a respected Mufti was wounded by guards quelling a mob complaining about a tax. Early in 1817 Daya Ram of Hathras in the Ganges-Jumna Doab seized police officers and had a force of 8,000 men. Lord Hastings sent enough artillery to capture his fortress. In Bengal a mob led by Jagbandhu revolted against government extortion and plundered Puri in 1817; martial law was proclaimed, and order was restored by reducing the assessment. In Benares a communal riot resulted in the death of about twenty people, and a general strike and petitioning was successful in getting a tax withdrawn.

The Gaikwar of Baroda had made a subsidiary alliance treaty with the Company in April 1805; but Major Walker kept Anand Rao Gaikwar and Fateh Singh Gaikwar under British guards. His successor, Captain Rivett Carnac, provoked resistance by Gaikwar Ranis. Peshwa Baji Rao II plotted to form a Maratha confederacy against the English. In 1814 the Peshwa conducted Gaikwar chief minister Gangadhar Shastri, who was a friend of the English, to Nasik, where he was murdered. Trimbakji Danglia was suspected, and Baji Rao reluctantly surrendered him to the British resident Elphinstone at Puna. Trimbakji escaped the following year, probably by the connivance of the Peshwa. Lord Hastings ordered Elphinstone to curtail the Peshwa, and Baji Rao II was compelled to sign the Treaty of Puna in June 1817. The article in the Bassein treaty obligating him to send a contingent force was annulled. The Peshwa renounced leadership of the Maratha confederacy, surrendered three forts, and ceded to the Company territory yielding 3,400,000 rupees for a maintenance force of 5,000 cavalry and 3,000 infantry. Lord Hastings himself commanded an army of 113,000 men with 300 guns. He expected Maratha chiefs to cooperate and warned any aid to the Pindaris would be treated as predatory aggression.

On November 5, 1817 Daulat Rao Sindia signed the Treaty of Gwalior, promising to provide 5,000 cavalry and help the English suppress the Pindaris. On that day the Peshwa burned the British Residency at Puna and attacked with 27,000 men Col. Burr's British army of 2,800, but he was defeated. The British occupied Puna, and Baji Rao fled. Amir Khan submitted by agreeing to be nawab of Tonk. Appa Sahib of Nagpur had about 20,000 men and 36 guns, but his forces were defeated at Sitabaldi. Appa Sahib gave up and apologized to Richard Jenkins, whose army forced the surrender of Nagpur. The Holkar regency wanted a treaty, but the Pathan war party murdered Tulsi Bai. In December, Jaswant's son Malhar Rao Holkar II attacked the British in the largest battle of the war at Mahidpur, but his army was routed by the combined forces of Commander-in-Chief Thomas Hislop. Holkar was forced to sign a subsidiary treaty in January 1818, giving up claims to the Rajput states and ceding territory south of the Narmada River.

Captain Staunton with 900 men ran into the Peshwa's army of 28,000 but survived with only 265 casualties while killing many Marathas. In February 1818 the British defeated and killed Maratha commander Gokhale, capturing the Satara raja who was descended from Shivaji. He was installed as the ruler of a very small Maratha kingdom at Satara. The Company army defeated Pindari leaders Karim Khan and Vasil Muhammad, and about 25,000 Pindari horsemen were eventually rounded up or dispersed. The greatest Pindari leader Chitu fled into a forest and was killed by a tiger. The Peshwa was pursued and finally surrendered in June 1818 to John Malcolm, who offered him an annual pension of 800,000 rupees, which was paid until he died in 1851. One by one the Rajput states accepted "defensive alliance" treaties with the British. The last Maratha fortress at Asirgarh did not surrender until April 1819. The blind Mughal emperor Shah 'Alam II on a pension died in 1806, and Lord Hastings told his successor Akbar II to give up all ceremonial pretensions. The British now had political supremacy over all of India except Assam, Sind, and the Punjab.

Indian historians have suggested various causes for the decline of Maratha power in India from Sarkar's opinion that Indian society had become rotten to Qanungo's view that aggressive British imperialism inevitably overcame the medieval feudalism of the Maratha chiefs. Major factors include diverse causes.

The Marathas overextended themselves by trying to conquer the north in the mid-17th century. Conflicts, such as the Sindia-Holkar rivalry, with each other and the Peshwa divided them. Maratha states had administrative anarchy with court corruption and excessive violence. Armies were the main government and mostly plundered, even their own people. Chiefs were won over by British money, and many sepoys served in the Company armies.

Maratha military forces were badly organized and poorly trained; they lacked the modern equipment and discipline of the Europeans. Marathas had declining national feeling as the proportion of mercenaries increased and included Arabs, Sikhs, Rajputs, Sindis, Rohillas, Abyssinians, Pathans, Topiwalas, and Europeans; even Napoleon called Perron a traitor to his profession for betraying Sindia's army. The Maratha state had a precarious agriculture dependent on rain, commerce that was frequently harassed, and little industry. Unpaid soldiers led to coercive protests. The feudal system only promoted local and temporary loyalties as peasants supported whoever protected them. Caste prejudices also weakened the social fabric.

Education was very limited, and even Persian influences dried up with the decline of the Safavids. The Marathas had no great leader after Shivaji, and after the death of Nana Fadnavis in 1800 the leaders were especially bad.

Sikander Jah had succeeded his father Nizam 'Ali in 1803 at Hyderabad, and his pro-British prime minister Mir Alam had such strong opposition that he took refuge with the British resident. When Mir Alam died in 1809, his Hindu deputy Chandu Lal gained the power and was also supported by the British. Company loans at high interest rates were used to spread corruption. By 1810 the outgoing resident Captain Sydenham advised taking over the administration; but the Directors still favored non-intervention. Resident Henry Russell added to the prodigal spending with a new brigade of over-paid officers. General Palmer's Eurasian son William and Director William Rumbold set up William Palmer & Co. to make money from loans as Bentinck had done at Madras.

Lord Hastings gave permission for loans at 25 percent interest. The firm made advances totaling £240,000 mostly to the Russell brigade, and in 1819 Chandu Lal asked to borrow £600,000. When Metcalfe became resident, he investigated the fraud and arranged for the British government to guarantee a loan at 6 percent. This scandal resulted in the resignation of Lord Hastings at the end of 1822.

SIKHS AND NORTH INDIA 1767-1800

Ranjit Singh was born November 13, 1780. His father died in 1792, and five years later he became chief of the Sikh misl Sukarchakia. At that time between the Indus and Setluj rivers were 27 Hindu states, 25 Muslim states, and 16 Sikh states. Ranjit Singh made political alliances by marrying a Kanahya princess in 1796 and a Nakai princess in 1798. The next year the citizens of Lahore invited Ranjit Singh to occupy their city, and Shah Zaman authorized him to govern it for the Afghans, enabling Ranjit Singh to take over Lahore with little resistance. In 1800 Governor-General Wellesley sent Yusaf Ali to persuade Ranjit Singh not to form an alliance with Shah Zaman. However, Shah Zaman was deposed and blinded by his brother Mahmud, who was overthrown by Shah Shuja in 1803. The Muslim Nizam-uddin Khan and the Bhangi Sikhs submitted to Ranjit Singh in 1801, and Nizam paid him a war indemnity. Maharaja Ranjit Singh led an army that attacked Amritsar in 1802 and conquered the Sikh religious center in a few days. Also that year the Maharaja invaded Multar and set the tribute at 120,000 rupees.

Though the Marathas and Sikhs were not united, the British feared the disciplined army of Perron and sent General Lake to capture Aligarh in August 1803. Bourquien was defeated the next month. Lake put the blind Emperor Shah Alam II under British protection, and in November, Daulat Rao Sindia was defeated at Laswari. Wellesley instructed Lake to win over the Sikhs from the Marathas. Ranjit Singh replied that he would cooperate with the British if they would accept his sovereignty over all the Sikh chiefs west of the Sutlej River. After the British conquered Delhi, they treated the Sikh sirdars and rajas as independent chiefs. In 1804 Bhag Singh of Jind and Bhanga Singh of Thanesar were the first Sikh sirdars to go over to the British. Bhag Singh was rewarded with tax districts. When Ochterlony warned Wellesley that Ranjit Singh was threatening the Cis-Sutlej chiefs, the Governor-General advised him to establish friendly relations with all the Cis-Sutlej chiefs. In February 1805 Ranjit Singh sent messages to all Sikh sirdars to join a united Sikh state under his leadership as Maharaja. In April, Ochterlony sent Burne to attack Gurdit Singh of Ladwa, the leader of the anti-British Sikhs who had been plundering the upper Ganga Doab, and Burne captured Karnal. By June most Sikh sirdars had agreed to be friendly with the British.

Jaswant Rao Holkar got support from Sahib Singh and asked for other Sikhs to join his anti-British efforts; but Ranjit Singh visited Lake's camp in disguise and promised him and Malcolm that he would not support Holkar. Ranjit Singh sent Fateh Singh Ahluwalia with Bhag Singh to help mediate a treaty between the British and Holkar in December 1805. These two emissaries also made a treaty for the Sikhs with the British the next month. Gian Singh was impressed by the discipline of the British army and compared them to the Mughals, Afghans, Marathas, and Sikhs, who laid waste to all the cultivation within thirty kilometers of the road; the British purchased what the others stole.

After Baghel Singh died in 1805, Ranjit Singh took over the territory of his widow Ram Kaur along with 2,400,000 rupees in cash. Ranjit Singh campaigned in the Cis-Sutlej region and took over 311 villages from Rani Nurulnisa in November 1806. Ranjit Singh continued his plundering the next year, expelling the Pathan chief of Kasur; but he alienated Lal Singh and Sahib Singh by not sharing his loot with them. He also antagonized his mother-in-law Sada Kaur by sending his general Mohkam Chand to take Dinanagar from her.

Ten Cis-Sutlej chiefs met in March 1808 and felt they were caught between the British and Ranjit Singh, but they sent their representatives to the British resident Seton at Delhi to ask for protection against Ranjit Singh. The exclusion of Holkar and the British from the Punjab had enabled Ranjit Singh to unite his kingdom.

Metcalfe was sent to Ranjit Singh and met him at Kasur to negotiate a confederation; Metcalfe complained when the Maharaja sent Karam Singh Chahal with 2,000 troops to seize Faridkot in October 1808. Metcalfe refused to accompany Ranjit Singh's army as he captured Ambala and Mulana from Rani Daya Kaur, seizing 50,000 rupees. Metcalfe went to Amritsar, and the Maharaja spent time there with his favorite dancing-girl Moran. A mob of Hindus burned down the houses of dancing-girls, and Ranjit Singh fled with Moran to Lahore, where Brahmins went on a hunger strike. Hindu-Muslim riots broke out in Amritsar and Lahore, but the Maharaja suppressed them by the end of 1808.

Metcalfe accused Ranjit Singh of duplicity and noted that he had repudiated his first wife Mahtab Kaur and their two sons, angering her mother Sada Kaur, who offered Metcalfe free passage for British troops. Seton and Metcalfe advised Governor-General Minto not to allow a Sikh kingdom on the British border. Minto sent a force under Col. Ochterlony, and the Maharaja's men evacuated Ambala. Ranjit Singh chose to negotiate with Ochterlony, who was censured, resigned, and reinstated. In April 1809 Ranjit Singh accepted the Treaty of Amritsar that gave the British the territory between the Yamuna and Sutlej rivers while recognizing Ranjit Singh's domain northwest of the Sutlej. Ranjit Singh withdrew his forces across the river, giving back Faridkot, and Bhag Singh surrendered Ludhiana to Ochterlony for his camp. The British declined to support the Gurkha general Amar Singh Thapa's invasion proposal and even offered to help defend Ranjit Singh.

In Afghanistan the Barakzai brothers of the Sadozai family and Durrani tribe deposed Zaman Shah and enthroned Mahmud Mirza in 1800, but he was overthrown by his younger brother Shuja-ul-Mulk three years later.

Shah Shuja ruled Afghanistan from 1803 until 1809 when he was replaced by his stepbrother Shah Mahmud because of the revolt led by the oldest Barakzai brother Fateh Khan and his brother Dost Muhammad. Shah Shuja escaped to the Punjab, where he was supported by Ranjit Singh. Shuja with help from Kabul vizier Fateh Khan conquered Peshawar, but in 1812 he was captured by Attock governor Jahan Dad Khan and imprisoned in Kashmir for a year. Meanwhile Ranjit Singh and diwan Mohkam Chand were subjugating Hindu and Muslim chiefs, and the road to Kashmir was prepared by seizing Bhimbar in 1811 and Rajauri in 1812.

Shuja's senior wife Wafa Begam offered Ranjit Singh the famous Kohinur diamond if he would protect her husband from Vizier Fateh Khan, who had proposed a campaign to overthrow his brother Ata Muhammad Khan in Kashmir. The Maharaja sent his top general Mohkam Chand to accomplish both tasks in 1813. Fateh Khan got to Kashmir before the Sikhs and refused to share the spoils with Ranjit Singh. Fateh Khan released Shah Shuja but lost the battle for the fort of Attock to Mohkam Chand and the Sikhs. Shah Shuja chose to live in Lahore, and Ranjit Singh got the diamond. In 1815 Shuja escaped from Lahore and made his way through Kulu to Ludhiana, where the British raised his allowance to 50,000 rupees. Ranjit Singh fined the Kulu raja 80,000 rupees for not capturing Shuja.

Maharaja Ranjit Singh's system of justice was to make the rich pay fines for the offenses of the poor in their village. Another Kashmir expedition in 1814 led by Ranjit Singh failed because of defense by its governor Muhammad Azim Khan, the mountain terrain, and the rain. The Maharaja lamented the heavy costs of this expedition. After Jodh Singh died, Ranjit Singh seized the estates and destroyed about 150 forts of the Ramgarhia Misl. The Maharaja continued to take over more territory and forced the chiefs to pay him tribute. He declined to help the Gurkha chief Amar Singh against the British. Ranjit Singh engaged in six campaigns into Multan over fifteen years before he could collect 130,000 rupees tribute in 1816; finally his Sikh army of 25,000 conquered Multan in 1818.

BRITISH EXPANSION 1818-36

After 1800 Thomas Munro spent seven years in Mysore developing his method of tax collection he had initiated at Madras. He returned to England and in 1812 persuaded the Directors to prevent the use of the permanent settlement in Madras and the Upper Provinces.

Munro went back to Madras in 1814 to implement annual settlements and reform of the judicial system. In 1820 he was made governor of Madras and applied his more traditional ryotwari settlements throughout the province for the next seven years. He believed that the natives were much more qualified than the Europeans for making judicial decisions, and Charles Metcalfe described the British-dominated courts as " scenes of great corruption" and "very unpopular."

Even Governor-General Lord Hastings bemoaned the inconvenience, expense, and delay of the civil proceedings. He let Munro experiment using village headmen (patels) for suits up to 250 rupees and village councils (panchayats) for larger ones; but they were all expected to work without remuneration and were not utilized. Munro believed in working with a prejudice in favor of native systems, instead of against them, so that they could learn to govern themselves. Although this judicial method failed, his revenue system was adopted throughout India. Metcalfe also warned that if the British empire kept its inhabitants in ignorance, their dominance would be a curse; but if they promoted enlightenment with arts and sciences to improve conditions, then the gratitude of India and the admiration of the world would accompany their name in the future.

Bombay governor Mountstuart Elphinstone adopted the ryotwari system. In 1819 he described two techniques used if the panchayat refused to hear a dispute. In takaza a man may restrain an equal or inferior from leaving his house or eating or compel him to sit in the sun until he makes some accommodation. If the debtor is a superior, the creditor may supplicate and lay on his doorstep, appealing to his honor and shame. A person may also sit in dharna by fasting on the other party's doorstep. Maratha troops often used the dharna method to extract back pay from their chiefs. Elphinstone revised the Bombay judicial system in 1827, using Zila (district) courts with one judge, whose decision could be appealed to the Sadar Diwani Adalat. Petty cases were tried in lower courts by Indians.

In Afghanistan after Dost Muhammad treacherously took Herat from Mahmud's brother Firuz-ud-din and insulted his harem, Mahmud's son Kamran murdered Fateh Khan in 1818. The next oldest brother Azim Khan asserted his claim, as Dost Muhammad seized Kabul and fought Shah Mahmud and Kamran, who now had Herat. Azim Khan turned to exiled Shah Shuja, and they marched on Kabul; but in a quarrel between them Shah Shuja was defeated and fled back to Ludhiana in 1821. Azim Khan and his Barakzai brothers ruled over all of Afghanistan.

Maharaja Ranjit Singh extended his Sikh confederation by conquering Multan in 1818, Kashmir in 1819, Dera Ghazi Khan in 1820, Mankera and Dera Ismail Khan in 1821, and Bannu and Tank in 1822. Some of these territories were taken from the Afghan empire, while the Indus River marked the boundary between his Sikh kingdom and Sind. Ranjit Singh imprisoned his mother-in-law Sada Kaur in 1820, but two years later the British restored her to the fort of Whadni. Because of his friendship with the British, Ranjit Singh refused to form defensive alliances with Nepal or Bharatpur. When

Peshawar governor Yar Muhammad Khan gave Ranjit Singh valuable horses, Muhammad Azim Khan disapproved and went to Peshawar, declaring holy war on Ranjit. The Sikhs won the battle in March 1823. Azim Khan died the same year, resulting in a struggle for power between the Barakzai brothers that lasted three years until Dost Muhammad captured Kabul, Ghazni, and Jalalabad; other brothers held Qandahar.

Concerned about a possible invasion into India by Russia, the British had concluded a treaty with Persia in 1814 in which they promised to provide military aid to Persia if they were invaded by any European power; but when Russia and Persia went to war in 1826, the English annulled the provision by paying Persia money. In the treaty Persia agreed to send forces if the British were at war with Afghanistan; but the British were not to interfere in an Afghanistan-Persian conflict unless both sides sought mediation.

Governor-General Wellesley had imposed press censorship; but the liberal Lord Hastings granted wide latitude to the Calcutta Journal, which James Buckingham began publishing in 1818. Three years later it was countered by the pro-government John Bull. The Government sued Buckingham for libel but lost. A financial scandal caused the Marquess of Hastings to leave India in early 1823. By then the Calcutta Journal had a circulation of a thousand. Senior councilor John Adam governed in Bengal for seven months until William Amherst arrived. However, when the Calcutta Journal satirized the appointment of a Scottish minister to a post in the Stationery department, Adam had Buckingham deported. England and the Netherlands signed a treaty in 1824 that ceded the Dutch territories in Bengal to the British.

Bishop's College was established at Calcutta in 1820 but did not admit non-Christians. In 1823 the General Committee of Public Instruction was formed in Calcutta, and Sanskrit College was founded. Rammohun Roy wrote a letter suggesting that more modern education was needed. The next year James Mill and the Court of Directors issued a dispatch urging education with utilitarian principles. A Calcutta madrasa (Islamic school) was established in 1826, but only two students passed the junior scholarship examination in the next 25 years. Cotton manufacturing in England reversed this trade as a nominal 2.5% duty allowed British goods into India. With the ending of the Company monopoly in 1813 unsold native cotton goods accumulated in Company warehouses. The cotton imports increased from 2,000 pounds in 1813 to 100,000 pounds ten years later. The British government protected its industry at home with tariffs while allowing free trade in India. In his ten years Lord Hastings increased the Company's annual revenue by nearly six million pounds.

East of Bengal, Burma was expanding its little empire. They seized Manipur in 1813. Rebels led by Khyen-byan attacked Arakan from 1811 until he died in 1815. Burmans installed in Assam a ruler who accepted their sovereignty in 1818. Burma demanded that the British deliver the rebels who took refuge in Bengal, or they threatened to annex Ramu, Chittagong, Murshidabad, and Dacca as part of Arakan. Hostilities escalated gradually because of border incidents involving British subjects. In September 1823 Burmans killed three British sepoys on the tiny island of Shahpuri, a place so unhealthy no one even wanted to leave a garrison there. Nonetheless, the British reoccupied it and put up stockades in November. Govinda Chandra had been driven away from his kingdom of Cachar by three brothers and appealed to the British, who declined to help; but the Burmans sent an army that reinstated him. Amherst wrote to the Directors that this pass was essential and recognized Govinda Chandra as a ruler protected by the British, sending a force from Dacca to Sylhet. Govinda Chandra accepted and promised to pay the British tribute.

The Burmese government sent a force of 4,000 from Assam, but a British force led by Major Thomas Newton defeated them in January 1824. After the Burmans captured the pilot of a British schooner and burned the hut on Shahpuri, the British declared war on Burma. The Burmese general Maha Bandula led a large army that caused the sepoys to flee from Ramu. The British withdrew to protect Chittagong, and the Burmans entered Cachar; but they left before Newton's force arrived. The youngest brother Gambhir Singh had joined the British but managed to conquer Manipur on his own. General Archibald Campbell with his army of 11,000 occupied Rangoon in May after the Burmans had fled with badly needed provisions.

Maha Bandula attacked them in December with about 60,000 men; but the British force managed to defend themselves as part of Rangoon was burned. Meanwhile an expeditionary force occupied Tenasserim. Sepoys at Barrackpur near Calcutta, upset that they did not have enough pay to buy bullocks to carry their cooking pots, refused to obey orders to march into Arakan. Commander-in-Chief Edward Paget ordered guns to fire on them; a few were killed, and some drowned in the Ganges. A court martial sentenced the 41 captured to death; twelve were hanged, and the rest had their sentences commuted to fourteen years hard labor.

In January 1825 the British army forced the Burmans at Rangpur to ask for a truce. When the British force occupied the capital at Arakan, the Burmans withdrew from that province. Because of fever and dysentery, the British withdrew from most of Arakan. Campbell's forces and a naval column attacked Donabew in April, and Maha Bandula was killed by a rocket. The Burman king's brother, Prince of Tharrawaddy, opposed the war with the British and evacuated the strongly fortified Prome to return to the capital at Awa and try to persuade his brother to make peace. Campbell cantoned his troops at Prome and under an armistice began negotiating, but King Bagyidaw refused to accept the terms.

The Burmans made another proposal, and a treaty was signed in January 1826; but the King refused to ratify it. Finally as the British army came near the capital, at Yandabo the King agreed in February to give up his claims to Assam, Cachar, and Manipur, ceding Arakan and Tenasserim to the English and promising to pay an indemnity of ten million rupees. They agreed to exchange envoys, and a commercial treaty was signed. Even the Company Directors had to admit that this war was caused by "trifling acts of insult and aggression" and that the invasion of lower Burma was not justified by military necessity. The number of those killed in battle was less than two hundred; but of 3,738 European troops in the Rangoon expedition 3,160 died of scurvy and dysentery, and of 1,004 in Arakan 595 died from malaria. All together on the British side about 15,000 died, and the war cost five million pounds.

In central India rumors that the British were withdrawing troops for the Burman war stimulated Pindari brigands, rebels, and ambitious chiefs to take up arms. Two days before Bharatpur ruler Baldeo Singh died in February 1825, Resident David Ochterlony invested the young prince as the heir. However, Durjan Sal as regent claimed the throne and took over the fort of Bharatpur. Ochterlony announced that his troops would rescue the boy before the fort could be defended; but when the Governor-General in council suspended his preparations, Ochterlony resigned. Charles Metcalfe was appointed resident of Delhi and formulated the imperialist policy that it would be hazardous for the British to relax their paramount influence in Malwa and Rajputana, arguing that the non-interference policy had failed in 1806. He denounced Durjan Sal and sent a large force that assaulted and captured Bharatpur in December 1825, killing at least 8,000 while suffering only 600 casualties; a treasury worth £480,000 was divided by the army as prize money. Durjan Sal was imprisoned at Allahabad, and Metcalfe installed the boy Bulwant Singh as raja.

In 1827 Governor-General Amherst visited Awadh nawab Ghazi-ud-din, who loaned the Bengal government fifteen million rupees before he died that October. Daulat Rao Sindhia died earlier in 1827 but had arranged for his favorite wife Baiza Bai to choose an adopted son to succeed. Major Stewart supported this, and as regent she loaned the British Company five million rupees.

William Bentinck returned to India as governor-general in July 1828 intent on applying utilitarian principles to reform India. Metcalfe left Delhi and as senior member of the Council became Bentinck's chief advisor. He warned that the only thing that was universal in India was the disaffection toward the dominion by strangers. Bentinck himself wrote that he wanted to reform the "monstrous rapacity" of four hundred strangers governing sixty million people. At the end of his term in 1835 he concluded that compared to the Muslims who intermixed and married the natives, the British rule was "cold, selfish and unfeeling" using the "iron hand of power" along with "monopoly and exclusion."

Because of the expenses of the Burma war, Amherst left India with a one-million-pound deficit his last year. Bentinck saved nearly a million by reducing military expenditures, and an interlude of peace along with special measures to protect the Government's lucrative opium monopoly created a two-million-pound surplus by the time he left. Although it only saved £20,000 a year, the officers resented his cutting in half their batta (extra pay). Bentinck allowed newspapers to criticize him and his government, but after a while he forbade them to mention the batta issue anymore. He adopted in Bengal the revenue administration pioneered by Munro in Madras, saved money by appointing Indian judges for 400 rupees per month, and let them handle more cases.

Company servant David Scott in Assam recommended annexing western Assam and recognizing someone from the Ahom dynasty. The Company did the former but procrastinated on the latter. Prince Gadadhar Singh rebelled in 1828, but he and his supporters were arrested and put in prison. The next year Khasi raja Tirat Singh regretted his agreement to help the British build a road, and his men killed two British lieutenants. During the rebellion the British burned Khasi villages. In 1830 Assamese nobles proclaimed Kumar Rupchand raja.

The British suppressed these insurrections by the Khasi hill tribes and the Singpho. Two rebels were hanged, and Rupchand was imprisoned for fourteen years. Tirat Singh eventually surrendered and spent the rest of his life in prison. Scott died in 1831, and two years later Purandar Singh was installed in Upper Assam; but his tribute was set at the exorbitant 50,000 rupees. After five years he was in arrears and was deposed as Upper Assam was annexed by the Company.

The British asked Cachar raja Govinda Chandra to cede his territory to the Company, but he refused. Cajar was invaded by Tularam on one side and by Manipur raja Gambhir Singh on the other. The British declined to help him and made him assign territory to both of them. After Govinda Chandra was assassinated in 1830 by a servant of Gambhir Singh, the British rejected all the possible rulers and annexed Cachar. Tularam was forced to pay tribute for his territory, which was later annexed three years after he died in 1851. The raja of Jaintia died in 1835, and his successor declined to pay the high tribute demanded; the best part of his territory was taken, and he gave up the rest. The Company also annexed other small territories in the late 1830s.

In Tenasserim some fanatical Muslims objected to Hindu idolatry and in 1830 plundered and burned their houses. They killed cows and forced Brahmins to eat beef. After a magistrate was forced to flee, soldiers came and killed nearly a hundred of the zealous Muslims, imprisoning and dispersing the rest. In Orissa and southwest Bihar native tribes objected to British taxes and settlers taking the best land; but their uprising with primitive weapons was suppressed by the military.

Sayyid Ahmad of Bareilly taught the doctrines of Waliullah and traveled from Delhi to Peshawar, where the governor was accused of trying to poison him. He aroused his followers to fight, and they defeated and killed Yar Muhammad in 1829; but Sikhs led by Prince Sher Singh and General Ventura helped Sultan Muhammad win back Peshawar. The Sikh troops withdrew, but Sayyid Ahmad led his forces across the Indus in 1830 to attack Sikhs led by Hari Singh Nalwa and General Allard. The Sayyid's holy warriors (Ghazis) withdrew, but a few months later they attacked Sultan Muhammad Khan and occupied Peshawar. Ahmad proclaimed himself caliph and minted a coin. His taxes on the peasants and decree that all young men must marry caused discontent, and he was killed at Balakot by a surprise attack in May 1831. The Usufzai tribe expelled his deputies, and the Ghazis dispersed.

In 1831 Bentinck visited Lucknow (Lakhnau) and tried to persuade the profligate Nasir-ud-din that if he did not reduce the corruption, he would be removed from power. The Nawab hired Hakim Mehdi to collect revenue, but the Indians and Europeans who disliked his reforms drove him from his office.

In 1835 the Directors ordered Bentinck to take over the government of Awadh (Oudh); but since he was leaving office, he just warned the Nawab. Bentinck did take over the government of Mysore from its unpopular ruler Purneah because he mistakenly thought the tribute was in arrears. Later in 1834 he visited the Raja and proposed his power be restored, but the British kept control over Mysore until 1881. Coorg was annexed by force because its raja had killed all his heirs. Bentinck tried to get the emirs to open up the Indus River, but Ranjit Singh believed it was too shallow.

Governor-General Bentinck and Maharaja Ranjit Singh exchanged state visits in 1831 with mutual respect, and the next year Captain Wade got Ranjit Singh to agree to let British traders use the Sutlej River. Sikhs led by Hari Singh defeated Afghan tribes above Attock in 1832. Shah Shuja tried to recapture his throne but could only get a four-month advance on his allowance from the British. After making a treaty with Ranjit Singh, Shah Shuja set out from Ludhiana in 1833 with 3,000 troops and 200,000 rupees. As he traveled through Shikarpur, he forced the Sind emirs to pay him 500,000 rupees. Shuja's forces besieged Qandahar in 1834, but they were defeated by Dost Muhammad Khan and his brothers. Shah Shuja returned to Ludhiana the next year with 250,000 rupees.

Bentinck made special efforts to end thuggery and sati (widow suicide). Thugs (robbers) had been active in India since the decline of the Mughal empire. They were also called Phansigars because they used nooses to strangle their victims. Mostly they were Hindus worshipping Kali, the goddess of destruction, but Muslims sometimes joined their gangs. They preyed upon travelers by pretending to befriend them before murdering them and taking their possessions.

They gave some of their loot for Kali ceremonies and to those who protected them. Bentinck sent special agents and established special courts to hear these cases, and in 1835 the Department of Thuggee and Dacoity was established. A law was enacted making membership in a thuggee band a crime. In six years more than four hundred thugs were hanged, and the roads became much safer. After Wellesley decreed that sati was legal if voluntary, the attendance by police officers to assure this seemed to give it more credibility. The number of sati deaths more than doubled in six years, reaching a high of 839 for the year 1818. Bentinck enacted a regulation in 1829 making burning or burying widows alive homicide. This reduced sati in Bengal, Bombay, and Madras, but it still was allowed in the native states.

The Company's charter to administer territories in India was renewed in 1833 for another twenty years because many believed that the Parliament would increase the corruption of patronage. The new Charter Act stated that the interests of the native subjects were to be preferred to those of the Europeans when they were in conflict.

The Governor-General was responsible for Bengal, Assam, and the Burman possessions, and Metcalfe was appointed governor at Agra. The English were now allowed to acquire land in India. Slavery was abolished in the West Indies in1833, and many planters moved their plantation system of exploiting labor to India.

The Governor-General and the Council could now make laws for all the Company's territories. A law member was added to the Council, and a Law Commission was appointed with Thomas B. Macaulay as its head. The Charter Act of 1833 also required the Company to divest itself of administering religious endowments, and participation in religious festivals was discouraged and in 1840 prohibited. Bentinck dismissed for corruption the residents at Delhi and Lucknow, and he transferred others he suspected.

Before he left India in March 1835, Bentinck announced that the British government should promote European literature and science by making English the language of higher education. Macaulay wrote his "Minute on Education" in which he argued that English should be taught instead of Sanskrit and Arabic. Thousands of Indians enrolled in English schools, and in two years the Calcutta School Book Society sold more than 30,000 books in English. According to an 1845 report to the House of Commons the number of students being educated at government expense included 13,699 Hindus, 1,636 Muslims, and 236

Christians. The Bengal government attempted to establish in each district an English school or a school using both English and the local language. Higher education was available in Calcutta at the Hindu College, which was only open to Hindus. In 1854 the government took it over and renamed it Presidency College, emphasizing the writings of Bacon, Johnson, Milton, and Shakespeare along with history, science, moral philosophy, and political economy.

Charles Metcalfe served as acting governor-general for one year. He believed in freedom of the press and removed the restrictions. F. J. Shore published his Notes on Indian Affairs in 1837, criticizing the government by the English Company for being "extortionate and tyrannical in practice" while professing to be benevolent and philanthropic.

The last Maratha raja, Pratap Singh, in 1835 tried to claim the six jagirs (tax districts) recognized by the treaty of 1819, but Bombay governor Robert Grant deliberately withheld a letter and honorary sword sent by the Court of Directors. Brahmins resented Pratap Singh for supporting the right of Prabhu Kayasthas to perform religious rites.

They intrigued to bring charges of conspiracy and treason against the Raja and two men for trying to seduce Indian officers from their allegiance to the British. James Carnac replaced Grant and asked the Raja to sign a memorandum agreeing to certain conditions for clemency on the charges; but Pratap Singh lost his throne at Satara in 1839, only because he had the integrity not to sign the document that would be admitting what was false.

RAMMOHUN ROY AND SOCIAL REFORM

Rammohun Roy was born into a Brahmin family near Calcutta on May 22, 1772. At Patna he learned Arabic and Persian, studying the Qur'an, Islamic law, and Persian poetry. By the age of ten he had two wives. Rammohun learned Sanskrit at Benares and studied Hindu philosophy for three years. He traveled, and some believe he studied Buddhism in Tibet. His father was a zamindar and collected taxes. Absorbed in Sufi and Vedanta philosophy, Rammohun criticized Hindu idolatry and soon became alienated from his traditional parents. Yet in 1796 his father gave him a house in Calcutta, and Rammohun began studying English. He loaned money to English employees of the East India Company.

His father died in 1803, and years later his mother tried to disinherit Rammohun for heresy. His friend John Digby introduced him to western literature, and in 1805 he began working for Digby and the Company. Rammohun's first publication was in Persian and affirmed the unity of God; he warned against idolatry and religious doctrines that deceive.

Rammohun may have witnessed a widow burned to death in sati at the funeral of his brother in 1812.

In 1814 Rammohun and a few friends began a friendship society called Atmiya Sabha. The next year he began translating some of the Upanishads and an abridgment of the Vedanta Sutra into Bengali and English.

In 1817 he helped Edward Hyde East and David Hare found the Hindu College; but Rammohun's name was not associated with it because some Hindus considered him a heretic. In debate Rammohun defended Hindu theism and argued that people are harmed by myths about gods and goddesses that do not stand up to reason.

In 1820 he began helping missionaries translate the Bible into Bengali to improve on Carey's version, and he published his book on the ethics of Jesus called The Precepts of Jesus, Guide to Peace and Happiness. In response to criticism, he wrote three appeals to Christians in which he argued that the humanistic ethics of Jesus is much more important than the miracles and theological doctrines on atonement and the trinity. Rammohun emphasized the oneness of God. Max Müller, the scholar who helped to found the modern study of comparative religion, said that Rammohun was the first person to synthesize eastern and western religion.

In 1818 Rammohun began an educational campaign to end the burning of Hindu widows (sati) by publishing and freely circulating a dialog between an advocate and an opponent. He wrote,

In times of want the wife works like a slave.

In times of affluence the husband takes another wife and enjoys worldly pleasures.

Very often the wife is beaten up, discarded, accused of disloyalty, all because the husband feels that he has the right to do so.

Rammohun argued that nowhere in the Hindu scriptures is it demanded that a widow must commit suicide or be murdered. He charged that one of the main reasons for sati was the avarice of relatives who wanted to avoid the cost of supporting a bereaved widow. He advocated the custom should be abolished for humanitarian reasons. Most of the widows dying by sati were in Calcutta, and the number in Rammohun's own district of Burdwan was barely second to Hughli. The number of such widow suicides in the six divisions of Bengal had gone from 378 in 1815 to 812 in 1818. These increases discouraged the efforts that were being made by the British government.

Rammohun managed to prevent some burnings by personal persuasion. His writing must have had an effect because in 1819 the number of widow burnings in Bengal was 650. In a second tract that year he defended the rights of women by showing that they are not inferior to men but in some ways even superior. Orthodox Hindus organized groups to defend the atrocious tradition of sati against his campaign, and the number only gradually decreased in the next decade to 464 in 1828. However, the new Governor-General Bentinck made any support for sati a crime in 1829, and in gratitude Rammohun sent him an anti-sati address on behalf of more than 300 supporters.

During its first year in 1821 Rammohun took over the editing of the Bengali weekly Sambad Kaumudi (Moon of Intelligence), the first newspaper published by Indians. Rammohun also founded and began editing a Persian weekly in 1822 called The Mirror of News (Mirat-ul-Akhbar). He wrote a brochure demanding that Hindu women should have the same property rights as their fathers and husbands. In 1823

Chief Secretary John Adam got a regulation enacted that was called Adam's Gag because it required every periodical to obtain a license signed by the Council's Chief Secretary before it could publish each issue. Rammohun closed down The Mirror in protest of this pre-censorship and sent a memorial to the Government. He explained why a powerful government should avoid censoring.

> *Another evil of equal importance in the eyes of a just Ruler, is, that it will also preclude the natives from making the Government readily acquainted with the errors and injustice that may be committed by its executive officers in the various part of this extensive country.*
>
> *Every good ruler who is convinced of the imperfection of human nature, and reverences the Eternal Governor of the World, must be conscious of the great liability to error in managing the affairs of a vast empire and therefore he will be anxious to afford to every individual the readiest means of bringing to his notice whatever may require his interference.*
>
> *To secure this most important object, the unrestrained liberty of publication is the only effective means that can be employed.*

When the British decided to spend its large grant for education on a Sanskrit College in 1823, Rammohun argued that Indians had a much greater need to learn science from Europeans. Just as the Baconian philosophy had replaced the medieval scholastics, India needed its own renaissance beyond its religious philosophy. Rammohun helped William Adam found the Unitarian Association, and with David Hare they started an Anglo-Hindu school with free tuition for Indians.

The Vedanta College was founded to study Hindu scriptures. In 1825 the Parliament passed an East India Jury Bill that only allowed Christians to serve on grand juries. Rammohun criticized this discrimination by writing articles for Sambad Kaumudi, and the next year he demanded equal treatment in the Native Petition to Parliament. In 1827 he published the Sanskrit work Vajrasuchi that criticized the caste system. He believed that the most important moral principle is the golden rule: "Do to others as you would be done by."

Rammohun and his friends began the Brahmo Sabha on August 20, 1828 based on the idea of one God, one world, one humanity. Devotional songs, mostly by Rammohun, were interspersed between the invocation, prayer, meditation, and sermons. When they moved into their own building on January 23, 1830, their purpose was defined in the Trust Deed as to worship "the Eternal, Unsearchable, and Immutable Being who is the Author and Preserver of the Universe." All kinds of people were welcome as long as they behaved in an "orderly, sober, religious and devout manner." No objects were to be worshipped. No person was to be reviled.

They aimed to promote "charity, morality, piety, benevolence, virtue, and strengthening the bonds of union between men of all religions, persuasions and creeds."3 The Brahmo Sabha did not recognize any priestly class as privileged mediators between God and humans. Their members worked on such reforms as abolishing child-marriage, polygamy, and caste persecution. They planned how to bring education to women and give them their proper status in society. Conservative Hindus led by Radhakanto Dev, compiler of a comprehensive Sanskrit dictionary, tried to counter their progressive ideas by forming the Dharma Sabha. Young Bengalis responded to Rammohun's practical synthesis of eastern and western education, freedom of thought, freedom of the press, and intellectual idealism. Rammohun protested against the Government's salt monopoly, the high taxes on the cultivators, and worked for many progressive reforms. He criticized the East India Company for taking two million pounds out of India to London each year. He encouraged Dwarkanath Tagore to set up small industries in the Bengal countryside.

In 1831 Rammohun went against caste rules and became the first prominent Hindu to visit England. As the envoy of Mughal king Akbar II, he gained him an additional 300,000 rupees for his budget. His memorial to the House of Commons to counter the petition to repeal the abolition of sati was successful, and he presented in writing his reform ideas before the next renewal of the Company charter. He proposed reductions in the rents of the ryots (peasants), and he suggested that the decrease in revenue could be balanced by hiring native collectors at lower salaries. In his Questions and Answers on the Judicial System of India, Rammohun recommended replacing Persian with English as the official language in the law-courts, appointing native assessors, using trial by jury and the traditional panchayat system, separating the offices of revenue collectors from judges, codifying the criminal and civil law of India, and consulting with local leaders before enacting laws. His efforts helped persuade the House of Commons to repeal the clause disqualifying all but Christians from serving on grand juries, and the Indian Jury Act of 1832 allowed the governments of Bengal, Bombay, and Madras to appoint qualified Indians as judges. He urged the Tories to support the Reform Bill currently being debated. He did not think that a commercial organization should be ruling another country and suggested that a proper government would be easier for the natives, even though it would still be a foreign one.

Rammohun Roy also visited France before he died at Bristol on September 27, 1833. He lived according to the great humanistic saying of Sa'di that he wanted as his epitaph, that the best way of serving God is to do good to humans. He was one of the first pioneers for the ecumenical unity of all religions, and his outstanding efforts for modern education and social reform led some to call him the father of modern India.

The Young Bengal movement had been inspired by the poet Henry Derozio (1809-31), who had taught at the Hindu College and founded the Academic Association in 1828. After Rammohun Roy died in 1833, his disciple Vidyavagish led the Brahmo Sabha; but it languished until Dwarkanath Tagore's oldest son Devendranath Tagore joined in 1843 with twenty of his associates. Dwarakanath Tagore helped found the Landholders' Society in 1838, and the next year Rammohun's friend William Adam started the British India Society in England. They eventually merged into the British Indian

Association, which paid agents to pressure in England and worked for reforms in local government. In 1846 Govindachandra Dutt denounced the unequal treatment of British and Indians before the law and urged the separation of the executive and judicial functions. Devendranath had founded the Tattvabodhini Sabha in 1839, and the monthly Tattvabodhini Patrika promoted Indian culture with western improvements.

They changed the name of Brahmo Sabha to Brahmo Samaj (God Society) and in 1850 began agitating for social reforms such as widow remarriage, monogamy, and temperance. Vidyasagar discovered a verse in the Parashara Samhita that approved of widow remarriage, and his book Vidhava Vivaha led to the passage of the Widow Remarriage Bill in 1856. That year Devendranath withdrew for two years to travel and be more reclusive in the Simla hills.

BRITISH INVASION OF AFGHANISTAN AND SIND

Tory minister Robert Peel persuaded the Directors to appoint the diplomatic Heytesbury as governor-general; but the Whigs replaced the Tories in 1835, and the new foreign secretary Palmerston did not want the former ambassador who was friendly with the Russians. Instead, George Eden, known as Baron Auckland, was chosen. He set out for the Upper Provinces with a retinue of 12,000 people and was not deterred from passing through the famished region between Kanpur (Cawnpore) and Agra in 1837. They did some relief work, but about 800,000 died of hunger and disease. Col. John Colvin began investigation for an irrigation project that led to the Ganges Canal nearly twenty years later. At Lucknow, Resident Col. John Low had used force to defeat the Begum's nominee as successor to Nasir-ud-din Haidar and put his uncle Muhammad 'Ali on the Awadh throne; but he had to agree to pay 1,600,000 rupees annually for an additional subsidiary force. The Directors later rejected the new treaty as unfair; but Auckland only told the new ruler he was released from the additional burden.

Ranjit Singh intrigued with the Barakzai brothers against Dost Muhammad, and Hari Singh led the Sikhs that seized

Peshawar in May 1834. Dost Muhammad declared a holy war on the Sikhs and marched on Peshawar; he asked for English aid, but they declined. Sultan Muhammad refused to take the Sikh envoys hostage for his brother Dost Muhammad and went over to Ranjit Singh, who gave him some tax districts after Dost Muhammad withdrew.

The British could not get the Khairpur emir to restrain the Mazaris from attacking the Sikh posts, and so in 1836 the Multan governor defeated the Mazaris and took over Rojhan and the Ken fort. The English sent Captain Alexander Burnes to negotiate commercial agreements with the countries bordering on the Indus River, and Captain Wade traveled to Lahore to reassure Ranjit Singh. Hari Singh occupied the Jamrud post at the Khyber Pass, but he was defeated and killed by Dost Muhammad's army from Kabul in 1837.

Russian envoy Simonitch encouraged Persia's Muhammad Shah to attack Herat, and the Persian army began a siege in November 1837. English envoy Burnes was in Kabul trying to persuade the Barakzai brothers to resist a possible Russian advance when Russian emissary Vitkevitch arrived to tell Dost Muhammad that Russia would fund his effort to expel Ranjit Singh from Peshawar.

In a treaty guaranteed by Simonitch the Persian shah transferred Herat to the rulers of Qandahar. Burnes negotiated with Qandahar and offered British help against the Persians, but the Government of India made him withdraw that. They offered to restrain Ranjit Singh from attacking Dost Muhammad if he would not make an alliance with another state. However, Auckland was afraid of losing the Anglo-Sikh alliance if he pressured Ranjit Singh. Since the British offered little, Dost Muhammad welcomed Vitkevitch to Kabul.

The British minister McNeill complained to the Shah in his camp that the siege of Herat violated their treaty, and meeting with the Herat ruler he arranged a treaty, which the Persian shah refused to ratify. So McNeill suggested that Auckland send a naval force to the Persian Gulf, and they occupied the island of Kharak. In August 1838 the British told the Shah he must withdraw from Herat to suspend British actions, and the next month the Persians retreated. The Russians said they were not aggressive and recalled Simonitch and Vitkevitch, who felt disgraced and committed suicide.

William Macnaghten in Lahore asked Ranjit Singh to help Shah Shuja regain his throne at Kabul, but the Maharaja declined to do so without British forces participating. Shuja promised to turn over two million rupees paid by the Sind emirs to Ranjit Singh, and all three signed the treaty by July 1838. Armies in Bengal and Bombay began preparing. In October the Governor-General issued a manifesto from Simla that even the press at the time exposed as a "collection of absolute falsehoods." Even though the siege of Herat had been ended, Auckland did not call off the campaign; his proclamation in November indicated his intention to replace a hostile power in eastern Afghanistan. The Duke of Wellington warned that the advance would be "a perennial march into that country." A Blue Book of dispatches was published in 1839, but they were carefully selected and edited to convey false impressions.

The British army gathered at Firozpur with 9,500 men in the Bengal division and 5,600 from Bombay, while Shah Shuja had 6,000 men. Across the Sutlej River were 15,000 Sikh troops, but Ranjit Singh would not allow the army to march through his country. So they had to go through Sind even though a military crossing of the Indus River was a violation of their 1832 treaty with the English. The Sind emirs were forced to pay Shah Shuja 2,500,000 rupees (25 lakhs), and he had to pass on 15 lakhs to Ranjit Singh. The Khairpur state made a treaty to cooperate with the British, who promised to protect them and occupied their fortress at Bukkur. Auckland also demanded that the Sinds pay three lakhs per year for the subsidiary force in their territories. Facing an attack by this army on Hyderabad if they did not comply, the Sind emirs signed two more treaties, paid the tribute, and provided supplies. Troops took over Karachi, and a British force was stationed to make sure that tolls were no longer collected on the Indus River.

As the army marched, Baluchi brigands harassed the rear, carrying off baggage, camels and bullocks, which were dying by the hundreds. In late March 1839 they reached Quetta, where commander John Keane established his headquarters. By then they were on half rations, and 20,000 baggage animals had been lost. Macnaghten began using money to give people compensation and bribe the authorities. Most Afghan tribes were won over by gold, and Qandahar surrendered on April 25. Shah Shuja was enthroned on a platform. Macnaghten and Burnes persuaded General Keane that the Ghazni fortress would also surrender, and so he left behind the large guns. Only because a nephew of Dost Muhammad deserted and told them of a weak gate were they able to blast through and take the fortress, killing many Afghans while suffering less than 200 casualties. Dost Muhammad and a few followers fled north into the Hindu Kush mountains. There he took refuge with Uzbek chief Wali of Kulun, who kept him prisoner. Keane's army marched into Kabul on August 7, 1839, but Shah Shuja was not warmly received. The Barakzai sirdars had been expelled from Afghanistan, and British soldiers occupied Qandahar, Ghazni, Jalalabad, and Kabul.

The Bombay army departed Afghanistan as did some of General Nott's Bengal troops. Macnaghten advised Auckland to order the Bombay division to punish Mehrab Khan for not restraining the Baluchi brigands, and three Khelat provinces were turned over to Shah Shuja. Ranjit Singh had died in June 1839, and his successors objected to Keane's army passing through the Punjab. Macnaghten paid them off, and he also found that the Ghilzai chiefs and Afridis had to be bribed to keep the mountain passes open. Baluchi tribes still attacked convoys and even Quetta itself in June and July 1840. Mehrab Khan's son Nasir Khan took over Khelat and forced the British puppet Shah Nawaz Khan to abdicate until General William Nott arrived with troops and forced Nasir Khan to flee to the hills. Yet a year later to avoid more trouble the British recognized Nasir Khan as the ruler of Khelat and the three provinces taken from his father.

The Afghans did not like Shah Shuja's government and blamed the British because of their military occupation. Auckland's council complained of the huge cost for this Afghan adventure. Macnaghten contemplated taking Herat but was restrained by Auckland. Dost Muhammad persuaded Wali of Kulun to support his attack on Bamiyan, but the British defeated them in September 1840 and won over the Wali with gold. Joined by some of Shah Shuja's troops, Dost Muhammad marched toward Kabul, but the British cavalry defeated him at Parwandurrah on November 2. Two days later Dost Muhammad rode up to Macnaghten and surrendered. Macnaghten kept him as an honored prisoner before sending him under guard to Calcutta, persuading Auckland to give him a pension of 200,000 rupees.

To save money Macnaghten reduced the stipends and subsidies he paid to Afghan chiefs. This caused resentment, and the eastern Ghilzais left Kabul to take up positions on the road to Jalalabad. Macgregor arranged truces, but they were to no avail. Col. Robert Sale was wounded in Khurd Kabul Pass, and many of his men and much equipment were lost in October 1841. On November 2, Afghans in Kabul attacked the house of Burnes, killing him and many others and taking the Shah's treasury. The gout-suffering General W. G. K. Elphinstone failed to reinforce the commissariat fort, and the British lost most of their provisions. Their troops often did not obey orders or fight. The Hindu sepoys resented their loss of caste, and the Muslim sepoys were reluctant to kill fellow Muslims. The freedom-loving Afghans also resented the way their women in Kabul had been seduced by the occupying army. The insurrection spread, and the garrison at the Laghman fort mutinied, left the fort, and marched to Kabul. Two British officers at the fort in Kohistan were murdered by their men. Ghazni was attacked, and the British garrison stayed in the citadel until March 1842, when they surrendered and were treacherously killed.

Auckland ordered a withdrawal, but Macnaghten was still optimistic and sent Mohanlal to spread around 50,000 rupees among the tribes. The army was demoralized and faced starvation, and Elphinstone urged Macnaghten to make peace. Macnaghten proposed the British evacuate Afghanistan unmolested; Shah Shuja would abdicate, and four British officers would remain as hostages. They evacuated Bala Hissar on

December 13. The Afghan chiefs brought provisions but asked the British to hand over their forts. They did so, but carriages were not arriving. Dost Muhammad's son Akbar Khan sent Macnaghten a proposal for Shuja to rule with Akbar as his well paid vizier. On December 23 Macnaghten went to meet Akbar with three officers; but Macnaghten and another were killed, and the other two were made prisoners. Now the Afghan chiefs required the British to leave behind all their guns except six along with all spare muskets and the coins in the public treasury.

They also wanted the married men to remain with their families as hostages; but none volunteered, and this was changed to a few men. The sick and wounded were left at Bala Hissar. In January 1842 the British left with 4,500 troops and 12,000 camp followers. In the Khurd Kabul Pass they were ambushed by Ghilzais, and about 3,000 were killed. The attacks continued, and more were massacred. A few officers forged ahead, but all were cut down or dispersed except Dr. Bryden, who reached the fort at Jalabad after a week of slaughter.

Brigadier Wild led four regiments from Firozpur to Peshawar but could not get Sikh support. In the January weather the sepoys refused to march to Kabul without gloves and coats, but Henry Lawrence prevented their execution and persuaded them. At the Khyber Pass they did not fight, and the Afghans took the Ali Masjid fort that commanded the Pass. Gen. Nott disobeyed an order to evacuate Qandahar and defeated some Afghans. In March 1842 Brigadier Richard England led a relief detachment from Sind but was defeated and fell back to Quetta. Col. Sale refused to evacuate Jalalabad and defeated Akbar Khan's Afghans in April.

On February 28, 1842 Baron Ellenborough (Edward Law Jr.) arrived at Calcutta and replaced Auckland. Ellenborough ordered an immediate evacuation but contemplated whether military operations should be undertaken to restore British honor. Generals George Pollock and Nott were given discretion to vindicate the military. Pollock defeated some Afghans in August and the next month occupied Kabul. In revenge the British demolished the marketplace. Shah Shuja had been murdered in April, and his son Fath Jung, who had been a tool of Akbar Khan, fled, surrendered, and abdicated. Shapur, another son of Shuja, was proclaimed king. General Nott entered abandoned Ghazni and destroyed the town, claiming he captured the gates from the tomb of the 11th-century conqueror Mahmud. Saleh Muhammad Khan released the British prisoners from Bamiyan for 20,000 rupees and a small pension. Dost Muhammad and other Afghans returned from India. Shapur fled to Peshawar in 1843, and the British recognized Dost Muhammad, the one they had overthrown, as the rightful ruler before they departed from Afghanistan.

To gain control over Sind, Governor-General Ellenborough sent letters to the emirs Nasir Khan at Hyderabad, Rustum Khan at Khairpur, and Sher Muhammad Khan at Mirpur, warning that if they were not faithful, their sovereignty would be taken away. Ellenborough replaced Major James Outram with Charles Napier as commander and ordered him to investigate the Sind emirs. They were accused of seeking secret alliances against the British and levying tolls. In November 1842 a treaty took away their right to coin money, and Karachi and Tatta were ceded to the British. Napier ordered British troops to occupy the left bank of the Indus from Rohri to Bahawalpur, and he marched on Khairpur to replace Rustum Khan with his brother, the compliant Ali Murad. Outram as commissioner was negotiating with the emirs in Hyderabad and advised Napier not to march on the unarmed city with troops. After Napier captured the Imamgarh fortress, thousands of armed Baluchis came and attacked Outram's residence, forcing him to flee to a steamer.

In February 1843 Napier's force defeated them in a fierce battle; 62 British and about 5,000 Baluchis were killed. Most of the emirs surrendered, and their property was confiscated and auctioned. Napier received about £50,000, but Outram declined to accept £3,000 and left the country. In March a similar battle was fought against Sher Muhammad of Mirpur, killing about 2,000 Baluchis. The British annexed Sind and appointed Napier governor, but Ali Murad ruled Khairpur as their vassal. Ali Murad tried to extend his domain with a forged treaty; but he was eventually caught, and his authority was diminished in 1851. In England Punch summed up Napier's conquest of Sind with the Latin word peccavi, which means "I have sinned." The Directors passed a resolution condemning his Sind takeover but decided that giving it back would cause more mischief. Outram testified that the emirs had been bullied and provoked into armed resistance because Napier did not halt his march even after they signed a treaty. Napier had confessed in his journal, "We have no right to seize Scinde; yet we shall do so, and a very advantageous, useful, humane piece of rascality it would be."4 Sind remained a deficit province for many years, and Napier governed it until 1847. Although Bentinck had abolished flogging in the Indian army, Napier continued to flog. He imposed martial law and tried cases by military commissions, deciding himself the capital cases. Captain Keith Young complained that he retried persons who had been acquitted. Using the Irish constabulary as a model, Napier established the Sind police under a European captain with native officers. This was the first modern police force in India that was independent of the military and revenue collections, and the Bombay Presidency adopted the system in 1852.

Ellenborough assigned Col. W. H. Sleeman to investigate the uprisings in the Saugor district of central India that occurred in April 1842. He found that the Revenue Board orders had been misconstrued, damaging the landowners. When their protests were ignored, they revolted. Ellenborough dismissed the officials. He also abolished many inland customs duties in Madras and the North-Western Provinces, raising the salt tax to make up the revenue.

When Jankoji Rao Sindhia died in February 1843, leaving behind no son and an 11-year-old widow, Ellenborough used the opportunity to take over the large Gwalior province. The Gwalior Durbar wanted Khasjiwalla as regent, but the British chose Mama Sahib, who was opposed by all the chiefs. The British government demanded that the influential Khasjiwalla be fined and banished. The Governor-General appointed Col. Sleeman as resident at Agra and went there himself. Warned that the British army was coming, Khasjiwalla surrendered. In December 1843 Ellenborough demanded a treaty be signed within three days. The Maratha troops fought for their independence and inflicted 790 casualties but suffered more than 3,000. In January 1844 the Governor-General dictated a treaty at Gwalior that provided for a larger British force and civil administration, 2,600,000 rupees from the Gwalior Durbar, a limit of 9,000 men in the Maharaja's force, and a British regent until the Maharaja came of age in 1853.

SIKHS AND PUNJAB SUBMIT TO BRITISH

Ranjit Singh died on June 27, 1839. His oldest son Kharak Singh became maharaja and let the British troops pass through the Punjab on their way back from Afghanistan. Sikh troops helped General Pollock get through the Khyber Pass on their way for vengeance against Kabul. Kharak Singh was considered a fool and an opium-eater; but his son Nao Nihal Singh took control after Dhian Singh murdered the Maharaja's favorite Chet Singh Bajwa in October 1839.

The three wealthy Hindu brothers of the Dogra tribe named Gulab Singh, Dhian Singh, and Suchet Singh had been made rajas in the province of Jammu. Kharak Singh died in November 1840; coming back from the funeral, Nao Nihal Singh was killed when an archway fell on him. Many suspected Dhian Singh even though he was also injured and his nephew was killed. Ranjit Singh's reputed son Sher Singh succeeded. He was a voluptuary and was challenged by Kharak Singh's widow Chand Kaur, who claimed to be regent for Nao Nihal Singh's son who was born later. Both sides offered the British and the Sikh army advantages. In January 1841 Sher Singh besieged the Rani (Queen) at the Lahore fort; Dhian Singh became his chief minister, as Chand Kaur retired with a tax income. Her Sandhanwalia supporters withdrew to British territory.

The Sikh army now felt its power and plundered houses of the wealthy in Lahore, killing several people. The disorders spread, and General Avitabile fled from Peshawar to Jalalabad. Kashmir troops murdered Col. Mian Singh, but Jammu raja Gulab Singh restored order and gained control over the valley in April 1841. However, his nomination to Peshawar was vetoed by a British agent later that year. Other commanders in Mandi,

Kulu, Hazara, and Amritsar were also assassinated. Sher Singh appealed to the British, and they prepared to send a force of 10,000, but Sher Singh changed his mind. The Lahore Durbar invited representatives of the army units and increased their pay; these committees of five were called military panchayats. The army had control and chastised those they considered traitors. In June 1842 female attendants beat to death Chand Kaur.

The British agent Clarke persuaded Sher Singh to recall the exiled Sandhanwalia sirdars, Attar Singh and Ajit Singh. Nearly a year later in September 1843 Ajit Singh shot Sher Singh dead while his uncle Lahna Singh killed his son Partap Singh. Then together they shot and killed Dhian Singh along with his bodyguards. Dhian's son Hira Singh and brother Suchet Singh aroused the army and stormed the fort, killing Ajit Singh, Lahna Singh, and several hundred of their troops.

Attar Singh fled with his son to the British. Hira Singh declared maharaja young Dalip Singh, the son of Ranjit Singh and Rani Jindan, who became regent with Hira Singh as prime minister. Suchet Singh supported two other reputed sons of Ranjit Singh, Kashmira Singh and Peshawara Singh; but his revolt was crushed, and Suchet was killed in March 1844. Another rebellion was quelled the next month as Kashmira Singh was killed.

Robert Peel appointed his secretary of war Henry Hardinge to be governor-general, and he arrived in July 1844. Multan governor Sawan Mal was assassinated in September and was succeeded by his son Mulraj. He quelled a mutiny in November by killing four hundred soldiers. Hira Singh's counselor Jalla Pandit offended Rani Jindan, and she caused the army to turn against them. Hira Singh and Jalla Pandit fled from Lahore and were killed in December 1844.

The Rani's debauched brother Jawahir Singh became the prime minister in May 1845, and her lover Lal Singh was influential. The panchayats did not like them and wanted Peshawara Singh as maharaja with Jammu raja Gulab Singh as vizier; but Chatar Singh Atariwala, whose daughter was betrothed to the young maharaja Dalip Singh, had Peshawara

Singh murdered. Jawahir Singh was suspected of having killed the prince and fled with Dalip Singh; but he was caught and executed by the angry panchayats in September 1845; his four wives died on his funeral pyre.

Lal Singh became prime minister with Tej Singh as commander-in-chief. Meanwhile Gulab Singh had extended his domains to include not only Kashmir but also Chach and Rawalpindi, while his military forces increased to 50,000 men with 200 guns. Gulab Singh and others secretly negotiated with the British, who promised they could keep their kingdoms. Meanwhile the British had been preparing by increasing their troops from 23,000 to more than forty thousand and by sending supplies to Firozpur, where they built a fort. Hardinge appointed the bellicose Major George Broadfoot, who did not like the Sikhs. He declared the Cis-Sutlej territories belonging to Lahore under British protection.

By the fall of 1845 two British armies were about to converge on Firozpur, and in December the Sikh army crossed the Sutlej to a piece of Sikh territory on the other side. The Sikh leader Lal Singh was secretly in communication with British captain Peter Nicholson and asked what he should do. He was told to delay the attack on Firozpur several days, and the Sikhs lost their advantage. After the British commander-in-chief Hugh Gough arrived with his army, the battle of Mudki began. Lal Singh deserted his army, and the Sikhs fell back. The sepoys were reluctant to fight against the Sikhs, and most of Gough's casualties were British. The Sikhs had a larger force, and about 2,000 were killed.

That night Sikhs killed the British left alive on the field. In the morning a fresh force led by Tej Singh missed an opportunity; he also fled to save the British army. While Gough needed fresh troops, Lal Singh and Tej Singh waited a month. However, Ranjodh Singh Majithia led a Sikh attack on Ludhiana. Harry Smith, who also fought in South Africa, led a relief force; but they were surprised at Baddowal in January 1846, were rescued by a British detachment, and won a battle at Aliwal. Henry Lawrence replaced the killed Broadfoot as political agent and continued to get secret information from Lal Singh. Gulab

Singh stopped sending supplies to the Sikhs. In February the British had the guns for an offensive. In the battle at Sobraon the traitorous Lal Singh and Tej Singh fled across the Sutlej and broke the bridge of boats so that their army would be destroyed. The British got revenge for their wounded having been killed at Firozpur by killing all they could; about half of the 20,000 Sikhs were killed or drowned.

The British sent a reserve unit into Lahore, and Governor-General Hardinge imposed a treaty on March 9, 1846. The British annexed the Jullundur Doab and sold the hill country between the Beas and the Indus rivers to Gulab Singh for five million rupees.

The Sikh army was reduced to 20,000 infantry and 12,000 cavalry. All guns were taken over by the British, and they were given permission to pass through the Punjab. The British promised not to interfere in the internal administration at Lahore, but this was not kept. Gulab Singh now had sovereignty over Jammu and Kashmir, and his nephew Hira Singh paid the indemnity from the Lahore treasury. Lal Singh was still prime minister, and he urged Kashmir governor Shaikh Imamuddin not to turn over the valley to Gulab Singh. Henry Lawrence marched there with troops, learned why, and returned to prosecute Lal Singh at Lahore. He was found guilty and exiled in December 1846, replaced as vizier by Tej Singh. That month Frederick Currie proclaimed the conditions Governor-General Hardinge was imposing on the Lahore government, and the Treaty of Bhyrowal was signed.

The British officer in Lahore was to have "full authority to direct and control all matters in every department of the State." Henry Lawrence was appointed the first Resident, and Rani Jindan was excluded from the administrative regency council. When the young maharaja Dalip Singh refused to invest prime minister Tej Singh, Lawrence had the Rani imprisoned in the fort.

Before he left office, Governor-General Hardinge reduced the native regiments by twenty percent, resulting in 50,000 less soldiers and saving more than a million pounds. James Ramsay (Marquess of Dalhousie) arrived in January 1848.

Henry Lawrence went home on sick leave, and John Lawrence replaced his brother Henry as commissioner of the Jullundur Doab. He reduced taxes and eliminated unnecessary duties. He proclaimed slogans against burning widows, killing infant daughters, and burying lepers alive. The Khalsa army was reduced from 27,764 to 22,005, and roads were built. Some of those unemployed turned to raiding. The outbreak in Multan stimulated other dispossessed rajas of Kangra, Jaswan, and Datarpur to rise up against the British also; but John Lawrence raised two divisions and crushed the insurgents by offering each village a choice between a pen or a sword, saying,

> *What is your injury I consider mine; what is gain to you I consider my gain....*
>
> *If your lands are heavily assessed, tell me and I will relieve you; if you have any grievance,*
>
> *let me know it, and I will try to remove it....*
>
> *If you will excite rebellion, as I live I will punish you.*
>
> *I have ruled this district three years by the sole agency of the pen and if necessary I will rule it by the sword.*

Mulraj was charged three million rupees for having succeeded his father as governor of Multan, but the British troops sent to collect it had been defeated in 1846. Mulraj wanted to resign, but John Lawrence persuaded him to wait a year. When Currie became resident, he sent Khan Singh Man to replace Mulraj with the British officers Vans Agnew and Lt. Anderson. Mulraj handed over his office; but someone threw a spear at Agnew, and fleeing Anderson was badly wounded. Mulraj's mother taunted him into leading the insurgents. The next day a Mazhabi boy was killed in shooting with Khan Singh's troops, and rebels murdered Agnew and Anderson.

The revolt spread to Bannu, Peshawar, and the northwestern Punjab. The miserable condition of the imprisoned Maharani also provoked discontent. Hazara governor Chatar Singh was a popular Sikh leader, and his daughter was engaged to Maharaja Dalip Singh; but the British kept postponing the wedding. Captain James Abbott accused Chatar Singh of conspiracy against the English and instigated Muslims against him, promising them three years without taxes if they expelled him. Sikh soldiers under Chatar Singh's son Sher Singh were deserting to Mulraj in large numbers. Chatar Singh resigned, and his son Sher also joined Mulraj in September 1848.

Upon Currie's advice not to declare war, Governor-General Dalhousie announced that the British government was occupying the Punjab province. Chatar Singh seized Peshawar at the end of October, and Commander-in-Chief Gough crossed the Sutlej and moved into Lahore. The armies met on the banks of the Chenab in November, but Gough waited for his troops from Multan. After news arrived that Chatar Singh's troops had captured Attock on January 3, 1849, the battle was fought at Chilianwala. The British forces lost 2,446 men, and both sides claimed victory. Meanwhile Multan was being assaulted, and Mulraj surrendered on January 22. Chatar Singh got 1,500 cavalry from Afghanistan's Dost Muhammad and joined his son; they fought the British again at Gujarat. General Whish had arrived from Multan, and the British had superior artillery. The Sikh army was routed and chased by the British cavalry for fifteen miles while Walter Gilbert's forces pursued the Afghans through the Khyber Pass. On March 12, 1849 the Sikhs surrendered and laid down their arms. An old Sikh soldier cried, "Today Ranjit Singh is dead." The prophecy of the great Sikh maharaja that the map of the Punjab would one day become all red (British) had come to pass.

Henry Lawrence returned as resident and opposed annexation; but Governor-General Dalhousie was determined, and in April 1849 he ratified the treaty in which Dalip Singh gave up sovereignty to the British for a pension. He and others later complained that those who had promised to protect him had taken away his sovereignty. Only one of the eight on the regency council had joined the rebellion, and the majority of the army had not revolted. Dalhousie had annexed the Punjab without consulting the home authorities. Maharani Jindan escaped to Nepal; she lost her property and lived there on a pension. Dalip Singh became a Christian in 1853 and went to England, but he returned to India in 1860. After he left India in 1886, he reverted to the Sikh religion.

Charles Napier was appointed commander-in-chief, and his inflammatory rhetoric had to be restrained by the Punjab board. A mutiny in Rawalpindi was solved by dismissing about a dozen men who refused to accept their pay in 1849. The next year Napier had to disband a mutinous regiment at Amritsar. He ordered that soldiers at Wazirabad be given dearness pay, making Dalhousie furious; Napier resigned and went back to England.

Governor-General Dalhousie established a board with Henry Lawrence as president but with John Lawrence to supervise finances and Charles G. Mansel (replaced by Robert Montgomery in 1851) over the judiciary. The liberal Henry and the rational John Lawrence worked together to improve the Punjab. They began with disarmament, and using the influence of the headmen 120,000 weapons were surrendered. Forts were leveled except in Peshawar, where defense against tribal raiders was needed. The Khalsa army of the Sikhs was completely disbanded and was replaced by a military of Sikhs and Muslims, a police force of mostly Muslims, and the Punjab Frontier Force. Dalhousie over-ruled Henry Lawrence and insisted that military grants be abolished. By 1852 Punjab soldiers were volunteering to fight for the British in Burma. Former soldiers took up plows, and large amounts of grain were produced. The market was flooded, and for a while transportation was difficult. Henry Lawrence talked to the peasants and got his brother John to suspend money payments. Despite reductions, more efficient taxation along with the sale of Durbar property produced annual surpluses. Eventually the Punjab became the bread-basket of India.

Henry Lawrence urged that roads, canals, and bridges be constructed. In four years 1,349 miles of roads were built; 2,487 miles were traced; and 5,272 miles were surveyed, not counting minor roads. Henry argued that the Sikh chiefs should have continued authority, but John disagreed and was supported by Dalhousie. After many arguments, in December 1852 both brothers resigned. John Lawrence was appointed commissioner, and Henry was sent as an agent to Rajputana. The people missed the kind Henry, but John continued the successful work. Edwin Arnold praised the results, writing, "Few could boast of having substituted in the space of four years, order for anarchy, obedience for irregular impulse, gardens for jungles, plenty for barrenness, peace for war."6

Between 1849 and 1856 twelve punitive expeditions suppressed raiding. The Pathans used guerrilla tactics, and so John Lawrence began giving cash allowances to influential chiefs and encouraged friendly contacts with officials. Herbert Edwardes negotiated a friendship treaty with Dost Muhammad's son in Kabul. In these seven years the Punjab spent thirty million rupees on public works. Many Sikhs already went to school, and Lahore had sixteen elementary schools for girls. In 1856 they planned to build 130 new schools, and most classes were conducted in Urdu. They established 104 Small Causes Courts that did not charge fees for legal advice.

DALHOUSIE'S ANNEXATIONS 1848-56

The annexation of the Punjab was only the beginning of Governor-General Dalhousie's annexations in India. He often used the doctrine of lapse as a reason for taking over states after a ruler died without a male heir. When deposed raja Pratap Singh died in exile at Benares in 1847, his brother Apa Sahib was allowed to inherit the Maratha state at Satara. He adopted a son the day he died in April 1848, but this time Dalhousie annexed that state. When Sambalpur's ruler Narayan Singh died in 1849, Dalhousie disregarded his widow and annexed the already surrounded state.

The Company took over a large part of Sikkim in 1850 to punish its ruler for mistreating British subjects. In 1852 the Mir of Khairpur was deposed. John Low persuaded the Directors not to let Dalhousie annex the Rajput state of Karauli because of Rajput feelings. Raja Raghuji Bhonsle III died without a male heir in 1853, but the reason for annexing the large Maratha state of Nagpur was to consolidate British military power and commercial resources. Low raised the only objection on the Council; he believed that these native states provided an outlet for the energies and ambitions of Indians who could not rise in British territories. Also in 1853 Dalhousie annexed Jhansi in Bundelkhand after its Maratha chief died; he too had adopted a son the day before he died. Under the subsidiary treaty the Nizam of Hyderabad came to owe the British Company some half a million pounds and was persuaded to sign over the management of his territory to the Company.

In 1837 a palace revolution removed Burman king Bagyidow, and he was replaced by his brother Tharrawaddy, who was an alcoholic. He refused to acknowledge the Treaty of Yandabo. The British were not welcome, and the Resident withdrew in 1840. Tharrawaddy was considered so insane that in 1845 he was put under restraint until he died the next year. In 1851 the British government decided to intervene on behalf of Europeans' complaints, and Dalhousie sent Commodore Lambert in a frigate to Rangoon. Burman king Pagan Min sent conciliatory letters and replaced the offending governor of Rangoon. In January 1852 Lambert sent interpreter Edwards to arrange a meeting with the new governor; but his deputation was put off when they were told the governor was asleep. Lambert gave asylum to British subjects on his ships and blockaded the rivers. Despite a warning that a yellow ship belonged to the king of Burma, Lambert seized it and refused to give it back even when the Governor offered to pay compensation for the grievances. Lambert provoked the Burman batteries to fire and then destroyed them. Dalhousie admitted that Lambert started the war by seizing the king's ship. Even though Dalhousie repudiated Lambert's action, he accepted responsibility and gave the king an ultimatum to pay one million rupees by April first. He sent the 38th Native Infantry by the Dacca road, because they were not required to fight overseas by their enlistment contract. John Lawrence later criticized Dalhousie for sending a commodore if he wanted peace, and Richard Cobden wrote a pamphlet on the origin of the Burman war, condemning the whole affair.

General Godwin arrived in Rangoon on April 2, 1852, and the war began. Rangoon was captured on April 14, and the British took Bassein in May. They captured the city of Pegu and installed a prince from an old ruling family. In July the British captured the fortress of Prome; but after the interlude of the rainy season these two places had to be recaptured in the fall. Dalhousie rejected a march on the capital at Ava and ordered annexation to somewhere beyond Prome. The Burman king declined to negotiate a treaty, and in December the annexation was proclaimed. In February 1853 King Pagan Min was replaced by his half-brother Mindon, who wanted peace; he ordered his officers to stop attacking British forces and released their prisoners. Major Arthur Phayre was appointed commissioner of the new province that extended fifty miles beyond Prome.

In 1847 Hardinge had warned Wajid Ali Shah of Awadh (Oudh) that he had two years to put his house in order or face annexation. Wajid Ali was an accomplished poet and liked to spend his time with musicians and artists. Dalhousie asked Resident William Sleeman to investigate, and he described the corruption and anarchy in the country. The property-owning Talukdars regularly terrorized the poor cultivators. Robbery and murder were common. The Awadh shah complained later that Sleeman had interfered with his administration by urging people to submit complaints and even gathered names on a list of those who wanted the East India Company to govern Awadh. Bishop Heber had described Awadh as a prosperous country in 1825, and the two British residents between 1839 and 1847 testified that Nasir-ud-daullah had improved agriculture, reformed the police, revenue, and the judiciary, encouraged commerce, and sponsored public works such as schools, colleges, tanks, and wells.

Wajid Ali Shah was open to improvements by British administration, and Sleeman advised the British government to help without taking over the revenues of Awadh. Henry Lawrence recommended letting Awadh be governed by its own people. Sleeman wrote about Dalhousie's intentions regarding annexation, "There is no pretext, however weak, that is not sufficient, in their estimation, for the purpose; and no war, however cruel, that is not justifiable, if it has only this object in view."7 Sleeman saw the danger and warned that the native states were the breakwaters. If the annexations swept them away, they would be left at the mercy of the native army, which they may not always be able to control. Dalhousie wanted to warn the king again; but the Council felt the risk of recalling British troops should not be taken. Finally in January 1856 the Court of Directors extended Dalhousie's term and approved his annexation of Awadh. He sent Outram with a treaty; but Wajid Ali told him that treaties were for equals, and being treated as an inferior he would not sign nor accept the pension. Annexation was proclaimed four days later. Many Talukdars lost their land, and cultivators suffered from high assessments. About 50,000 sepoys were dismissed. The tax on opium was increased, and prices generally went up.

In October 1855 the last Karnatak nawab Muhammad Ghaus Khan died without a son, and Dalhousie would not recognize his uncle Azim Jah as nawab. That same month Raja Shivaji of Tanjore also died without a male heir. The Court of Directors declared that no daughter of a Hindu sovereign could succeed, and Dalhousie avoided deciding about the claim of the senior widow. The next Governor-General Canning decided to restore the property but not the regalia of the family.

Dalhousie also implemented internal reforms and promoted western education, planning three universities. In Bengal the Santals rebelled against harassment by police and revenue officials. Bengal had been under the busy Governor-General. The Company Charter was renewed again in 1853, and the new Charter Act created a lieutenant-governor to oversee Bengal, Bihar, Orissa, and Assam. Since 1833 complaints had been made that the Indians were not appointed to higher positions, but the 1853 Act did little to remedy that. Competitive examination for the Company's covenanted service took away patronage from the Directors; their number was reduced from 24 to 18, and six were to be appointed by the Crown. The Act abolished the Military Board and transferred public works to a new department that was staffed with engineers as well as military men. A system of railroads was planned, and the first 150 miles were constructed. A telegraph system was created and extended wires for nearly 4,000 miles. Reformed postal facilities fixed a uniform rate for letters. Charles Wood took responsibility for improving education. Forest conservancy and tea plantations were established, and jails were reformed. Military force was used to suppress human sacrifices in the hills of Orissa.

Schools were taught in the vernacular languages at the lower levels with English used more in the colleges. The Educational Dispatch of 1854 proposed an administrative department of education, universities in the three Presidency cities, institutions for training teachers, increasing government schools and colleges, establishing middle schools, increasing vernacular elementary schools, and providing grants. During 1857 universities were incorporated in Calcutta, Bombay, and Madras. Their faculties were in the arts, law, medicine, engineering, and science. Lahore University was established in 1869.

MUTINY AND REVOLT 1857-58

The English Company had been ruling more and more of India for a century since Clive's conquest of Calcutta in 1757. The British may have had economic success, but the people of India were suffering from ruined industries, oppressive land tax, and lack of education for most of the people. The law courts were not impartial; police were more feared than respected; and prisons were wretched. The large Indian population had become passive and had little influence on administration. English officials were not very accessible to people, who could not present their grievances as they had before. British administration was less personal, slower, delayed, and frequently changing. Most Indians did not understand English law, and Muslims particularly disliked the use of English instead of Persian in the courts. Worst of all, Indians were systematically excluded from higher offices in government and the military. Even well educated Indians could not sit on legislative councils or be given covenanted service.

Economically British commerce exploited the Indians. High tariffs were erected in Britain against Indian goods, while importation of English products into India was encouraged. The importation of British cotton goods ruined millions of Indians involved in manufacturing and trade. India was used as a cheap source of materials. Raw cotton exports went from 9 million pounds in 1813 to 32 million in 1833 and 88 million in 1844. Wool increased from 3,700 pounds in 1833 to 2,700,000 pounds in 1844. Linseed increased more than a hundredfold in the same period. The importation of British muslins into India went from 6 million yards in 1824 to 64 million in 1837. Millions of Indian artisans, spinners, weavers, potters, tanners, smelters, smiths had to find work in agriculture because of the industrial revolution and manufacturing capitalism in England. In 1852 the Inam Commission was set up to require titles from landowners, and in the next five years more than 20,000 estates were confiscated in the Deccan, just as many Talukdars lost their property after Awadh was annexed.

The Charter Act of 1813 had unleashed proselytizing Christian missionaries, and gradually Indians came to fear that the British wanted to convert all of India to Christianity. Sayyid Ahmad Khan complained that the famine of 1837 had been used to make orphans Christians, and some believed the Government was reducing people to poverty so that they would adopt Christianity. In 1839 Christian missionaries petitioned the Company's government to stop supporting Hindu temples and caste regulations. The Religious Disabilities Act of 1850 made conversion easier by protecting converts from forfeiting their property or civil rights. Conservative Hindus also resented the Widows Remarriage Act of 1856 that removed legal obstacles to marrying again.

Many rebellions had broken out in various places since the end of the Maratha wars in 1818. Bhils revolted in 1819, 1825, 1831, and 1846. Rumors about the Burma War 1824-26 stimulated rebellions in various places. In 1830 and 1831 revolts broke out in Vizagapatam and among the Singphos, Titu Mir, and the Kols. Gumsur rebelled in 1835. Hindu College students began demanding more offices for Indians in 1843, and ten years later Ram-gopal Ghosh called for opening the civil service to Indians. Kolhapur revolted in 1844 as did the Khonds two years later. Moplah insurrections occurred four times between 1849 and 1855. That year the Santals began a revolt that went on for two years. The British had been fighting in the Crimean

War, China, and against Persia over their taking of Herat in Afghanistan again, though by April 1857 the British envoys made peace with the Persians in Paris.

The Company's army had English officers with natives called sepoys (from sipahi for soldier) as most of the rank and file. The Indians in the army outnumbered the British by more than five to one; but all the top officers were British, and most of the expenditures were for them. Sepoys complained of low salaries and little chance for promotion. Hindus objected that going outside of India violated their caste rules, and Muslims did not want to fight those of their religion in Afghanistan and other places. The Madras governor promised the Bengal army a special allowance for going to Sind; but this was not fulfilled because it was against Bengal regulations. In 1856 the new Governor-General C. J. Canning implemented the General Service Enlistment Act requiring all new recruits to serve abroad; he did not think it would cause bad feelings. In Awadh more than 60,000 troops had been recently dismissed with small gratuities, and ill Commissioner James Outram was replaced by the insensitive Coverley Jackson, who ignored complaints, delayed paying grants and pensions, treated Talukdars harshly, approved heavy assessments on cultivators, and lived in the ex-king's palace. In January 1857 Henry Lawrence replaced Jackson.

In January 1857 Brahmin sepoys at Dumdum became concerned that the new Enfield rifles required them to bite open cartridges that were smeared with grease from the fat of hogs and cattle. Muslims are forbidden to eat pork, and Hindus do not eat beef. The rumor spread to Barrackpur, where they complained to General Hearsey. He let them use their own grease, and the Government approved. However, the Adjutant-General wired back that such concessions would increase the suspicion; he said that the sepoys had been using cartridges greased with mutton fat for years. The sepoys suspected that cow and pig fat were being used in order to convert them to Christianity, and they began to set fire to officers' bungalows at Barrackpur. On February 26 the 19th Native Infantry refused to accept percussion caps. The Governor-General ordered the

19th N. I. disbanded. On March 29 Mangal Pandey of the 34th N. I. shot at two officers, tried to shoot himself, and was put in the hospital. Other sepoys said that he had taken too much bhang (cannabis). He and another were tried and executed, and later many called the mutineers Pandeys. The 34th was disbanded, but discontent and acts of arson spread.

On May 2 the 7th Awadh regiment refused to bite the greased cartridges. Commissioner Henry Lawrence learned of threats to kill officers, and he persuaded the mutineers to lay down their arms. Rumors also spread that bone dust from cows was being put in flour and wells. At Mirat forty miles north of Delhi, 85 troopers from the Third Cavalry had refused to touch the cartridges on April 24. They were tried by a court martial and sentenced to ten years. On parade before other unarmed sepoys they were stripped of their uniforms and shackled as armed British soldiers watched. On the Sunday night of May 10 while the British were in church, sepoys from the Third Cavalry released their comrades from jail. The 20th and 11th infantry regiments seized their muskets and killed Col. Finnis. After that, the sepoys and freed convicts killed Europeans, plundering and burning their houses. The sepoys decided to go to Delhi, but the British commander did not pursue them. The Sepoys from Mirat reached Delhi at dawn, entered the Red Fort, and proclaimed elderly Bahadur Shah II emperor. Delhi had only three regiments of sepoys; they joined the mutiny, killed officers, and plundered Europeans, who fled. A few British officers led by Lt. George Willoughby managed to explode much of the ammunition magazine. The uprisings spread down the Ganges to Bihar and south to Gwalior, Jhansi, and Bundelkhand. The Madras and Bombay presidencies were fairly free of revolt, which was concentrated in Delhi, Awadh, and Rohilkhand.

Bahadur Shah II at Delhi played both sides by protecting British fugitives and communicating secretly with the British at Agra; he offered to help the British troops enter the fort if they would recognize his position. Bahadur became a virtual prisoner of the plundering sepoys who made him help them. The revolt was chaotic as the cavalry and others demanded more pay. When the sepoys found that the Emperor's advisor Ahsan Ulla had 52 European prisoners, they killed them with swords. Bahadur Shah was deposed after a week on May 17, when prince Abu Bakr was elected. Bahadur still claimed to be king, but sepoys refused to serve under his commander-in-chief, Bakht Khan. A main motivation for the revolt was religious, and proclamations were made to kill all the infidels. Hindus and Muslims tried to stay united but sometimes turned against each other. Gradually the anti-English fervor faded, and magistrate Sayyid Ahmad was able to hold Bijnor for the British without any military forces.

Lucknow learned of Mirat and Delhi on May 14. Henry Lawrence was able to suppress an uprising on May 31, but the mutiny spread throughout Awadh. The Talukdars quickly acted to regain their lands and secure their forts. The last nawab was in British custody at Calcutta, but his queen Begam Hazrat Mahal and her son Birjis Quadr were chosen as the new rulers. They gave offices to Hindus and Muslims while many local chiefs established independent kingdoms in Awadh and in Rohilkhand. Henry Lawrence fortified his Residency at Lucknow as a refuge for Europeans. While Lawrence was ill, Financial Commissioner Martin Gubbins disarmed the sepoys and sent them home. Lawrence learned of it and managed to get some 600 sepoys to return. Lawrence tried to command the army, but on June 11 the military police joined the mutiny. Lawrence advised a defensive strategy, but Gubbins urged an attack on the rebel army. Desertions caused Lawrence to order a retreat, which became a rout. The Residency was besieged on June 30. Three days later Lawrence was mortally wounded by a shell, but 1,700 British soldiers, civilians, and the loyal sepoys held out against a rebel army that grew to 100,000. The Residency was relieved in September, but Lucknow was not re-occupied by the British until March 1858.

Rohilkhand had no British regiments and was taken over by mutineers in Bareilly on May 31. Khan Bahadur Khan was the grandson of Rohilkhand's deposed nawab, and he had tried to warn the British commissioner of the coming mutiny. He quickly joined the mutiny as Bahadur Shah's viceroy and ordered all the English executed. He began organizing revenue collection and appointed Hindus as well as Muslims. However, communal conflict erupted, and Hindu officers were despoiled. Sepoys plundered the rich and looted the shops. Khan Bahadur Khan governed Rohilkhand for nearly a year. He hired the poor, raising an army of 40,000 troops.

In Bengal only troops at Dacca and Chittagong mutinied. Several mutinies broke out briefly in Bihar led by Kunwar Singh, but the Deccan was quiet except at Kolhapur. Mutiny attempts at Ahmadabad in Gujarat and Hyderabad in Sind failed, and the one at Karachi was quickly put down. The mutinies were generally spontaneous and local without coordination. After killing and plundering, many sepoys went home with their loot; some mutineers set out for Delhi as the center of the revolt. Maulavi Ahmadulla of Faizabad had actually called for a holy war against the English infidels in January 1857, but the Muslims in Madras did not really act on this. So Ahmadulla went north. Sambalpur was ripe for rebellion because British annexation had raised their taxes from 8,800 rupees to 74,000. Imprisoned Surendra Sal was freed and led the revolt there that lasted until 1862.

In the Punjab most of the sepoys were disarmed. At Lahore 600 Europeans disarmed 2,500 sepoys on May 13. Some resisted at Firozpur. At Peshawar the 55th regiment fled; of the 120 caught 40 were executed by cannons. John Lawrence was in Rawalpindi and worked to raise loyal troops to retake Delhi. The English officers took control of the forts at Phillaur, Govindgarh, Kangra, Attock, and Multan. Gurkha regiments disobeyed and seized the treasury at Kasauli; but they returned to their barracks when their demands were met. News of the mutiny stimulated raiding by the Ranghar and Gujar tribes. Lt. Col. John Nicholson and Frederick Cooper led forces that tracked down mutineers and executed hundreds of prisoners to deter revolt in the Punjab. Brigadier Hodson recruited 200 Punjabis for each of 74 regiments; half of them were Sikhs. However, only Jat Sikhs were recruited, as the lower castes were excluded; Mazhabis were hired to build roads and dig canals. By the end of August 1757 a total of 34,000 Punjabi troops had been raised. Ahmad Khan led an uprising in Multan in September that lasted two months. George Lawrence managed to keep the Rajputana region under control.

Before the telegraph wires were cut, Governor-General Canning got word of the mutiny on May 14. He summoned European troops from Madras and Bombay, and an expedition about to leave for China was called back. Col. James Neill brought the First Madras Fusiliers to Calcutta and was sent to disarm Benares and Allahabad. Hasty planning at Benares on June 5 resulted in some sepoys picking up their arms and firing on approaching Europeans. Cavalry arrived during the confusion, but by evening all the mutineers not killed had dispersed. News of this slaughter provoked a mutiny at Allahabad two days later. They waited until evening and then murdered six officers and eight teenage cadets. The British still held the fort at Allahabad, and on June 11 Neill arrived to put down the insurgency with indiscriminate killing, plundering of houses, and burning of villages.

Brigadier Archdale Wilson led troops from Mirat that managed to take the Ridge overlooking Delhi but did not have enough men to attack the city. Believing the prophecy that the British would only rule India for a century, on the centenary of the battle of Plassey (June 23) the sepoys attacked the British on the Ridge but could not overcome them. More troops arrived from the Punjab, and more than twenty battles were fought. Nicholson arrived in August, and the siege train enabled them to storm and take the Red Fort on September 20. Bahadur Shah surrendered on the condition that his life would be spared; but Hodson shot three princes himself because he feared the mob would rescue them. A few days later 21 more princes were hanged. The plundering of Delhi by the British, Sikhs, Pathans, and Gurkhas was compared to the sacking by Persian conqueror Nadir Shah in 1739. Bahadur Shah was convicted of murdering Europeans and was sentenced to life imprisonment; he was transported to Rangoon and died in 1862 at the age of 87.

The mutiny of the sepoys was gradually transformed into a rebellion led by chiefs. Nana Sahib claimed to be the Peshwa's heir at Kanpur (Cawnpore) on June 26. Mutineers surrounded the garrison of about four hundred British soldiers, who surrendered when they were offered safe conduct to Allahabad. However, their boats were fired on, and only four men escaped. Also 211 women and children were eventually put to death by the sepoys under Nana Sahib and Tantia Topi, a Maratha Brahmin who led 20,000 mutineers from Gwalior. Henry Havelock led a force that defeated Nana's troops on July 16. After Neill occupied Kanpur, Havelock went on to relieve Lucknow but swung back to attack and defeat Tantia Topi on August 16. Tantia survived and gathered more sepoys at Gwalior to seize Kalpi. In Bihar mutinous sepoys from Dinapur followed Kunwar Singh, the Talukdar of Jagdishpur. Nepal's Jang Bahadur sent a Gurkha army that defeated rebels in Azamgarh and Jaunpur in July. That month the Nizam's chief minister Salar Jang used artillery to defeat a fanatical Muslim mob that was attacking the Residency at Hyderabad.

Nana's nephew Rao Sahib persuaded Tantia to take Kanpur back from the British troops left there under Windham. He did so in November while British commander-in-chief Colin Campbell was evacuating civilians from Lucknow. Campbell then won Kanpur back on December 6 Campbell spent the next month hunting down rebels in the Ganges-Jumna Doab and recapturing Fatehgarh. He appointed a commissioner, who was known as "Hanging" Power because of his death sentences for dozens of prisoners.

General Campbell assembled a large army of 30,000, including Sikhs, Punjabis, and 9,000 Gurkhas led by Jang Bahadur himself, for the retaking of Lucknow. This was accomplished on March 21, 1858; but while they looted and destroyed Lucknow, about 60.000 armed rebels scattered throughout Awadh. Governor-General Canning proclaimed that all proprietary rights in Awadh would be confiscated except for six he named and others who could prove their loyalty. As James Outram predicted, this had the effect of causing the Talukdars to fight a guerrilla campaign instead of helping to restore order. Outram mitigated its effect somewhat by circulating a letter that cases of land confiscated after annexation would be reheard. Ellenborough, President of the Board of

Control, was so outraged by the proclamation that he wrote a scathing letter to Governor-General Canning in which he reminded him that influential landowners had been deprived of their property and that the hostilities in Awadh had "rather the character of legitimate war than that of rebellion."8

The widowed Rani Lakshmi Bai of Jhansi had had her kingdom annexed by Dalhousie. When the sepoys mutinied in Jhansi, they slaughtered dozens of Europeans; they threatened the Rani, took her money, and departed for Delhi, leaving her in charge of the administration. She wrote two letters to the commissioner of Saugor, who asked her to govern Jhansi on behalf of the British. She fought against an invasion by the chiefs of Orchha and Datia by forming an alliance with the rebel raja of Banpur. She sent more letters to the British that were not answered. Jhansi was attacked by Hugh Rose's army of about 6,000 on March 30 when Tantia Topi arrived with 20,000 men. Rose managed to attack them, causing Tantia to flee. Then his British forces stormed the fort at Jhansi on April 4 and slaughtered about 5,000 people. The Rani escaped dressed as a man. She and Rao Sahib were joined by Tantia Topi near Gwalior and won over Sindhia's army to take that fort, proclaiming Nana Sahib peshwa. However, Rose defeated these rebels at Gwalior. Rani Lakshmi Bai was one of the few rebel chiefs to be killed in battle, and Rose called her the bravest of the rebels. Tantia was eventually captured, tried, and hanged in April 1859. Rao Sahib was not arrested and hanged until 1862.

Campbell's army defeated Khan Bahadur Khan's army of 40,000 near Bareilly on May 5, 1858, ending the rebellion in Rohilkhand. Maulavi Ahmadulla, Begam Hazrat Mahal, and other rebel leaders continued to fight. After Ahmadulla proclaimed himself king and threatened Shahjahanpur, the Governor-General offered a reward of 50,000 rupees for his arrest. The Maulavi was shot dead at Powain on June 5, and the raja cut off his head and took it to the Shahjahanpur magistrate, who paid him the reward. That month Canning passed an Act to control the Calcutta press that equally applied to English as well as Indian publications. The Arms Act of

September required licenses for firearms, swords, and other weapons. His Clemency Resolution was designed to stop the indiscriminate hanging of sepoys for merely being part of a mutinous regiment, but the vindictive derisively called him "Clemency Canning."

Ben Madho was defeated, but he left a fort with 15,000 men and continually managed to escape. Colin Campbell had to destroy 1,572 forts in order win back the province of Awadh. He organized 5,000 police to help civil authorities after his army departed. On November first a full pardon was promised to all rebels who had not murdered British subjects and would return to their homes by the end of December. Most of the remaining rebels were driven toward the border region of Nepal by the end of 1858. Jang Bahadur announced that Nepal would not give refuge to rebels, and more than 2,000 were turned over to the British. Nana Sahib took refuge in the jungles of Nepal and probably died there. Many in England and India wanted more vengeance, but the Governor-General wisely limited the prosecutions. Later Viceroy Curzon commended Canning's clemency because the government that punishes revengefully loses the respect of its subjects.

The India Bill of August 1858 ended the century of rule by the East India Company, replacing the Court of Directors and Board of Control by putting the British government in charge using a secretary of state and a council of fifteen with a majority having ten years experience in India. On November 1, 1858 Queen Victoria proclaimed that Canning would be the first viceroy and that they would respect the rights of native princes and ancestral land-owners; they would not discriminate on the bases of religious faith or observances; all were to have equal and impartial protection of the law; those in authority must abstain from interfering with religious belief or worship; all Indian subjects regardless of race or creed, should be admitted to offices according to the qualifications of education, ability, and integrity. The Queen's proclamation was called the Magna Carta of the Indian people.

The causes of why the mutiny and revolt erupted have been discussed; but why did the revolt fail when the Europeans in India were so greatly outnumbered? The British had already established their control by government over most of India and thus had their power structures in place.

Their technology was superior, and especially the new breech-loading Enfield rifles that the sepoys were rejecting gave the British using them a tremendous advantage over the old muzzle-loaded muskets. The new telegraph lines helped the British react quickly to the emergency, and many mutinies were headed off by disarming the sepoys. Although there were serious grievances and legitimate reasons for Indian independence, a revolutionary movement with intellectual education had not yet developed.

The first mutiny and most of those that followed freed convicted criminals and were lawless riots involving mass murders, robbery, looting, and chaotic destruction. Although some ancestral kings were selected as rulers, the rebellion suffered from pervading disorder with little or no coordination between rebel groups in different localities. In addition to the lack of political leadership, the military strategies were also inept. Most of the rebels gathered at Delhi and Lucknow, where little of strategic importance was accomplished. Because of the lawless behavior and lack of principles, the civil population was not inclined to support the rebels. Thus many Indians remained loyal to the British government, especially in areas where it remained in force. Essentially, unrestrained violence and the lack of ethics doomed the revolt. In the next century the inspired campaigns led by Mahatma Gandhi would show that the cleanest revolutions can be best accomplished without violence.

RECONSTRUCTION OF BRITISH INDIA 1858-76

In 1804 the eighth Dalai Lama died, and Regent Tenpai Gonpo Kundeling provided needed food and exempted from taxes those who had suffered during the Gurkha war. He mediated between Tibetans protesting Chinese domination and the new Manchu emperor Jiaqing (r. 1799-1820). The two Ambans (Qing representatives) were investigated and replaced. The Chinese and the three big monasteries of Drepung, Sera, and Ganden urged the Tibetan government to ban foreigners

Thomas Manning used a disguise to visit in 1811 and criticized the poor quality of the imperial representatives in Lhasa. The ninth Dalai Lama died in 1815.

Raja Ran Bahadur Shah ruled Nepal so badly that he was denounced by the people and fled to Benares in 1800. He asked the Governor-General to loan him ten battalions, but instead the English signed a friendship treaty with Nepal in 1801. Wellesley sent Captain Knox to negotiate a commercial treaty, but the Nepalese already resented the treaty that forced them to accept a British resident at Kathmandu. The senior Rani (Queen) took control and appointed Damodar Pande her chief minister. Knox left Kathmandu, and the Company renounced the 1801 treaty. This enabled Ran Bahadur Shah to return to Nepal; but he ruled so cruelly that he was beheaded in 1804 before the Durbar by his own brother Sher Bahadur, whom he had threatened to execute. The widowed Tripur Sundari Devi acted as regent and appointed Bhim Sen Thapa prime minister. The Nepal army invaded the west and killed the Garhwal chief. The Gurkhas penetrated into the region between the Sutlej and Jumna rivers until Ranjit Singh conquered the fortress at Kangra in 1809.

In 1813 Col. Ochterlony protested that the Gurkhas were taking over villages belonging to Butowley, but he did not think they were worth waging a war. Company troops peacefully occupied the disputed lands. In May a Nepalese force attacked three villages in Butwal and killed a chief. When the Gurkhas occupied all of Butwal, the Gorakhpur magistrate withdrew the troops from Sheoraj. Governor-General Hastings declared war even though Col. Ochterlony wrote to Metcalfe it was "the most impolitic measure we have ever attempted." Three out of the first four expeditions failed. In October 1814 the British led by Col. Mawley occupied Dehra Dun. Lord Hastings reluctantly approved the policy of destroying crops to force the enemy to withdraw from Tarai in Butwal. General Marley's advance on Kathmandu with 12,000 troops failed after he fled.

By 1815 the Company had 34,000 troops battling about 12,000 Gurkhas. Ochterlony captured forts at Nalagarh and Ramgarh and then blockaded the Gurkhas' best general, Amar

Singh Thapa. Col. Gardner and Captain Hearsey attacked Kumaon and threatened the capital at Almora, and in April the Gurkhas surrendered the whole province and withdrew east of the Kali River. Amar Singh Thapa's troops deserted, and he surrendered the Malaun fort to Ochterlony in May. Ochterlony marched with 20,000 men to Kathmandu, and in November 1815 the Treaty of Sagauli was signed. The war party in Nepal refused to ratify the treaty until the Nepalese were defeated again in February 1816. They ceded Garhwal and Kumaon to the British and withdrew from Sikkim. The Sikkim raja signed a protective treaty in February 1817, giving the British a buffer between Bhutan and Nepal, which was allowed to be independent and became an effective ally of the British. The British had won a war to secure a few villages in Tarai.

In 1822, even though the tenth Dalai Lama had been selected in the usual Tibetan way, Regent Jampel Tsultrim Tsemonling announced that he had been chosen by lottery between candidates as the Chinese required. A study of agriculture and families in the province of U was conducted that helped the Regent to improve revenue collection. In 1832 Regent Tsemonling sent troops to capture robbers led by Junang Dzasa, who was brought to the Dalai Lama and submitted. Two years later troops were used to make the people in southwest Kham pay taxes. The tenth Dalai Lama was only 21 years old when he died in 1837. Two candidates were selected in 1841, and it was reported that the eleventh Dalai Lama was chosen by lottery.

In 1834 the Dogra raja of Jammu had forced the Ladakh king to flee into Tibet. Kashmir maharaja Gulab Singh sent vizier Zorawar Singh with troops into Ladakh in support of the Dogra army. Ladakh minister Ngodup Tenzin surrendered to Zorawar, and he replaced the Ladakh ruler Lala with Ngodup, who agreed to pay 5,000 rupees annual tribute to Kashmir. However, in 1840 Zorawar Singh returned to Ladakh with 6,000 troops to depose Ngodup and reinstate Lala. The next year Zorawar Singh and Lala invaded Tibet with Sikh and Ladakhi forces. Lala died and was succeeded by his cousin while Zorawar's Sikhs advanced into Purang. Tibetan reinforcements were sent and defeated and killed Zorawar. They also killed 3,000 Sikhs and took 700 prisoners as the rest fled to Ladakh. Gulab Singh sent 8,000 more Sikhs in 1842, and about sixty Tibetans were captured. A treaty was made, and the Tibetans withdrew; about a third of the Sikh and Ladakhi prisoners elected to remain in southern Tibet.

In 1844 the Tibetan Council (Kashag) and officials from the three largest monasteries deposed Regent Tsemonling, and the Panchen Lama governed at Lhasa for nine months until Yeshe Gyatso Rating was appointed as regent. Tibet made a trade agreement with Ladakh in 1853.

The eleventh Dalai Lama was 17 when he assumed power in 1855, but he died eleven months later. The Kashag recalled Regent Rating. Complaining of trade violations, the Gurkhas invaded Tibet and occupied Nyanang, Rongshar, Dzonka, and Purang again. Tibetan troops were unable to regain the territory, and monks volunteered; but a treaty was negotiated in 1856. The Tibetan government agreed to pay the Gurkhas 10,000 rupees annually and stop collecting duties from Gurkha traders, and the Gurkhas gave back the four districts.

Nepal's prime minister Bhim Sen Thapa made sure that the English Resident could only communicate through him. When the regent Tripur Sundari Devi died in 1832, the young Rajendra Bikram Shah rebelled against his tutor and prime minister Bhim Sen and began favoring the exiled Pandes faction. The Orientalist Brian Hodgson had become resident at Kathmandu in 1829, and in 1834 he negotiated a reciprocity agreement; the Resident would make no claims on the Durbar that he would not admit if they made them.

In 1836 acting Governor-General Metcalfe would not return eleven slave girls who had taken refuge in Tirhut because the British opposed slavery. The Pandes faction accused Bhim Sen of various crimes. He denounced the papers as forgeries, but he was arrested in 1837 and, threatened with torture, committed suicide. In 1840 the Raja sent a message to his mutinous army that he had no money to pay them because he was saving it to fight the English. Although the British were busy with the Afghan war, Resident Hodgson persuaded the king of Nepal to dismiss the Pandes faction in favor of the Brahmin Raj Guru and the Chautariyas family. An army of 20,000 men was made available to the Resident at Kathmandu to protect the Company's northern frontier. In December 1843 Major Henry Lawrence replaced Hodgson and informed Nepal of the Company's neutrality; they were not concerned with Nepalese politics but only trade. The Company followed international law in not handing over political refugees.

When the senior Maharani died, the young Surender Vikram Shah began oppressing the people of Nepal. The Chautariya prime minister Fateh Jung presided over a meeting with 675 responsible people in which the young king signed over his powers to the junior Maharani; but she wanted her son to be king and appointed General Matabar Singh prime minister in December 1843, as most of the Pandes were exterminated. Yet in May 1845 she had Matabar shot dead and appointed General Gagan Singh. Jang Bahadur was promoted to commander of the army, and Gagan Singh was assassinated in September 1846. In a tumultuous assembly about 150 nobles were murdered, killing the rest of the Pandes and the Chautariyas.

The junior Maharani got Jang Bahadur appointed prime minister. He made a speech that won over the army despite the officers lost. When the Maharani gave him a written order to kill two princes, Jang Bahadur sent back a letter explaining he could not obey an illegal order. After discovering her plot against his life, he arranged for the Maharani to go to Benares; her son Rajendra Vikram Shah went with her despite Jang Bahadur's request for him to stay.

Rajendra's son Surendra Vikram Shah was installed as raja in May 1847. Rajendra Vikram's plan to invade Nepal was foiled by Jang Bahadur, who banished him to Bhatgaon. In 1850 Jang Bahadur became the first Hindu political leader to visit England. He met with Queen Victoria and was impressed by her courtesy and lack of vanity. His requests for artillery engineers, a treaty for the reciprocal surrender of criminals, and direct communication with the Company directors were all denied. Jang Bahadur also visited President Louis Napoleon in France, but all his requests had to go through the British embassy because of their tributary treaty. Realizing the industrial and military strength of Britain, Jang Bahadur would not oppose the English in India.

When Lhasa officials did not respond to his complaints about the bad treatment of Nepalese by Tibetans, Jang Bahadur went to war with Tibet in 1854. The British resident agreed to a treaty on reciprocal treatment with Nepal in 1855. The Tibetans sued for peace and signed a treaty at the home of Jang Bahadur on March 24, 1856. Both countries agreed to restore conquests, prisoners, and booty taken in the war.

Tibet agreed to pay Nepal 10,000 silver coins annually, and Nepal promised to help defend Tibet if they were attacked. Jang Bahadur resigned in July and let his brother Ram Bahadur govern until he died a natural death in May 1857. Then Jang Bahadur responded to the popular demand for his resumption of service. He offered Gurkha troops to help quell the revolt in Awadh and personally led 9,000 troops in the British recapture of Lucknow in March 1858. According to the treaty he had to hand over criminals escaping into Nepal, but he ordered that only those who had definitely killed a British woman or child were to be surrendered; the others received political asylum. In gratitude for the Gurkhas' military aid, in an 1860 treaty the British returned the Tarai lands to Nepal.

SRI LANKA 1707-1800

The English East India Company and the Crown had dual control over Sri Lanka from 1798 until it became the British crown colony of Ceylon in 1802. When Rajadhi Rajasimha died of illness in 1798 with no heir, the leading minister Pilima Talauve enthroned 18-year-old Konnasami as Sri Vikrama Rajasimha.

The late king's brother-in-law Muttusami also claimed the throne of Kandy, but Pilima Talauve arrested him and his sisters. Pilima Talauve was close to the British but could not control Vikrama Rajasimha. The first British governor, Frederick North (1798-1805), proclaimed in 1801 that all rajakariya (royal service) was abolished and replaced it with a tax of one-fifth of their produce on low land and one-tenth on high land. North declared himself head of the salagama caste and appointed Robert Arbuthnot head of the karava caste.

The Judicial Charter limited the governor's autocracy by establishing the Supreme Court and High Court of Appeal. The Dutch possessions in Sri Lanka were formally ceded to the British in the 1802 treaty of Amiens, but the English Company still retained a monopoly on the colony's trade. Agents were put in charge of lucrative pearl fisheries, cotton plantations, salt, and tobacco monopolies. In the first three years the government received £396,000 from pearl fisheries. This made up for the lower price of cinnamon because of Dutch stocks in Amsterdam. Buddhists of the salagama caste objected to restricting the upasampada ordination to the goyigama caste, and in 1802 they sent a mission to Burma that was followed by other delegations from the karava and durava castes. The Amarapura Nikaya was open to all castes and spread in the first half of the 19th century.

In January 1803 a British force led by General MacDowell marched to Kandy and found it evacuated. They installed Muttusami, but he was not respected. The British were surrounded by hostile people, lacked food, and suffered disease. MacDowell became ill and left Major Davie in charge. The British abandoned Kandy, and the sick left behind were put to death. Kandyan forces defeated the retreating British at the Mahavali River, executing Muttusami and all the British prisoners except Davie and three others. This Kandyan war lasted for two years because Governor North continued to send forces to the frontiers. When General Thomas Maitland became governor in 1805, he took a defensive posture. He restored the rajakariya labor requirements based on caste, and their services were used for constructing roads.

In 1806 the British removed the religious disabilities affecting Catholics in Ceylon. Because those in the Dutch Reformed Church refused to swear allegiance to the British, most of their converts abandoned that sect. The English took over their schools and used their own evangelical indoctrination.

Maitland tried to introduce merit into Ceylon's civil service system in 1808 with fixed salaries to prevent bribes, but this was resisted by those who preferred using seniority. The next year the Governor restricted the High Court's civil jurisdiction to Colombo.

In 1810 the Charter of Justice gave the Chief Justice more power and introduced jury trials in criminal cases, though caste restrictions were applied. That year Vikrama Rajasimha removed Pilima Talauve from office and, when he revolted, had him executed. Starting in 1812, Europeans were allowed to purchase or receive land grants of up to 4,000 acres.

In 1814 the Company's contract was renewed, but the colony gained a guarantee of £101,000 income per year on cinnamon. Pilima's nephew Ahalepola also intrigued against the King in 1814 but had to flee to the British, leaving behind his wife and children, who were put to death. John D'Oyly advised that enough Kandyan chiefs opposed the King to warrant British intervention.

After royal troops chased insurgents across the Sabaragamuva border, Governor Robert Brownrigg used this as an excuse to lead his planned invasion, proclaiming the British were protecting the Kandyan people from a tyrant. The King's commander Molligoda had defected, and the British troops entered Kandy in 1815, capturing the fleeing Vikrama Rajasimha. The Kandyan Convention formally ceded the kingdom to the British; but the Kandyan chiefs and monks insisted on clause 5, which declared that the Buddhist religion was to be maintained and protected. In 1816 British officials persuaded slave-owners to emancipate all children of slaves.

Most Kandyans only wanted their unpopular king removed and resented British rule. The provinces of Uva and Vellasa were not subjugated, and in 1817 the ex-monk Vilbave claimed to be the Nayakkar prince Doraisami. Kappitipola led the rebellion in Uva and presided over the new king's initiation in May 1818. Every chief except Molligoda joined the rebellion or was in British custody. The British overcame the guerrilla tactics of the Kandyans by terrorizing the villagers that harbored them, by stopping their support for the guerrillas, and by destroying food and crops. These scorched-earth tactics also destroyed the irrigation works in Uva. They subdued Uva and Vellasa by September, and reinforcements from India helped defeat the remaining divided rebels.

Some Kandyan aristocrats remained loyal to the British and were rewarded. Vilbave was exposed as an impostor, and many believed that the British recapture of the tooth relic was a sign that they were meant to rule the Kandyans. When the Supreme Court questioned the legality of using rajakariya service, Governor Brownrigg enacted a law enabling the government to exact labor. In November 1818 the British proclaimed the unity of Sri Lanka and the reduction of chiefs' privileges.

Governor Brownrigg (1812-20) demoted chiefs to stipendiaries carrying out the orders of British officials. The East India Company lost its contract for the cinnamon monopoly to the Colony of Ceylon in 1822. In the first thirty years of the 19th century the per capita consumption of coffee in England increased twenty-fold. Governor Edward Barnes (1824-31) exempted coffee land from taxes and abolished the export duty on coffee.

The monopoly on salt gave the Government some profits over a thousand percent. The lower castes were put to work making roads under the traditional rajakariya corvée system that was already using the salagama caste for peeling cinnamon. In 1820 the Supreme Court granted an appeal by a slave who was sentenced to flogging by a collector in Jaffna, but Barnes decreed that collectors could flog slaves for any offense. Commercial banks extended credit to planters, and the Colony gave them land grants.

The Colonial Office employed a commission to inquire into the colonies at the Cape of Good Hope, Mauritius, and Ceylon. William Colebrooke was the only commissioner left when he arrived at Ceylon in 1829. A year later Charles Cameron joined him to investigate the judiciary, while Colebrooke reported on the other branches of government and the administration. Governor Barnes was reluctant to cooperate and had to be pressured by the Colonial Office. Colebrooke wrote four reports on the administration, revenues, expenditures, and a confidential report on the compulsory labor system; Cameron wrote one on the judiciary. The governor of Ceylon had been autocratic, although sometimes the Supreme Court resisted.

Colebrooke proposed unifying the government by bringing in the Kandyan territory as a province along with Colombo, Gale, Jafine, and Trincomalee. He suggested forming an executive and a legislative council to assist the governor so that he would no longer have complete control over finances. The executive council would be composed of the Government's Secretary, Treasurer, Auditor-General, Collector of Customs at Colombo, and the Colombo Agent. The governor had been originating all legislation, but now he would have to share this with the legislative council, which would include non-officials and could subpoena documents, hear witnesses, and direct investigations. The Supreme Court would have the power to certify that new laws were in accordance with English laws. Colebrooke suggested reductions with civil servants that would cut expenditures by a third. In 1831 Robert Wilmot Horton had commented that only 14 of 31 civil servants were definitely competent. The civil service was to be opened to local leaders, and thus education in English for the elite was also instituted. Officials were to be given land grants so that they could live on lower salaries. Colebrooke was influenced by the free-trade movement and recommended that the rajakariya service be abolished. He suggested that the Government withdraw from economic activities, and a Bank of Deposits was to be established to grant loans on reasonable terms.

Cameron proposed changes in the judiciary so that all people could gain their rights easily in a court of law and to prevent courts from being used to injure others. He wanted litigants to be able to act without a lawyer and not have to pay any fees. To help the European judges understand local conditions he suggested each should have an assessor when hearing suits. The judicial branch was to be autonomous so that the executive would not interfere. Most of the Colebrooke-Cameron reforms were adopted by the Colonial Office, though some were altered; starting in 1833 Ceylon became perhaps the most liberal of the British colonies. After rajakariya labor was abolished in 1833, irrigation works had to be maintained by cultivators. That year the Government ended land grants and began selling land to planters by auction. The British discouraged slavery in the 1830s by requiring registration, and it was formally abolished in 1844. A year earlier caste distinction in jury selection had been ended. Yet lower castes in the Tamil north still could not enter Hindu temples. In 1840 the Government enacted the Crown Land Encroachment Ordinance No. 12 to claim all land that had not been previously granted. A later modification allowed the peasants in the Kandyan highlands to establish their title to their chena lands, forests they had cut and burned for cultivation.

By 1840 so much rice was being imported by Ceylon that the revenue from duties on rice and paddies surpassed the grain tax. Attempts to collect arrears on grain taxes for a decade had been difficult. Coffee plantations spread rapidly in the 1840s, and thousands of laborers made the dangerous journey from India through the malaria-infested dry zone. One effect of the Colebrooke reforms was that fewer civil servants with lower salaries caused many to neglect their duties and engage in plantation activity. In 1844 Colonial Secretary Anstruther began the effort that ended civil servants' participation in trade and agriculture. In 1845 coffee prices started falling while in three years the acreage of coffee plantations doubled, causing many bankruptcies. Colonial Secretary J. E. Tennent published his Report on the Finances and Commerce of Ceylon in 1846 to remove restrictions on industry and secure free trade. He suggested that reduced or abolished export and import duties as well as grain taxes could be replaced by a land tax, as in India. In the midst of this depression Governor Torrington instead chose new taxes that fell mostly on peasants and the local population.

The Road Ordinance was resented by Kandyans as a revival of compulsory labor, and they rebelled in 1848. The irrigation works were in bad shape, and they also objected to the British encouraging of taverns. Aristocrats objected to the attempt by the Government to break its promise to protect Buddhism.

Riots also broke out in Colombo, where they were influenced by European radicalism. Governor George Anderson (1850-55) tried to balance island finances by limiting spending, but rising prices and demand improved the economy.

The School Commission was established in 1834, and by 1839 the Government was sponsoring 39 English schools and five Tamil schools. In 1837 the Secretary of State for Colonies advised Governor Mackenzie to encourage Christian missionaries. Dissenters complained, and Anglican privileges in education, registering births, marriages, and deaths, and state-subsidized church building were eventually eliminated. In 1841 the Government began giving grants to Christian schools, and they replaced some public schools. A campaign in England persuaded the Ceylon government to sever its connection to Buddhism in 1847, and by 1853 the pledge to protect Buddhist institutions was formally ended.

5

British India: The Great Religious Identities

The research done so far on the nationalist movements of the 1920s and 1930s has generally focused on a particular region, on a single ethnic or religious community.' Evaluation of their role is commonly based on their contribution to the nationalist movement and the anti-colonial struggle overall. While there is an abundance of comparative studies on the contemporary period, the comparative aspect of ethnic and religious conflict before 1947 has so far received scant attention.' Little is known about the independent motives of these movements and what kind of conditions facilitated their formation and furthered the ascent of ethnopolitical conflict in colonial India.

In the context of this paper, religious movements are subsumed under ethnic movements if and when they display characteristic features of clearly delineated regional group structures and identities.

A conceptual debate on pre-independence ethnic and religious identities may be helpful in verifying the contemporary concepts of nationality formation for South Asia which have mainly been developed using the experience of post-independence developments.' This paper discusses various approaches towards identity-building in South Asia during the colonial period, tentatively grouping arguments around the catchwords of 'unonolithic nationalism', 'religious nationalism', and 'e'litist nationality formation', and would suggest a conceptual alternative, called an 'interaction approach'.

MONOLITHIC NATIONALISM

There is a standard viewpoint which is particularly popular in Indian historiography, that the nationalist movement was comparatively coherent and uniform, meaning that it \vas mainly a single constitutional process aimed at state building. Cultural and social sub-divisions are relegated to the background. Majumdar stressed that the national awakening of India was based on 'the unity of India as a hole'.

Qanungo rejected the notion supposedly implied in the Communal Award 'that India was not a nation but a congeries of groups (religious, cultural, racial, caste, class and interet)'.If it is not overtly assumed that ethnic and religious movements or conflicts were invented or instigated by the British, it is at least alleged that they manifested themselves mainly after independence when the grand coalition of the nationalist movement broke apart.

There is no reason to deny the profound impact of the all-India nationalist movement on the political project of the nation state as embodied in the development of India and Pakistan. The compulsion to confront the colonial administration made it necessary for all opposition forces to unite on a single political platform. However. there was a vast gap between claim and reality. It is argued here that the high point of the nationalist movement was also the formative phase of the regionalization of politics in ethnic and religious terms.

It was in the 1920s and 1930s that the drive against colonial rule over India entered the new phase of mass politics. That period saw not only the rise of the all-India nationalist force to prominence but also the formation of its different composite parts into separate ethnic and religious movements, rivaling each other enviously. This happened both inside and outside the two major parties, the Congress and the Muslim League. The kind of state nationalism that was pursued by the Indian National Congress and the Muslim League was closely echoed by regional Clites and spurred the rise of ethnic nationalism. Where the nation-state project seemed to attract the all-India political classes with its prospects of power and prosperity, the same goals were followed at the level of local government. The major nationalist forces, the Congress and the Muslim League, were ihemclvecomposed of regional groups which owcd their identity to ethnicity and religion. Congress had emerged from three regional organizations, the Indian Association of Calcutta (1876), the Madras Mahajan Sabha (1884), and the Bombay Presidency Association (1885), developing along the lines of the three Presidencies of British rule in India with strong Bengali, Tamil and Marathi overtones.

A new upsurge of the Swadeslzi movement to boycott imported goods in 1905-08 (mainly in response to the partition of Bengal), the major movements of non-cooperation and civil disobedience in 1920-22 (boycott of titles, schools, courts and councils) and in 1930-34 (no-rent and no-tax campaigns, courting arrest, etc), as well as the Khilafat movement of the 1920s revealed strong regional and ethnoreligious features and disparities.' Since the creation of separate Congress provinces on linguistic grounds as a result of the 1920 Nagpur session, Congress tried to mobilize public opinion through the very means of ethnolinguistic identities, as it saw no alternative to reach the broad, mainly illiterate masses but through the medium of their native tongue and culture. Regional disparities and contradictions were also major features of the Muslim movement and had long prevented the Muslim League from gaining an undivided hold on Indian Muslims.' After the Muslim League had been profoundly defeated during the 1937 provincial elections, it had to execute a special mass-contact campaign to overcome the regional divisions and to gain a foothold in the 'majority provinces' where Muslims constituted the bulk of the population.

At the same time, autonomous regional ethnic and religious movements had emerged which operated in a framework of their own, irrespective of their interaction with Congress or with the Muslim League. The Sikhs and the Pathans, for instance, developed autonomous movements in the 1920s. In both cases these movements constituted a particular cultural response to the capitalist transformation of the colonial society. Since 1921 the Sikhs were fighting against the Mahants, a particular sect which was looking after the Sikh temples and the shrines. Under the British, they had come to regard these religious places as their property and started using them for commercial purposes.

In many areas the Mahants closely collaborated with the local authorities. The Sikhs who in Punjab mainly hailed from agricultural castes such as the Jats had also come under severe pressure as a result of the agricultural policies of the colonial government. Rising taxes and a slack in crop prices left them with little surplus. In addition, Sikh political pride was greatly hurt when those who had fought prominently in the Anglo-Indian army during World War I had returned to India not to a hero's welcome with a pronlise of an independent India but to political repression and suspicion embodied in the Rowlatt Act. After the Sikhs had been 'gainfully' employed to defend the British Empire they were now made redundant. The Jallianwala Bagh massacre of 1919 that aroused wrath all over India naturally stirred the Punjab as well. In this way the Sikh movement for temple control was a regional response to growing social and political polarization.'

The Pathan movement of the Red Shirt volunteers was the political offspring of the Congress-led civil disobedience campaign, scheduled to start in 1930. Though it aligned itself with Congress, those links were rather formal and it retained its distinct ethnocultural identity throughout the 1930s and 1940s. Originating in the countryside, it also strongly featured social reform. When its leader, Abdul Ghaffar Khan, who had taken to politics with the Khilafat movement in 1919, compared the situation of the Pathans to the status of other peoples and regions in India he saw backward social customs like the permanent tribal feuds as the main reason for the weakness of the Pathans.'

The brigades which were formed in many villages acted as a sort of social worker. They judged feuds and promoted schools and sanitary living conditions. Similar to the Sikh movement, the Red Shirts mobilized their followers, ie mainly small farmers and landless labourers, against a social group on which the British relied heavily for their rule over the province, the rich and big Khans. Economically, agrarian unrest in the Frontier Province reflected the concern over increased revenue assessments by an average of 2210 and a drop in agricultural prices by 50-70%."' Politically, the Afghan war of 1919 had left behind a great deal of tension and discontent in the Frontier province where the British had massively deployed troops not only to fight the Afghans but also to suppress tribal discontent and resistance.

The South Indian non-Brahmin movement did not originate in the countryside. Its leaders came from the new urban professions which had been patronized by the British. They felt threatened by the prospect of the Congress movement gaining the upper hand. They regarded the Congress as Brahmin-dominated and sought the protection of the British-Indian administration against it. Though coming from an urban background, the movement depended on landlord finance.

Its social base was the intermediate castes, not confined to urban professions. E. V. Ramaswami Naicker, who joined the Justice party in 1935, conducted a Self-Respect movement in the 1920s that sought to put an end to Brahminism and became particularly known for its atheistic marriages without Brahmins. He tried to associate peasants, weavers, and local merchants with the movement.

In the non-Brahmin movement the regional appeal at first was hardly recognizable. But the treatment of Brahmins as 'foreigners' and outsiders from the north provided the link and a convenient base for a South Indian, Dravidian regionalization of the movement. When Congress had dislodged the Justice ministry in the Madras Presidency in 1937, its Hindi-first policy combined with growing popular discontent over agrarian and urban economic problems in the aftermath of the Great Depression hastened the resort to Dravidian and Tamil slogans in the course of the anti-Hindi movement led by the Justice party. In 1944, it was transformed into the Dravida Munetra Kazhagam.

The movements to create the linguictic provinces of Andhra, Assam, Orissa, Bihar and Sindh, which-with the exception of Andhra-were subsequently granted by the British through the re-demarcation of the provinces, also betrayed a strong sense of identity. Ethnonationalist sentiments ruled movements in Bengal, in Baluchistan and in Kashmir.

The sudden flowering of political diversity confirmed that secular nationalism was never monolithic. The dichotomy of state and ethnic nationalism showed the ambiguily in identity-building: On the one hand, a sense of community anlong Indians of various ethnic groups and religions was real. Time and again, syncretism manifested itself in daily life, particularly in the villages, when people of different communities took part in cultural ceremonies, and sometimes even adopted them. On the other hand, increased political awareness almost always drew on a heightened sense of 'native' ethnic identity to contrast with the 'alien' colonial polity.

RELIGIOUS NATIONALISM

Secular nationalism was mainly territorial nationalism, based on the reference to India as a nation-state. This concept was introduced into India from Britain and France after the French Revolution and the era of 'Enlightenment' in the 18th and 19th centuries. Contrary to territorial nationalism, or rather in addition to it, the Indian nationalist movement developed nationalist variations in which a sometimes dispersed religious community was taken as a reference basis for nationalist aspirations instead of an ethnic group or a political territory with comparatively fixed boundaries of geographical settlement. Religious nationalism, which had long outlived its utility in Europe, had become a very important and efficient tool for mass mobilization in South Asia since the middle of the 19th century. When the nationalist ideas reached South Asia at the beginning of the 19th century it was Hindu social reformers like Rammohan Roy (1772-1833) who defined nationalism in terms of a renewal of religious tradition.

Nationalism and religion thus became intertwined right from the outset of the nationalist movement. At first the Brahmo Samaj, inspired by Rammohan Roy, tried to reform Hinduism on a unitarian, universalist note which was actively propagated by Keshub Chandra Sen. After the Brahmo Samaj split in 1866, its conservative wing, the Adi Brahmo Samaj, then turned to the defence of cultural nationalism. Its leader, Rajnarian Bose (1826-99), lectured on the superiority of Hinduism to all other religions."

The Arya Samaj. whose founder Swami Dayananda (1824-83) wanted to combat the influence of Christian missionaries more actively and who tried to rationalize Hinduism and free it from idolatry, became the proponent of a Hindu nation. Dayananda even dreamed of a world order in which the Arya (Hindu) nation would assume the leadership of all other nationals and Aryavauta (India) would have sovereignty over all other countries." This concept was aggressively advanced by the Hindu Mahasabha after the 1920s.

The latter demanded a universal and undivided Hindu Raj in the subcontinent. On the Muslim side of the political spectrum the religious approach corresponded to Muslim nationalism that mainly took its roots from the Aligarh movement. Saeed Ahmad Khan (1817-98) had strongly pleaded in favour of a separate Muslim nation and demanded that Muslims be treated equally with the Hindus, grossly inflating the actual weight of Muslims in India, who constituted roughly 20% of the population. In Muslim politics there were mainstream nationalists as well, like Abu Kalam Azad, regarding Indian and Congress culture as a composite culture. They had the emphasis put on an all-India nationalism and were called nationalist Muslims.

It was the vehicle of religion that brought the idea of the mainstream freedom movement down to the masses of the Indian villages when the high-sounding statements and ideas were transformed into simple symbols of mainly religious tradition.

In his book Young India, written in 1915, Lala Lajpat Rai, Congress politician and activist of the Hindu revivalist Arja Samaj, explains that 'this interpretation of the old images of gods and goddesses has imparted a new meaning to the current ceremonialism of the country, and multitudes, while worshipping either Jagatdhatri, or Kali, or Durga, accost them with devotion and enthusiasm, with the inspiring cry of Bande Mataram'." He describes 'neo-Vedantism', a refined, reformist variation of Hinduism, especially popularized by Swami Vivekananda (1863-

1902), as the 'spiritual note of the present Nationalist Movement in India'."

The Muslim point of view, though apparently diametrically opposed, was actually quite on par with the Hindu-nationalist position, as far as the appropriation of religion for nationalist sentiments was concerned. The Famous poet and politician, Mohammad Iqbal, remarked that 'the construction of a polity on Indian national lines, if it means a displacement of the Islamic principle of solidarity, is simply unthinkable to a Muslim'." At the same time, Iqbal embodied the layered and composite nature of Indian identity as he had supported the essential unity of India on many earlier occasions.

The influence of the religious heritage was so strong that secular nationalism based on territorial loyalties could not free itself from the generic influence of religion. Many of the territorial nationalists, ie, proponents of an Indian nation-state, derived their justification of it from religious sources. They preached nationalism and meant Hinduism or I lam.'

Even radical nationalism would occasionally, though unwillingly, lend credence to the claims of religious nationalists. The radicals had some definite convictions in common with 'religious nationalists' like Jinnah, Malaviya and Lajpat Rai. All of them aspired for single political representation of their nationalist group at an all-India level and regarded each other as the main impediment towards this goal.

Bipan Chandra argued in his Communalism in Modern India that 'the national movement did succeed in overcoming or making passive, at least for the time being, all other antagonisms but the communal one. Moreover. among all such divisive ideologies and movements, communalism was the only one that was all-India in its scope'.19 Rejecting sub-national and ethnic divisions in India, this viewpoint practically supported the claim of religious movements to a special status, alongside with all-India nationalism.

Both camps regarded their brand of nationalism as indivisible. Indivisible nationalism first and foremost was a claim to power which was not to be divided or weakened by competing demands. Congress considered the Indian national movement indivisible which meant that its stake to power was also indivisible. This prevented Congress leaders from coming to terms with the Muslim League in 1937 and thereafter, until it was too late for an amicable settlement. Things were made even more complicated because leaders like Nehru and Gandhi, no matter how sensibly and carefully they behaved in most cases, or how hard they tried to unite all Indians and all religions on a common platform against colonialism, could not shed the religious cloth of their nationalist aspirations entirely.

Gandhi, on a unitarian note, incorporated Hinduist values like non-violence and the reverence of the chakra (wheel) into the nationalist movement which helped it spread out among the masses, but which also gave political leaders of religious movements a pretext for confrontation.

Gandhi argued that the practice of religious pilgrimage which involved the visiting of sacred centres in various parts of India, linked people from many regions into a cultural unity. 'We were one nation before [the British] came to India.'" Indian civilization, culture and nationhood all predated the British arrival. 'India . . . has nothing to learn from anybody else." India did not cease to be one nation because different religious groups or foreigners lived in it, he maintained.

India 'must have a faculty for assimilation'." He supported the introduction of Hindi in either Persian or Devanagari characters as a compulsory medium of instruction with optional English courses all over And Nehru, explaining the 'Psychology of Indian Nationalism' in a Swiss newspaper in 1927, declared:

The modern idea of nationhood is of recent growth even in the West, and India in the past certainly was not, and is not even now wholly, a nalion like France or England is today. It was too vast a country to develop on those lines before the advent of the modern methods of communication. But even in the remote past there has always been a fundamental unity of India-a unity of a common faith and culture. India was Bharata, the holy land of the Hindus, and it is not without significance that the great places of Hindu pilgrimage are situated in the four corners of India. . .

Sanskrit was the language of the learned throughout the length and breadth of the country and the provincial languages in the North were all derived from Sanskrit and were closely allied. the four principal southern languages being greatly influenced by Sanskrit.'"

Jinnah's case was probably somewhat different. Unlike Nehru, he did not refer to religion as the unavoidable and natural form of social consciousness in India but as a political weapon to wrench his share of power, his 'pound of flesh', from Congress. On the basis of the concept of 'Muslim nationalism' (which is not to be discussed in detail here) he argued that India was not homogeneous, but consisted of two nations, Hindus and Muslims.

Muslim nationalism was operating on the same level as 'monolithic nationalism': beyond the religious Hindu-Muslim polarization it did not recognize any further divisions. Once, competing claims would cut into the flesh of the League or were prone to create additional problems for the League, for example, in the case of the demand for Azad Punjab by the Sikhs, or the demand for Dravidanadu by the Justice Party. Jinnah rejected these, or at least declined to support them. And, once Pakistan was created, he was the first in the subsequent line of leaders who tried to put down the sub-nationalist aspirations of the Bengalis in East Pakistan, also of the Pathans in the Frontier Province. He extorted his countrymen that they 'are now all Pakistanis, not Baluchis, Pathans, Sindhis, Bengalis, Punjabis and so on'. They should be 'proud to be known as Pakistanis and nothing ele'.'

ELITIST NATIONALITY-FORMATION

The standard western approach to ethnicity and nation-building seems to contrast starkly with 'monolithic nationalism' and 'religious nationalism': plurality is widely accepted. While historiographic concepts of 'monolithic nationalism' and 'religious nationalism' could easily be traced back to particular political trends on the ground, the fact. that the pluralistic approach was also manifest in some way in the Indian polity was often overlooked. It was the British administration that vigorously contended that the Indian races were too diverse to ever unite, a position which suited the imperial interests of the British at the time. On the subject of Indian Councils reform back in 1861, Sir Charles Wood maintained in the House of Commons that an Indian electorate was bound to be so deeply divided as to preclude the emergence of a recognizable political consensus. He insisted that 'you cannot possibly assemble at any one place . . . persons who shall be the real representatives of the Native population of that empire'

Modern historiographic debate in the light of sociocultural plurality tends to revolve around the polarization between the 'structuralists' or 'primordialists' like Francis Robinson, who attached major importance to the 'givens' of the human conditions like birthplace, kin, religion and language, resulting in a life attachment of man's personality to these values." and the 'instrumentalists', who saw ethnicity like Brass 'as the pursuit of interest and advantage for members of groups whose cultures are injnitelj malleable and manipulable by elites'" (emphasis added). Discussing thc issuc on the factual basis of developments in South Asia, one feels that both approaches are highly selective. They reflect important, mutually complementary features, which alternately dominate one or the other situation.

Middle class Muslims of Uttar Pradesh analysed by Robinson, may be psychologically more constrained by their ties of religion and language (script) than Punjabis who could sometimes choose to be either Hindi- or Punjabi-speaking, either Hindu- or Sikh-oriented, in order to cater to their social and political needs, as analysed by Brass. However, both concepts proceed from the assumption that ethnicity is decided by the actions and ideas of the Clite; in the case of the structuralists it is the 6lite which would accept the inherited pattern of loyalties. and in the case of the instrumentalists it is the Clite that would initiate action. according to its needs.

Yet, could they appeal just to any loyalty? How wide would their choice, their room for manoeuvring have been? In order to get effective mass support the leader was constrained in his or her choice of ethnic and religious symbols by the loyalties known to the masses and accepted by them, which meant by the inherited loyalties. The leader was also constrained by the symbols and loyalties known to and accepted by him or her personally. Thus, symbols and loyalties, though changing over time, tended to be comparatively stable at any given moment. And it was social intercourse which itself was inseparable from a regional economic cycle of production, distribution and consumption, that made symbols and loyalties known to people and accepted by them. That means that leaders would have been further constrained in their choice of symbols by economic regionalization which often tended to correspond to ethnic settlement patterns.

Sumit Sarkar in his history 'from below' gave several examples of this kind of interaction of socioeconomic and political as well as ideological factors. The 'tumult' of the Munda tribes around 1900 was the discernible result of the erosion of the traditional land system of joint holdings by tribal lineages through merchants and moneylenders coming from the northern plains.

The Moplah revolt largely resulted from the British insistence on landlord rights. This re-established and vastly enhanced the position of the Hindu upper-caste Namboodri and Nair, but worsened the situation of the mainly Muslim leaseholders and cultivators locally known as the Moplahs. The bulk of the 15,506 Akali volunteers listed in a government report of January 1922 came from the Jat Sikh peasantry who were dissatisfied with their indebtedness to mainly Hindu moneylenders, with low returns from sales to Hindu traders etc. The Dravidian movement reflected discontent with the dominant position of Brahmin castes in the Madras Preidency.'Moneylenders, revenue collectors, newly made landlords and administrators often belonged to separate ethnic andlor religious andlor caste groups.

INTERACTION APPROACH

Given the wide range of often contradictory concepts, the correlation between identity-building and socioeconomic factors needed further exploration. For this purpose a theoretical approach was required that would explain the context of ethnic and religious polarization. both under conditions of independent development and under colonial rule. Coming from a background of Marxist-related reaearch it was felt that a careful analysis was needed to understand what parts of the Marxist theoretical legacy could be discarded or retained and where this fitted into the conceptual framework on ethnicity and identity-building evolved in the West. Georg Elwert has discussed various concepts of ethnic and religious identity-building and radical instrumentalism (Nationalism and Ethnicia on the formation of identity-groups, 1989), and has identified the influence of the Marxist legacy.

It was Otto Bauer (1881-1938) who discussed this nexus of economy and consciousness in his 1907 work Die Nationalitatenfrage und die Soialdemokrcie (The iVutionulities Question and Social Democracj). 'But because of his Marxist reference scheme established research (which reacts to Marxism rather allergicly) quoted him only from secondary source.

A Marxist theory on ethnicity and nationalism worth the name never came into being. It was rejected and twisted by orthodox Marxism of later years, including the mainly tactical and political approach which Lenin took towards ethnonationalist movements, as temporary political allies in the struggle for power inside the Soviet Union and on a global scale against Western imperialism.

Bauer had been severely criticized by many Marxists and socialists for his clichC of the Schicksalsgemeinschaft (community of fate) being the essence of the nation by which he was supposed to have fallen into the trap of bourgeois nationalism, mythologizing the substance of the nation. Because of the political implications of this approach at his time, his underlying concept was overlooked by both critics and supporters alike. What he meant was, in fact, the commonality of experience. of shared history which was the result of the interaction of a group of people over a period of time. For his thesis, Bauer referred to Immanuel Kant's understanding of the community (Gemeinschaft) as being constituted by continuous interaction of its members (durchgangige Wechselvirkung untereindander)."

Taken in this context, Bauer's idea of the Schicksalsgemeinschaft did not look static any more. Fate was embodied in common history, in the circumstances of living together.

Responding to the dilemma of choice between different factors that determine conflict patterns and identity, an 'interaction approach' is suggested that louId want to avoid a stagnant assessment and try to understand the interaction of various factors in the course of a dynamic process.

FAREWELLS TO THE PEASANTRY

This discussion is about a theoretical issue that has obsessed me, on and off, for many years: how to understand the conditions of existence of those people termed 'peasants', or collectively 'the peasantry', within the world of mature capitalism.

Any pursuit of the theme immediately confronts an issue that plagues the social sciences as much as it does everyday dispute: it all depends on what you mean by 'peasantry'. Indeed it does, and this is notmerely a semantic issuebecause different conceptions of thepeasantry, and its fate in modern capitalism (and once socialism), resonate different interpretations of modernity and 'development' and the dramatic dialectic that attaches to them of destruction and creation, in short, the dialectic of progress (Berman 1983). The central analytical issue atstakehere iswhether 'the peasantry' constitutes a general (and generic) social 'type' (entity, formation, class, and so on). That is, whether there are qualities of 'peasantness' applicable to, and illuminating, different parts of theworld in different periods of their histories, not least the poorer countries of Latin America, Asia and Africa today, and their processes of development/ underdevelopment.

The view that there are such qualities is termed 'peasant essentialism'. Those qualities include such familiar notions as household farming organised for simple reproduction ('subsistence'), the solidarities, reciprocities and egalitarianism of (village) community, and commitment to the values of away of life based on household and community, kin and locale (and harmony with nature, a motif revived and privileged by current 'green' discourses). The qualities of an essential 'peasantness' can thusbe constructed in economic, sociological or cultural terms, or some combination of them, in order to specify what makes peasants different and special, and to contrast them - explicitly or implicitly - with (rural) proletarians on one hand, market- oriented and entrepreneurial 'farmers' on the other. Such essentialist constructions acknowledge the relations of peasants with other social groups and entities - landlords, merchants, the state, the urban in general - which they typically view as relations of subordination and exploitation that also define the peasant condition and generate the politics of peasant resistance.

The most important and enduring claim (or assumption) of peasant essentialism is that the core elements of peasant 'society' - household, kin, community, locale - produce (or express) a distinctive internal logic or dynamic. It follows that the relations of peasants with powerful others amount to various forms of appropriation and oppression external to that essence of peasant existence, which, in principle, can thus not only survive their demise but subsequently, andconsequently, flourish. It is more difficult to construct a generic 'peasantry' in sociological and cultural terms that travel across different types of society and historical periods with much plausibility, than it is to do so in terms of conventional economics with its postulate of a universal matrix of human behaviour.

Arguably the most rigorous formal attempt to the oriseasuigener is peasantry is the model of peasant economy of the great Russian agrarian scholar AV Chayanov (1966). The originality, and indeed peculiarity, of Chayanov's model consists inits combination ofaclaimfor 'peasantry' as aspecific and generictype of economy, akinto a mode of production in Marxistterms, and staking that claim on a marginalist analysis of thebehaviour of the peasant household as both unitary farming enterprise and site of (biological) reproduction.

The plot now thickens because ideas of peasant essentialism do not attach to any one ideological position or programme, in my view. First, essentialist conceptions lurk in both Left and Right versions of the disappearance of the peasantry necessary to economic, social and cultural progress ('development'). Second, they can inspire varieties of populism that celebrate 'resistance' to urban-industrial civilisation and its discontents ('anti-development'); or, third, that advocate aprogramme of development that frees the productive energies, and social and moral virtues, of the peasantry from its historic condition of subjugation and exploitation. The last has probably never been better expressed than in Chayanov's definition of neo-populism: 'a theory for the development of agriculture on the basis of cooperative peasant households, apeasantry organised cooperatively as an independent class and technically superiorto allotherforms of agricultural organization' (Bourgholtzer 1999:3, 16).

HowChayanov envisaged asociety built on these foundations is set out in his strange novella, written in 1920 and set in 1984, The Journey of My Brother Alexei to the Land of Peasant Utopia. There, among other good things, Alexei discovered that he 'was positively crazy about Utopian women'! (Chayanov 1976:83). The Utopia of peasant socialism in a post-Soviet Russia in 1984 was presented by Chayanov as a 'third way' of development, a desirable alternative to both capitalism and Bolshevism, and one he portrayed in strongly modernist terms of the development of technology and social regulation, as well as in aesthetic and even mystical terms. If Chayanov pinned his hopes of progress on the return of the peasantry, I refer next to another scholar whose modernism bids farewell to the peasantry with no apparentregret. In his Age of Extremes, EJH. obsbawm declared that 'For 80 per cent of humanity, the Middle Ages ended suddenly in the 1950s... the most dramatic change of the second half of this century, and the one which cuts us forever from the world of the past, is the death of the peasantry' ('which had formed the majority of the human race throughout recorded history') (Hobsbawm 1994:288-9, 415).

Hobsbawm locates the disappearance of this truly world-historical anachronism inthe 'revolution of global society' or 'global transformation' from the 1950s that extended industrial capitalism beyond its historic heartlands of Western and Central Europe andNorth America. 'Only three regions of the globe remained essentially dominated by their villages and fields:

sub-Saharan Africa, South and continental South-east Asia, and China' - although 'admittedly' these regions of 'peasant dominance' comprisedhalf the world's population inthe 1990s (Hobsbawm 1994:291). The 'deathof the peasantry' is thus somewhat exaggerated, even according to Hobsbawm's idiosyncratic demographic accounting, and 'even' though these regions 'were crumbling atthe edgesunder the pressures of economic development' (Hobsbawm 1994:291).

Let me reprise briefly different versions of the 'death of the peasantry'. First, there are denials ofthis event, and oftheinevitability ofprocesses that produce it: views ofthe 'persistence' ofthepeasantry inthe world of mature capitalism. Such 'persistence' maybe celebrated invariousforms of agrarian populism as the effect of qualities ofpeasant resilience and 'resistance'. Or itmayberegretted, inbothMarxist andbourgeois versions of modernisation. Second, the prediction of the 'death of the peasantry' may be maintained, and again whether this outcome is regretted or welcomed, as it is by Eric Hobsbawm albeitwith arecognition thatthe deaththroes aremore protracted than once believed (and that this itself is an historical puzzle). What these positions share, despite alltheir other differences, are typically essentialist views of 'the peasantry' as pre-capitalist.

Isadifferent approachpossible,withoutanyassumption of'the peasantry' as anachronism or exemplifying 'backwardness', and without any trace of peasant essentialismandromanticism? I believe that it is. My argument also entails a farewell to 'the peasantry',but in a different manner to those which deny, confirm orpredictitsdemisefrom essentialist premises. I start from the other direction, as it were. Rather than seeking to explain the 'persistence' of a pre-capitalist socialform as an historical puzzle, as cause for celebration or regret, I ask whether andhow those termed 'peasants'/'peasantry' in the contemporary world can be theorised by investigating their conditions of existence, and reproduction, through the categories of the capitalist mode ofproduction: the social relations, dynamics of accumulation, and divisions of labour of capitalism/imperialism. I attempt to answer this by considering the specificities of, first, petty commodity production, and, second, agriculture, in capitalism. A third step concern show 'peasants' inthe South and'family farmers' in the North are located in the international divisions of labour of imperialism and their mutations.

First, then, the concept of petty commodity production. This specifies a form of small-scale - 'family', 'household' or individual - production in capitalism engaged in more or less specialised commodity production and constituted by a particular combination of the class places of capital and labour(Gibbonand Neocosomos 1985).The agents of this form of production are capitalists and workers at the same time because they own or otherwise command means of production and employ their own labour. This specification of a form generic to the capitalist mode of production is necessarily highly abstract. It does not distinguish agricultural from non- agricultural enterprises nor their locations in the social divisions of labour of the South and the North. 'Peasants' become petty commodity producers in this sense when they are unable to reproduce themselves outside the relations and processes of capitalist commodity production, when those relations andprocesses become conditions of existence of peasant fanning and are internalised inits organisation and activity. That historical moment is satisfied when 'forced commercialization' (Bharadwaj 1985), typical of early colonialism, gives way to the reproduction of commodity production andproducers through 'the dull compulsion ofeconomic forces' (in Marx's term). And that, I would argue, was the case for the vast majority of 'peasants' by the end of the colonial era in Asia and Africa.

The theory of petty commodity production suggests that its 'spaces' in the socialdivision oflabour arecontinuously (re)createdaswellas destroyed in processes of capitalist development, a dynamic likely to be particularly accentuated in agriculture for reasons I return to. Here a distinction is necessary between the destruction of petty commodity production in particular branches of activity (for example, the emblematic fate of hand- loom weavers in both nineteenth-century Britain and colonial India, as a consequence of British industrialisation) and the demise of individual enterprises as the effect of competition betweenpetty commodity producers and thepressures on their reproduction as both capital and labour. This also points to the vexed issue of class differentiation.

For Marx, whoseresearch centred onthe original transition to capitalism in Britain, the transformation of agriculture was charted above all through the displacement or dispossession of peasant by capitalist farming, what might be called the enclosure model or effect. Lenin's emphasis on the tendency to class differentiation of peasants (and other petty commodity producers) was a fundamental addition to understanding paths of agrarian change, identifying the possibility of the dissolution of the peasantry throughthe formation ofdistinct classes ofagrarian capitalandwage labour from its ranks. Lenin's argument, of course, is strenuously contested by versions of peasant essentialism inherent in agrarian populism. It is also often misunderstood theoretically, hence misapplied empirically, by its adherents as well as its opponents. The tendency to class differentiation arises from thepeculiar combination ofthe classplaces ofcapital and labour in petty commodity production, hence its 'exaggerated form of instability' (Gibbon and Neocosmos 1985). Poor peasants are subject to a simple reproduction 'squeeze' as capital or labour, or both. Their poverty and depressed levelsofconsumption (reproductionas labour)commonly express intense struggles to maintain their means of production (reproduction as capital), loss ofwhich entails proletarianisation. Middle peasants are those abletomeetthedemands of simple reproduction; while rich peasants are able to engagein expanded reproduction: toincrease theland and/or other means of production at their disposal beyond the capacity of family/household labour, hence hiring wage labour.

I want to emphasise two further aspects of the class differentiation of the peasantry. One is that the class places of capital and labour which combine to constitute petty commodity production in capitalism are not necessarily distributed symmetricallywithin 'family' or 'household' production. Indeed, they areunlikely to be so as they typically follow the contours of gendered (and otherunequal) divisions ofproperty, labour andincomein 'family' and kinship structures. The other aspect is that class differentiation of peasants can proceed via the increasing 'entry' or reproduction costs of petty commodity enterprise, resulting in the dispossessionVproletarianisation of weakerproducers/poor peasantswithout anynecessary formation of classes of rich peasants or capitalist farmers. This is emphasised because the presence/reproduction of 'family farmers' (in the USA and Europe) or of middle peasants (in the imperialist periphery) is so often, and mistakenly, understood to signal an absence of differentiation rather than one kind of outcome of class differentiation, generated by the levels of capitalisation necessary to the simple reproduction of farming enterprises.

The abstract ideas I have presented are necessary to provide a theoretical point of entry and basis for considering 'peasants' in the capitalist mode of production, and in imperialism as its modern global form. They suggest (and help explain) class differentiation of 'peasants' (as of other petty commodity producers) as atendency with in capitalism,not as an inevitable and uniform empirical trend. This tendency contains its own distinctive complexities and contradictions, as I have noted, which are compounded by introducing other, more concrete observations.

First, many-no doubt the great majority - of 'peasants' today are not engaged exclusively in farming but combine agricultural petty commodity production (including so-called' subsistence' farming) with a range of other economic activities. They rotate between different locations in social divisions of labour constituted variously by agricultural andnon-agricultural branches of production,by rural and urban existence, and by the exchange of labour power as well as its combination with property in petty commodity production. Of course, these diverse combinations of farming with other activities are also structured by class relations.

Poor peasants are most likely to engage inwage labour and in the more marginal (and'crowded') branches of non-agricultural petty commodity activity, in other words pursue 'survival' in conditions of extreme constraint; middle peasant households also typically diversify sources of income (including from wage labour) to reproduce their means of production (reproduce themselves as capital); rich peasants frequently pursue diversified accumulation strategies, with investment 'portfolios' in crop trading and processing, money lending, rural transport, tractor renting, and village shops and bars (this can help explain why agrarian accumulation by rich peasants often does not proceed beyond certain limits).

A second and related observation is that rural labour markets are pervasive in most areas of peasant production and much middle peasant farming (as well as rich peasant farming) depends on hired labour. The rural labour question is complicated by the fact that some middle peasant households sell as well as buy labour power (and even poor peasant households occasionally hire labour), and that the boundaries between the poorpeasantry and the rural proletariat are typically blurred. Nonetheless, the prevalence and importance of labour hiring to agricultural petty commodity production (and its implications) is often overlooked as is the intensity of class struggle it generates in some areas of peasant capitalism. Third, if the poor peasantry is typically an important component of the reserve army of labour in the countrysides of the imperialist periphery, all classes of the peasantry are likely to have links, albeit of different kinds,with urban centresan markets.

The framework sketched points tothe great diversity of 'peasants' in the history and current period of capitalism/ imperialism. It shouldbe clear that 'the peasantry' is hardly a uniform, or analytically helpful, social category in contemporary capitalism,whether by anachronistic reference (the survival of' the world of the past') or in seeking to understand changes in agriculture andrural social existence generated by imperialism/ globalisation. The same stricture necessarily applies to views of 'the peasantry' as a (single) 'class' ('exploited' orotherwise) common in agrarian populism.

I move now to the second theme, that of specific structural sources of diversity (and instability) in the characteristics of agriculture as well as of petty commodity production in capitalism, hence in the ways that they intersect in 'peasant' production (as well as other 'family' farming). A common assumption, inherited from classical political economy (and its roots in England's distinctive, indeed unique, path of transition to capitalism) is that the capitalist agricultural enterprise - the farm - is homologous with the mode of production, that it necessarily consists of capital and 'free' wage labour.

By analogy with manufacturing industry, capitalist farming should increase its scale (concentration of capital), technical divisions of labour (formation of the collective worker) and productivity of labour (development of the productive forces), in line with the laws of motion of capitalism.

Already in the late nineteenth century, this expectation was contested by reference to the strong 'persistence' of small-scale ('family') farming into the era of industrial capitalism: in Europe in the form of peasantries of feudal provenance (by contrast withthe fate of pre-industrial artisans), and in the USA in the form of mechanised grain production in the prairies by family (rather than wage) labour farms.

The particular unevenness of the capitalist transformation of farming has thus long been remarked, and attempts to explain it in general terms typically start from the conditions of transforming nature peculiar to agriculture, and their implications for capital. While manufacturing industry transforms materials already appropriated from nature, agriculture only transforms nature throughth every activities of appropriating it, and thus confronts the uncertainties of natural environments andprocesses and their effects for the growth of plant and animal organisms.

Accordingly, it has been suggested that capital is inhibited from direct investment in farming for several reasons. One is that this tends to be riskier than investment in other branches of activity; the normal risks of market competition are compounded by the risks inherent in the environmental conditions of farming.

A second reason, derived from Marxian value theory, is the non-identity of labour time and production time: production time exceeds labour time because of the growth cycles of plants and animals during which capital is 'tied up' and unable to realise profit (Mann and Dickinson 1978). Another argument from value theory emphasises the burden of ground rent which capital tends to leave to 'family' farmers to absorb, similar to their absorption of risk and the delayed realisation of surplusvalue (Djurfeldt 1981).

Yet other arguments centre on labour markets and labour processes: capitalist agriculture is unable to compete for labour as economic development raises wage rates, giving family labour farms a 'labour-price advantage' (Koning 1994:172);the labour process argument is that it is much more difficult, hence costly, to supervise and control the pace and quality of wage labour in the field than in the factory (Nolan 1988).

These are, of course, very general reasons advanced to explain a tendency, the accentuated unevenness of capitalist transformation of forms of production in farming. At the same time, they point to two features of agriculture in capitalism that are key to the formation and mutations of its international divisions of labour, especially in the era of globalisation.

The first is the drive of technical innovation to simplify and standardise the conditions of agricultural production: to reduce the variability, obstacles and uncertainties presented by natural environments to approximate the ideal of control in industrial production. This means to produce yields that areas predictable as well as large (and fast maturing) as possible - by acting on soils, climate,the attributes of plant and animal organisms, parasites and diseases, weed growth, and so on.

The second, and related, feature is the increasing integration of farming by capital concentrated upstream and downstream of production on the land. 'Upstream' refers to capital in input production, above all chemical corporations which dominate seed development and production as well as that of fertilizers and other agricultural chemicals; 'downstream' refers to the giant corporations in food processing/manufacturing and distribution.

The provenance of such corporations is in the industrialised capitalist countries, and they tend to be the more concentrated, them or developed the agricultural sector (and economy in which it is located). These corporations are now engaged in anew wave of globalisation, inways that affect the fortunes and prospects of many different kinds of farmers, including 'peasants' in the imperialist periphery. Of course, a strategic implication of the features of agriculture in capitalism outlined isthat the diversity of types of farming is much greater than that of the (globalising) branches which integrate the backward and forward linkages of fanning.

Farming enterprises in contemporary capitalism, within as well as across North and South, exhibit great diversity in their size, scale, social organisation and labour processes (forms, and combinations, of family labour, free and unfree wage labour), their degree and types of capitalisation and mechanisation, and their forms of insertion/integration in markets and commodity chains.

The third element of my argument entails aperiodisation of imperialism and agriculture from the 1870s, to sketch the differential locations of 'peasants' (inthe South) and 'family' farmers (intheNorth) in international divisions of labour.

The last three decades of the nineteenth century were as momentous in the formation of global capitalism as the current period since the 1970s, marked as they were by the 'Second Industrial Revolution', the new wave of internationalisation of capital and final major phase of European colonial expansion emphasised in Lenin's analysis of imperialism, and the formation of the first 'international food regime' identified by Harriet Friedmann's remarkable project on the international political economy of food (Friedmann 1978,1982a, 1982b, 1993; Friedmann and McMichael 1989).

The basis of that regime was the massive growth of grain (and livestock/meat) production on the vast internal frontiers of 'settler' states- Argentina, Australia, Canada, and above all the USA. In a (relatively) open international trade order, the exports of these countries, especially of wheat, competed directly with the temperate agriculture of the European heartlands of industrial capitalism, by contrast with the complementary tropical agricultural exports of Asia and Africa whose colonial incorporation was completed in the same period. For the agrarian economies of the imperialist periphery, this period was marked by three broad types of change. One was the emergence of the 'industrial plantation' which replaced earlier types of plantation in Asia, the Caribbean, and parts of Latin America, generated new plantation 'frontiers' (in Indochina, Malaya, Sumatra) and greatly enlarged the scale and volume of highly specialised world market production of rubber, oil palm, sisal, sugar, cocoa, tea and bananas.

Latin America, which was mostly independent of colonial rulebefore the international hegemony of industrial capitalism, also experienced a second type of change; central to its massive agricultural export boom in the same period was a new phase of commoditisation of the originally colonial hacienda, involving further land grabbing from peasant communities and the expansion of a servile labour force.

The third kind of change, pervasive in much of Africa and most of Asia where colonialism didnot dispossess the varied peasantries it encountered, was the increased incorporation (in scale and intensity) of peasant farmers in capitalist economy as producers of export crops (cotton, oilpalm, coffee, cocoa, tobacco, groundnuts), of (sometimes new) food staples for domestic markets and of labour power via migrant labour systems (including indentured and corvee labour) to build the railways and roads, and to work in the plantations, mines and ports.

Of course, these processes manifested a great variety of forms of land tenure and differential access to land, labour and markets, reflecting both diverse pre-colonial agrarian structures and the complex ways in which colonial rule and commoditisation incorporated and changed them.

Following the (first) 'golden age' of globalisation (1870s-1914), the inter war period plunged the first international food regime into crisis. During the uneven recovery of the world economy in the 1920s, the agriculture of the developed capitalist economies again started to experience the effects of overproduction (still one of their definitive features). With the advent of the Depression of the 1930s the major capitalist countries embarked on a course of agricultural protectionism.

In the Asian and African colonies, the instruments of agricultural protection introduced in Europe (like marketing boards) were adapted to extract the maximum transfers from peasant export agriculture to imperial exchequers.

In the revival and unprecedented growth of the world economy from the 1950s to early 1970s, anew and quite different 'international food regime' was established, under American hegemony and turning on the 'Atlantic pivot' of the USA and Europe. This both maintained the farm support policies of the pre-war years and added the export of American maize and soya (the definitive field crops of the postwar 'second agricultural revolution') for animal feeds.

The production of meat and of high value-added manufactured foods ('food durables') for mass consumption became the leading international agribusiness sectors in the developed capitalist world as the postwar economic boom accelerated. In return for its openness to US exports of raw materials for feedstuffs (and US corporate investment in their manufacture in Europe), the EU was able to maintain high levels of protection for other branches, notably wheat and dairy products.

In effect, this generated systems of national agricultural regulation by which European countries sought to replicate US agricultural growth through a combination of import tariffs and export subsidies,without similar limits on the movement of agribusiness capital- an unstable combination of the freedom of capital with restriction on trade, as Friedmann (1993) puts it.

The USA also deployed its surpluses of subsidised grain (and soy oil) for strategic foreign policy purposes through foreign aid and export promotion (dumping), which stimulated dependence on (cheap) American wheat in areas of the imperialist periphery hitherto largely self-sufficient in staple food production. In turn this facilitated the further specialisation of the latter in the production of industrial and (mostly non-staple) food crops for world markets, as did the ambitious development plans of the newly independent former colonies of Asia and Africa, for most of which the earnings of primary commodity exports (agricultural and mineral) were the principal source of foreign exchange for import-substituting industrialisation. This created the conditions of a potential scissors effect for many poor,primarily agricultural, countries, one blade being increasing food import dependence,the other the fluctuating but generally declining terms of trade for their historic export crops.

Agricultural production in the imperialist periphery thus became increasingly internationalised in this period: through the quasi-public investment of aid agencies, notably the World Bank, to create more systematically commoditised and productive export-cropping peasantries in Asia and Africa in the name of 'national development'; through American (and later European) strategic food aid and/or commercial dumping; and, reflecting post-war Malthusian fears of mass famine and starvation (hence pursued alongside population control), through (international) research and development of new high-yielding hybrid grain varieties (in order of importance, of rice, wheat and maize) to boost food production in poor countries: the 'Green Revolution'.

The conjuncture of the 1970s appears, in retrospect, to have been as definitive a moment of subsequent structural shifts in the world economy as that of the 1870s a century before (similarly manifested in a dialectic of global recession, adjustment, and massive expansion of international flows of money and commodities). This applies to the collapse of the prevailing international food regime no less than to the end of international monetary stability, the declining competitiveness of US industry, or the subsequent global(ising) ascendancy of neo-liberalism. The proximate cause or trigger of that collapse was a brief episode of 'a sudden, unprecedented shortage and sky-rocketing prices' in world grain markets, linked to enormous (and preferential) US grain sales to the USSR in the early 1970s (Friedmann 1993: 40). This stimulated greatly increased borrowing by American farmers to expand production, paving the way for the US farm crisis of the 1980s when the structural nature of overproduction reasserted itself. US grain exports now faced increasing competition - in wheat from the EU (above all France), and in soya, and especially processed soy products, from what Friedmann (1993) terms New Agricultural Countries (NACs). In short, the basis of the relatively stable post-war international food regime was undermined as the EU and the NACs successfully replicated the American model.

The increasing weakness and then demise of the Soviet Union and its bloc further undermined a key strategic rationale of the Atlantic pivot. As is well known, the Uruguay Round from 1986 established agricultural trade and its liberalisation as central to the agenda of GATT (now the WTO) under pressure from the USA, which had hitherto blocked its subjection to GATT processes and rules.

The most fundamental structural shift Friedmann points to - and one familiar from widerdebates about contemporary globalisation-is that from the ruins of international (Atlantic-centred) regulation emerged transnational agro-food corporations as 'the major agents attempting to...organize stable conditions of production and consumption which allow them to plan investment, sourcing of agricultural materials, and marketing', that is, as integrating various sites of production and consumption through global private (corporate) regulation (ibid: 52). This occurred in a conjuncture in which the debt of the imperialist periphery, escalating since the 1970s, became the key lever of structural adjustment lending and trade liberalisation with a renewed emphasis - for the poorest countries- on their comparative advantage in agricultural exports.

In addition to this agricultural 'export platform' dynamic, globalisation also impacts on countries of the imperialist periphery with sufficient demand to attract agribusiness production for domestic markets, whether as an element of wage goods (e.g. certain parts of Latin America and North Africa) and/or luxury consumption.

India provides a perhaps surprising, hence instructive, example of the latter. Despite its levels of poverty, both rural and urban, but given the size of its population and inequality of income distribution, since liberalisation of its economy in the early 1990s India has become an arena of intense competition between transnational agro-food corporations. They seek to locate new food processing and manufacturing plants in rural areas lacking histories of worker organisation, where they can also be sourced by converting adjacent farm land to production of the raw materials they require, often through contract farming arrangements (Banaji 1996).

The enhanced connections of sites/forms of production and consumption in a globalisation of agriculture driven by transnational corporations might seem a compelling manifestation of 'the pressures of economic development' observed (if not specified) by Hobsbawm (1994; 291). The effects are likely to be uneven and contradictory for the kinds ofreasons I suggested earlier.

Some forms of globalisation undoubtedly generate expansions of capitalist agriculture that displace peasant farming (the enclosure effect), for example, large-scale mechanised cultivation of feed grains in Mexico together with increased grain imports for human consumption, and otherwise reduce or marginalise the contributions of their own farming to the incomes/ reproduction of especially poor, but also many middle, 'peasants' and/or accelerate tendencies to class differentiation. Not surprisingly, the costs of entry into such new activities as contract farming of high value 'non- traditional' crops (fresh fruits, vegetables, cut flowers, decorative house plants) for global markets, are beyond the reach of most peasant farmers (while expanded production of these commodities generally stimulates the demand for rural wage labour).

In short, while it is impossible to generalise about the impact of (uneven and diverse forms of) globalisation on (differentiated) peasantries, itis likely that in this current phase of imperialism, most poor peasants confront an increasing simple reproduction 'squeeze', as indeed dothe great majority of the poor in both South and North.

Together with the landless rural proletariat, poor peasants form part of an expanding reserve army of labour in the countryside and in the cities and towns of large areas of the imperialist periphery, given the prevalence of rural-urban links which include regular migration in search of wage employment as 'footloose labour' in Jan Breman'sterm (Breman 1996). This doesnot, however, indicate any uniform or linear route to an inevitable destination: the general or definitive demise of agricultural petty commodity production.

The impulses to economic change generated by globalisation, and how they are mediated by the diverse class structures and dynamics of the imperialist periphery, can consolidate certain spaces for agricultural petty commodity production, and create new spaces as well as destroy existing ones. Indeed, pressures on industrial and urban employment, and the immiseration that results, may generate tendencies to 're-peasantisation' in some instances.

Latin America again provides some notable examples, like the former tinminers, historically the vanguard of the Bolivian working class, now turned coca growers (Petras 1997:26-9), and the Landless Workers Movement in Brazil {Movimiento Rural San Terra) which James Petras (1998:124) considers 'the most dynamic rural social movement in Latin America' today.

6

The Policy of Religious Conversions

According to the 1901 census, Bihar and Uttar Pradesh combined contained about 72 million people. Of that number, over 44 million were officially classified as shudra, untouchable, or, more precisely, according to the very limited degree of social contact they were allowed with the twice-born. The Ramanandi sampraday provided in the nineteenth and twentieth centuries an institutional context within which members of those stigmatized communities could acquire a modicum of social and religious dignity. By the late nineteenth century a parallel and qualitatively different brand of social reform had begun to emerge that was, strictly speaking, independent of any direct institutional connection to the Ramanandi or any other Vaishnava sampraday. Rather, this new reformism originated in the jatis assigned shudra status and was for the most part spearheaded by articulate, educated members of those stigmatized communities.

Whereas shudra and untouchable involvement in Vaishnava religiosity, whether as lay devotees or as sadhus, was predicated on a Ramanandi disdain for status, these new jati reformers sought personal and community dignity on their own by the unqualified assertion of status. Such assertions occurred among a broad range of agricultural and artisanal jatis who had in common an ascriptively shudra past, and the discussion in this chapter reflects that socio-occupational variety. Of particular interest, however, given their centrality to Gangetic agriculture and relative demographic strength, were the kshatriya campaigns mounted by Kurmi, Yadav, and Kushvaha peasants. Hence, I pay particular attention to these groups.

Though the various new kshatriya organizations that began to appear after the late nineteenth century were institutionally separate from the Ramanandi or any other Vaishnava sampraday, they did evince, as I will argue, a distinctly religious character in both form and content that can only be described as Vaishnava. This is most evident in the very strategy employed in claiming high status: the ex-shudras asserted kshatriya status on the basis of genealogical ties to either Ram or Krishna, the well-known avatars of Vishnu. In addition, much of the reform urged upon the jati communities by their leaders involved abstinence from meat and intoxicants so as to inculcate a "pure" lifestyle, tactics which echoed those utilized in Buchanan's day as the hallmark of Vaishnava (particularly Ramanandi) respectability.

The language and rhetoric of kshatriya reform also reflected an unmistakable Vaishnava texture, which I explore in some detail. Finally, though Vaishnava monasticism was not integral to kshatriya reform, Ramanandis, and particularly Ramanuja-oriented Ramanandis, did on occasion become involved as proponents of kshatriya identity. The intersection between Vaishnava monasticism and kshatriya reform is particularly revealing given the disputes over caste and tradition in the Ramanandi sampraday in the twentieth century.

The most broad-based kshatriya reform movements occurred among Kurmi and Yadav peasants. Yadav and Kurmi-kshatriya advocates maintained important roots in the Gangetic core of Bihar and eastern Uttar Pradesh, but gained wide support throughout northern and western India. The less well-known Kushvaha-kshatriya movement, meanwhile, experienced its greatest successes among peasants in the Gangetic core; other analogous peasant and artisan-based reform programs experienced similar regional concentrations of activity. Notwithstanding their broad regional appeal, the Kurmi and Yadav movements have received only limited, descriptive attention in the historical literature. By contrast, more attention has been given to the movement to inculcate a kshatriya identity among the smaller but more influential Kayasth community, which has been well represented in the professions, the civil service, and politics.

Because many jati reformers encouraged vegetarianism, abstinence from spirituous liquors, Sanskrit education, and wearing of the sacred thread among their members, it is possible to see in the kshatriya reform movements a significant degree of what the anthropologist M. N. Srinivas has called "Sanskritization."

However, it can be argued that the focus on Sanskritization has led scholars to emphasize the cosmetics of ritual and behavioral transformation and obscured from view the more significant, underlying meanings of ideological change implicit in social reform. Underpinning the ceremonial concerns, emphasis on classical education, and advocacy of pure living that characterized these reform efforts was, I argue, a complex and highly ramified Vaishnava discourse that extended throughout and beyond Gangetic India. Indeed, the history of kshatriya reformism described here suggests that a Vaishnava ethic of reform had become institutionalized in the everyday lives of ordinary people by the turn of the century. Examining the nineteenth-century antecedents of kshatriya reformism, exploring its complex dimensions in the twentieth century and its occasional intersections with Ramanandi monasticism, and discerning some of its broader political and cultural implications, are the objectives of the remainder of this book.

STATUS AND THE NINETEENTH CENTURY

The concern with personal dignity, community identity, and caste status reached a peak among Kurmi, Yadav, and Kushvaha peasants in the first four decades of the twentieth century. But widespread, though sporadic, apprehensions over such issues extended well beyond those who cultivated the soil and emerged well before 1900. That a concern for status and dignity was not restricted to peasants is evident from the official record: by the end of the nineteenth century two influential, landed communities of ambiguous social rank in the Gangetic core, Bhumihars and Kayasths, had already made claims to superior status, and as a result their official position was in doubt. While the 1901 census was in the compilation stage, Bhumihar associations filed numerous representations with E. A. Gait, the director of census operations for Bengal and Bihar, which argued that, for the purposes of the census, the term "Babhan" should not be used to describe them and instead they should be classified as Bhumihar, or landed, brahmans.

Ninety years earlier, in his survey of what later became Patna and Gaya Districts of Bihar, Buchanan had noted with some disdain that Bhumihars (to whom he referred as Magahi and military brahmans) "have betaken themselves entirely to agriculture and arms, and cannot be considered as belonging to the sacred order." He consequently ascribed to them kshatriya status. Gait followed suit in his census report at the turn of the century, though he left the question of Bhumihar status officially unresolved: "The best opinion at the present time is perhaps in favour of the Brahmanical origin of the Babhans, but it would be incorrect to say that they are, therefore, Brahmans still. In the eyes of the general Hindu public they constitute a separate caste, which is generally, but not always, regarded as slightly superior to that of the Rajputs [regarded as kshatriya]."

By contrast, Kayasths had been classified as pure shudras by Buchanan in the beginning of the nineteenth century. As a result of their very public campaign for kshatriya status in the last quarter of the century, not to mention their substantial economic and political clout, Kayasths were classified along with "Babhans" and Rajputs as "other castes of twice-born rank" in the 1901 census hierarchy for Bihar. Herbert Hope Risley, who devised the hierarchy, noted elsewhere that "the social position of the Behar Kayasths is unquestionably a high one," inasmuch as "popular opinion ranks them next in order to the Babhans and Rajputs."

The problem of ambiguous status implicit in the many claims for high caste was not restricted to Bihar. Risley also designed a complex hierarchy guide for the Uttar Pradesh census that acknowledged disputed claims by delineating such intermediate categories as "Castes allied to Brahmans and who are considered to be of high social standing"; "Castes allied to Kshatriyas, though their claim is not universally admitted"; and "Castes allied to Vaishyas, but their claim is not universally admitted." Additional intermediate categories reflected the broader incongruity between social practice, particularly regarding the consumption of food and water, and varna theory. Such categories included "Castes of good social position, superior to that of the remaining classes"; "Castes from whom some of the twice-born would take water and pakki [prepared food], without question"; "Castes from whom some of the twice-born take water while others would not"; "Castes from whose hand the twice-born cannot take water, but who are not untouchable"; "Castes that are untouchable, but do not eat beef"; and "The lowest castes eating beef and vermin."

Indeed, Risley's hierarchy for Uttar Pradesh was far more elaborate than that for Bihar, suggesting that contending claims of social respectability may have been more deeply entrenched in the western half of the Gangetic Plain. In any case, it is clear from a perusal of Buchanan, writing ninety years before Risley, that status claims predated the creation of the Indian census; neither were they restricted to the powerful landed and professional jatis. For instance, Buchanan observed that in south Bihar,

> Although the Rajputs are here universally admitted to be Kshatriyas, there are, as in Bhagalpur, other pretenders to that rank whose claim is not generally admitted . . . by those who are not in their power. It must however be observed, that their claims to a descent from the original regal tribe is probably as well founded as those of the Rajputs....In fact, every military tribe that had sufficient power, seems to have been admitted by the Brahmans into the regal caste, so soon as it became subject to their authority, and betook itself to a pure life.

These "other pretenders" to rank included, most prominently, Kurmi and Goala peasants. The two italicized phrases point out not only Buchanan's awareness of the influence of brahman opinion in his depiction of Gangetic social differentiation, but the awareness among those aspiring to elite status that the complicity of brahmans (as venerated scholars) was a valued requisite. Perhaps to redress the brahmanical weight of his own presentation, Buchanan was willing to cite (often with considerable sympathy) cases of dissenting claims to status in the regions he surveyed, noting especially the religio-mythical account given by "Goala" peasants (who would later claim Yadav-kshatriya status) regarding their own origins: "These people, however low they may be held by the Brahmans, pretend to considerable dignity on account of their connection with the god Krishna, who, although a Kshatri of the family of the moon, was adopted by a Goyala, and many of his wives (1600) are said on some authorities to have been of the Goyala tribe."

Buchanan observed similar localized claims to high status among Kurmis in the Gangetic core, based on an Ayodhya-centered consciousness. The significance of Ayodhya here derives not so much from the importance of that site as a growing Ramanandi monastic center as from its position as the mytho-historical kingdom of Ramchandra (though of course the two are closely related) and hence as an increasingly important geocultural hub of Vaishnava belief.

Buchanan noted that so-called Ayodhya Kurmis, especially in the Bhojpur region of western Bihar and eastern Uttar Pradesh, claimed superior status and even spurned certain economic and agricultural roles on the basis of that assertion. One case dating from the late eighteenth century concerned a group of influential, land-controlling Ayodhya Kurmis who lived in the Parraona environs of northeast Gorakhpur District and upon whom Asaf ud-daula, the fourth Nawab of Awadh, attempted to bestow the title of "Raja" and thus kshatriya status.

The Kurmi avowal of noble status ultimately seemed to fail due to united Rajput opposition in Asaf's court. Ironically, the Rajput constituency of Awadh itself composed a "group of newcomers to the court, who had been peasant soldiers only a few years before. They were called, half sarcastically, the 'Tilangi Rajas' [or] 'trooper rajas'-the people described by the shocked Muhammad Faiz Baksh as the new Nawab's courtiers:

'Naked rustics, whose fathers and brothers were with their own hands guiding the plow . . . , rode about as Asaf ud-daula's orderlies.'" In other words, the Rajputs of Awadh, who along with brahmans constituted the main beneficiaries of what historian Richard Barnett characterizes as "Asaf's permissive program of social mobility," were not willing to let that mobility reach beyond certain arbitrary sociocultural boundaries.

Notwithstanding a lack of success at the nawabi court, however, Kurmis still managed to craft for themselves a sophisticated identity. Indeed, Buchanan's description indicates that some wealthy Kurmis in the early nineteenth century were on the verge of rejecting entirely the physical labor inherent in a peasant-cultivator existence:

> The families most nearly connected with the chiefs of Parraona, and some others, who were Chaudhuris [chiefs] of Pergunahs [precincts], are reckoned Ashraf [high class], and scorn the plow. While a great many of [them] have become ashamed of the term Kurmi, and reject all additions to the names above mentioned, . . . many of them are not ashamed of this name....The families reckoned Ashraf, perhaps 110 houses, can read and write [and] unless exceedingly poor, will not hire themselves as plowmen, nor on any account act as domestics.

Later data, from early twentieth-century village note surveys in Patna District, suggest that Kurmis in Bihar possessed an Ayodhya-centered consciousness as well. According to this detailed survey, Awadhia (a Persianized version of Ayodhya) Kurmis were the dominant community in a large tract of villages in the Barh precinct of northeast Patna District; as an example, in one village the surveying officer noted that "there are 9 families / 60 people of Awadhia Kurmis who wear the sacred thread since a long time." Likewise, according to officials northwest of Patna in Saran District, among Kurmis "Ayodhias were particularly singled out as the 'substantial farmers and . . . the most influential sub-caste.'"

Similar claims to status prevailed among many Muslim peasants in Bihar, who appropriated the title Shekh, implying highly coveted Arab origins. Buchanan remarked that "even though every low fellow assumes this title, . . . he is [nevertheless] not admitted to any rank." Purnea District, in the northeasternmost section of the Gangetic core, possessed the greatest concentration of Shekhs claiming "descent from the gentry of Arabia." Buchanan insisted, however, that "a few alone can boast of this distinction, and the greater part are not to be distinguished from the Hindu peasantry of the vicinity. These Sheykhs are in general cultivators, and seem much fonder of the plough than of any other profession."

Shekhs were more evenly spread throughout the Gangetic districts to the west of Bihar, and here similar doubts were raised by colonial observers as to their exact history. Of particular note were concerns not unlike Buchanan's raised in the late 1860s by Henry Miers Elliot. Elliot divided Muslims into two large categories, viz., the nobility descended from "foreign invaders" and the commoners who descended from or were themselves Hindu converts, whom he referred to as "Mahommedans."

The nobility comprised four ethnic groups, "Sayyid, Mughal, Pathan, and Shaikh"; but for Elliot, the last of these terms represented a conceptual, classificatory stumbling block: "Any ordinary Musulman who belongs to none of the three above-named classes [Sayyid, Mughal, and Pathan], is called Shaikh. A vast number of the converts from Hinduism give themselves this title, which from being so promiscuously used has long ceased to have any special meaning or value as a title of honour." In a later, more detailed consideration of the subject, Elliot confessed an inability to pinpoint the "true" identity of Shekhs, observing that while many were descended from low-caste Hindu converts, many others could be regarded as "the lowest class of the descendants of the invaders." Like Buchanan, Elliot was forced to base his conclusions on information provided by informants and on his own first-hand observations of the apparent racial stock of a given community.

Hence Elliot observed that "[the Shekh] is often of Affghan descent, though his forefathers were not of sufficient social standing to acquire the title of Khan. There is also much Persian, Bokhariot, and Turki blood in his veins. Judging from the appearance of this class on the whole, one would say that the non-Aryan element preponderated considerably."

Claims of this sort, grounded in the racial assumptions of the nineteenth century, were resorted to as a way of resolving the inevitable ambiguities that plagued colonial classification. In this case, those ambiguities indicate that a significant number of Muslim peasants sought to achieve a modicum of self-respect through the articulation of a noble past, expressed here as an identity with the Arab crucible of Islam, regardless of whether that identity was called into question by colonial observers. This process, boiled down to its essentials, is analogous to the changing identities among Kurmi, Yadav, and Kushvaha peasants, aspirations that begin to crystallize into full-fledged movements by the 1890s.

The divergent claims to status in the nineteenth century (and earlier) illustrate the point that for non-Muslims, while varna was generally accepted as the basis for identity, on the whole little agreement prevailed with respect to the place of the individual and the jati within a varna hierarchy. Srinivas, describing social relations in the mid-twentieth century, regarded such a "lack of clarity in the hierarchy" as "one of the most striking features of the caste system," adding that "it is this ambiguity which makes it possible for a caste to rise in the hierarchy." Such ambiguity only becomes a striking feature, however, when observers expect to see the opposite, that is, a complete congruity between theory (varna) and practice (jati). Such expectations were increasingly palpable in the late nineteenth and early twentieth centuries, when India became for nascent (imperial) anthropology a "laboratory of mankind," wherein scientific methods of observation (anthropometry among them) were expected to produce clear and straightforward sociological (and racial) patterns that conformed to varna-derived theories. But if the claims to status confronted by Buchanan were at all remarkable, it is because they appear so commonplace, as if they were not at all unexpected given the all-too-obvious dysfunctions between theory and practice.

What is perhaps more significant, given the foregoing, is that a popular concern with status predated the rise of an imperial census apparatus and the colonial obsession with caste. Rather, claims to personal and community dignity appeared to be part of a longer discourse that did not require European political and administrative structures.

This should not be taken to imply that the role of the state generally was of no significance. Status predicated on the presence of an interested state as arbiter was clearly evident in the political culture of Mughal India and Awadhi north India, but only served to give added political credence to attitudes that already possessed substantial popular appeal. The role of the British in the late nineteenth and early twentieth centuries was to further solidify the discourse of caste into a hierarchical "caste of mind," at least for those on the perceiving end. Even as this occurred, however, kshatriya identities were coalescing in peasant society that would, ultimately, threaten to undermine the systemics (if not the principle) of hierarchy by the middle of the twentieth century.

BUILDING A KSHATRIYA PAST

"The world is full of change!" declared Dilipsinha Yadav in 1914, as he exhorted his jati brothers to reform their lives. The early twentieth century was an age of change indeed, as sporadic and localized claims to status coalesced into regional and national peasant organizations in cities and towns across north India. Such organizations met annually to define their community identities and espouse their reformist causes. Leading members would give speeches in festive gatherings, contrasting past glories with their degraded present; the assembled congregation would pass resolutions expressing the urgent need for social, religious, and educational reform; occasionally a peasant jati mahasabha (great association) would mobilize enough funds to build a school to educate its sons (and, sometimes, daughters) or build a press to publish a jati newsletter.

Despite their diverse jati nomenclature, most of these organizations articulated a common historical vision: an ancient past of kshatriya distinction that had long since deteriorated into present-day shudra dishonor. The vision for the future was embodied in appeals for a return to the heady days of the kshatriya past.

A striking feature of these peasant-based social movements in the late nineteenth and early twentieth centuries is the quality of their leadership. A new educated elite, which had begun to penetrate the lower and middle rungs of government service, provided the organizational frame for the status claims among communities formerly identified as servile. This is most evident among Kurmis, the first peasant community to organize a campaign for kshatriya identity. By the 1890s the Kurmi-kshatriya movement was being coordinated on a broad, transregional level. The mantle of leadership in this phase befell the well-connected Ramdin Sinha, a government forester who had gained notoriety by resigning from his official post to protest a provincial circular of 1894 that included Kurmis as a "depressed community" and barred them therefore from recruitment into the police service.

The governor's office was flooded with letters from an outraged Kurmi-kshatriya public and was soon obliged to rescind the allegation in an 1896 communiqué to the police department: "His Honor [the governor] is . . . of the opinion that Kurmis constitute a respectable community which he would be reluctant to exclude from Government service." Ten years later, Devi Prasad Sinha Chaudhari, a Kurmi-kshatriya writer and lecturer, would make a special point of acknowledging in his work the sponsorship of a large number of wealthy Kurmi kshatriyas, including Kashi Ram Varma, a zamindar of Unnao District on the southwest border of Lucknow; Amarnath Sinha, a zamindar and municipal commissioner in the town of Barh, south of Patna; and Ramkishor Sinha, subinspector of police in Tikari thana, Patna District.

Though the official government recognition in 1896 of Kurmi respectability represented a major, and early, victory for the Kurmi-kshatriya movement, especially vis-á-vis its critics, it represented only one component of the complex history of kshatriya identity. The close ties between the new kshatriyas and the colonial government were not restricted to the Kurmis, nor was the battle for respectability fought solely with government petitions and interdepartmental circulars. The peasant communities that would begin to articulate formal kshatriya identities in the early twentieth century had also developed through the nineteenth century distinct ties with the local apparatus of empire. Gopas, Goalas, and Ahirs, who would by the early 1900s begin referring to themselves as Yadav kshatriyas, had long sought and attained (after 1898) recruitment as soldiers in the British Indian Army, particularly in the western Gangetic Plain. Koiris and Kachhis, who would identify themselves as Kushvaha kshatriyas after about 1910, had long been the preferred cultivators of government poppy (and consequently the recipient of many interest-free government loans) for the production of crude opium in the Patna and Banaras regions through the nineteenth century.

Kurmis, whose local conferences in the 1870s and 1880s coalesced into a pan-Gangetic phenomenon in the 1890s, expressed kshatriya status in terms of Vaishnava mythology. At an 1895 meeting in Lucknow, for example, one Ganesh Swami Sadhu traced the genealogical descent of Kurmis from his study of the Skanda Purana and argued that the terms Kurmi, Kunbi, and Kanbi all derived from the name Kurm, the tortoise incarnation of Vishnu who supported the earth while the gods churned the ocean of milk for the nectar of immortality.

Unlike Yadav and Kushvaha kshatriya reformers, the Kurmi reformers in the early twentieth century did not specify a single genealogical line but rather many lineages through which Kurmi kshatriyas could have descended. Thus Devi Prasad Sinha Chaudhari, an early Kurmi publicist of Lucknow, listed in 1907 over sixty kshatriya lineages denoting Gangetic and Maharashtran lineages "in which Kurmis are found." Chaudhari based much of his discussion of what he termed the "famous kshatriya branches" almost entirely on "Kitts' Compendium of Hindu Castes and Tribes and other English books."

Advocates of Kurmi-kshatriya identity broadened their social base to include influential agricultural communities throughout India, most notably Kunbis, Kulambis, and Marathas of Maharashtra; Patidars and Patels of Gujarat; and even

Naidus, Reddis, and Okkalingas of South India. Chaudhari maintained in his 1907 tract that most Kurmis descended from Ramchandra's two sons, Kush and Lav. He added, however, that some Kurmis were descended from Krishna and other notable chiefs involved in the epic Mahabharata wars. Given the relatively early datc (1907) of Chaudhari's booklet and the emergence as early as the 1870s of diverse Kurmi organizations, it is likely that Kurmis were simply amassing the maximum number of possible routes to kshatriya status. In later years, Koiris, Kachhis, and Muraos (as Kushvaha kshatriyas) would assert genealogical links with Ramchandra via his son Kush, while Goalas, Ahirs, and Gopas (as Yadav kshatriyas) would likewise affirm a descent from Krishna.

As with Kurmis and the early expression of an Awadhia/ Ayodhya consciousness, the Goala association with Krishna and his Braj homeland was evident long before the formal articulation of a Yadav-kshatriya movement in the early twentieth century. By the 1910s, however, the diffuse assertions of Krishna kinship had coalesced into a concerted call for kshatriya status based on a claim of descent in the ancient lineage of Raja Yadu (hence Yadav), of which Krishna was the most famous progenitor. As with Kurmis, the newly delimited Yadav-kshatriya community expanded its geographical horizons to incorporate not only Goalas of Bihar and eastern Uttar Pradesh, but Ahirs, Gops, Gopals, and Sadgops-closely related and/or synonomous jati communities throughout the Gangetic north that combined cultivation with the herding of cattle and dairy farming.

By the 1930s, Yadav-kshatriya historians held that "Yadavs [were] the ancient citizens of the land of the Aryans [and] have their origins in the main Chandravamsh [lunar line] branch of kshatriyas, . . . and as the Suryavamsh [solar line] is known for its original ancestor Ramchandra, the Yadu line is famous for its original progenitor Lord Krishna." In the reconstructed history of the Yadav kshatriyas, the devastation of the Mahabharata wars signaled the onset of jati decline, Yadav unity began to give way to factionalism, and drinking and gambling corrupted once-noble jati morals. The standard Yadav-kshatriya account concluded with the final stages of cultural decline, marked by mass conversions to Buddhism and the requisite repudiation of the sacred thread.

The Kurmi and Yadav-kshatriya movements of the twentieth century both possessed distinct early nineteenth-century antecedents in the form of a geocultural association with historical manifestations of Vishnu-Ramchandra and Ayodhya in the case of Kurmis, Krishna and Mathura-Vrindaban in the case of Yadavs.

By contrast, the nineteenth-century antecedents of the Kushvaha-kshatriya movement reveal distinct cosmological associations with Shiva and his divine consort, Parvati. Kushvaha-kshatriya identity was espoused by agricultural communities well known throughout the Gangetic north for an expertise in small-scale vegetable and (to an increasingly limited extent after the turn of the twentieth century) poppy cultivation. Prominent among them were Kachhi and Murao agriculturalists of central Uttar Pradesh, Kachhvahas of western Uttar Pradesh, and Koiris of Bihar and eastern Uttar Pradesh.

Made up of such skilled agriculturalists, these communities had long since come to the attention of colonial administrators and ethnologists. Both W. W. Hunter in the 1870s and H. H. Risley in the 1890s recorded the legend that Koiris and Kachhis were created by Shiva and Parvati to tend the vegetable (Risley mentions in particular radishes, murai, hence Murao) and flower gardens of Banaras, a mythological reflection of the importance to their identity of both agricultural skill and Shaiva belief. Indeed, Risley characterized the majority of Koiris in Bihar as Shaiva or Shakta (followers of shakti, the female personification of cosmic energy) and observed that "Vaishnavism has hitherto made little progress among them." Buchanan, eighty years earlier, had noted that most Koiris in Bihar followed Dasnami sanyasis, while many in the Gorakhpur region adjacent to Ayodhya as well as in Purnia in the east had already begun to look to Ramanandis for spiritual guidance.

By the early 1920s, the ideology of social reform began to displace the commitment to Shaiva-Shakta origins and replace them with a kshatriya identity based on an historical association with Ramchandra. According to Gangaprasad, a resident of Banaras and an outspoken proponent of reform, Koiris, Kachhis, Muraos, and Kachhvahas were inexorably connected to the roots of Vaishnava history through linear descent from Kush, the son of Ramchandra. Gangaprasad argued therefore that the proper designation of the greater north Indian jati should be Kushvaha kshatriya.

The early twentieth-century reconstruction of the past, here recounted by Gangaprasad, linked the history of the jati with the ill-fated cause of the defense of Hindu India.

The descendants of Kush, the reader was told, eventually found military service in the courtly ranks of Raja Jaichand, whose north Indian armies were subsequently defeated in battle by Sultan Shahabuddin Ghuri at the close of the twelfth century, during the consolidation of Muslim rule based in Delhi. Gangaprasad blamed all the ills of the subsequent eight centuries on Muslim persecution, citing particularly the fear of Muslim atrocities as the sole reason Kushvaha kshatriyas fled to the forests in disarray, discarding their sacred threads, so as not to be recognized as erstwhile defenders of the "Hindu" faith.

The jati history concludes with a rueful account of social degradation, disorganization, and dispersal throughout north India; Kushvaha kshatriyas then became known by the more familiar local designations of Kachhvaha, Kachhi, Murao, and Koiri.

Movements for kshatriya identity were by no means restricted to the major peasant jatis, but included a wide range of less populous communities that often combined "traditional" occupations with agriculture. Examples include Kahars (palanquin bearers and household servants), Tantis (weavers), Sonars (goldsmiths), Malis (flower-gardeners), Tambulis (betel-leaf traders), Kalwars (distillers), and numerous others.

This fact was not lost on Nirgun Sinha "Khali," author of several Yadav kshatriya tracts, who by the end of the 1930s called repeatedly for greater ideological flexibility in allowing these claims on the grounds that an augmented kshatriya population would "bolster the defense of Hinduism." His comments on the plethora and diversity of jati reform movements in the early twentieth century give some indication of the heady transformations that marked this period: "In these changing times jatis that we would have considered shudra twenty or twenty-five years ago are now educating scholars who are proving that their communities are not only vaishya and kshatriya, but even brahman! Only a few jatis today fail to become agitated when called shudra; most become quite stern and angry at the mere mention of the term."

A heightened sensitivity to caste, identity, and the past marked the social and cultural transformations of this period. A popular verse of the time, attributed to one Bharat Bharati and cited in at least two reform pamphlets, urged its audience to reflect,

> *Who were we, what has happened, and where are we going now?*
>
> *Gather round everyone and ponder these questions together.*
>
> *If we fail to appreciate the entirety of our past, we may never realize who we really are.*

Jati reformers of the early twentieth century took this poetic counsel particularly seriously and spent endless hours reconstructing, indeed reinventing, the pasts of their communities. But what they were saying and the ways in which they were saying it are two distinct and equally significant phenomena.

On the surface these publicist-reformers understood, or at least represented, the past in terms of a familiar Vaishnava mythological framework; the myth-history that resulted began with the primeval battle between good and evil that set the groundwork for the cosmological origins of the Hindu world, continued with the epic lineages of Vishnu's avatars, and concluded with the alleged civilizational chaos that accompanied the Muslim invasions and the rise of British power. However, the rhetoric beneath the profusion of mytho-historical detail can tell us a great deal more about the quality of social and cultural change in this period.

RHETORIC AND REFORM

Kshatriya reform depended not simply on a Vaishnava mythological framework, but on the institutionalization of a belief in Vaishnava morality, pervading day-to-day affairs. The repeated references in kshatriya reform literature to Vishnu, Narayan, Rama, Krishna, and related Vaishnava personages (such as Lakshmi, Sita, Radha, Hanuman, etc.), the frequent use of Vaishnava terms in common discourse, and the occasional allusions to the changing institution of Vaishnava monasticism (particularly the Ramanandi sampraday), all reflect this institutionalization process. And from the perspective of the new kshatriyas, the central social imperative of Vaishnava morality was caste reform. An example of this can be seen on the cover of a 1920 pamphlet advocating the kshatriya status of Kahars, where the maxim, "This world faces innumerable challenges, but no one of them is greater than jati reform," is attributed to Ramchandra himself.

The lives of Ramchandra and Krishna were frequently held up by jati reformers as the standard for morally correct attitudes and behavior, even at the risk of criticizing contemporary Vaishnava institutions. A didactic technique often utilized by the jati publications was a mock dialogue between two or more people. One particularly telling "conversation" was contributed to the Kurmi Samachar ("Kurmi Newspaper") by a correspondent in 1895. The piece portrays a discussion between a social critic by the name of Vichar Sinha and one Bhagat-ji, meant to represent mindless obedience to religious custom.

The dialogue begins with Bhagat-ji's enthusiastic description of a lavish wedding he has just had the pleasure of attending. Sinha responds by attacking the "foolish expenditures" and "corrupt practices" seen during marriages, such as the spectacle of fireworks and, especially, dancing girls:

VS: You surely have read in the Ramayan that all the gods, sages, seers, and great men came and attended the grandeur of Raja Ramchandra Maharaja's wedding. Well how could they possibly stomach seeing those prostitutes flaunt themselves and hearing those filthy songs they sing at our weddings today?

Bh: I suppose you're right. But nowadays people even arrange for dancing girls in the temples. In fact, they even perform on the birthday celebrations of Krishna and Ramchandra. Nobody goes if there aren't any dancers.

VS: Exactly. By constantly allowing these dancers to perform we have allowed our judgment to become perverted, and now we can't seem to enjoy worshipping God without them. Oh, what a state our country is in!

This portrayal of the corruption of temple worship, whether real or imagined, was gauged to shock the Kurmi kshatriya readership into promoting prudent expenditures during family ceremonies such as weddings; the financial savings that would thus accrue could then be directed toward the betterment of the jati as a whole.

The editor of the Kurmi Samachar, Babu Bhagvandin, may have been troubled by the risqué content of the criticism and prefaced the dialogue with the cautionary note that "the editor chooses to make no comment here." Nevertheless, the puritanical Vaishnava tenor of the piece reflects the willingness of kshatriya reformers to address religious issues directly, even to the extent of caricaturing contemporary religion itself as little more than mindless custom.

Also typical of kshatriya reform were frequent textual allusions to Vaishnava festivals and Ram and Krishna bhakti. For example, Nauvat Ray, a proponent of Kahar status in western Uttar Pradesh, noted the significance of the publication day of his 1920 jati-reform booklet with the declaration, "Today is the great day of vijay dashmi-this is our special festival, the auspicious day that commemorates the victory of the stately and revered Bhagvan Ramchandra-ji.

It was on this day that he killed Ravana, the very embodiment of evil, and hoisted the banner of victory." Vijay dashmi, literally "victory on the tenth," also refers to the tenth day of the moonlit half of the lunar month of Ashwin when, during the annual performance of the Ram Lila, or the "play of Ram," Ramchandra destroys the evil king Ravana in a dramatically reenacted battle. Nauvat Ray and his publisher,

Fakirchand, incorporated the historic meaning of Ramchandra's epic battle against the forces of evil directly into the struggle for kshatriya status. In a supplicatory aside, the publisher also noted the auspicious date and prayed to Ramchandra to support their cause, identifying the opponents of the Kahar movement for kshatriya status with the evil Ravana:

> Then [when Ramchandra defeated Ravana] it was tretayug, now it is kaliyug. Since then our condition has deteriorated. At that time you killed the evil Ravana, freed the world from sin, restored the dignity of dharma, and spread contentment and tranquility. Why will you not come back now, when dharma has all but disappeared from the world and we are oppressed by Ravana in the form of our detractors? Bhagvan! Please come, slay the demon, and restore completely the dignity of dharma and hoist the banner of victory. Unite through love brahman, kshatriya, vaishya, and shudra, fulfill your own visions, and everyone will extol you and abide by your directives.

The commitment of Kahars to Ram was equally powerful in south Bihar. In 1906, the Kahars of Gaya-who styled themselves Ramani Kahars-organized a Ramani Dharma Pracharani Sabha (Association for the Spread of Ramani Dharma) and, under its auspices, produced a short pamphlet of rules, regulations, and fines to counter the "many crude practices that had, over time, corrupted the jati."

More interesting than the elaborate punishments prescribed for offenders of jati dignity are the names printed on the register of officers and members of the jati sabha itself. Listed as vice-chairman of the organization was one Ram Das, "a noted resident of the neighborhood of Geval Bigha in Gaya."

Others included a bookseller named Ram Kishan Das who was listed as the consultant for the association, and Chhote Ram Das, both of the same neighborhood. As noted in chapter 2, "das" means "servant" or "slave" and was commonly assumed as a suffix by many Ramanandi sadhus (especially prior to 1918) to signal their symbolic relationship to Ramchandra; here it would appear that Kahars had begun adopting the suffix for their own purposes, regardless of any connection to the sampraday. Even more remarkable were the names of many of the remaining members. The associate chairman, his assistant, and fully forty-nine of the fifty-eight general and associate members possessed the surname Ram.

The institutionalization of Vaishnava language was not restricted to personal nomenclature, however. The author of a 1924 publication, again from Gaya, which advocated the Kanyakubja-kshatriya status of Sonars (goldsmiths), pointed out that the universal importance of Vaishnava belief could even be seen by the frequent colloquial use of the names of Vishnu's avatars in popular language: "Let us now turn to the subject of popular language. Even the most boorish peasants, who don't know anything, immediately cry out 'Ram Ram' upon meeting one another.

The Thakurs say 'Jay Radho-ji ki' [victory to Radha]. When this spread into popular usage among the four varnas is not in fact known....If someone stumbles while walking along, "aré Ram" [oh Ram] immediately escapes from his lips." Such terms were also brought to bear in peasant politics, most notably during a tense three-year period of peasant activism in Awadh beginning in 1919.

Baba Ramchandra, who both espoused Kurmi reform and came to lead the peasant outcry against landlord tyranny, introduced the language of Vaishnava devotion in Awadh peasant politics to advance the notion of a just political economy crafted around the ideal of Ramchandra's Ayodhya. According to historian Gyanendra Pandey, Baba Ramchandra recalled some years later that he actively promoted the use of the egalitarian greeting, Sitaram, in the place of the hierarchical salaam, an act that was soon to earn him the ire of "many of the praiseworthy and respectable folk of the upper castes."

Similarly, Vaishnava symbols and vocabulary adorned the textual frame of jati reform literature, including such literary constructions as the names of publishing houses, illustrations, dedications, and prefatory benedictions. A typical example was a collection of exhortational songs and prayers on the subject of social reform among Goalas. This short tract, entitled Jatiya Sandesh (Jati Message), was published by one Swami Nathu

Bhagat Yadav and printed by the Haribhakt Narayan Raja Press in Darbhanga, North Bihar.

The facts that the publisher was himself a Yadav and a religious figure (as reflected in the title "Swami") and that the name of the press was composed of a phrase signifying devotion to Vishnu (Haribhakt Narayan) only serve to underline the complementarity of peasant-kshatriya reform and Vaishnava rhetoric. Inscribed on the cover page is the initiatory mantra or chant for worshipping the conjoined image of Radha-Krishna (Shri Radhokrishnabhyanamah) followed on the inside cover by a picture of the divine couple. Likewise, a compendium of social rules for Yadav kshatriyas was published in 1928 from the Gokul Press, Gokul being the remembered home of Krishna, Radha, and the cowherds around Vrindaban and Mathura in western Uttar Pradesh. And, as a final example, separate editions of a prominent historical tract on Yadav-kshatriya history were published in Etawah and Lucknow from the Krishna Press.

The reformist kshatriya dedication to a Vaishnava ethic even extended, in some cases, to pugnacious attacks against competing religious traditions. Jamuna Prashad Yadav, in a 1927 pamphlet published in Jhansi and directed at caste members in his native Chhattisgarhi region as well as "for the benefit of the entire Ahir jati," condemned what he termed the "lewd, sex-ridden" rituals and practices of "vam margis" (a pejorative term for practitioners of a particular kind of Shaiva-Shakta tantra) and exhorted Yadavs to follow the correct worship of the Vaishnavi devi (goddess). Although Chattisgarh in what is now Madhya Pradesh is some distance removed from the Gangetic core, J. Yadav's remarks mirrored in tone as well as content a Ramanandi polemic directed against the so-called vam-margis published in Prayag (Allahabad) ten years later and widely available in north Bihar.

In this publication, entitled Devivali Pakhand (The Heresy of Sacrifice to the Goddess), Janki Ballabh Das launched a thoroughgoing invective against Shaiva-Shakta tantra, with particular criticism of the worshipers of the goddess Durga (the main proponents of which he alleged were Maithil brahmans, that is, belonging to the dominant land-controlling jati of North Bihar) for their animal sacrifices, but shifted quickly to accusations of everything from pedophilia, ritual sex, and incest to the consumption of beef, alcohol, and far more reprehensible substances, all allegedly performed during tantric rituals.

However, the most explicit indication of the Vaishnava rhetoric of social reform in the early twentieth century was the affirmation by kshatriya ideologues of the upright morality of their jati constituents. This was best expressed by Gangaprasad, the Banaras-based proponent of Kushvaha-kshatriya identity, who described his jati brothers as "followers of the Vaishnava path" and noted that "devotees made certain their children received proper spiritual initiation and education."

Gangaprasad added that all Kushvahas "receive the mantra from their family gurus and sing those verses every morning and evening" and that "in the month of Kartik or Shravan they worship Mahabir [Hanuman, the embodiment of true devotion to Ram and Sita], wear the sacred thread, and offer bread and sweets."

Similarly, Baijnath Prasad Yadav's compendium of rules for Goalas not only prescribed upright decorum and proper methods of celebrating a variety of household and public festivals, but also condemned the various "evil" attitudes and practices of caste members such as illiteracy, child marriage, drinking, gambling, and wasteful expenditures.

When reformers were not citing the extensive Vaishnava credentials of their jati members, they were marshaling a wide array of sectarian institutional sanction to back their claims of kshatriya status. In Maharashtra and Gujarat, associated Kunbis and Kanbis solicited and received this certification from the head abbot of the Dasnami order in Nasik, northeast of Bombay, and from his Ramanuji counterpart in Kanchi, southwest of Madras. Kurmis of the Gangetic north, however, sought the Vaishnava backing of Radhacharan Goswami of Vrindaban, who presided over a debate of Banaras scholars on the subject of Kurmi status that took place under the auspices of the Kurmi association of Bharehta village south of Banaras in 1907.

In defense of the Kurmi claim to kshatriya status, Radhacharan Goswami cited a range of positive attributes, including the fact that "this jati has built many temples in which brahmans have performed the image consecrations and wherein all people pay respectful homage to God by taking the water with which the feet of the image has been washed." Caste-based temple construction occurred most prominently in the major Vaishnava pilgrimage centers. In Ayodhya, for instance, a multitude of "caste temples" erected in this century would buttress the kshatriya status claims of jati organizations; these include temples built by Kurmis, Yadavs, Kahars, Kayasths, Barhais, Malis, Murais (Kushvahas), Sonars, and many others.

KSHATRIYA REFORM AND RAMANANDIS

Kshatriya reform in the early twentieth century was built on a Vaishnava mythological foundation, espoused a strict Vaishnava morality, employed a rich Vaishnava symbolic vocabulary, and even contributed materially to the success of Vaishnava pilgrimage centers. Taken as a whole, then, the history of kshatriya reform in the late nineteenth and early twentieth centuries reflects the institutionalization of Vaishnava belief as a generally agreed-upon Hindu framework for social change, regardless of one's specific sectarian commitments.

In this sense, the kshatriya reform campaigns as a whole can be seen as ideological heir to the Vaishnava reform mentalities of the nineteenth and twentieth centuries, particularly as manifest in Ramanandi liberalism with respect to caste. But while the Ramanandi sampraday has long evinced a marked disdain for questions of status, particularly in the twentieth century, the whole point of kshatriya reform campaigns was the enhancement of status. This major ideological difference, explains the unevenness of Ramanandi participation in the forefront of kshatriya reform campaigns.

However, the Ramanandi sampraday was not ideologically monolithic, and many Ramanandis harbored views on caste wholly divergent from what became the dominant position in the sampraday in the twentieth century. More precisely, those sadhus who chose not to accept what I have termed the "radical" Ramanandi guru parampara after 1921 and who consequently were labeled Ramanuji, not only took a conservative approach to the question of Ramanand's monastic antecedents by insisting on the retention of Ramanuja in their guru parampara, but insisted on the maintenance of caste boundaries in monastic life. Based on their willingness to admit the relevance of varna in religious affairs, it would not have been ideologically inconsistent for a "Ramanuji Ramanandi" to promote the pursuit of status implicit in movements for kshatriya reform.

In this section we will examine two such individuals, kshatriya ideologues with Ramanuji links to the Ramanandi sampraday, to throw light on how the travails of being Vaishnava informed the politics of becoming kshatriya, and vice versa.

The first of the two, Raghunandan Prasad Sinha Varmma, a proponent of kshatriya status for Sonars (goldsmiths), published a booklet from Gaya in south Bihar in 1924, three years after the Ujjain decision, which declared that Ramanuja was not included in the guru parampara of Ramanand. Even though his name suggests a nonascetic status, Varmma's lay partisanship in the parampara dispute is made immediately clear in his work: both above the title on the cover page and prior to the introduction are dedications to Ramanujacharya.

In addition, he notes that he received the help of one Babu Aditya Narayan Sinha (of Chaudharani Tola, Village and Post Office Mokama, District Patna), a devotee of Swami Ramprapann Ramanujadas.

Ramprapann Ramanujadas, it may be recalled, represented the south Indian Shri Vaishnava side in the debate against Bhagavadacharya at the Ujjain kumbh in 1921. Varmma also assured the reader that in addition to shedding light on the "ancient pedigree of the Sonar jati," he would "elaborate some of the mysteries of Shri Vaishnava dharma."

After devoting the next forty-six and a half pages to the "Kanyakubja-kshatriya" identity of Sonars, Varmma turned to "the importance of Shri Vaishnava dharma," prefacing his remarks with the core Ramanuji tenet that "the swami of Shri

Vaishnava dharma is Vishnu and the acharya is Shri Lakshmiji." This was certain to enrage any radical Ramanandis who happened to read the tract, inasmuch as the 1918-1921 dispute was sparked by the unwillingness of Ramanujis to worship the images of Ram and Sita.

Varmma was only warming to his Ramanuji task, however; he next made reference to the universal acceptance of Shri Vaishnava symbols by "other sampraday": "Regardless of membership in any particular sampraday, the obligation of any auspicious ceremony, such as marriage or the birth of a child, requires the correct application of tilak [a marking of vermilion or sandal] powder in a vertical fashion [on the forehead]. This is inevitably called the marking of Shri Vishnu. When followers of other sampraday follow such obligations they take that very name, they wear his very sign."

Varmma chose not to mention Ramanandis here by name; however, since Ramanandis and Ramanujis employ nearly identical tilak markings, it is clear that this was a calculated affront and that radical Ramanandis were the main target. His objective was to position those loyal to the memory of Ramanuja as "high" Vaishnavas, within which exist the various-and by implication hierarchically inferior-sectarian divisions. To this end, Varmma hypothesized that since "so many other sampraday rely on our literature (Gita, Ramayan, Bhagvat, etc.) and we read or take no interest in the literature of any other sampraday, we must be the most superior."

He asserted, in addition, that no other sadhus were so pure, a reference no doubt to the "acharya" status long maintained by Ramanujis and to the commensal restrictions that were alleged to have been the cause of Ramanand's expulsion from the fraternity of Raghavanand's disciples in the fourteenth century.

Far more detailed mention was made of Ramanandi-Ramanuji divisiveness by Swami Dharnidharacharya, the author of a 1930 history of Bihar-based Kurmis who styled themselves "Awadhvamshiya" (of the lineage of Awadh) kshatriyas. Prior to addressing the subject of kshatriya identity in his booklet, Dharnidharacharya focused on "sampraday matters," citing his guru-given name as Dharnidhar Ramanujadas, his guru's place as the Totadri Math (the center of south Indian Vaishnavism), and finally his guru-parampara, which includes Ramanuja but makes no mention whatsoever of Ramanand.

The actual text begins with supplications to Ramchandra and Ramanuja, followed by a few words on the author's name and village; Dharnidharacharya then takes up a detailed disquisition on the history and religious dimensions of the Awadhia kshatriyas. Included here are such topics as the origin of kshatriyas; the genesis of the kurmm vamsh; the spread of the kshatriyas from Ayodhya to modern Bihar and eastern Uttar Pradesh; the tale of Ramchandra's birth and the birth of his two sons, Lav and Kush; the correct ritual observations for pregnancy, birth, menstruation, eating, sacred thread investiture, marriage, and death; and the traditional roles of each of the four varna.

The author then returns to matters of personal and sampraday concern, the narrative of which I shall recount here in some detail. Dharnidharacharya was born in 1891 to an Awadh-kshatriya family of Patipur village, not far from the town of Nandalalabad in Patna District, south Bihar. He reveals little of his youth, aside from the fact that his given name was Dhanraj Sinha Varmma and that he was married at the age of fourteen. Soon thereafter and against the wishes of his parents, Dhanraj (the young Dharnidharacharya) left home.

Crossing the Ganga, which forms the northern border of Patna District, he wandered northward for about one hundred miles and eventually found himself in a village near the town of Sitamarhi in north Bihar; there he remained for six months, in a small establishment of a local naga jatadhari (a sadhu who wears long, matted hair).

Finally, afraid that his parents would be able to locate him and force him to return home, Dhanraj set off for Nepal with a group of wandering monks and from there undertook a lengthy pilgrimage route that led him all over north India. He visited such sites as Mukti Narayan, Damodar Kund, Tansen Pahar, Gangasagar, Puri, Prayag, Chitrakut, and finally ended up in

Ayodhya, by then well known as one of the most important pilgrimage centers in the Gangetic region. At this point in his life, probably around 1910, Dhanraj decided to remain in Ayodhya and began the study of nyaya (logic, one of the six traditional schools of Indian philosophy) and related subjects under the tutelage of Saryudas, a noted Ramanandi scholar.

Dhanraj passed the next several years furthering his studies under various teachers connected to the rasik strain of Vaishnava bhakti, when in 1918 the controversy over Ramanuja and the Ramanandi parampara erupted in Ayodhya and, subsequently, throughout north India. The ensuing debates were particularly all-consuming in Ayodhya, and few if any there remained aloof from the turmoil. The author was certainly no exception: the ties Dhanraj formed with individuals in the south Indian Vaishnava tradition at this time ensured that he would be caught in the throes of sampraday discord. Dhanraj eventually supported the Ramanuji view and even went so far as to become the disciple of a major Shri Vaishnava figure from south India visiting Ayodhya at the time; indeed, it was during his initiation that he even was given the name Dharnidhar Ramanujadas, or "Dharnidhar, slave of Ramanuja."

If Dhanraj had achieved by this time a fraction of the scholarly respect he was to garner in the 1930s, the new title of this young Vaishnava intellectual-not to mention his recent initiation with a south Indian guru-was sure to have raised the ire of more than a few Ramanandis. Dharnidhar itself means "mountain"; as a result of the author's growing prominence in the 1930s, he became regarded generally throughout Bihar and eastern Uttar Pradesh as Swami Dharnidharacharya.

By the 1920s prevailing opinion in Ayodhya had tipped in favor of the radical Ramanandi view, and the memory of Ramanuja was being purged (at least officially) from sampraday records. Naturally, Dharnidharacharya was deeply disturbed by this development, and his recollections of Ayodhya in this period are full of bitterness. But it is his response to the radical position that is of particular interest, because the evidence he marshaled to prove that Ramanuja, and not Ramanand, was the founder of the Shri Vaishnava sampraday consisted primarily of prophetic Sanskrit hymns composed by ancient rishis (seers) well before the advent of either Ramanand or Ramanuja.

These texts shared in common the prediction that the four main divisions of Vaishnava sampraday, or chatuh-sampraday, would be founded by Vishnuswami, Madhvacharya, Ramanujacharya, and Nimbarkacharya. Dharnidharacharya warned that "anyone who opposes such proof would in the end come to ruin."

In response to the Ramanandi claim that the literature of the Ramanujis offended Ramchandra, he asserted, on the authority of the Brihadbrahm Samhita (part 2, section 7, verses 1-71), that "it is well known that Shri Ramanuja Swami is the originator of the Ramtarak mantra [an invocation to Ram as savior]." Dharnidharacharya urged Ramanandis to "renounce obstinate factionalism....If not, the loss will be on their own heads, since it is well known that 'the mantras of the man who is without a sampraday will bear no fruit.'"

Notwithstanding these remonstrations, however, there was little Dharnidharacharya could do to check the gradual rise to prominence of radical Ramanandis in Ayodhya. In fact, he was so dismayed by the turn of events that at some point in the early 1920s he contemplated leaving Ayodhya altogether and undertook another lengthy pilgrimage to put the controversy behind him.

Again his travels took him all over the northern half of the subcontinent, but also to Totadri and Venkatesh, the former his guru's place and both important Ramanuji sites in the southern peninsula. Nevertheless, Dharnidharacharya found himself yearning for Ayodhya, which had become a home to him notwithstanding the many reminders of the quarrel that had disrupted his life, and he returned there in 1924. Eventually, with the assistance of a friend, Dharnidharacharya took up residence at the Uttar Totadri Math (the northern branch of the south Indian Totadri math) in Ayodhya, an institution clearly in sympathy with the Ramanuji position. Ensconced in the idyllic setting of the monastery's Venkatesh temple bordering on Vibhishan pond, and thereby insulated from the haughtiness of predominantly Ramanandi Ayodhya, the author gained a reputation of high scholarly ability and began to accept students, to whom he devoted his full attention.

It was in all likelihood the reputation as an energetic young Vaishnava intellectual of Ayodhya that attracted to Dharnidharacharya the attention of kshatriya ideologues in the late 1920s, and by 1930 he had published his jati study. The boy who had run away at the age of fourteen or fifteen thus found himself returning home, both geographically and genealogically, in his thirties and forties. Dharnidharacharya's role as a monk addressing issues of caste status for individuals outside the world of sampraday was an appropriate one and, indeed, was endorsed and even emulated by a number of Dharnidharacharya's peers throughout the Gangetic region. Three individuals in particular who appear in the prefatory pages of Dharnidharacharya's Shri Awadhvamshiya Kshatriya Martandah merit a brief mention here: Ramtahaldas, Hanuman Sharan, and Videhanandani Sharan.

The first, Ramtahaldas, in a letter expressing his deep appreciation for the work that Dharnidharacharya had done in advancing the cause of the Awadhvamshiya kshatriyas, described himself as a "Shri Vaishnava pandit" of Daraganj near Prayag.

The others, Hanuman Sharan and Videhanandani Sharan, were described in an adjoining felicitation as the successive heads of the Rajapur Thakurbari (abode of god) in Patna and praised for their work on behalf of both Vaishnava belief and the Awadhvamshiya kshatriya sabha; the former, Hanuman Sharan, was in all likelihood born an Awadhvamshiya kshatriya. It is also worth noting that Hanuman Sharan claimed guru-parampara descent from Swami Balanandacharya, the eighteenth-century Ramanandi of Jaipur who is credited with organizing the Vaishnava naga armies. This conforms, incidentally, with the suggestion that soldier monasticism in the eighteenth century drew on a nonelite, shudra base; in the early twentieth century, Awadhvamshiya kshatriyas would refute the imputation of shudra-ness and, indeed, would use the Rajapur Thakurbari in Patna (along with the Uttar Totadri

Math in Ayodhya) as informal distribution centers for Awadhvamshiya-kshatriya propaganda.

Besides providing a recollection of the Ramanandi crisis of memory and ensuing Ramanandi-Ramanuji animosities that bears striking, if predictable, contrasts to that given by the radical Bhagavadacharya (recounted in the previous chapter), Swami Dharnidharacharya's reminiscences afford a sense of the networks that allowed him and others of the north Indian Ramanuji mold to remain active in Gangetic Vaishnava culture. Perhaps more importantly, the experience of Swami Dharnidharacharya leads to broader speculation regarding the intersections of sampraday and caste in the Gangetic region. According to Dharnidharacharya, an extensive Ramanuji network spanned the religious topography of Bihar and Uttar Pradesh, a network that eventually supported and sharpened the identity of reformist kshatriyas claiming Awadh as a place of origin.

Indeed, a similar network seemed to be in place as well to nurture a Kanyakubja-kshatriya identity for Sonars, and it is likely that there were other examples of Ramanuji sadhus involved in kshatriya reform, because those Vaishnava monks who became Ramanuji by force of circumstance after 1921 were by definition more attuned in general to the ideological demands of varna commensality. While all Ramanujis were not invariably enmeshed in the kshatriya campaigns of the early twentieth century, Ramanujis were more likely to respond positively to the concerns being raised by the widespread kshatriya movements of peasants and artisans long labeled shudra by the social elite. Others less concerned about jati, varna, and personal purity-whatever their imputed status-and more interested in developing an aggressive, egalitarian social vision within the dominant monastic order of Gangetic India (the Ramanandi sampraday) could be expected to have sided with Bhagavadacharya and the radical wing. These latter, of course, would not be and were not precluded from advocating the cause of jati reform in the late nineteenth and early twentieth centuries, but they would have been less likely to do so given their disdain for issues of status in general.

While I have argued that the crisis of tradition that divided the Ramanandi sampraday after 1918 can only be understood in terms of caste in colonial India, it would be difficult to make a related argument, namely, that kshatriya reform in the early twentieth century can only be understood in terms of caste attitudes expressed in the Ramanandi sampraday. However, it is clear from the foregoing that attitudes toward caste expressed in north Indian Vaishnava monastic circles were not restricted to the realm of sampraday but were applied to the "outside" world. Hence, not only was an institutionalized Vaishnava discourse inherent in the dialogue of social change, certain Vaishnava monks were willing and able to act as intellectuals on behalf of agricultural and artisan communities. Indeed, kshatriya identity seemed at least as important to Dharnidharacharya and his associates as their status as Ramanuji Vaishnavas.

The eventual dominance of radical Ramanandis in Ayodhya may also help to explain the overt dedication of Ramanujis to the cause of kshatriya campaigns. Men like Dharnidharacharya probably saw the growing kshatriya movement as an outlet for political and intellectual expression, which for them had been quashed to a large extent within the sampraday by the group of young Ramanandi radicals spearheading the "Gangeticization" of Vaishnava tradition. Kshatriya reform gave Dharnidharacharya and other Gangetic Ramanujis the opportunity to organize, to espouse a group identity, and perhaps most significantly, to express their own opinions regarding the crisis in the sampraday itself through the forum of local jati publications.

Before concluding this section, it is important to note that the involvement of Vaishnava monks in kshatriya reform was not restricted to the Ramanandi sampraday. The other mainstream Vaishnava orders in Gangetic north India were oriented primarily toward the worship of Radha and Krishna and included the relatively small Radhaballabhi community and the more populous Gauriya (followers of Chaitanya) and Nimbarki sampraday. These sampraday were concentrated in western Uttar Pradesh, particularly the Mathura-Vrindaban region, and Bengal proper and were only very sparsely represented in the central and eastern Gangetic districts between Lucknow and Patna, what I have referred to generally as the Gangetic core. If kshatriya reformers, particularly those claiming descent from the chandra-vamsh (lunar lineage) of Krishna in western Uttar Pradesh, wished to enlist the intellectual and religious sanction of Vaishnava sadhus, they would have been as likely to turn to these sampraday. However, if kshatriya reformers in the Gangetic core required Vaishnava monastic confirmation of their kshatriya status claims, they would have to seek out sadhus from what was essentially the dominant Vaishnava order there: namely, the Ramanandi sampraday.

Likewise, there is no reason to presume that Ramanandi devotion to Ram and Sita would have restricted their kshatriya reform activity to those movements that sought a genealogical link with Ramchandra's suryavamsh (solar lineage). Though Ram and Sita were central to Ramanandi identity, Radha-Krishna bhakti also figured prominently in Ramanandi worship and literature.

Buchanan noted on several occasions that Ramanandis were willing to instruct lay followers in the worship of any of Vishnu's avatars, most particularly Ram and Krishna. Such devotional flexibility was evident even in Ayodhya itself, where, Buchanan observed, the Ramanandis "do not scruple to deliver the form of prayer, by which Krishna is addressed." The Ramanandi focus on Krishna extended as well to hagiographic and mythological literature; for example, the Bhaktamal, a text of major importance for all Vaishnavas, recounts numerous stories and legends pertaining to saints famous for their vigorous devotion to Ram as well as Krishna and their attendant pantheons.

The main Bhaktamal scholars in the nineteenth and early twentieth centuries, as noted in the previous chapter, were associated with the Ramanandi sampraday, most notably, at the turn of the century, Sitaramsharan Bhagvan Prasad. Indeed, Bhagvan Prasad was also well known for his poetry describing the life of Mirabai, the legendary Rajput princess whose adorations of Krishna superseded her matrimonial obligations. In addition, Ramanandis in Bihar have long considered the Bhagavata Purana, which among other things recounts the life of Krishna, and the Bhagavad Gita, comprising Krishna's discourses to Arjuna on the battlefield, texts of major doctrinal importance.

Hence, chandra-vamshiya kshatriya reformers could partake of the monastic and religious world of Ram without compromising their commitments to a social identity focused on a descent from Krishna and his historical antecedents. The most articulate, numerous, and best-organized kshatriya reformers claiming descent from Krishna in the early twentieth century were Yadavs, and indeed there are indications of strong Yadav involvement in both Ram worship and the Ramanandi order after 1900.

For example, van der Veer lists a number of "caste temples" built in Ayodhya in this century, among which is one founded by Yadavs. Freitag notes that during the annual Ram Lila festival in Banaras in the early twentieth century, Yadavs were prominent among those who served to carry the huge images of Ram and his brother Bharat in the Bharat Milap (reunion with Bharat) procession. And I have cited in the conclusion to the previous chapter a 1935-1936 poem published in a Ramanandi magazine and authored by one Ramavatar Yadav "Shakta" Visharad (or Ramavatar Yadav, learned in Shakta doctrine), which praises Ramanand's efforts on behalf of the downtrodden masses.

RACE, DIGNITY AND LABOR

A compelling theme addressed by much of the kshatriya reform literature through the early twentieth century was the redefinition of agricultural labor in terms of ancient pedigree and personal dignity. The ideas formulated in this literature challenged the brahmanical notion of physical work that girded the notion of a "plowman boundary" separating the shudra and untouchable mass from the varna elite.

The rhetoric employed by the jati reformers bore a relationship to that devised by Swami Dayanand in his attempt to cast a new Arya Samaj (literally, "Aryan society") according to what he saw as the "original" meaning of the ancient Vedic corpus. Dayanand posited a varna system based not on birth but merit that, according to the historian Kenneth Jones, held great attraction for those "frustrated by the conservatism of the Hindu world." However, notwithstanding these and other shared themes (most notably around the idea of an "Aryan" people) between kshatriya reform and Arya Samaji ideology, the relationship between kshatriya reformers and the Arya Samaj was often troubled.

For kshatriya reformers, the arguments for a reconsideration of social differentiation and dignified work were woven together with protohistorical accounts of the influx of an Aryan race into the south Asian subcontinent. As a Kushvaha-kshatriya ideologue put it,

The country we live in is named Aryavarta; it is called Aryavarta because in the beginning the Aryas settled here.... The place of origin of the Aryas is Tibet, and the Aryas that crossed the mountains did not discriminate among themselves. Rather, those who worshipped and sang hymns to god received great respect and were called rishis. There were also those who ruled, handled administrative affairs, and fought wars, and those who practiced agriculture, while those who were stupid did daily work.

They were chosen to serve. Over time the priests were called brahmans, the rulers were called kshatriyas, agriculturalists were called vaishyas, and the stupid who could not learn were given the name shudra. However, they were all sons of the same father, and to facilitate the smooth functioning of Aryan society the names of these four varna-brahman, kshatriya, vaishya, and shudra-were institutionalized.

The articulation of Aryan racial origins would commingle with that of Vaishnava genealogies and would vary only in detail, not in scope. Hence the reconstellated Kurmi-kshatriya identity of the 1920s extended the genealogy back into the Vedic age to include descent from the so-called Indra jati, that is, partisans of the Vedic god Indra.

The Indra jati, it was contended, was one among several semidivine communities who inhabited the Tibetan plateau in the north and fought incessant wars against hideous demons to the west. The conclusion inevitably reached following this representation of the "golden age of Aryavarta" held that originally one's varna was determined by one's abilities, not by one's deeds in a previous life (karma).

This rendering of "Hindu" history and the aggressive interpretation of varna in racial terms were hallmarks of Arya Samaji reform in late nineteenth and early twentieth-century Punjab and western Uttar Pradesh. In fact, one such Kushvaha-kshatriya pamphlet was authored by a teacher of the local Dayanand Anglo-Vedic high school in Banaras. Not surprisingly, that work's overtly Arya Samaji stance in no way contradicted the standard Vaishnava conception of varna and labor outlined in the jati reform literature of the early twentieth century. Significant inroads had been made by Arya Samajis into the Yadav-kshatriya movement as well, especially in western Uttar Pradesh and Delhi, where many villages and towns with large Yadav populations came to have Arya Samaji temples, priests, schools, and publicists.

A close inspection of the Gangetic reform literature reveals, nevertheless, a great ambivalence on the part of most jati reformers regarding the proper role of the Arya Samaj in Indian society in general and in social and religious change in particular. The comments of two jati reform authors reveal the conflicts between what they and others were beginning to define as sanatan dharma, the "eternal religion" to which they avowedly subscribed, and what was increasingly being characterized as the offensive, "non-Hindu" programs of the Arya Samaj. Dilipsinha Yadav, whose writings were influential among Yadav kshatriyas throughout U.P, attacked Arya Samajis as "Vedic believers in name only, who have, for the sake of their own greed and self-aggrandizement, granted initiation to Chamars and Muslims."

While the propagation of Arya Samaji ideas by men like Swami Krishnanandji, a self-described Yadav kshatriya, who toured the Punjab, Uttar Pradesh, and Bihar, certainly must have had a significant impact on jati reform rhetoric, it would be an overstatement to contend that the Arya Samaj was a leading force in kshatriya reform.

Raghunanandan Prasad Sinha Varmma, the Kanyakubja-kshatriya ideologue on behalf of Sonars (cited in the previous section for his views on Vaishnava sampraday), was more explicit in his condemnation of the followers of Dayanand:

> These days Dayanandis, also known as Arya Samajis, are secretly gaining entrance into all jati mahasabhas, are gradually scandalizing the sanatan dharma, and are devoting all their efforts to the subversion of the varna system. The varna system is the very foundation of sanatan dharma. The important point is that these atheists have even worked their way into the Kanyakubja-kshatriya jati society and are very influential; their articles have already been published, the name of one is "Svarnakar Koi Jati ya Varna Nahin Hai [Sonar is not a Jati or Varna]." It is with great sorrow that I must report that . . . our Kanyakubja-kshatriya brothers pay not even the slightest heed to this [threat]. It is impossible to gauge the effect these godless essays will have in the future. We hereby inform our Kanyakubja-kshatriya brothers-whosoever should read such an article or hear such a speech should immediately refute it!

From the tone of these remarks, published in 1924, it is clear that while the Arya Samaj had made significant inroads into the jati reform movement, those inroads were severely resented by what had become, by the early twentieth century, "orthodox" opinion. This, of course, begs the questions of what constituted orthodoxy and how certain elements of Hindu belief came to be considered orthodox. In partial answer, Philip Lutgendorf has recently described the bland, universally acceptable Hinduism that was being promoted as sanatan dharma in north India by such men as the Hindu nationalist Madanmohan Malaviya, the publicist Din Dayal Sharma, and the Ramayana scholar Pandit Jwalaprasad Mishra. Lutgendorf's main emphasis here is on the overriding importance of the immensely popular Ramcharitmanas of Tulsidas to the success of the sanatan dharma agenda, an agenda closely allied to the desire to create an Indian identity built on Hindu ideas.

Tulsidas' Manas thus became the Sanatani scripture par excellence-a devotional work which still preached reverence for cows and Brahmans; offered a veritable catalogue of sacred rivers, pilgrimage sites, and popular rituals; presented a harmonious synthesis of Vaishnavaism and Shaivism; and in the minds of devotees managed at one and the same time to stand for religious egalitarianism, the maintenance of the social status quo, and (later on) even nationalism and swadeshi (the boycott of British products, especially textiles), since it offered an inspiring vision of a powerful and self-sufficient Hindu state.

Sanatan dharma was (and remains) a loose enough amalgam of religious concepts to represent all things to all Hindus, for Lutgendorf an "old-time religion" of sorts, self-conscious, conservative, vague, and, most importantly, exclusivist, by enabling adherents to delimit those who were not "orthodox."

On the question of the acceptability of certain forms of labor, however, kshatriya reformers unambiguously asserted that actual agricultural work was in no way undignified, a conclusion of no small significance given the elite aversion for physical labor-an aversion only reinforced by colonial replications of varna as irrefutable caste hierarchy. Ascriptive caste based on a principle of social hierarchy was attacked in the name of a distinct kind of racial equality, the logic of which dictated that since all Hindus are of the same race (i.e, Aryas), all Hindus are equal. Devi Prasad Sinha Chaudhari asserted in 1907 that "Kurmi kshatriyas practice agriculture as a livelihood and since it is associated with the earth it is therefore a noble vocation." According to the Rgveda, he continued, "in ancient times well-born men took up the plow, cultivated, and were known as Aryas."

Swami Abhayananda Saraswati elaborated on this sentiment twenty years later when he noted that according to the Ramayana, "Maharaja Janak and his queen [i.e., Sita's foster parents] practiced agriculture and protected their subjects" and that therefore farming "cannot be considered an obstacle to being kshatriya." J. Chaudhari of the Anglo-Vedic

High School in Banaras insisted that "there is nothing undignified about plowing a field," and suggested that people who argue otherwise are either exposing their ignorance of the ancient texts or, more likely, "simply do not want to work." He further noted that "in Bihar Rajputs and in some places even Bhumihars plow the fields. Konkani brahmans and farmer brahmans of Mewar also work the plow. Rajputs plow in Rajputana [Rajasthan] and Garhwal as well....So long as these brahmans and kshatriyas don't become shudra by plowing, Koiris will not relent [in their demands for kshatriya status]." At the 1907 debate over the viability of a Kurmi-kshatriya identity, the Vrindaban scholar Radhacharan Goswami even cited the fact that Kurmis were "almost entirely landowners and cultivators, and are quite powerful," as evidence of their kshatriya status.

Similar arguments were constructed for nonagricultural and marginally agricultural communities claiming professional dignity in this period. Raghunandan Prasad Varmma urged his jati brothers not to be at all ashamed of their scientific and technical skills as goldsmiths and pointed to the scientific achievements that made America and Germany great. He added that three out of four of Kush's sons (i.e., Ramchandra's grandsons) were said to have become skilled in handicrafts and architecture. Lalji Lal of the Tanti (weaver) community in Bihar argued that cloth production was a noble occupation, especially given the efforts by Mahatma Gandhi to elevate the practice of spinning to a patriotic pastime-a campaign that made the spinning wheel the symbol for the nationalist movement. Likewise, the tedious profession of hauling water received critical consideration by Kahar reformers. Nauvat Ray refused to refer even to water-hauling as an occupational birthright (pesh) but insisted on it as professional wage labor (mazdur) because he did not consider it an act that only a certain section of society had the ability to perform. His argument employed and inverted classic varna logic:

These days, a section of uneducated people in this jati provide the service of drawing and carrying water, and this is a kind of task that everyone in Hindu society himself must perform every day to some extent at one time or another....And yet this is not even degraded work, because high jatis in Hindu society also perform this very mazduri. On railway station platforms and in temple water-booths one can hear the pandit calling for water. How could a brahman perform this task if this is such lowly work?

This argument may appear simplistic, but its implications were to prove enormous for the political economy of varna in the village: by consciously rejecting the assumption that the physical act of hauling water (or palanquins, for that matter) was an inherent corporeal component of being Kahar, Ray rendered impotent the claims of elite society on Kahar labor as a matter of varna prerogative. Rather, Ray demanded that a hauler of water should be rewarded not with the satisfaction of knowing that he has lived up to his full potential in life as a Kahar, but with hard cash, and then should be left to pursue other callings. Ray added that many Kahars were cultivators, others had found employment in the military and in commerce, and those who were educated had attained high rank in civil and military service. He encapsulated the Kahar struggle for noble kshatriya origins in an allegorical tale of a prince who, through a turn of fate, was raised in a poor family and unaware of his true origins. The prince grew up learning how to farm and do physical labor when, one day, his true identity was revealed to him. The prince's whole bearing immediately changed as he assumed the mantle of dignity; yet he remained a peasant, well-versed in the art of cultivation.

If the twice-born held sway over shudra and untouchable by virtue of their greater control over the product of the land, the hierarchy such an ideology implied had long been reinforced by an ideology of physical work. Indeed, the stigma attached to labor was so powerful in Gangetic India that the very act of ploughing (chasa) constituted an important social delimiter, distinguishing the upper classes from the lower in the early nineteenth century. The many descriptions in the district gazetteers of Gangetic Uttar Pradesh and Bihar make it abundantly clear that the elite prescription against ploughing held through the nineteenth century and into the twentieth.

For example, in Ballia District in eastern Uttar Pradesh, H. R. Nevill noted that "high caste tenants seldom do the actual cultivation themselves, generally sub-letting their lands"; he added, however, that "they get less out of the soil, whether they sublet it or cultivate it themselves or employ hired labour, than do the Koeris and Kurmis."

Physical labor represented the point of convergence between social identity and economic exigency; as such, the simple act of cultivating a field-and the logic of agricultural production to which that act is inexorably tied-constituted the arena of historical possibilities for both economic and social change. It is not surprising, then, that the idea of labor was of such great importance to kshatriya reformers. As is evident in the leadership ranks of their various organizations, increasing numbers of first-line tenant cultivators were acquiring productive power and occasionally property rights over increasingly larger amounts of land. Now, in the early twentieth century, the physical boundary that upheld political, cultural, and social hierarchy was being questioned by reform-minded intellectuals. Indeed, some radicals went so far as to dispense with the boundaries entirely. Examples of the profound-and often violent-economic, political, and social consequences that would ensue are provided in the following chapter.

CONCLUSION

The profusion of jati reform movements in the late nineteenth and early twentieth centuries implies a changing universe of political and ethical concerns, expressed nevertheless in terms familiar to the Vaishnava religious milieu. The most explicit Vaishnava contour of kshatriya reform was the detailed cooptation of the dynastic genealogies of Ramchandra and Krishna, both as historical figures and as gods in their own right. But the articulation of kshatriya identity went beyond the reification of a specific Vaishnava historical framework. The very language, rhetoric, and texture of kshatriya reform reflected the institutionalization of Vaishnava belief, so much so that in some cases the kshatriya reformers themselves emerged from the universe of Vaishnava monasticism, in particular, from the monasticism centered on Ayodhya, the Ramanandi sampraday.

This is not surprising: the Ramanandi sampraday was and is north India's largest Vaishnava monastic community, and Ramanandis had long been known for their open-mindedness on the question of caste. As we have seen, however, not all Ramanandis were inclined to lend their support to social movements whose ideologies, by implication, reinforced caste attitudes.

If the assertions of kshatriya identity, the claim to uniracial (Aryan) equality, and the insistence on the dignity of physical work (not to mention the recognition of the fundamental economic necessity of labor) cannot be understood independently of Vaishnava reform, neither can it be understood independently of the economic expansion of the nineteenth and early twentieth centuries.

Many peasants and artisans appear to have been edged (if not catapulted) into positions of financial prosperity and were able thus to mount coordinated kshatriya identity campaigns. Ultimately, the dignity-of-labor rhetoric, grounded in a racial interpretation of varna, would constitute a significant challenge to the political economy of caste hierarchy.

To many observers within and beyond kshatriya reform, the political economy of caste was predicated on a moral understanding of physical work-particularly the act of preparing a field by maneuvering a plow while walking behind a cow or bull-as personally degrading. However, an ideological redefinition of labor would eventually pose a philosophical dilemma for kshatriya reformers themselves (not to mention their communities), forcing a choice between kshatriya status (and the continued systemics of varna that such a status implied) and the Vaishnava assertions of the dignity of labor (which ultimately undermined the systemics of varna and rendered the need for a kshatriya identity obsolete).

Such choices would be made in the context of dramatic political change, as nationalist and peasant politicians would look to the kshatriya organizations after 1920 in an effort to cultivate a rural base. The trajectories of such ideological and political movements and the manner in which they intersected are explored in the remainder of this study.

Finally, it is worth pointing out that as kshatriya identities centered on Ayodhya gained ideological and organizational strength in the early twentieth century, and particularly among the sizable Kurmi and Kushvaha peasant communities, Ayodhya also began to emerge on the north Indian political landscape as the place where God was born as Ramchandra. It has been argued recently that the current political turmoil over Ramchandra's birthplace (Ramjanambhumi) has its roots in a colonial historiography that was all too quick to perceive and assert an age-old enmity between Hindus and Muslims as the driving force of Indian history.

Overlooked in this argument are the social and religious contexts of the early twentieth century: the ideological need for a birthplace of Ramchandra can also be understood as symptomatic of the historiography of kshatriya ancestries grounded in a Vaishnava discourse. In other words, at some point claims of genealogical descent from God demand the physical presence of the remains of God. The recent controversy over a mosque built in Ayodhya in 1528 by the Mughal emperor Babar and the allegation that it not only occupies the site of Ramchandra's birth but was built with construction materials taken from the ruins of a temple marking that birth, demonstrates the extent to which the heightened communal consciousness of the twentieth century bleeds into debates over status in society, monastic or otherwise.

7

Status of the Ganga and Nearby Areas

Kshatriya reform represented an aggressive Gangetic populism in which a newly formed peasant and artisanal elite encouraged a full-scale examination of the historical and mythological underpinnings of their personal and jati identities. Among those engaged in this reform effort, Yadav, Kushvaha, and Kurmi kshatriyas were the most visible and numerically powerful. Strong in numbers and agrarian skill, many were small landholders and powerful tenants, but their numbers included a few large landowners as well as tenant-laborers. Most of them had toiled for generations in the rich Gangetic alluvial soils and as a result of that hard work and an intimate knowledge of local agricultural practice, had amassed significant rural wealth and power.

This newfound influence is what enabled them, by the early 1900s, to mount the claim that they were not shudra but kshatriya, descended from the proudest and oldest families imaginable, the families of Ramchandra and Krishna, and to sustain that claim with annual meetings and colorful publications. Yet the language of varna-in which brahmans were expert and upon which British understanding of Indian society relied-continued to describe these communities as shudra, or servile, by virtue of the physical labor implicit in their professions.

But increasingly the voices of the peasants could be heard above the din of imputed identities, voices asserting a new conception of themselves. By demanding a modicum of personal dignity and by claiming and articulating a noble kshatriya past, the ideologues of these communities challenged both the political economy and political culture of Gangetic India in a language that everyone was sure to understand. This challenge was quick to draw immediate attention and equally quick attempts at refutation from the social elite. Perhaps the first printed manifestation of this emergent antipathy was an anti-kshatriya reform booklet in both English and Hindi in 1907 authored by Kunvar Chheda Sinha, published and widely circulated by the Rajput Anglo-Oriental Press.

In what must have seemed an infuriating manner to the new peasant kshatriyas, Sinha bemoaned the fact that "even after a century of English rule and the spread of Western education the question of jati is still so heavily debated, especially given the fact that modern education and progress have given some jatis not only the opportunity but also the right to better their lot." Sinha ignored the cultural and economic transformations that had occurred to bring about social reform; rather, he tied the rising concern with caste pedigree to policies of hierarchical ranking in the census office and to a desire on the part of jati activists to attain high posts in the colonial government. In so doing, he inverted the arguments of the kshatriya reformers themselves, who cited military and government service by leading community figures not only as a professional aspiration but as evidence of the distinct abilities of the jati as a whole.

Sinha's logic, which endowed the colonial, census-based discourse of caste with historical agency in social and religious reform, has been employed in more recent analyses of caste movements in colonial India. Most striking in this regard is the assertion that "the censuses themselves instigated mobility aspirations and they do not necessarily reflect the actual processes taking place in society." This general argument has been widely circulated and characteristically describes the 1901 census as "a powerful stimulus to the formation of modern, provincewide and even countrywide caste associations and the development of broader solidarities." The perception that the colonial fixation with status inspired jati reform relies for the most part on an aggressive interpretation of census department records, particularly those sections of decennial reports that detailed the very real concerns of jati activists with the official representation of regional caste hierarchy. Of particular importance are the reflections of officials like L. S. S. O'Malley, director of the 1911 census in Bengal, Bihar, and Orissa, who noted that

> *there was a general idea in Bengal-that the object of the census was not to show the number of persons belonging to each caste, but to fix the relative status of different castes and to deal with the question of social superiority.... The feeling on the subject was largely the result of castes having been classified in the last census report in order of social precedence....Many castes were aggrieved at the position assigned them, and complained that it lowered them in the public estimation....Others thought it was a good opportunity to advance new claims.*

The question that must be raised, of course, is whether census classificatory practices actually inspired the campaigns for respectability and status or, conversely, whether such census practices merely attracted the attention of reformers, thus inspiring them to bury the responsible census officials in supplicatory memoranda. There is nothing in the observations of O'Malley to suggest the former case. The tendency was, rather, for colonial administrators to acknowledge that the hierarchical mindset of the census "greatly agitated" communities undergoing social and religious reform.

The assessment of social and religious reform as a reaction to census whims does point, however, to the importance of official opinion for kshatriya publicists. Some kind of authoritative sanction was crucial for the assertion and maintenance of social status, and the frequency with which kshatriya-reform memoranda were dispatched to the census office reflects the ease with which elite representatives of peasant jatis could enter into a sensitive dialogue with British officialdom. Indeed, notwithstanding the sharp contrast between those who composed the "memorials" in a showy panegyric that bordered on sycophancy and those who received and read them with a highly skeptical eye, the correspondence over varna status in the census should be seen as part of a larger process of colonial culture in the making.

To argue that census opinion alone inspired and directed movements for social reform not only suggests that the reform ideologies implicit to the kshatriya movements were somehow inauthentic but ignores the religious dimensions of the history of social reform and the very real fact that a new elite had emerged among the peasantry that sought to avail itself of connections to the colonial political arena. As I have argued in the preceding chapters, social reform on behalf of shudras and untouchables in the Gangetic north was manifest in a semiorganized form at least since the early nineteenth century under the rubric of Vaishnava (and primarily Ramanandi) monasticism. In addition, sporadic peasant claims to kshatriya status had been articulated as early as the late eighteenth century in Awadh and the early nineteenth century in Bihar.

The institutional heirs to such early reform efforts were the caste associations (mahasabhas) of the late nineteenth and early twentieth centuries, which combined the demand for high (usually kshatriya) status with a potent Vaishnava rhetorical content. Kshatriyatva (the essence of being kshatriya, or valor) constituted an important component of this new political framework for reform, in part because the martial element contained therein fit a colonial ideology that placed a premium on virility and power.

In this light, the formulation that "the censuses themselves instigated mobility aspirations and they do not necessarily reflect the actual processes taking place in society" deserves closer scrutiny. The profusion of census-directed jati memorials are depicted as false indicators of social change, and historians are therefore encouraged to ignore the wider cultural history that both occasioned and accompanied that change.

The argumentation employed by Sinha in 1907 and refined by historians and sociologists in the 1970s and 1980s presents an image of entire caste mahasabha organizations involving countless thousands of members devoted only to garnering the crumbs of status and position from the British imperial table.

There can be no doubt that kshatriya reformers were all too concerned with the political legitimization of their sociocultural identity, but this must be seen primarily as a symptomatic feature of the larger movement for respectability. The image of the scurrying, low-level babu (clerk) overlooks, consciously or unconsciously, the main agenda of these organizations: education, religious reform, economic frugality, physical integrity, and most important of all, personal dignity. These are goals that generally would not have been made explicit in petitions to census officials but which emerge clearly in the vernacular literature espousing both the religious and social reform movements of the late nineteenth and early twentieth centuries.

FROM COWHERD TO KSHATRIYA

Despite the challenge to the social status quo implicit in kshatriya reform movements among groups heretofore accorded low status, kshatriya reformers saw themselves as an integral part of a larger Hindu universe. The rupturing of ties to superordinate groups was secondary to the object of community respect expressed in terms of kshatriya identity. Nevertheless, the increasing urgency of claims to kshatriya status served to offend many established high-status communities, primarily because of the social and cultural proximity such claims implied. Social reform would thus inevitably produce social strife. Strife, however, implies past cohesion. Such cohesion can be seen to have existed in the 1890s at certain levels, and was expressed in a particularly ardent manner by Goala peasant-pastoralists as a cultural solidarity with the landed, social elite during cow-protection agitation. Three decades later, that agrarian cohesion would be rendered obsolete by the strident call for Yadav-kshatriya identity.

Organized primarily in opposition to the slaughter of cows and the consumption of beef during Muslim festivals and holidays, the cow-protection-or gauraksha-movement represented an important phase of a growing political and cultural activism in late nineteenth-century north India. This activism, the historian John McLane has suggested, was evident as well in the mobilizational systemics of the early Indian National Congress and in the increased competition between Hindu and Muslim elites for secular power. National elite competition became intertwined with popular religious practice at the regional level, a combination that ultimately erupted in the Gangetic heartland over the issue of cow slaughter. This controversy peaked in 1893 as angry Hindus attacked entire Muslim village centers, assaulting butchers as well as low-status Hindus viewed as complicit in marketing beef. The cow-protection cause found enthusiastic support in cities and towns as well as villages, as agitators employed both local trade networks and powerful religious symbols to divide Hindus from Muslims as well as the British. As gau-mata (mother cow) evolved into a unifying "Hindu" political symbol, the urban elites that peopled the Indian National Congress increasingly looked to it to develop a rural base, "despite the refusal of Congress leaders to allow the Congress to support cow protection." McLane even suggests that it became "inevitable that the Congress, standing as it did for majority rule and parliamentary government, should have attracted advocates of restrictions upon cow slaughter."

The shifting agrarian tensions that accompanied the late nineteenth-century price rise in the Gangetic north, it has been argued, made cow protection an opportune issue for a kind of makeshift agrarian unity involving increasingly less powerful Hindu zamindars and increasingly more assertive Hindu tenants. Gyanendra Pandey has investigated the nature of that agrarian unity from the perspective of the tenants and has argued that "the prevention of cow-slaughter became a major object of the Ahirs [generally synonymous with Goalas] as they advanced their bid for a higher social status." Pandey's data and observations concern the Bhojpuri region of eastern Uttar Pradesh and western Bihar where, he argues, "the agitation appears to have acquired its greatest social depth and an unexpected militancy."

Citing official reports of the physical participation of Goalas in mob violence directed against Muslims and others involved in the sacrifice of cattle, as well as records of subsequent trials in which Goalas received sentencing, Pandey suggests "that we have evidence here of a relatively independent force that added a good deal of power to cow-protection activities in the Bhojpuri region-marginally 'clean' castes who aspired to full 'cleanness' by emphasizing the purity of their faith and the strictness of ritual adherence to it on the issue of cow-slaughter. In the case of the Ahirs this motive would certainly have been reinforced by their traditional and continued association with the business of tending cattle." Pandey's observations reflect the importance of cow-protection violence to Goala/Ahir conceptions of status and identity, expressed here as a function of ritual cleanliness. His use of the term "marginal" highlights the notion that Goalas, like other peasants, straddled the fine line between shudra and elite in the political economy of the Gangetic heartland and were committed to the exploitation of that precarious stance to their fullest advantage.

Pandey makes brief reference to agitation in Patna and Gaya Districts and argues that these districts-adjacent to the eastern extension of Bhojpur into Gangetic south Bihar-experienced significant cow-protection activity in the early 1890s. The evidence of official reports bears out this assertion and, as in eastern Uttar Pradesh, Goalas played an important grassroots role in advancing the cause of gauraksha.

For instance, of the twelve cases of forcible seizure of cattle reported in the first five months of 1893 in Gaya District, six cited Goalas as the offending party (of the remaining six cases, four failed to identify the jati of the accused). Inasmuch as most of the twelve incidents occurred during or after the Bisua village cattle fair held that year on April 12, it is not unlikely that Goalas, as cowherds and dairy farmers, were involved in some of the other incidents as well. The following description of an incident at the mela, extracted from the judicial record, is typical of the activities of Goalas working for cow-protection:

In this case the complainant, who is a [Muslim] butcher, says he bought two cows at the Bisua Mela [fair] for Rs. 7-1 through one Dodal Chamar, because he was afraid that Hindus would not sell cattle to Muhammedans. The first purchase was duly recorded by the owner of the Mela, and the usual receipt checque was granted. But when the Chamar was going back along with both cows to have the second purchase recorded, he was suddenly stopped by the accused [Gopi Goala] and several others, and accused of buying cows for butchers. The cattle were snatched and carried off by the accused. Sub-Inspector Zahir Khan, of town Gaya, having received information that the accused and cattle were near the place where cattle sales were being recorded, went to the spot and managed to arrest accused Gopi Goala.

This description, and others like it, characterize Goalas as the shock troops of cow protection. The above case is of added interest because of the complicity of Dodal Chamar, an untouchable, in purchasing the cattle for the butcher Mangor Kassai, a Muslim. Such alliances were apparently not uncommon in the Gangetic core: in eastern Uttar Pradesh "the Chamar, far from being actively involved in the Cow-Protection movement, was in fact the target of a good deal of Gaurakshinist vilification and attack."

Consequently, a list of sixteen rules drawn up at a meeting of cow-protection activists in Gorakhpur District included the explicit message that "Chamars and others buy cows and sell them to butchers; and Musalmans and others are the very cause of the slaughter of cows. Cows shall not be sold into the hands of any such persons, and if any kind of cow die the owner shall sell its skin to a proper person, and apply the money to cow-protection."

Ironically, inasmuch as Chamars worked with leather, they would also be the "proper persons" to which the manifesto refers. By supporting the "Hindu establishment" in its cause célèbre, the protection of cows, Goalas symbolically allied themselves with the landed and powerful while distancing themselves from those socially and economically beneath them ("Chamars and others") in the Gangetic core. Goala aspirations in the 1890s drew on the cowherd ethos of Krishna's childhood milieu, albeit at the expense of Muslim religious custom. So long as Goala participation in cow-protection agitation remained devoid of any specific transformative, status-oriented rhetoric, the tenuous agrarian unity between landlord and tenant remained intact. However, a loosely expressed dedication to the Vaishnava world of Krishna would soon evolve by the early 1910s and 1920s into a commitment to a historical exegesis of that world in the form of Yadav-kshatriya identity, an identity that would serve to drive a wedge between Goalas and other cultivators on the margin of land control, on the one hand, and the landed elite on the other.

Conflict between the landed elite and marginal cultivators became manifest as physical confrontation in the teens and twenties of the present century. Official police reports of the 1920s describe in substantial detail the tensions and occasional violence between Goalas forwarding a Yadav-kshatriya identity and the landed elite who felt threatened by that new identity. This threat was perceived as economic as well as social, inasmuch as the systemics of varna provided the cultural justification for the agrarian perquisites demanded of cultivating tenants. While the Muslim elite also challenged the Yadav-kshatriya identity, they did so on purely economic and not religious grounds, and Yadav kshatriyas responded in kind. These tensions culminated with the threat of serious bloodletting on May 27, 1925, when a group of three thousand "Goalas" (Yadav kshatriyas) and an equal number of heavily armed "Babhans" (Bhumihar brahmans) faced each other at Lakho Chak village near Lakhisarai town, Monghyr District, in central Bihar. Though official reports tended to employ the appellations Goala and Babhan, I have chosen to refer to the two parties in my description of this extended conflict simply as Yadavs and Bhumihars, terms that reflect both their own conception of themselves as well as the current usage. These and other reports make clear that the Lakho Chak showdown was only the most visible manifestation of a conflict that had been simmering for several years.

The Lakho Chak riot itself was precipitated by the decision of local Bhumihar zamindars of Monghyr District to attack a panchayat (council meeting) of Yadavs that had convened in the village of Lakho Chak to discuss jati reform. The description of the riot in the official report indicates the formidable force brought to bear by the Bhumihars and that, if not for the timely intervention of local and district police to protect the peaceable Yadav meeting, serious violence would have been the likely result.

On the morning of the 27th, before the arrival of the armed police at Lakho Chak, a large body of rioters advanced upon the village. The local police intervened to expostulate and were at once surrounded, the Sub-Inspector and Chaukidar [village watchman] received grievous injuries and the other constables of the party were hurt. After ill-treating the local police, the rioters retired temporarily but returned to the attack soon after the arrival of the S.P. [Superintendent of Police] with his force. The Superintendent and S.D.O [Subdivisional District Officer] went out to meet the advancing rioters and attempted to parley with them. The attacking party, however, to the number of about 3000 armed with lathis [heavy, metal tipped bamboo truncheons], axes, and spears continued to advance and the police were forced to fire to protect themselves and the Goalas. Although temporarily checked by the fire, the Babhan party continued to advance as they outflanked the police on both sides, the police were forced to retire fighting to the village site three or four hundred yards to their rear. The retirement was effected in good order and after the defending party reached the village the rioters withdrew.

The dramatic crisis that unfolded in 1925 under the hot May sun on the outskirts of Lakho Chak village was in fact the most recent and explosive act in the construction of a Yadav-kshatriya identity that had begun in the nineteenth century with claims of genealogical ties to Krishna. The movement took on a more urgent and organized form throughout the Gangetic north in the early twentieth century with the emergence of large-scale associations and active propaganda. In a lengthy note to his superior Y. A. Godbole, the district officer of Purnea, S.D.O Phanindra Nath Mukherji noted that he "first came across the Goala movement in the Patna district in the year 1912."

The leader was Babu Damodar Prasad-a Goala landlord of Pachchimdarwaza in Patna City. A huge meeting called the "Gope Jatiya Mahasabha" was held in Kankarbagh and domestic service was eschewed except for tending cattle, sacred threads taken-and ceremonial purity was, I believe, put down at 15 days. I have to depend on memory-other meetings were held at Dinapur, Maner, and Mussorhi [Masaurhi]. I do not know if the movement had preceded elsewhere but I read in the papers of meetings in the United Provinces of Agra and Oudh and elsewhere.

Mukherji provided the above description by way of historical background. His subsequent portrayal of his own experiences in dealing with the "Goala movement" in Purnea District in 1924 and 1925 demonstrate both the importance of economic advancement to Yadavs as well as the subtle techniques employed by them in mobilizing a kshatriya identity.

The movement in this district has spread within the last year or so. The material condition of the Goalas in the western and southern portions of the district is very prosperous. In fact in wealth measured in terms of cattle, land, etc. they are in no way inferior to the average Bhumihars and Brahmins and Chhatris [local variant of kshatriya, in reference to Rajputs]. The movement in this district was I used to hear being fostered by Babu Swyambara Das, late Deputy Inspector of schools in this district. He had lecturers brought in from other districts and there were meetings held at Ghansurpur, Dhamdaha, Rupauli and several centres. The Goalas began to call themselves Jadavs, took sacred threads and gave out that they will do the ceremonial purification of Sradh after 13 days. The Bhumihars resented this as did the Brahmins and Chhatris. An attempt was made to break up the meeting at Ghansurpur but the police got timely notice and occurrence [sic] took place. The Bhumihars later refused to allow the Goalas to draw water from the village wells and I had to go to Ghansurpur. I warned the leading Bhumihars and with my privilege as a Brahmin I pointed out to them that the Bhumihars themselves had reduced the period of ceremonial purification from 15 to 13 days in several districts within living memory and that . . . their ancestors called themselves Bavans [variant of Babhans].

Mukherji noted in addition that in many villages in Purnea District the dominant caste-whether Bhumihar brahman,

Maithil brahman, or Rajput-organized a social boycott of Yadavs, with the object of making it extremely difficult for the latter to perform the rituals prescribed for kshatriya status. This obstacle was circumvented without much difficulty, as "the richer sections [of Yadavs] have come to the help of the poorer section and have either got Brahmins from Madhipura in Bhagalpur district where there are many Goala landlords or managed to win over opposition by making it worthwhile for the Brahmins and barbers to officiate." It is clear from Mukherji's description, then, that pockets of Yadav economic power in Bihar played a large role not only in inspiring changing attitudes toward their sociocultural identity but in ensuring that the new identity being advanced stayed alive despite rural pressure to obliterate it.

Nevertheless, economic contradictions internal to the Yadav community inevitably became manifest as, according to Mukherji, "The better off wanted to insist that the women-folk of the poor section will not sell Goetha (fuel cakes made from cowdung) or milk in the hats (weekly markets) and bazars. And that the women should follow in all respects the practices of the women of the higher castes. This gave rise to a few criminal cases but then the inexorable economic laws acted and the women folk of the poorer section are again selling cowdung cakes and milk." The conclusion that must be reached, then, is that in the short term the consolidation of Yadav-kshatriya identity succeeded only to the extent that economic considerations allowed. Better-off Yadavs could not entirely subvent the incomes of their less-fortunate jati brothers and, importantly, sisters, but they certainly were able, as Mukherji's observations on ritual officiates indicate, to at least mobilize the wherewithal either to bring brahmans from a neighboring district or to increase the economic reward for local brahmans and hajjams (barbers) to perform the necessary ceremonial functions.

This glimpse into the household economics of Yadavs struggling to live up to a new Vaishnava and kshatriya ideal of dignity introduces an important element of caste reform, namely, a strictly circumscribed redefinition of acceptable female social, religious, and economic behavior. Such an imposition of male control over female lives is all the more striking given that many of the peasant families involved in the identity campaigns had benefited economically from the lack of any cultural proscription of women working in the field as well as in the home-in stark contrast to the mores of elite society. Hence the mid nineteenth-century adage, "A good caste is the Kunbin [Kurmi woman]; with hoe in hand, they weed the fields together with their husbands."

However, kshatriya reformers generally viewed the centrality of women in the economic success of the peasant family as an entrée to female independence and thus a serious threat to the integrity of not only the immediate household but the entire jati community. Baijnath Prasad Yadav of Banaras claimed, not atypically, that "the root cause of all the needless household expenses is the fickle greed of women" and urged "men to put a halt to the rule of women in the home." Yadav also argued against allowing women to sing in public, against permitting women to view the barat (the procession of the groom with his friends and male family members), and "against allowing women to attend the big festivals, where they would run the risk of being dishonored by one of the many low jatis that roam the crowds, which would thus bring dishonor upon our jati." Extending this particular line of reasoning, he vehemently criticized women who purchased glass bangles from "lascivious vendors, who are only too willing to grab our women's wrists and help them try on their wares." Swami Abhayananda Saraswati, also of Banaras, cautioned Kurmis against educating their women, maintaining that such education could only have a negative effect on the children, on household work, and on the development of a loving relationship between a husband and wife.

While women did take part in the reform movements, the greatest challenge they faced was to redress the growing male conceptualization of women as property to be manipulated and polished for the sake of a positive and powerful kshatriya image. The participation of women in the organizational apparatus of kshatriya reform rhetoric was relegated, in the main, to the activities of mahila sammelans (women's conferences), which usually occurred in conjunction with the regional and national meetings of the jati. These organizations pushed for government legislation against polygamy and for mahasabha resolutions providing for the education of boys and girls. Nevertheless, it is doubtful that women involved in upgrading their gender status made much headway vis-à-vis the kshatriya-focused attitudes of their fathers, brothers, husbands, and sons.

That the control over the life and death of women was of paramount importance to the success of kshatriya identity can be seen in the boast by Nauvat Ray, the Kahar ideologue of Agra, that "many of our women even become sati," which can mean both becoming loyal wives and immolating themselves upon the husband's funeral pyre (the tone of the passage indicates that the latter meaning is intended). This conceptualization of women as martyrs to the cause of community status extended as well into the nascent Hindi literary movement.

An example is Gangaprasad, the Kushvaha-kshatriya historian cited in the previous chapter, who also published historical fiction under the name Gangaprasad Gupta. One of his novels, entitled Vir Jaymal (Valiant Defense), glorified the courage of Rajputs in battle against Muslims during the reign of Akbar. Of particular note, however, was his narrative of the death of Raja Prithviraj of Delhi and the self-immolation of his bereaved queen, Sanyogita, entitled Vir Patni (Brave Wife). Gangaprasad portrayed female martyrdom as an important embodiment of a kshatriya tradition that combined steadfast loyalty to husband with patriotic devotion to country, a evocation of the sacrificing female that he also perceived to be extant in Victorian literature of the previous century. Hence his translation of "The Young Fishermen," a story by the Victorian romance author George W. M. Reynolds (1814-1879), which Gangaprasad entitled Kile ki Rani (Queen of the Fort).

While economic power enabled Yadavs to forge a kshatriya identity campaign, it is equally the case that a major aim of that campaign was an improvement of the economic position of Yadavs vis-à-vis superordinate landlords. This dilemma, in a sense, reflected the essence of the marginal status of Yadavs in society: having tasted some of the fruits of economic strength, they demanded more. The forced, unremunerative labor known as begari was the ground on which the battle for equal economic status was fought.

The caste implications of begari were such that elite landlords expected it of nonelite (whether shudra or untouchable) fellow villagers. Labor in this context referred not only to agricultural work but, especially in the Yadav context, to nonremunerative efforts such as providing milk and ghi (clarified butter) at reduced rates or even free of charge. Thus, S. A. Khan, a district officer of Bhagalpur, noted in an official correspondence that "The low caste Hindus generally do some kind of 'begari' work for their landlords. A people wearing the sacred thread are taken as respectable and are exempt from gratis service of this type. They would also take it to be very much derogatory to work as daily labourers or even as hired ploughmen."

The official record tells of an important meeting convened by Babu Shri Ballab Das in 1921 that was attended by approximately sixteen hundred Yadavs. Among the resolutions passed at this meeting was a plea to the government to take note of conflict "between the zamindars (landlords) and the Gope Jotiya having arisen over the begari question over which the latter have been oppressed by the zamindars, so much so that in several places several lives have been lost."

This file also tells of a related incident several months earlier in which a rural council of Yadavs in Islampur Thana, Patna District, refused to allow members of the jati to provide ghi and goats to a Muslim landlord for a wedding feast. However, in contrast to the earlier cow-protection activity, anti-Muslim rhetoric was severely curtailed in the language of the resolution. The meeting specifically stated that "in the coming Bakr-Id this community will not create any disturbance in connection with the cow-killing and if, unfortunately, any engineered by other caste [sic] would happen, this community would have no hand in it."

Two factors are important in understanding the Yadav disavowal of the anti-Muslim stance that they had so strongly advocated during the cow-protection agitation. First, and probably most importantly, the calculated and willful articulation of a kshatriya identity called for a refinement of the Yadav sociocultural position vis-à-vis superordinate and subordinate actors in the agrarian environment. No longer would it be sufficient to express vague designs for high status through open attacks on Muslims; a well-crafted kshatriya identity immediately placed Yadavs (and other cultivators) in social, economic, and cultural conflict with the twice-born elite, requiring a realigned, refined political program devoid of any content directed against a particular religious community.

Naturally, those likely to be most offended by the culture of upward mobility implicit to Yadav identity would be the dominant Hindu groups. Second, and closely related, the characterization of the Yadav movement in positive class terms relative to zamindars was more likely to win the official support of the colonial administration, primarily because Yadavs could easily portray themselves as the victims of socioeconomic oppression rather than as perpetrators of anti-Muslim mob violence.

The simple assumption of an aggressive kshatriya identity by Yadavs placed the onus upon superordinates to react violently, thereby casting the latter in the role of lawbreakers. This tactic had near-immediate results; according to the sociologist Hetukar Jha, "The reports [contained in file 171 of 1925] though written by government employees are not biased in favour of zamindars or in favour of government officers. The reporters did not hesitate to point out when they found that an officer of the rank of S.D.O. had sided with the zamindars at Samastipur (then a subdivision of Darbhanga) against peasants without conducting a proper enquiry."

The essentially nonpartisan judgment of district officers in itself constituted a major victory for marginal peasants. Indeed, if anything, the reports expressed a significant degree of sympathy for the aims of the kshatriya reformers. It has already been noted that the local police force of Lakhisarai and the district police of Monghyr had come to the aid of the Yadav meeting being held in Lakho Chak village in 1925. In addition, Subdivisional District Officer Phanindra Nath Mukherji, cited at length above, had gone to great pains to convince the Bhumihar landlords of Purnea District to refrain from harassing Yadav peasants; indeed, he even lorded his own brahman status over the Bhumihars to remind them of their own upward social mobility.

Most reports described the begari demanded by the landlords not as customary and benign agrarian perquisites but as oppressive "exactions." Commenting on what was perceived as an unjust economic arrangement, Commissioner J. A. Hubback of Bhagalpur Division noted caustically that "the higher castes (in that tract [South Monghyr] mainly Babhans) derive livelihood from the land, and do as little as they can to earn it." Hubback's phraseology indicates that he was not simply directing a pointed criticism at Bhumihars but was describing what he perceived as a nonproductive elite class that survived off the sweat of "sturdy" peasants.

These official characterizations reflected the subtle alliance that was being forged between the new kshatriya peasants on the one hand and regional and local administrators (the former mostly British, the latter mostly Indian) on the other. This alliance was spurred along by frequent appeals to and representations of "sarkar" as a benevolent, caring government. The efforts by government as sarkar to protect the new kshatriyas from the abuses and threats of physical violence by the outraged elite, and at the same time to mollify that outrage with reasoned pleas for peaceful behavior, make clear that district officials and cultivators at the productive core of Indian society were speaking to and regenerating each other in ideal terms.

This emergent alliance extended as well into the agrarian political context described above, as marginal peasants reacted favorably to what they understood as the nonpartisan spirit of British rule and the judicious exercise of administrative force. The most telling example of this perception in the jati reform literature is without question the contention of Gangaprasad, who wrote on behalf of Kushvaha kshatriyas, that "now this is the age of British rule. The lion and the lamb can drink from the same pond and no one can say to another, 'thus a shudra is born.'" Another example of this sentiment is found in a pamphlet arguing kshatriya status for Kahars authored by Nauvat Ray, who praised British rule as "an age of light from which darkness can only flee."

Notwithstanding what they perceived as the benevolence of British officials, however, the new kshatriyas still had to contend with opposition to their social, cultural, and economic advancement organized by the established landed elite. Perhaps the most galling element of this form of resistance to Yadav-kshatriya identity were the "abuses, taunts and jokes . . . hurled on the Goalas."

Particularly insulting, according to S. A. Khan (a district officer of Bhagalpur), were ten thousand printed copies of a leaflet of Bihari verse "sung by hired boys in the mofussil [countryside]," in which "Goalas are asked to stick to their old faith and customs." The author of this leaflet gave his name as Bahuran of Ram Patti village north of Singheshwar dham [pilgrimage center] near Saharsa in northern Bhagalpur District and described himself as "a reputed Brahman." The distributor of the leaflet, however, was listed as one Raghunandan Jha (Jha is a well-known Maithil brahman surname) of the same address, suggesting Bahuran's likely identity.

Bahuran prefaced his verse with a short Sanskrit dedication to Radha and Krishna, which he concluded with the patronizing affront that he was merely "narrating the conduct of the Gopas to increase their knowledge." Indeed, throughout the leaflet Bahuran referred to Yadavs as Gopas, the traditional term for the idealized, innocent cowherds of Krishna's mytho-historical boyhood in Mathura-Vrindaban.

After dedicating several lines to descriptions of the eminence of Radha and Krishna and their exploits, Bahuran settled down to the serious business of persuading the Yadav community to renounce its upstart behavior. His efforts concentrated on several themes, the most important of which was the Yadav practice of donning the sacred thread and performing the shraddh funerary ceremony only thirteen days after the death of a family member:

While you flaunt a sacred thread on your shoulders,
your women wake up to milk cows and herd calves.

You work the plough while wearing the thread, and
force your women to labor in the fields.

You've bought up all the weavers' cotton, and the scarcity
has made cloth dear.

Gwalins [Goala women] sell milk and curd all day long,
they wouldn't know how to spin thread.

......

[How can] two opposing customs prevail in one family:
one-month shraddh and thirteen-day shraddh?

......

Read the Laws of Manu wherein Gopas are said to be
shudra, and abandon shraddh after thirteen days.

Be united and accept a one-month shraddh, this should
be the only reform of the Gopa jati.

......

Your ancestors in Kashi, Vrindaban, Awadh, and Gokul,
have crammed full the stomachs of all the sadhus.

[This is how] they are allowed to wear the sacred thread
and perform thirteen-day shraddh.

......

Think for yourselves in groups of ten or twenty, and give
up the spread of the sacred thread.

As a purposefully insulting document, Bahuran's verse reveals much about the political economy of caste in the Gangetic north. His reference to Goalas ploughing, milking cows, and performing other menial tasks while wearing the sacred thread reflects the profound socioeconomic challenge that the kshatriya (not to mention Vaishnava) reconsideration of dignified labor held for the social elite. His advice to gather in "groups of ten or twenty" was surely calculated to foment divisiveness within the Yadav-kshatriya movement, the periodic meetings of which were attended by Yadavs numbering in the thousands. The reference to 'Gwalins' spending their entire days milking cows, chasing cattle, and marketing their wares was surely meant to ridicule Yadav women as immodest and Yadav men as lazy good-for-nothings who relax while their wives do all the work. On this point, Bahuran chastised Yadav men for letting their "mothers cut grass" and their "sisters sell milk in the villages, towns, and markets." But he could not have been more derisive than with the taunt that

> *When your elder brother dies, you make his widow a happy bride.*
>
> *Whenever the husbands of your daughters and sisters expire, you once again marry off their wives.*

Another important theme in the text of the verse centered around Bahuran's claim that the root cause of the Yadav-kshatriya campaign was the work of Swami Dayanand and the Arya Samaj. However, while Dayanand's ideas probably influenced kshatriya reform, there was a great deal of institutional ambivalence regarding the role of Arya Samajis in the reform movement itself. It is in this context that Bahuran's comments should be understood. He pointedly accused Yadavs of having "abandoned your family duties for the ideas of Dayanand and . . . thus destroyed your good name," and he urged them in turn to "abandon the ways of Dayanand, Gopas, for difficult times lie ahead." These verses were intended as an affront to Yadav sensibilities, semantically calculated to imply that support for kshatriya identity was synonymous with an affinity for the Arya Samaj.

Goala unity, which emerged in the political arena in 1893 as an amorphous dedication to Krishna and cows and expressed itself in anti-Muslim rioting, had become by 1925 a well-organized call for a Yadav-kshatriya identity that offended the twice-born sensibilities and socioeconomic power of village elites.

As the new kshatriyas-Yadavs as well as Kurmis and Kushvahas-flexed their social, economic, and cultural muscles in the early twentieth century, they began to take a closer look at the political landscape around them. From their agrarian perspective, the most important political institutions were the Bihar Provincial Kisan Sabha (peasant association) and the Indian National Congress, especially insofar as each body developed an "agrarian program." That they responded to those dominant organizations by joining together to form their own political front, the Triveni Sangh, confirms the increasingly independent posture of kshatriya reformers in the early twentieth century.

POLITICAL PEASANTS

Mahatma Gandhi's great achievement was to revitalize the Indian National Congress in the late teens and twenties of this century by drawing in the support of what historians and political scientists-with some important, and relatively recent, exceptions-have called "the masses." Thus Lloyd and Suzanne Rudolph write that Gandhi transformed "the Indian National Congress from a body narrowly concerned with the interests of an anglicized elite to a socially concerned mass organization" by using "traditional symbols and language to convey new meanings and to reconstitute social action."

It cannot be denied that the rich cultural idiom that Gandhi drew upon throughout his political career proved profoundly effective in providing the Congress with a much broader base. Nevertheless, the "masses" that became involved in the Congress were far from undifferentiated. The aim of this section is to review the class dimensions of Indian nationalism and the caste dimensions of peasant radicalism, and to discern how both intersected with the sociocultural agenda of kshatriya reform.

Perhaps the best evidence of this fact in the Gangetic core is the growth in the 1920s and 1930s of the Kisan Sabha, which came to articulate a distinct peasant interest in contrast to the agrarian policies advanced by the Congress. An understanding of the political events of this period hinges to a great extent on the ideas and work of one remarkable man, Swami Sahajanand Saraswati. Born Navrang Ray in 1889, a Jujhautia brahman of Ghazipur District, Sahajanand Saraswati took the vows of sanyas at the age of eighteen (1907) and became a Dasnami sanyasi. Sahajanand became involved in social reform activity when, in 1914 at the age of twenty-five, he was asked to address the annual conference of the Bhumihar Brahman Mahasabha held at Ballia in eastern Uttar Pradesh.

After some determined reflection on his role as a sanyasi involved in social action, Sahajanand decided to devote himself fully to the cause of defining and maintaining a Bhumihar brahman identity for "Babhans." In response to the denigrations of Bhumihars by Maithil brahmans and others, Sahajanand cited a broad range of Sanskrit and orientalist authorities to argue that "the acceptance of charity and the discharge of priestly duties are not inevitably necessary for the brahmans." Rather, "even for the brahman, agriculture is preferable to the priesthood, and only in the absence of agriculture does the brahman have the right to perform the functions of the priest." However, being brahman required a knowledge of Sanskrit and priestly ritual (karmakand), two assets in short supply among the Bhumihar community. Therefore, the founding of the Sitaram Ashram [sanctuary] to train students at Bihta, about sixteen miles west of Patna on the East India Railway line, signified the culminating achievement in Sahajanand's efforts to build a Bhumihar brahman identity.

Sahajanand's role in the political history of Gangetic north India was, to a large extent, a reflection of his unsurpassed ability to bridge differences in sociocultural, religious, and economic background. And he was able to overcome those barriers in exciting ways, creating new patterns of social and political organization.

For instance, even though Sahajanand was a Dasnami sanyasi, it is clear from his own work that he was heavily influenced by the Vaishnava discourse of reform. And it was precisely the social imperative of that Vaishnava discourse that pushed him increasingly toward political radicalism. According to the historian Walter Hauser, Sahajanand's reading of the Bhagavat Purana, a text central to Vaishnava bhakti, "made it explicit that to serve the people was like service and devotion to God."

Sahajanand also wrote a commentary on the Bhagavad Gita, published as Gita Hriday (The Heart of the Gita), which still stands as a remarkable personal testimony of socialist idealism founded on core Vaishnava tenets of correct social action.

Sahajanand was influenced by Vaishnava belief in more mundane ways as well. The land and buildings that formed the original nucleus of the Sitaram Ashram Sahajanand received from a Bhumihar Ramanandi named Sitaram Das, whose wish in old age was to "create a brahmacharya [student] ashram where Bhumihar brahman boys can come to study the Vedas, Shastras, and other sacred texts." However, the Swami's principled dedication to the common man and his keen commitment to social and economic justice no matter what the cost thrust him increasingly into a position contrary to that of the Bhumihar Brahman Mahasabha's image as an organization designed to represent the "aristocratic, powerful, landowning elite." This emerges nowhere more clearly than in Sahajanand's own remarks describing the formative events of 1927:

The countless Bhumihar brahman benefactors, who in fact kept the ashram from closing with their total yearly subscriptions of thousands of rupees, nevertheless eventually became the sworn enemies of the ashram. Indeed, many of them lived near the ashram itself. This [their hatred] was due to the fact that I sided with the anguished Goalas and other kisans [peasants] who came to me, and raised a storm against their oppressive zamindars. If anyone goes to that area today to see for themselves the downtrodden people there, regardless of their jati or religion, he will be in total agreement with me and, therefore, the ashram. Indeed, there the question of jati does not arise.

From this point on, Sahajanand would only perceive agrarian conflict as that between landlords and peasants: "Caste and class had merged into a single category of social and economic exploitation. The Sitaram Ashram had become in his words a 'symbol of revolution.'" It will be remembered that the term "Sitaram" possessed symbolic power in nearby Awadh during the Baba Ramchandra-led peasant struggle of 1919-

1921. The name of the ashram alone may well have played a significant role in convincing many local cultivators of western Patna District that, in fact, the Swami would lend a sympathetic ear to their complaints. That the buildings and land for the ashram had been donated by a Ramanandi sadhu could only have furthered this perception. To complete the image, the Swami had by this time already developed a begrudged reputation among his landlord critics of being "nothing if . . . not progressive."

While it is exceedingly difficult to arrive at any clear sense of the socioeconomic composition of the Bihar Provincial Kisan Sabha, it is likely-especially given the willingness of local Yadav tenants to seek the aid of the Swami in the transformative year of 1927-that peasants on the tenancy/proprietorship margin became involved in one way or another through the late 1920s and 1930s.

This impression is reinforced by Hauser's own earlier reading of the caste dimensions of the leadership of the Kisan Sabha, which included a dominant group of Bhumihars in addition to Rajputs and Kayasths, "with occasional Muslims and lower caste cultivating peasants, primarily Kurmis and Koeris." Emphasizing the anti-landlord, pro-tenant stance of the organization, Hauser points out that "While most Kisan Sabha leaders were Bhumihars, so were most of the major zamindars, including the ones who came under sharpest attack by the Kisan Sabha. On the other hand, while there are some Bhumihar tenants in Bihar it is estimated that upwards of 90 per cent are not, and of course many of the best peasant cultivators in the province are Kurmis and Koeris."

Nevertheless, while the Kisan Sabha may have satisfied temporarily the political aspirations of many marginally elite cultivators, the rise of the Triveni Sangh organization confirms that many Kurmi, Kushvaha, and Yadav kshatriyas felt a growing need for distinct political representation. Though the precise chronology of the emergence of the Triveni Sangh is as yet unclear-one scholar placing its organizational origins in the mid-1920s, other observers dating the formal naming of the organization to 1934-early signs of political cohesion between

Yadavs, Kurmis, and Kushvahas can be seen as early as 1930. In that year a district-level meeting of Kushvahas and Yadavs was held in the village of Garve in central Shahabad District in southwest Bihar and was presided over by Sheopujan Prasad Singh, a Kurmi-kshatriya leader.

Individual Kushvahas (Tapsi Ram of Begampur, Raghu Vir Singh of Dumraon) and Yadavs (Sheopujan Singh of Jitaura, Nandkishore Singh of Tenuni) cooperated in contesting the local district board elections in that and the following year, but fared badly. The Triveni Sangh was formally constituted in 1934 at another Shahabad District conference. A third district conference was held in 1936, when membership was estimated at approximately one million based on the number of Kushvahas, Yadavs, and Kurmis who had paid the four-anna (one-quarter of a rupee) fee to join the organization.

The movement expanded to the provincial level-partly in an effort to court Congress support in the upcoming elections of 1937-under the leadership of Guru Sahay Lal (who would later become a "backward caste" leader and who, according to one account, had suffered severe personal humiliation by the high-caste elite) and Dasu Singh (a Kurmi). Meanwhile, after 1935 the Congress was busy forming the Backward Classes Federation to counter what they viewed as the dangerous class features of the Triveni Sangh and Kisan Sabha movements. This federation groomed future "backward" leaders by co-opting men like Birchand Patel (a Kurmi), Sheonandan Mandal, and later Ram Lakhan Singh Yadav.

Having thus guaranteed its "backward class" "vote bank," the Congress subsequently refused to grant Triveni Sangh candidates tickets to contest the upcoming elections. Furious at what they could only perceive as the underhanded trickery of local Congress party bosses, the Triveni Sangh leaders pledged electoral war against the "cursed Congressites." Following a hotly contested election in which two Triveni Sanghis emerged victorious in Shahabad District (Tapsi Mahto from Arrah constituency and Nandkishore Singh from Piro constituency), the war that had been waged with the ballot reverted to more violent means as high-status landlords reigned vengeful terror on whole Kurmi, Kushvaha, and Yadav villages. Conversely, in areas where the Triveni Sangh had not won, supporters consoled themselves with the ominous solace, "we lost by the vote, but we hadn't lost our lathis."

The rift between Congress and the Triveni Sangh, while sizable, was not insurmountable, as the latter merged with the Congress-sponsored Backward Classes Federation in 1948. While this certainly signified the end of the Triveni Sangh as a distinct political entity, it should not be viewed as the decline of Kushvaha-Kurmi-Yadav political power. Triveni Sangh leaders were being given posts in the Bihar Congress as early as 1940, and Kurmis, Kushvahas, and Yadavs contested seats in the 1946 election on Congress tickets. Thus, what Triveni Sanghis lost in terms of the symbolic power inherent in their kshatriya identities they gained in terms of direct access to political power. And while Congress gained access to a formidable rural vote bank, the social and economic tensions they were able to contain during the heady days of the new republic would eventually rise to the surface to define the quality of Indian politics in the post-1947 era.

Conversely, the failure to produce any sort of union between the Kisan Sabha and the Triveni Sangh in the 1930s, despite common economic interests, can only be explained by the historical antagonisms that existed between powerful Bhumihar landlords on the one hand and marginal Yadav, Kurmi, and Kushvaha peasants on the other. This basic enmity surfaces in a politically and socially charged description of the tenuous relationship between the Sangh and the Sabha:

> The bridge between the Bhumihar messiah, Swami Sahajanand Saraswati, and [the] ideologues of the Triveni Sangh was never built. Despite the fact that members of the Sangh flocked to listen to the Swami's message of common struggle, the Bhumihar label stuck. When Kesari "Master" [a Triveni Sangh leader] visited the Swami's ashram at Bihta in Patna district, night had fallen. Looking around he saw that those who surrounded the Swami were all upper-caste Bhumihars. Horrified, the backward-caste leader crept away under the cover of darkness.

This episode is recounted in a language and tone familiar to observers of late twentieth-century Bihar politics, but adjectives like "backward-caste" would have had little meaning in the 1920s and 1930s, when Sahajanand was making his overtures to the broad base of tenant-cultivators and the tenant-cultivators themselves-the new peasant kshatriyas-were joining to explore new modes of political expression. Master Keshari, the hardened Triveni Sangh orator, shrank from the overpowering Bhumihar presence in Sahajanand's Sitaram Ashram not because they were "upper-caste Bhumihars" and he was a "backward-caste leader," but because the memory of staunch Bhumihar opposition to peasant-kshatriya reform was too fresh in the minds of all Kurmis, Kushvahas, and Yadavs. Only in the 1940s and especially after Independence did such politically inspired labels as "backward" and "forward" become superimposed on the older and, by then, antiquated conflicts over varna.

IDENTITY AND CLASS

The 1890s began with the rise of anti-Muslim mob violence, perpetrated in large part by gangs of Goalas set on associating themselves with what they perceived as the respectable desire to prohibit the slaughter of cows. As such, this phenomenon constituted an expression, albeit vague, of Goala solidarity with the landed elite who led the gauraksha movement. This tenuous solidarity began to develop cracks by the beginning of the twentieth century, as marginal elites in general and Goalas in particular launched campaigns articulating kshatriya identities. At the core of the kshatriya reform movements resided a direct challenge to the social and economic supremacy of the twice-born elite, and as these movements progressed, cultural confrontation became physical conflict.

Importantly, however, as old solidarities grew obsolete, new cohesive forms began to emerge. The Triveni Sangh represented the political union of Bihar's three most populous peasant communities-Yadav, Kushvaha, and Kurmi kshatriyas. In addition to the fact that they possessed common economic interests, these three communities had exercised a common cultural logic to regenerate their identities. The electoral power of this union was clearly demonstrated in 1937, as was its potential for class formation. As we shall see in the next chapter, nationalist politicians, anxious to minimize the growth of class antagonisms that would not only threaten the fragile unified opposition to British rule but also their own superordinate status, worked successfully to co-opt Triveni Sanghis as part of an undifferentiated "backward class" component of the Indian National Congress.

But if it can be argued that the Congress benefited electorally from what those elite members of Congress saw as a broadly agrarian class element in its organizational structure, the counterargument can certainly be made that the new peasant kshatriyas gained in proportion access to power and policy formation. Indeed, the political power that ex-Triveni Sanghis wielded in the elite Congress ranks would have been understood reflexively as another example of the heights to which they themselves had successfully aspired in their programs for social reform. And when the limits of Congress's political vision (not to mention social semantics) could no longer accommodate the aspirations of its "backward" contingent, the latter would break away to create new political forms to articulate, once again, a distinct economic and social message. This is evident most recently in the emergence of the Janata Dal (People's Party) and in the increasingly independent political action of leaders like Ram Lakhan Singh Yadav, the late Karpoori Thakur, Mulayam Singh Yadav, and Laloo Yadav. In a sense, and understandably given the urgency of the nationalist movement, Congress leaders sacrificed long-term political cohesiveness for the short-term goal of delaying political discontent among peasants.

Social and cultural conflict did not end, therefore, with independence in 1947. Kurmis, Kushvahas, and Yadavs first flexed their unfettered political muscle in the late 1970s with demands for greater representation in the state bureaucracy under the controversial extension of the "reservations" policy for a vaguely defined list of "other backward classes." The reservation of political offices, administrative posts, and educational opportunities for "depressed communities" was enshrined in the Indian constitution, but only made explicit in state-by-state lists ("schedules") for untouchables and tribals; "other backward classes" would include a heavy preponderance of Kurmi, Yadav, and Kushvaha kshatriyas. Following the cessation of sporadic violence engendered by and in response to the backward classes movement, the 1980s would witness the emergence of overt, armed warfare over the control of land, spearheaded by the Communist Party of India (Marxist-Leninist).

Termed "Naxalite" after the initial experiments in militant landgrabbing conducted in the Naxalbari area of west Bengal, the movement now features Kurmis, Yadavs, and Kushvahas in Bihar as both victims and perpetrators of violence (though, significantly, never in the same case) directed against the landed, and retaliatory attacks by the landed against the landless. Historically, Kurmi, Yadav, and Kushvaha kshatriyas have been positioned on both sides of the margin of land tenancy and land ownership. This is a socioeconomic fact that, to a large extent, has hindered the formation of subordinate and superordinate class groups purely on the basis of jati distinctions.

The Yadav move from cowherd to kshatriya from the 1890s to the 1920s and the politics of Kurmi, Kushvaha, and Yadav involvement in agrarian radicalism from the 1920s to the 1940s together reveal the shifting nature of the caste fissures that inform the history of Gangetic north India.

Whether or not the "mobility aspirations" of low-status peasants and artisans reflected "actual processes taking place in society," kshatriya reform brought about real political and cultural change. And the degree to which kshatriya reformers were successful in creating an impression among those poised above them in the political and social economy of Gangetic north India can be measured by the willingness of agrarian elites to respond to their claims both with harsh words and violent deeds, and by the fact that the politics of kshatriya identity determined to a large extent the history of agrarian politics in the 1930s and 1940s.

CONCLUSIONS

This study has been concerned in particular with the ideological options that confronted those branded shudra, or servile, by the twice-born elite in the nineteenth and twentieth centuries. At this level of social-historical experience, the access to personal dignity afforded shudras by Ramanandis via the Vaishnava religious mainstream represented an important rupture in the culture of caste.

Through the course of the nineteenth and twentieth centuries, and despite what were at times fractious internal differences of opinion, Ramanandi monks were not only willing to overlook social stigma in administering religious teachings and directing worship, but even welcomed shudras as equal members of the monastic community. This was particularly the case after 1918, when the Ramanandi sampraday would find itself embroiled in debates over the question of religious and social elitism in monastic society, eventually leaning toward a distinctively egalitarian stance. Given the increasingly high profile of Ramanandis in Gangetic society during this period, this constituted an important rejection of the boundary between twice-born and shudra.

For many ordinary people, however, the culture of caste remained too overpowering to be subverted by the weight of monastic opinion, however authoritative. This did not necessarily mean, however, that they succumbed to its epistemological weight. Rather, by the early twentieth century many former shudras (including, most importantly, millions of peasants) began to refashion themselves en masse as the kshatriya descendants of divine royal lineages and hence as equal members of the very elite that despised them.

As part of that populist reform, and aimed directly at the caste systemics of agricultural and artisanal production, the new kshatriyas sought to transform the meaning of physical labor by questioning the social stigma attached to it. This would have dramatic-and often violent-repercussions in the countryside, as rural elites expressed resentment at the usurpation of their social and, hence, economic prerogatives. The history of kshatriya reform confirms, then, that as one descends to the perspective of those who suffer the brunt of social stigma, caste loses its epistemological force and is treated as ideology.

The variety of arguments put forward in peasant and monastic redefinitions hinged on the histories and hagiographies of important Vaishnava personages. Among monks, Ramanand and the chain of gurus that preceded and succeeded him assumed major importance; among peasants, Ram and Krishna and their genealogies became paramount. Not unexpectedly, there was significant overlap. On occasion, individual monks played a role in reformist campaigns for kshatriya identity, but their decision to do so depended on their perception of the relevance of caste in monastic life which, in turn, was a function of their specific sampraday identity.

More importantly, becoming kshatriya was in large part predicated on being Vaishnava-in behavior, belief, language, and diet. This history should be understood, then, as two socioreligiously related but distinct cultural processes: For radical Ramanandis, Vaishnavism entailed a philosophical stance against all forms of elitism, social or religious; for Yadavs, Kurmis, Kushvahas and many other "reformed kshatriyas," Vaishnavism provided the discursive and historical frame for a new, elite status that drew on a hierarchical ideology to subvert a hierarchical world. In this sense, though the ideological poles of this study stand in rigid opposition, both represented reasonable and compelling options for the millions of ordinary people long stigmatized by the term shudra.

Print technology and the rise of local publishing houses played an important role in the articulation and evolution of both radical Ramanandi and kshatriya reform viewpoints. Indeed the increasing number of competing commentaries on a major hagiographical text, namely, the Bhaktamal, in the latter half of the nineteenth century served to quicken the pace and heighten the intensity of philosophical and theological disputes within the Ramanandi sampraday.

There is no doubt that published religious tracts became a major means of expressing Ramanandi doctrinal opinion, superseding or working in tandem with such periodic assemblages as the kumbh. A similar argument can be made with reference to kshatriya reform, namely, that the ability to print several thousand inexpensive Yadav, Kurmi, or Kushvaha-kshatriya histories, along with guidebooks prescribing correct religious and ritual observances (complete with advertisements from shops in major towns willing to sell sacred thread to the aspiring kshatriya), contributed to the viability of the movement as a whole.

The popularization of printing presses certainly allowed for one remarkable feature of kshatriya reform, namely, the ability of educated individuals in the stigmatized communities to usurp to some extent the role of monastic gurus as local spiritual guides, by disseminating reformist propaganda with high levels of religious content. Given the strong Vaishnava dimension of that religious content, it is easy to understand how Hindi-language publishing quickly became associated with what Christopher King has called the "Hindu heritage," and what that meant in more specific sectarian terms. Prior to the rise of kshatriya reform, the publication of religious texts was directed for the most part to an expert readership which could then dispense religious teachings via oral disquisitions based on those texts.

The best example of this is the Bhaktamal, which was written for a select class of religious and literary adepts in a restricted Vaishnava sampraday context. With the popularization of kshatriya reform, religious instruction was often boiled down to a few essentials-vegetarian diet, proper worship, appropriate behavior (particularly for women), the schedule and performance of life-cycle rituals-to serve the interests of social and political mobilization, and was transmitted directly to large social groups independently of any mediation by a local religious adept. Appropriately, therefore, the genealogical concerns of kshatriya reform were not with sampraday-related guru parampara (Ramanandi or otherwise), but with the royal lineages of Ramchandra and Krishna.

The vast scope of kshatriya-reform publishing also served to popularize a historical message that would have major political and religious implications in the decades to come, namely, that Muslim invaders over the previous millennium were responsible for destroying the same sacred royal lineages in which the new kshatriya readership was being persuaded to claim descent. Given the colonial historiography of religion, this would have constituted an eminently believable, not to mention politically acceptable, way of explaining the degraded state of once-proud kshatriya communities in the early twentieth century. The communalist potential of kshatriya reform literature shared as well a great deal with historiographical themes raised in radical Ramanandi writing in the early twentieth century. Perhaps this is one reason, long after the passing of kshatriya reform and the political culture that nurtured it (to which we will turn momentarily), this convenient history lesson, with Ayodhya and Mathura-Vrindaban as its geocultural epicenters, remains embedded in the mental world of ordinary north Indians.

FORWARD AND BACKWARD

In retrospect, it would appear that the populist, peasant-based call for a kshatriya past suddenly lost its voice after the 1940s. Certainly one hears little mention today of the kshatriya antecedents of Kurmi, Yadav, and Kushvaha political identity. In fact the shift from the cultural politics of the early twentieth century to the political culture of the 1990s is not one that occurred as a sharp break at Independence in 1947 but has been much more gradual, indeed, almost imperceptible. The implications of that shift are profound, however, signaling the demise of a political culture based on an ideology of martial power and the rise of politics based on democratic, demographic realities.

Of all the reformed kshatriyas, Yadavs maintained the highest political profile after 1940. The following decades saw the increasing political engagement of such organizations as the All-India Yadav Mahasabha, the All-India Yadav Youth League, and the Bharatiya Yadav Sangh. Despite this upsurge in Yadav political activity, however, the period witnessed increasingly fewer calls for a detailed investigation of the martial history of Yadavs.

Indeed, even the brief but intense pressure by Yadav leaders in the 1960s for greater representation in the Indian armed forces and the creation of a Yadav regiment was supported not by a renewed elaboration of the ancient kshatriya glories of the community but by focusing on the participation of Ahirs in the 1857 rebellion (remembered now as the first war of Indian independence), the subsequent recruitment of Ahirs/Yadavs into the British-Indian army, and the valor of Yadav soldiers during the 1965 Indo-Pakistan war.

While Yadav organizations were becoming politically more active (if less avowedly kshatriya) after 1947, the analogous Kurmi bodies seemed to be in absolute decline. The All-India Kurmi Kshatriya Mahasabha, which had held twenty conferences between the years 1894 and 1933, held half as many conferences between 1934 and 1971, with a gap of over ten years between the twenty-fourth (1948) and twenty-fifth (1958) meetings. The 1971 meeting was of particular significance in that Dahya Bhai Patel, a socialist member of parliament who presided over the session, successfully advocated the deletion of the term 'kshatriya' from all conference announcements-a decision which engendered substantial ill-will on the part of jati elders. This same conference also saw increased ties between the Kurmi and Kushvaha communities, perhaps a spillover from the days of political cooperation in the 1930s; however, one hears almost no reference at all to Kushvaha-kshatriya organizations.

What occasioned the decline of the kshatriya political idiom among Yadav, Kurmi, and Kushvaha peasants between 1940 and the present? While this question reaches beyond the scope of this study, the answer can be found in the changing politics of India or, more precisely, in the new politics of independent India. The previous chapter ended with the three main peasant movements for kshatriya identity co-opted by the late 1930s via the Triveni Sangh into the Backward Classes Federation of the Indian National Congress and, hence, into the struggle for independence from British rule. Triveni Sangh leaders no doubt based this strategic shift on the perception that the future of Indian political patronage was to be dictated by nationalist leaders dedicated to a quasi-socialist democracy and, in that context, committed to the amelioration of social and economic injustice. For Kurmi, Yadav, and Kushvaha leaders, this would represent a sea change in Indian political culture, since a kshatriya identity only had meaning in the context of a colonial political system crafted around visions of martial grandeur. In independent India politics would be predicated instead on universal adult suffrage and a commitment to the welfare of the nation's citizenry and would be played out by Indian party politicians seeking Indian votes. The questions for the leaders of reformed kshatriya communities were, how to conceive of themselves in the new politics? how to relate to Indian social democracy?

In retrospect, the first indication that the prospect of an independent, social-democratic India would have a measurable effect on the Yadav, Kurmi, and Kushvaha identities could be seen in the nationalist conception of these peasant communities as components of a federation of "backward classes." This would lead to constitutional safeguards in the form of reserved legislative seats, administrative and educational appointments, and other protective discriminations adopted by the first parliament on behalf of untouchables ("scheduled castes"), tribals ("scheduled tribes"), and "other depressed sections" of society. Specific clauses in articles fifteen and sixteen (entitled "Prohibition of Discrimination on the Grounds of Religion, Race, Caste, Sex, or Place of Birth" and "Equality of Opportunity in Matters of Public Employment," respectively) of the Constitution gave the government of India the power to legislate in favor of "the advancement of any socially and educationally backward classes of citizens or for the Scheduled Castes and the Scheduled Tribes."

To throw moral and political weight behind these clauses, Prime Minister Nehru included in the "Objectives Resolution" (a memorandum outlining the philosophy behind the Constitution) the assurance that "adequate safeguards shall be provided for minorities, backward and tribal areas, and depressed and other backward classes." But while the question of identifying scheduled castes and scheduled tribes was settled before 1947 (in large part due to the efforts of B. R. Ambedkar, the author of the constitution), exactly who composed the backward classes-or, as Nehru put it, the "other backward classes"-was a question left for subsequent generations. This constitutional uncertainty, and the mixed record of government attempts to resolve it, would fuel the backward-classes movement after 1950.

The first attempt to identify the backward classes emerged in 1953, with the appointment of the Backward Classes Commission by the president of India.

The commission, in a report submitted after two years of deliberation, indicated that caste was an important measure of "backwardness" and, as such, drew up a list of 2,399 castes they believed to be backward.

However, five of the eleven members of the commission-including the head of the commission itself, the widely respected legal scholar Kakasaheb Kalelkar-voiced strong objections on philosophical grounds. In a dissent attached to the report, Kalelkar expressed his frustration that while "the caste system is the greatest hindrance in the way of our progress towards an egalitarian society, . . . the recognition of the specified castes as backward may serve to maintain and even perpetuate the existing distinctions on the basis of caste."

Thus, for many educated Indians, applying caste as a delimiting tool in the struggle to eradicate the inequalities of caste represented a philosophically self-defeating exercise. Their critics would charge that this philosophical dilemma was simply a convenient (and typically Gandhian) upper-caste ploy to delay indefinitely the pressing need to redress the millennia-old social injustices of caste. With this dilemma in mind, not to mention other more pressing political factors, the central government rejected the 1955 report on the grounds that the commission had not applied more objective criteria, such as income, education, and literacy, to determine backward status.

In the following decades, numerous state commissions were formed to devise methods of identifying "backward" on the basis of a regional caste list combined with a battery of social, educational, and economic litmus tests. In 1978 a new central government Backward Classes Commission was created, headed by B. P. Mandal. According to the Mandal Commission report, submitted at the end of 1980, fully 3,743 castes representing over 52 percent of the population of India were identified as "backward"; the commission therefore recommended additional reservations of 27 percent (so as to keep the combined total reservations for scheduled castes, scheduled tribes, and "other backward classes" under the constitutional limit of 50 percent).

The central and state governments would deal with the backward classes issue in a variety of ways, some more aggressive than others. Even the Congress Party, since the 1970s viewed as a bastion of brahman conservatism on the backward classes issue, would gradually inch toward a grudging recognition of the political necessity of granting reservations according to their own reading of the Mandal Commission recommendations.

If a turning point can be discerned, it was the announcement in August 1990 by then Prime Minister V. P. Singh that his government would begin implementing the Mandal recommendations. This act set off a firestorm of vigorous "forward-caste" protests, including a rash of self-immolation attempts by university students, and even brought down V. P. Singh's National Front government. However, it effectively ensured that every major party would have to address the issue directly, not simply make gratuitous reference to it in campaign manifestos.

If reform on behalf of the backward classes posed a set of philosophical and logistical problems for the administrative and political elite, it posed an entirely different sort of dilemma for communities within the backward classes movement itself. The dominance of the "backward" rhetoric has meant, for members of many newly designated "backward" castes, that communities long engaged in sophisticated campaigns to garner self-respect as kshatriyas-reformed, educated, and socially advanced-had now to begin representing themselves as disadvantaged.

While one object of jati mahasabha relations with government-whether British or Indian-remained the same, namely, the agitation for greater job opportunities, the entire tone of the relationship with government changed. No longer would caste leaders dispatch memorials to government bureaucracies elaborating the proud histories and extensive abilities of their communities as a justification for increased employment; the post-1947 leaders of the same communities have agitated for the passage of backward classes legislation-and hence symbolically important reservations for jobs, university admissions, and seats in legislatures-as a political and social obligation of government, so that the beneficiaries of that legislation, conceived as the downtrodden members of an oppressive society, can lead their brothers and sisters out of the abyss of institutionalized inequality.

The demise of kshatriya reform politics does not mean, however, that the religiously potent politics of kshatriyatva (martial valor) are no longer to be seen in north India. That political idiom still survives, but has been taken up by what is generally referred to as the "Hindu right," manifest in Uttar Pradesh and Bihar as the Sangh Parivar (the family of the Sangh): the Bharatiya Janata Party (BJP), the Vishwa Hindu Parishad, and the Rashtriya Swayamsevak Sangh.

Consequently, we still hear a great deal about the martial qualities of Ramchandra and, increasingly, Krishna, though they are not articulated in terms of the genealogical antecedents of the communities that have come to be known as "backward," but as the basis for a new moral politics and a utopian social vision centered in particular on the birthplaces of those divine personages. Given the political topography of north India, it is generally assumed that the "backwards" keep the Hindu right at arm's length.

This is due to the quasi-socialist leanings of most backward-class leaders as opposed to the generally procapitalist leanings of the BJP (which has in the past, collective wisdom tells us, relied upon the financial contributions of small urban shopkeepers and the occasional major financial concern). It is also often held that cadre support for the BJP is drawn largely

from the upper castes who inhabit the burgeoning economic middle classes in the cities, a social composition that would alienate the backwards. However, BJP leaders make no secret of their desire to attract a greater peasant following, and to do this they would naturally seek to exploit the by now near-forgotten claims to kshatriya status by Yadavs, Kurmis, and Kushvahas of yesteryear.

It is in this context that the Yadav identity of Bihar's chief minister, Laloo Yadav, was called into question after his jailing of the BJP leader Lal Kishan Advani, during the latter's "chariot ride" through north India to "liberate" the birthplace of Ram (Ramjanambhumi) in 1989. The implication is that if Laloo Yadav had been true to the Vaishnava dimensions of his Yadav-kshatriya roots, he would have supported the Ramjanambhumi movement and allowed Advani's procession to make a grand entrance into eastern Uttar Pradesh from Bihar. As yet it is unclear how "backwards" are responding to such rhetoric, though the successes of the Hindu right at the polls in the past decade and the support the Ramjanambhumi movement attracted in the rural areas indicate that the new articulation of kshatriyatva is resonating with more than just the urban middle class and the rural elite.

The emergence of backward and kshatriyatva politics reflects not only the changing nature of politics but the changing political culture of India. In ideological terms 1947 represented a clear break with the past, a watershed in terms of how individuals perceived themselves as part of the Indian body politic. Fundamental to this ideological change is the fact-explicit in the constitution with reference to universal equalities and implicit in any political system organized around democratic processes-that from the point of view of government (as distinct from politicians, political parties, and voters themselves), caste no longer constituted the basis of an individual's political and legal being, as it had in British India. However, moving from a political culture based firmly on caste to one that repudiates casteism is easier said than done. Scholars will be left to speculate on the effect of such legal reorientations on mass politics and individual people; there can be no doubt, however, that the effects on both were interconnected and, as yet, are unresolved.

The backward class movement was connected to the rise of a socialist-democratic state and reflected the popular perception that that state would respond to those who portrayed themselves as sufficiently needy. The new politics of kshatriyatva reflect, by contrast, a broad-based frustration with the nature of the moral order (or lack thereof) implicit to that state. The slow abandonment of the socialist components of the Indian state that now seems to be taking place is a process that of necessity reduces the extent to which the state can provide what it may have deemed in the past socially desirable employment, representation, and education.

The issue that faces Yadavs, Kurmis, Kushvahas as the twentieth century draws to a close is whether they should relinquish the politics of "backwardness" altogether in favor of a return to their kshatriya reformist roots. If they were to do so, it would be natural for them to articulate kshatriya reform politically as kshatriyatva.

HISTORY AND CONSCIOUSNESS

If I do not describe the history of kshatriya reform or Ramanandi radicalism in terms of subaltern consciousness, it is because to do so would be to understand the actors as perpetually put upon and to understand their ideologies in fundamentally negative terms-at best as forms of resistance destined to fall short of their utopian visions, at worst as predetermined national failures.

Kshatriya reform and radical Ramanandi ideologies were predicated on social change (whether real or imagined) and, as such, sought to inculcate new epistemologies, particularly at the level of popular religious consciousness. An understanding of political insurgency as the only worthwhile mode of peasant expression implies a theoretical frame that is impervious to such shifting social and mental worlds. This may appear as a critique of the subaltern studies project from the right. In fact, it is not unlike a recent reflection from within.

Fortunately, historical actors are not burdened by the theoretical paradigms and social categories that constrict social scientists, and social historians in particular. When we listen to what those historical actors have to say, we learn that significant, if commonplace, transformations took place on a regular basis throughout the nineteenth and twentieth centuries. Perhaps these transformations are more easily discerned if we understand them as the crossing of boundaries. Such boundary crossings included the commonplace entry of shudras into north India's largest Vaishnava monastic order, the Ramanandi sampraday, and the radical (and largely successful) attempts by some in that sampraday to foster a more egalitarian monastic spirit.

The crossing of boundaries also included the rejection by peasants and artisans of the shudra status that had for so long been ascribed to them, in favor of a kshatriya identity rich with Vaishnava meaning. Ramanandi and kshatriya reform each reflected a particular kind of consciousness predicated on the creation, maintenance, and definition of community, whether religious (sampraday) or social (jati).

Both Ramanandi radicals and kshatriya reformers went about their programs by engaging in intellectual labor and propaganda and by articulating their views in popular presses throughout the Gangetic north. Their aggressive posture occasioned moments of conflict and sometimes even violence, but unlike subaltern consciousness, their voices did not require moments of conflict to be discernible. And though they lacked the glamour and grandeur of a rebellion or revolution, Vaishnava and kshatriya reform possessed their own kind of rebellious, revolutionary content, howsoever incremental and subtle it may have been.

The history of the Ramanandi sampraday and kshatriya reform in the nineteenth and twentieth centuries affords an insider's view of caste, an idea that has long been presumed to reside at the heart of India, rendering that place and its inhabitants unchanging, even timeless. Though caste may have become integral to British imaginings of India, the caste of varna remained politically real and culturally pervasive, if not religiously sacrosanct. Like race, varna did not exist beyond history but remained well within it, was not rigid and monolithic but flexible, indeed malleable. Because the social and cultural systemics of identity had long involved repeated reconciliations of varna and jati-the ideal and the real-the tools with which to manipulate caste were readily available. All that was required was a familiarity with royal or religious genealogies, the ability to apply them to present-day identities, and the wherewithal to present them in the language of history as an ancient present.

Social history, particularly peasant history, is too often written as if the actors do not think-or if they do think, that their thoughts and beliefs do not matter in the long run-and as if the only force that propels them through history is a concern with the contents of pocketbook and stomach. Basic common sense, however, tells us that historical change can on occasion be dependent upon moral principles and a sense of social justice.

To write history, to engage opponents on the battleground of the past, to reform fundamental social groups, whether sampraday or jati, according to a new vision of the past-these were the accomplishments of thinking peasants and monks in Gangetic north India. For peasants history served identity, for monks history served hagiography. But for both, their discourses of history were rife with vital meaning. The constant, self-directed questioning of history by peasants and monks-

Who were we, what has happened, and where are we going now?

Gather round everyone and ponder these questions together.

If we fail to appreciate the entirety of our past, we may never realize who we really are.

or,

Who could have exposed the fallacy of high and low if such a sadhu had not entered the world?

Who else could have inspired the notion that no one is impure amid the tranquility of God's realm?

-confirms that to write about the past, whether in terms of ancient kshatriya origins or in terms of the life of Ramanand, justified action in the present. The past was alive for peasants and monks in British India.

This was not disinterested history. Indeed, many times here I have referred to elements of it as polemic and propaganda. Yet it served an important historical purpose by allowing ordinary people to debate the merits of status and equality. Peasants ultimately wished for a society that did not deride individuals as shudra, and they therefore advocated reform. But they did this in what appears to have been a roundabout manner, namely, by asserting kshatriya origins in the ancient past and, hence, elite status in the present.

This elitist strategy was remarkably effective, not to mention threatening, because of its epistemological implications. As one interested observer put it in 1925: "When everybody is somebody, then nobody is anybody." Or, as a friend put it in 1987, "we used to be shudra, then we were kshatriya; now I'm not sure what we are."

Bibliography

Bakker, Hans: *Ayodhya*, Groningen, Egbert Forsten, 1986.

Bhagvan Prasad, Sitaramsharan: *Shri Bhaktamal: Tika, Tilak, aur Namavali Sahit,* Kashi [Banaras], Chandraprabha Press, 1903–9.

Bahura, Gopal Narayan, and Chandramani Singh: *Catalogue of Historical Documents in the Kapad Dwara [royal warehouse], Jaipur*, Jaigarh Public Charitable Trust, 1988.

Bhandarkar, R. G.: *Vaishnavism, Saivism, and Minor Religious Systems*, New Delhi: Asian Educational Services, 1987.

Chaturvedi, Parshuram: *Uttari Bharat ki Sant-Parampara [The North Indian Sant Tradition]*, Allahabad, Leader Press, 1972.

Casey, Edward S.:*Remembering: A Phenomenological Study*, Bloomington: Indiana University Press, 1987.

Chaudhari, Devi Prasad Sinha: *Kurmi Kshatriyatva Darpan [Reflections on Kurmi-Kshatriya Valor]*, Lucknow, Kashi Ram Varma, 1907.

Cohn, Bernard S.: *An Anthropologist among the Historians and Other Essays*, Delhi, Oxford University Press, 1990.

Dasgupta, Atis K.: *The Fakir and Sannyasi Uprisings*, Calcutta: K. P. Bagchi, 1992.

Das, Janki Ballabh: *Devivali Pakhand [The Heresy of Sacrifice to the Goddess]*, Prayag, J. B. Das, 1937.

Growse, F. S.: *Mathura: A District Memoir*. 1880, Allahabad: Northwest Provinces and Oudh Government Press, 1883.

Ghurye, G. S.: *Indian Sadhus. 1953,* Bombay, Popular Prakashan, 1964.

Gupta, Gangaprasad: *Kile ki Rani [Queen of the Fort]*, Banaras, Durga Prasad Khatri, 1915.

Hess, Linda, and Shukdev Singh: *The Bijak of Kabir*, Delhi, Motilal Banarsidass, 1986.

Harlan, Lindsey: *Religion and Rajput Women: The Ethic of Protection in Contemporary Narratives*, Berkeley and Los Angeles, University of California Press, 1992.

Jones, Kenneth W.: *Arya Dharm: Hindu Consciousness in Nineteenth-Century Punjab*, Berkeley and Los Angeles, University of California Press, 1976.

King, Christopher R.: *One Language, Two Scripts: The Hindi Movement in Nineteenth-Century North India*, Delhi, Oxford University Press, 1994.

Kashinath (Pandit): *Varnvivek Chandrika [Moonlight of Varna Wisdom]*, Bombay, Shri Venkateshwar Press, 1898.

Mishra, Jvalaprasad: *Jatibhaskar [Illuminations on Jati]*. Bombay, Khemraj Shri Krishnadas, 1917.

McLeod, William H.: *The Evolution of the Sikh Community: Five Essays*, Delhi, Oxford University Press, 1975.

Ray, Nauvat: *Kahar Jati aur Varnavyavastha [The Kahar Jati and the Varna System]*. Firozabad, Agra, Fakirchand, 1920.

Ram, Karu: *Ramani Nirnay [Rules of the Ramanis]*, Gaya, Magadha Shubhanker Press, 1906.

Saraswati, Sahajanand (Swami): *Gita Hriday [The Heart of the Gita]*, Allahabad, Kitab Mahal, 1948.

Sahay, Shivpujan: *Hindi Sahitya aur Bihar [Hindi literature and Bihar]*, Patna: Bihar Rashtrabhasha Parishad, 1960–1984.

Sitaram (Lala): *Ayodhya ka Itihas [History of Ayodhya]*, Prayag (Allahabad): Hindustani Academy, 1932.

Sharma, Sachchidanand: *Udasi Sampraday aur Kavi Sant Rena [The Udasi Sampraday and the Poet-Saint Rena]*, Dehradun, Sahitya Sadan, 1967.

Vaudeville, Charlotte: *Kabir*, Oxford, Oxford University Press, 1974.

Index

AGEING IN NORTH EAST INDIA

MAGNITUDE OF THE PROBLEMS OF ELDERLY PERSONS IN MIZORAM

AGEING IN NORTH EAST INDIA

Magnitude of the Problems of Elderly Persons in Mizoram

Edited By:

LIANZELA

VANLALCHHAWNA

AKANSHA PUBLISHING HOUSE

NEW DELHI

AKANSHA PUBLISHING HOUSE
4649-B/21, Ansari Road
Darya Ganj, New Delhi - 110 002
Email: ektabooks@yahoo.com
Ph. : 23263193 / 9811582579

Ageing in North East India : Magnitude of the Problems of Elderly Persons in Mizoram

First Published 2007

Reprint 2026

ISBN 978-81-8370-102-0

PRINTED IN INDIA

Published by M.P. Misra for Akansha Publishing House, New Delhi and Printed at Aryan Enterprises, Delhi.

FOREWORD

Ageing or becoming old is a global phenomenon in the sense that it is experienced by all the societies in all generations and all countries but its magnitude and manifestations are not the same everywhere. It has been observed that science and technology, industrialization, modernization and globalization like improved health care, improved nutrition and improved standards of living make people live much longer than expected and thereby there has been an increase in the growth of elderly population in all societies. The United Nations Principles for Older Persons in 1991 emphasized that *in all countries, individuals are reaching an advanced age in greater numbers and in better health than ever before.* The rise in the population of the elderly was thought to be a concern only of the developed countries but now it has become an equally important issue even in the developing countries as well. The population aged 60+ is increasing rapidly in our country that it is expected to be 177 million by 2025. This growth in the population of the elderly will certainly change the aspect of life for individual and societies.

It is a known fact that the old people in the past especially in our country commanded respect because they controlled the sources of power, wealth, land, political office, and the fate of other family members. However, it has been observed that there have been some changes in the society as new generations perceive a different outlook in life which are due to the pressures of urbanization, increasing migration from rural to urban areas, change in occupation patterns and perhaps a change in life styles too. Old age is also generally accompanied by a number of problems that the elderly have to face and adjust with in varying degrees. The problems of elderly are generally rooted in physical debility, loneliness and depression. Thus their physical resources vary according to their age, life-style, genetic build and destiny. The important variables for the elderly are health and income. Therefore, the loss of economic independence and physical vigour and the emergence of various types of degenerative diseases, such as, hypertension, diabetes, rheumatism, gout, prostate, cardiac problems, spondylitis, lumbago, cancer, etc., often change an elderly from an independent self-supporting individual to one who needs help from his children, members of the family and the society in general. Absence of common interests and lack of extensive and regular interaction with the younger members in the family may result in social isolation and loneliness of the elderly.

There has been a time when the elders were kept in high esteem and phrases such as *old is gold; the older the wiser; country needs older people; you held our hands when we learnt to walk; now, as you enter the autumn of your lives, society is prepared to hold your hands*; etc., were appreciated much. While in some societies, the elders were neglected, left alone uncared when the children got married and separated. Where as in other societies there were joint families where parents and married children lived together sharing everything together. However, this culture has now slowly broken in many conservative societies. Time and life has changed so fast due to science and technology and even the Gandhian philosophy of simple living and high thinking have become redundant in many families. With no income and incapable of working, many aged people become a burden on their children. Even if they are well looked-after, they suffer from a guilt complex. As a result elders are neglected for some generations and suffer physically and mentally at the fag end of their life. In a befitting manner the former U.N Secretary General, Kofi Annan, in the second world assembly on ageing in Madrid emphatically declared:

We have neglected the elders for many years. From now on, all the countries of the world should think to give proper respect to the senior citizens, in the last phase of their life, while making national development plans – social, political and economic.

It is heartening to note that, the UPA government is preparing a bill to improve the condition of the elderly persons in India. The bill that is on the anvil should certainly address the problems of the old people.

In the recent years, much literature on Northeast India has been published by the scholars of this region on various issues related to the people and the region as a whole. However, the issues related to ageing and the elderly persons of this region are not properly addressed so far. Although every 1st October is being observed as the International Day for the Elderly, yet the magnitude of the elderly persons in Northeast is not properly addressed neither in myriad seminars organised by various academic bodies and the NGOs nor their problems and aspirations are documented. Considering the lacunae in this field, the Indian Council of Social Science Research, North Eastern Regional Centre (ICSSR-NERC) took the initiative to bridge the gap by organizing a day long seminar on the Magnitude of the Problems of the Elderly persons in various States during the year 2006. This book has its origin in one of the seminars organized by the Department of Economics, Mizoram University on 19th October 2006. Professor Lianzela, Head, Department of Economics, Mizoram University and his colleagues in the department took the keen interest in the seminar not only in organizing it but also compiling and revising the papers presented in the seminar in the present book format.

This book deals with a number of issues pertaining to the aged from a multi-disciplinary approach emphasizing on the status, welfare and problems of the elderly persons particularly in Mizoram and it will be a useful source of information and reference to academicians, scholars and social workers and government agencies alike.

C Joshua Thomas
Acting Director
ICSSR-NERC
Shillong

CONTENTS

Annexures

LIST OF CONTRIBUTORS

Desai, Kalpana, Reader, Department of Social Work, Mizoram University.

Lalbiakkimi, District Social Welfare Officer, Aizawl District (West), Social Welfare Department, Government of Mizoram.

Lalhriatpuii, Lecturer, Department of Economics, Mizoram University.

Lalmuanpuii, Research Scholar, Department of Social Work, Mizoram University.

Ralte, Dr. Jane R., MBBS (LHMC), MHA(AIIMS), OSD (Health)-*cum*-Focal Point, (WHO sponsored community based health care for the elderly), Department of Health and Family Welfare, Government of Mizoram.

Thanga, James L.T., Senior Statistical Assistant, Department of Economics, Mizoram University.

Thangchungnunga, Professor, Department of Economics, Mizoram University.

Thanseia, Editor MUP Journal, Mizoram.

Vanlalchhawna, Reader, Department of Economics, Mizoram University.

INTRODUCTION

Lianzela and Vanlalchhawna

Ageing of the population has become one of the most pressing socioeconomic concerns across the world including India. People are living longer with the increase in the expectation of life at birth. In India, the proportion of persons 60 years and above in the total population has increased from 5 per cent in 1901 to 6.7 per cent in 1991 and will be around 9 per cent by the year 2016. Improved life expectancy has contributed to the increase in the number of old age persons. From only 12 millions in 1901 the number of persons aged 60 years and above in India has increased to 57 millions in 1901 which will be around 113.5 millions by the year 2016 as projected by the Technical Group of Population Projections. Demographic ageing is also evident from the faster decadal growth rate of the elderly as compared to the growth rate of the total population. The demographic ageing of population has implications at the macro as well as at the household level. The sheer magnitude of numbers is indicative both of the huge human reserve and also of the scale of endeavours necessary to provide social services and other benefits. In contrast to developed countries, developing countries have hardly any provisions for taking care of their elderly population. As such, there is need to study the social as well as the demographic aspects of ageing population in India.

Though the Mizoram Senior Citizens' Association (Mizoram Upa Pawl, MUP in short) was formed way back in 1961 in Mizoram, no serious academic discussion on the problem of ageing was ever conducted in Mizoram. The said Association was affiliated to the Federation of Association of Senior Citizens of India (FASC). In spite of the numerous activities taken up by MUP, the general awareness of the people about the ageing and its associated problems did not get much headway. Therefore, it can be said that the need of the hour as in Mizoram is to educate the people about ageing and the related problems faced by different countries in the world in general, and India in particular.

It was the Director of Indian Council of Social Science Research, North Eastern Regional Centre (ICSSR-NERC) who initiated the idea of holding seminar on the issue of ageing in the state of Mizoram. The idea was introduced to the Head, Department of Economics, Mizoram University (MZU, Aizawl). A meeting of the teaching faculty of the department was then convened to discuss thoroughly the feasibility of holding seminar on old age and the related problems. The meeting resolved to hold the seminar on "The Magnitude of the Problems of Elderly Persons in Mizoram" subject to the availability of fund from ICSSR. After getting the approval from the said organisation the seminar was finally organized on 19th October 2006 at Aizawl.

The seminar was attended by various organizations such as political parties, members from state-level NGOs, prominent citizens, academicians and students. The seminar was well represented. In all, 52 delegates from various sections of the concerned people attended the seminar. The seminar had three sessions viz., inauguration, technical session I and II. Professor A.N. Rai, the Vice Chancellor of Mizoram University (MZU) graced the Inaugural Function as Chief Guest. Keynote Address of the seminar was delivered by Professor

Lianzela, Head, Department of Economics and convener of the seminar. Dr. C.J. Thomas, Director, ICSSR (NERC) also delivered a speech.

Papers presented in the seminar include the followings:

1. **Magnitude and Growth of Elderly Population in Mizoram**

   Dr. Vanlalchhawna, Reader, Department of Economics, Mizoram University

2. **Social and Economic Status of Elderly Persons in Mizo Society**

   Prof. Thangchungnunga, Department of Economics, Mizoram University

3. **Ageing Gracefully: Role and Activities of Mizoram Upa Pawl**

   Mr. Thanseia, Editor, MUP Journal

4. **Health Conditions and Access to Health Care Services by Elderly in Mizoram**

   Dr. Jane R. Ralte, Department of Health and Family Welfare, Government of Mizoram

5. **Social and Economic Security Programme for Elderly Persons in Mizoram: Role of State Government**

   Ms. Lalbiakkimi, District Social Welfare Officer, Social Welfare Department, Government of Mizoram

6. **Social Work Intervention with the Elderly**

   Dr. Kalpana N.Desai, Reader and Head, Department of Social Work, and

   Lalmuanpuii, Research Scholar, Dept. of Social Work, Mizoram University.

In his paper, Vanlalchhawna examined the growth and magnitude of elderly population in Mizoram. The paper stated that people 60 years and above have an increasingly larger share in the total population. The share of 60 years and above population increased from 4.42 per cent in 1981 to 5.52 per cent in 2001. The elderly population grew much faster than the total population over the last three decades. The number of elderly woman per elderly man is also rising. Compared to 1981 census, the number of centenarians increased in 1991. The dependency ratio, i.e., number of elderly persons aged 60 years and above divided by the number of persons in the age group of 15-59 years, is gradually increasing. The socio-economic characteristics of the elderly persons such as work status, literacy, level of education, marital status, etc. are important indicators of their general well-being, happiness and contentment. The paper highlights some of the selected indicators of the socio-economic status of the elderly population in Mizoram, based on 1991 census. It was pointed out that a good number of the elderly persons continued to remain economically active even after retiring from regular employment. This has been possible with the improvement of the health condition of the aged persons. The 1991 census figures show that the proportion of workers was 53.22 per cent for the elderly as against 48.91 per cent for the total population. This percentage was 66.93 for elderly males and 38.81 per cent for elderly females. The female's work participation rate is seen to be much lower as compared with the elderly males. The work participation rate in the rural and urban areas was 55.58 per cent and 50.08 per cent respectively. About 75 per cent of the economically active elder population are cultivators.

Thangchungnunga analysed the role of elderly persons in social and economic aspects in the context of Mizo society. He stated that the place of old people in traditional Mizo society was associated with some special characteristics of an asset in its culture. Their usefulness in the performance of chores, skill in certain arts and storytelling, control of property rights, power in the family, useful experience or extensive knowledge belonged to the most valued asset of the community. In Mizo society, the authority of elderly people on moral questions is highly respected and they are looked upon as preserver of tribal values and chivalry. In the past, there was no fixed age at which one should retire, but today, the modal role for older men is retirement, not work. Though some lucky ones continue to work with great efficiency, many of them appear to accept with contentment their new role of retired persons. Since, political influence is so widespread in the society, older people also, even those with little education, are involved in politics and they are better represented among the political elite. At the same time, they are not found to be vocal enough on the question of their own economic self-interest. However, they formed a state-level organization with branches in all villages and localities through which they could express their interest and build up a self help group. With regard to economic activity, older people are comparatively disadvantaged on the average although individual variations are plenty. There is a clear trend now that the aged couples with their inclination to live separately from children are likely to depend primarily upon each other, turning to relatives only under conditions of special need.

Besides the government, several non-government organisations are increasingly involved in helping the aged people in society. In this regard, the services rendered by Mizoram Upa Pawl (Mizoram Senior Citizens Organization) could not be overlooked. The paper summarising the activities of the organisation was presented by Thanseia, one of the activists of the organisation. The organisation, founded as a non-government body in 1957, works exclusively for the cause of the elderly in Mizoram. Members of the organisation are actually engaged in finding out destitutes among their fellow members in particular and the poor and needy in general within their local limit and give them financial assistance from their own contribution and sometimes by rendering physical work. The organisation has instituted MIZO MEDAL to be awarded to those who exhibit extraordinary bravery, scholarship, high quality of social work etc. In political and economic fields the organisation tries to create awareness among the general public of the need of having good and clean administration where the rule of law could reign and where economic self-sufficiency could be achieved. The organisation declared 2006 as "Year of Anti-Corruption". Representatives of the organisation have often special interactions with Ministers and high officials of the state giving them constructive advice on issues concerning public interest. The MUP at present has more than 500 units, 67 areas and 4 Sub-Headquarters all over the state. The organisation has never been involved in party politics. Any Indian citizen who has crossed 50 years of age residing in Mizoram could become a member. There is no discrimination on the basis of community, creed, rich and poor. Recently, it constituted CHARITY FUND amounting to at least Rs. 50 lakhs to assist the needy members of the association. In this way the association has been trying its level best to be a blessing for others.

Dr. Jane R. Ralte, in her paper observed that the understanding and practice of the special health care needs for this vulnerable category of the population are still inadequate and need to be developed at all levels from primary health care level through secondary to tertiary care levels. While highlighting the health conditions of the elderly in Mizoram, the paper found that the major health problems are visual impairments (24.85%) followed by problems associated with ENT, namely hearing impairment (20.58%). There are very limited special provisions for the elderly in the current health care services in the state. Health care delivery structure needs to gear up their services in order to provide appropriate health care for the specific health needs of the elderly persons in the society. This would entail provisions of appropriate technology through training of medical and para-medical staff, procurement of equipment necessary for application of the technology and providing hospitals, which are "geriatric friendly".

The State Government, recognising the importance of the older persons and their contribution to the society as a whole, has taken various steps for their welfare. Ms. Lalbiakimi gives a broad overview of the welfare measures taken by the State Government for the elderly people in the state. The paper highlights that, besides the provision of old age pension and old age home, the state government also assists and aids the Mizoram Upa Pawl and other NGOs working for older persons, some of them are running Day Care Centres for Older Persons. The paper also outlines the importance features of State Policy for older persons (SPOP), which was formulated in 2003. The author observes that the assistance and facilities given to the aged in our state are still inadequate. She argues that, since the aged have given all their productive days to raising children and family, and worked for the betterment of the society as well as the government, we should probe deep about the reason why the aged who made immeasurable sacrifices to the community during their time are subjected to having to live in old age homes and why they have to be given old age pensions. It is now time to plan innovative welfare programmes for the aged keeping in view the changing environment and lifestyles.

Gerontological social work is concerned with maintaining and enhancing the quality of life of older adults and their families. It is particularly concerned with ameliorating those physical, psychosocial, familial, cultural, ethnic and racial, organisational, and societal factors which serve as barriers to physical and emotional well-being in later life. Gerontological social work interventions are directed at enhancing dignity, self-determination, personal fulfilment, quality of life, optimal functioning, and ensuring the least restrictive living environment possible. Interventions that enhance older adults' coping and problem-solving capabilities are perhaps the most basic and crucial aspect of gerontological social work. Because services are typically sought at times of crisis, gerontological social workers give special attention to the psychosocial meanings of change and loss, as well as to underlying biological, psychological, cognitive and social factors experienced by the older adult and family. Social Work operates within the framework of a bio-psycho-social perspective and sees all problems or challenges from this angle. Kalpana Desai and Lalmuanpuii outline some conceptual and definitional aspects related to ageing. It views the older persons as belonging to different categories since their needs and challenges at different decades of life (in older ages) differ depending on their residual strengths. The paper further explores the scope of gerontological social work and highlights some psychosocial issues that the old population is compelled to contend with. In this regard, it refers to dissertations so far conducted in Mizoram and present some findings. The paper concludes by describing the scope of Social Work Intervention across institutional and non-institutional settings.

Paper presentation was followed by a lively and educative discussion. Main issues discussed were highlighted in the Rapporteurs' report given in Annexure I.

KEYNOTE ADDRESS

Lianzela

Becoming old (ageing) has become a global problem, an issue associated with a number of problems. It is a natural process involving every human being born to this world. The very thought that we will become old one day makes many people sad and sick. But the fortunate thing is that the Bible does not see old age as all curses. It says "Wisdom is with aged men, with long life is understanding" (Job 12:12). Again, the Bible says "The silver-haired head is a crown of glory, if it is found in the way of righteousness" (Proverb 16:31). Whether we agree with those statements or not is for us to decide.

In the editorial of the Hindu - Business Line Saturday, July 15, 2006 issue under the theme "We are greying faster with far less to bank on" we see the following lines - "It is not surprising that nobody likes to talk about the aged. For, "Crabbed age and youth cannot live together", as the Bard sings in a sonnet. "Youth is full of pleasance, age is full of care; youth of summer morn, age like winter weather; youth like summer brave, age like winter bare", he'd add, "Youth is full of sport, age's breath is short; youth is nimble, age is weak and cold; youth is wild, and age is tame."

Crisis associated with old age has been experienced more in the Third World/Less Developed Countries (LDCs) than in the Developed Countries. Ageing crisis might also differ from country to country, state to state, place to place and even from tribe to tribe. Even though the magnitude and manifestations of old age problems are not the same everywhere, no country or no state can claim that they are at all free from the problem.

The rapid increase in the population of the elderly in the world has caught the attention and concern of the United Nations and in its World Population Prospect, Estimates and Projections, the aged/elderly population (over 60 years of age) was estimated at 5.3 per cent in 1980 and is expected to jump to 7.7 per cent in 2000 and 13.3 per cent by the year 2025. The rise in the population of the elderly was earlier thought to be a concern only of the developed countries but it has now become more or less equally important issue even in the developing countries as well.

Recognizing the importance of this particular age group, in 1990, the UN General Assembly designated October 1 as the *International Day of Older Persons* for celebrating and acknowledging the contribution of older people to society. The United Nations' Principles for Older Persons, adopted in 1991, are best summed up in the logo: *To add life to the years that have been added to life.* Conceptual Framework for International Year of Older Person (IYOP), which is based on the International Plan of Action on Ageing (1982) and the Principles for Older Persons (1991), was formulated and submitted by the Secretary General to the 50th session of the General Assembly in 1995. The 1997 Operational Framework also assisted in setting the scene for the International Year of Older Persons, 1999.

UN Population Division predicts that the elderly population in India will rise from 85 million to over 300 million in about four decades, an increase of almost three and half times. India is not only greying at a pace faster than many of the industrialized societies but also with very limited resources both physical and financial according to Kanchan Chopra, Director, Institute of Economic Growth.

India being a developing country with a large population, one of the many challenges facing the country is the growth of elderly population which is growing much faster than the overall population itself. According to the Research, Reference and Training Division, Ministry of Information and Broadcasting, Government of India, the population of older persons of 60+ in India ranks fourth highest in the world and by the end of the present century it will be second only to China. Today India is home of one out of every ten senior citizens of the world (Research, Reference and Training Division, Ministry of Information and Broadcasting, 2001). According to Indian Census figures, the proportion of elderly persons in India has risen from 5.63 per cent in 1961 to 6.58 per cent in 1991, to around 7.08 per cent in 2001 and will be somewhere 9.87 per cent in 2021. India has a National Policy on Older Persons (NPOP). However, many of the provisions described in this policy document await proper implementation. The main reason for this neglect is the lack of necessary understanding about the issues of ageing.

Thus the population of 60 years and over is assuming an enormous size and the tremendous growth of the population of the elderly and its growing proportion in the total population are creating new problems for the society and for themselves. Old age is generally accompanied by a number of problems that the elderly have to face and adjust with in varying degrees. Loss of economic independence and physical vigour and the emergence of various types of degenerative diseases change an elderly from an independent self-supporting individual to one who needs help from his children, members of the family and the society in general. Absence of common interests and lack of extensive and regular interaction with the younger members in the family may result in social isolation and loneliness of the elderly.

Since the time the United Nations dedicated the year 1999 to the aged/elderly as the International Year for Older Persons, a large number of literatures have flooded the global print market focusing on a wide range of issues and concerns related to the elderly population of the world. India for its part has not been lagging behind in its approach to its elderly. This is reflected in the amount of literature appearing regularly. But as far as the Northeast is concerned, there is very little information on issues regarding the elderly. We have not found any book relating to the elderly from the Northeast except for a few articles and reports appearing here and there.

It is rather difficult to know how the states in the North Eastern Region take up the problems of old age in their respective states. It is reported that some associations have been formed in NE states which take up welfare activities for their members. For example, Pensioners' Association formed in different states in the North East rendered welfare services to their members. Assam has one such association called Government Pensioners' Association which has 52 branches. The said association also has a Women's wing. Likewise Meghalaya also has an association which has a registered members of 1500 in all. Tripura has Government Pensioners' Association, Tripura, which has 9570 members with 26 units of branches. The Mizoram Civil Pensioners' Association (MCPA) has in all 96 branches (52 in Aizawl and 44 in rural areas). They have sub-headquarters at Kolasib, Mamit, Serchhip, Champhai, Lawngtlai and Saiha. The total numbers of members of the association stand at 5000 at present.

Other than MCPA, in Mizoram there is one Non-Government Organisation called *"The senior citizens*

Association of Mizoram" (MUP in Mizo) which is affiliated to the Federation of Associations of Senior Citizens of India (FASC). The said Association was established in 1961 and has more than 50,000 members all over the state. Presently it has 512 units. More than 5 units can form an Area. Now there are 69 Areas. The Areas within a district are joined together as the sub-headquarters. There are 6 (six) sub-headquarters. The MUP Headquarter is at Aizawl, the capital of Mizoram.

All males and females above 50 years of age could become members. As MUP is a purely voluntary association, there is no racial, religious and communal discrimination. A member should be a permanent resident of Mizoram. Most of the members of MUP are living in the interior places of Mizoram. They are still economically backward and depending mainly on cultivation viz shifting cultivation or jhuming. In many places, elderly people who are above 60 years could not be spared from working in the jhum. As such they have to live a very hard and tiring life.

The motto of MUP is *"Be a blessing to many others"*. Members in each and every unit are helping their fellow members in every possible way. Aims and objects of MUP are :-

(i) To help the senior citizens to identify, assess and evaluate their problems and to look for solution so that they could continue to enjoy a healthy and happy life;

(ii) To help, advise and assist public leaders;

(iii) To maintain, as far as practicable and uphold Mizo customary laws, cultures, tradition and practices from time immemorial and if necessary to help amend or improve those, which, on careful examination are found no longer suited to the existing practices of the Mizo society;

(iv) To offer opinions and advice to the concerned authorities in matters concerning economic development of the state;

(v) To be very watchful of the political, social and economic life of the Mizos and to help guide the people if found following wrongful and undesirable ways to better and more correct ways;

(vi) To offer advice whenever the association feels it necessary to the State Government for efficient management of any of its machineries;

(vii) To be ready when situation demands to work together with other NGOs for a common good cause.

Members of the MUP in every unit and area are actively engaged in finding out their members who are in abject poverty, needing help. To them they give financial as well as physical assistance in whatever way they can. Sometimes they organize picnics/functions where enjoyable and interesting items are shown and performed. Recently the MUP has started a Charitable Trust in aid of poor and destitute needing kidney transplantation, cancer treatment etc. For this, each member of the association contributes Rs. 20 every year.

According to the figure provided by 2001 census, in Mizoram, there are 49023 persons in the age group of 60 years and above. Males are 24800 and females 24223. Rural people in the same age group are 25683, urban dwellers are 23340. Again, in the age group of 75 years and above, there are 10710 persons of which males are 5117 and females 5593. The distribution of their dwelling is 5591 rural and 5119 urban respectively.

In the past, the Mizo had a high regard and respect for the old people. They never, so to say, mistreated them. The advice of the elderly people were generally valued and taken as wise and meaningful. There are some sayings that reflect the honour and respect attributed to the old people. One of the sayings is *'Upa Sakah'*. The meaning is that special share/benefit is given just because he is older. For example in a hunting expedition two hunters fired at a wild animal. And it was difficult to know which bullet hit the animal. In that circumstance, the advantage is given to the one who is older. Another act which reveals that elderly people are respected is that at the time of eating unless the eldest starts, others never start the eating. It is also a cultural practice for male adults to sleep together in Zawlbuk (Bachelors' dormitory) to get necessary instruction. They also used to sleep together in the home of the bereaved family to console them. As a mark of respect for old people, the best place to sleep is spared for the eldest.

Till today, in Christian churches a prominent seating place is given to the elderly people. Not only that, in any public gathering (in times of joy or sorrow) elderly people are always given a place to sit. Even when it is a houseful situation, some one would leave his seat to just give it for old and the elderly. In the bus also people would just vacate their seat to accommodate the old people. The conductor would not collect bus fare from the elderly people (who are above a certain specified years). Besides, on some special occasion like Christmas celebration or some eventful celebration, old people are often given special treatment by giving a special dish with special seating arrangement. Some times they are given special presents just for being aged.

But due to the fast, rapid changes in the mind and attitude of the people, brought about by socio economic development, globalisation, and development in information technology, etc. the attitude towards the old people has, it appears, undergone changes. At some corners, the young start regarding the old people as those who are always nagging, who are ungrateful, unwise and rather foolish. They do not show respect or due regard to their advice and counseling. They seem to feel that old people live in a different world, which is outdated, not having any common thing and any relevance to theirs. Since this kind of attitude became more and more prominent in the society, particularly among the younger generation, the aged people, on their part experienced more problems than before. They had the feeling of being unwanted or unneeded, neglected and burdensome. They often felt very lonely as their life long partner left them long before and also because they did not find enough people to talk to or to listen to their problem. They lived in the past world, had a fond memory of their past youthful and happy years. They found difficulty in adjusting with the changed life and situation. They enjoyed telling the past stories which the youngsters found boring and not interesting.

Even when there are families who are so kind and well-treat elderly members, because of the nature of work and the style of living in this dynamic world it is harder to give time to them. Time at their disposal just does not permit that, it seems.

In the light of the current discussions, at the national, at the regional and more particularly at the state (Mizoram) level certainly a good deal of things needs to be done. In this very seminar issues should be raised and addressed so that old age people would lead a more happy and worthwhile living. Some of the issues to be addressed to during the seminar may be put forward as follow:-

(i) How to help the elderly people feel that they are wanted, needed and important in the family, that they have a place in the family and they should not feel that they are simply a liability;

(ii) How to solve their problem of loneliness, insecurity and frustration;

(iii) How to provide better recreational facilities both in the urban and rural areas. The statistics shows that concentration of elderly people is more in the rural areas in Mizoram than in the urban area;

(iv) Since elderly people, in their working age were engaged in the unorganised sector or informal sector, they might not have joined social security schemes or contributed for their pension etc.

(v) How to help them solve their financial problem;

(vi) How to render better health care facilities to them;

(vii) How to make the world, the society better for them to live in;

(viii) How to change the attitude of the people so that more old age homes be constructed and people should think that putting the aged people in the said Home is not a crime;

(ix) Unorganised workers require social security or health insurance when they become unproductive in thcir old agc;

(x) Though the Government of Mizoram has announced its state Policy for the Elderly People, the policy has not yet been properly implemented. This issue may be raised to the authority;

(xi) As directed by Article No. 96 of National Policy on Elderly People, the MUP be declared as the Nodal Agency of the State Government in looking after the elderly people within the state of Mizoram. This issue can be brought to the notice of the Government of Mizoram.

The role to be played by the government and non-government organizations, health care organizations, financial institutions, policy makers and researchers in highlighting the problems faced by the aged and initiating certain policy decisions to protect the rights and interests of the aged may also be addressed to.

CHAPTER 1

Magnitude and Growth of Elderly Population in Mizoram

Vanlalchhawna

INTRODUCTION

The world's population is ageing rapidly. The ageing of population refers to the increasing proportions of old people in the total population of a nation. The global ageing process that first took place in the developed countries has now become a worldwide phenomenon. Over the past few years, the world's population witnessed a continued transition of high birth and low death rate to one characterised by low birth and high death rate. The growth in the number and proportion of older persons characterised this transition. Today, one out of every ten persons is 60 years or above; by 2050, one out of five will be 60 years or older; and by 2150, one out of three persons will be 60 years or older. One significant aspect of the global ageing process is that the 80 years or over age group is the fastest growing segment of the population. In terms of the total population, 80 or above people today constitute a little more than 1 per cent, the proportion is expected to increase to 4.1 per cent in 2050. Globally, the average annual growth rate of persons aged 80 years or over, (3.8 per cent) is currently twice as high as the growth rate of the population over 60 years of age (1.9 per cent). In 1950, 1 in 15 persons aged 60 or older was 80 or above. In 2000 the ratio increased to 1 in 9 and by 2050 it is expected to increase to approximately 1 and 5. The most remarkable increase is expected to occur in Japan where, in 2050 more than 1 in every 3 persons aged 60 or over will be at least 80 years old. Most people above 80 years now live in the more developed region, the majority will soon live in the less developed regions. In some developed countries today, the proportion of older persons is close to one in five. The proportion will reach one in four and in some countries two during the first half of the 21st century. Currently, six countries account for 54 per cent of the total number aged 80 years or over. They are China (12 million), United States of America (9 million), India (6 million), Japan (5 million), Germany (3 million) and Russian Federation (3 million).

Although the proportion of the people who live beyond the age of 100 is still very small, their number is growing rapidly. In 2000, there were an estimated 180,000 centenarians throughout the world. By 2050, their number is projected to be 3.2 million, an increase of about eighteen times. Although less developed countries accounted smaller proportion of centenarians, a significant increase in the absolute number of persons in this age group is projected to take place in these regions over the next 50 years. The number will increase from 40,000 in 2000 to more than 1 million in 2050. Within the more developed countries, Japan will witness the most remarkable increase in the number of centenarians over the next half century. From less than 13,000 in 2000 to almost 1 million in 2050, Japan is expected to have the world's largest number and proportion of centenarians, constituting roughly 1 per cent of Japan's population.

Women make up a significant proportion of older population because their life expectancy is greater than men's. In 2000, the global sex ratio of the population aged 60 or over was 81 males per hundred females. There were 63 million more women aged 60 years or older than there were men of the same age. Since female mortality rates are lower than male rates at older ages, the proportion of women in the older population grows substantially with advancing age. In 2000, women outnumbered men by almost 4 to 3 at ages 65 or older and by almost 2 to 1 at ages 80 or above. Over the next half-century, the sex ratio of the older population is expected to increase. The evidence on which the projections are based suggests a somewhat faster growth in life expectancy among men than among women. In 2050, the global number of men per hundred women is projected to rise to 85 at ages 60 or over, to 81 at ages 65 or over, and 61 at ages 80 or over.

A process known as the "demographic transition" in which mortality and then fertility decline from higher to lower levels determines the global population ageing. Decreasing fertility along with lengthening life expectancy has reshaped the age structure in most part of the world by shifting relative weight from younger to older group. The primary determinant of population ageing is the decline in fertility rate across different parts of the world. Over the last five decades, the total fertility rate decreased globally by almost half, from 5.0 to 2.7 children per woman. The rate is expected to drop to the replacement level of 2.1 children per woman over the next half century. Due to sustained decline that occurred during the twentieth century, the average fertility rate is already well below the replacement level in almost all advanced countries. The rate has decreased from 2.8 children per woman in 1950-1955 to an extremely low level of 1.5 children per woman in 2000-2005. In some industrialized countries, the rate is under 1.3 children per woman.

In the developing regions, fertility decline started later, but it has proceeded much faster than the industrialized countries. Over the last 50 years, the average fertility rate dropped by more than 60 per cent, from 6.2 children per woman in 1950-1955 to 2.9 in 2000-2005. However, great disparity exists among the developing countries. In the least developed countries, the average fertility rate is now 5.2 children per woman while in some African countries, it remains in excess of 5.5 children per woman. In South Central Asia, South America and the Caribbean, the current rates are 2.5 children per woman or less. In 18 developing countries, the rate is already under replacement level.

Mortality decline at older ages assumes an increasingly important role in the population ageing after fertility decline. People are now living longer. More people also survive to older ages. In proportional terms, gains in life expectancy are expected to be higher at older ages. In developed countries where low fertility rate has prevailed for a significant period of time, relative increases in the older population are now determined by improved chances of surviving to old ages. Over the last five decades, life expectancy at birth increased globally by almost twenty years, from 46.5 years in 1950-1955 to 66.0 years in 2000-2005. The average gain in life expectancy at birth was 23.1 years in the less developed regions and 9.4 years in the more developed regions. Over the next 50 years, life expectancy at birth is projected to increase globally by 10 years, to reach 76 years in 2045-2050.

United Nations Principles for Older Persons

The United Nations World Assembly on Ageing, held at Vienna in 1982 formulated International Plan of Action on Ageing, which was endorsed by the General Assembly on 3 December 1982. The Action Plan gave high priority to research related to developmental and humanitarian aspects of ageing. In 1991, the Principles for Older Persons were formulated that aimed to ensure that priority attention will be given to the situation of older persons. The Principles address some core issues like independence, participation, care, self-fulfilment and dignity of older persons and encourage Governments to incorporate them into their national programmes whenever possible.

Independence

1. Older persons should have access to adequate food, water, shelter, clothing and health care through the provision of income, family and community support and self-help.
2. Older persons should have the opportunity to work or to have access to other income-generating opportunities.
3. Older persons should be able to participate in determining when and at what pace withdrawal from the labour force takes place.
4. Older persons should have access to appropriate educational and training programmes.
5. Older persons should be able to live in environments that are safe and adaptable to personal preferences and changing capacities.
6. Older persons should be able to reside at home for as long as possible.

Participation

7. Older persons should remain integrated in society, participate actively in the formulation and implementation of policies that directly affect their well-being and share their knowledge and skills with younger generations.
8. Older persons should be able to seek and develop opportunities for service to the community and

to serve as volunteers in positions appropriate to their interests and capabilities.

9. Older persons should be able to form movements or associations of older persons.

Care

10. Older persons should benefit from family and community care and protection in accordance with each society's system of cultural values.

11. Older persons should have access to health care to help them to maintain or regain the optimum level of physical, mental and emotional well-being and to prevent or delay the onset of illness.

12. Older persons should have access to social and legal services to enhance their autonomy, protection and care.

13. Older persons should be able to utilize appropriate levels of institutional care providing protection, rehabilitation and social and mental stimulation in a humane and secure environment.

14. Older persons should be able to enjoy human rights and fundamental freedoms when residing in any shelter, care or treatment facility, including full respect for their dignity, beliefs, needs and privacy and for the right to make decisions about their care and the quality of their lives.

Self-fulfilment:

15. Older persons should be able to pursue opportunities for the full development of their potential.

16. Older persons should have access to the educational, cultural, spiritual and recreational resources of society.

Dignity

17. Older persons should be able to live in dignity and security and be free of exploitation and physical or mental abuse.

18. Older persons should be treated fairly regardless of age, gender, racial or ethnic background, disability or other status, and be valued independently of their economic contribution.

Growth of Elderly Population in India

The ageing of population in India has started since 1961 which marked the process of the beginning of sharp decline in the overall death rate and also in mortality levels in the older age groups (age 60 and above). This has since accelerated after 1971 when the fertility level also started declining. The elderly population increased from 12.06 million in 1901 to 19.61 million in 1951, an increase of about 63 per cent. Between 1951 and 1971, the number of elderly persons increased by about 67 per cent, reaching 32.70 million by 1971. During 1971-81, the increase in the aged population was about 32 per cent as against the increase of 24.7 per cent recorded for the total population during this period. During the decade 1981-91, the old age population increased by 13.5 million with a decadal growth rate of 31 per cent. The proportion of population aged 60 years and more was 5.1 per cent of the population in 1901; this rose to 5.4 per cent in 1951 through 6.4 per cent in 1971, and is expected to be 7.7 per cent of the total population in 2001. The Technical Group on Population Projections estimated that the likely number of the elderly by the year 2016 will be around 113 millions.

The elderly population has registered a higher growth rate as compared with the total population. During 1981-

91, the number of persons in the age group 60 and above increased by 31.31 per cent while the total population by 23.85 per cent. The growth rate of the persons in the age group 60-69 was 28.63 per cent while the age group 70-79 recorded 29.41 per cent and for persons in the age group 80 and above, it was as high as 54.47 per cent.

About 78.1 per cent of the elderly population in India live in rural areas as against 74.3 per cent of the total population living in urban areas. The age structure of the elderly, which is an indicative of the concentration of the older population in the specific higher ages, shows that the number of elderly persons declines with increase in the age. In 1991, 62.82 per cent of the elderly population were in the age group 60-69 and 25.93 per cent in the age group 70-79. For other age group, the figures are- 9.06 per cent in 80 to 89 years, 1.92 per cent in 90 to 99 years and 0.27 per cent in 100 years and over.

The mortality rate for the elderly, as obtained from the scheme of the Sample Registration System (SRS), indicated that the mortality rate in the 60+ in 1996 was 50 per 1000 elderly population. This was 55 for males as compared with 46 for females. The expectation of life at birth in India has increased significantly over the years due to better medical facilities, control of epidemics and other infectious diseases resulting in appreciable decline in the level of mortality. The expectation of life at birth for Indians has increased from 49.7 years during the period 1970-75 to 60.3 years during the period 1991-95. The increment in the extra years of additional life at different old ages namely, 60,65 and 70+ are not very significant. At age 60 this increase has been from 13.8 years to 16.2 years during the period 1970-75 to 1991-95. At 70 and above, this increment is seen to be from 8.9 years to 10.6 years.

The impact of population ageing is increasingly evident in the old-age dependency ratio. The dependency ratio for the elderly is the number of persons aged 60 years and above per 100 persons of the age group 15-59 years. Between 2000 and 2050, the old-age dependency ratio will double in more developed regions and treble in less developed regions of the world. The potential socioeconomic impact on society that may result from an increasing old-age dependency ratio is an area of growing research and public debate. The old age dependency ratio in India has increased from 10.9 per cent in 1961 to 12.1 per cent in 1991. The dependency ratio is higher in rural areas as compared to that from urban areas. A refined dependency ratio for the elderly may be taken as the ratio of non-workers aged 60 years and above to workers in the age group 15-59 years. For the elderly population the number of non-workers per 100 economically active persons was 15 in urban areas and 11 in rural areas. The ratio varies from 3 in Nagaland to 22 in Kerela. Kerela has the maximum of old age dependents.

Demographic Profile of the Elderly in Mizoram

Mizoram, covering 21081 sq. km, had 888,573 of people in 2001 Census, and it occupies 30th position in terms of population size among the 35 states and union territories. The state consists of 8 districts with 22 RD Blocks and 817 villages, out of which 707 are inhabited and 110 are uninhabited. The urban areas of the state in the 2001 Census comprise 22 statutory towns. The rural population consists of 50.4 per cent of the total population while 49.6 per cent lives in urban areas. Mizoram is one of the highest urbanized states in the country, next only to Delhi. The state has registered 28.8 per cent growth rate of population during 1991-2001 compared to 39.7 per cent during the 1981-1991. The growth rate of the population in 1991-2001 is higher than the national growth of 21.5 per cent.

Among the districts, Aizawl has registered the highest growth of population at 38.1 per cent, followed by Kolasib with 28.1 per cent. Mamit district has recorded a negative growth in the population (2.8 per cent) during 1991-2001. In 2001 Census, the density of population in Mizoram is 42 persons per sq. km. as against 33 in 1991. It has the second lowest density among the states and union territories of the country. Among the districts, Aizawl has recorded the highest density of 91 persons per sq. km while Mamit district has the lowest density of 21 persons per sq. km. in 2001.

Mizoram is predominantly a tribal state with 839,310 (94.5 per cent) of the total population as Scheduled Tribes. The Scheduled Caste population was 272 (0.03 per cent) as per 2001 Census. There are no indigenous Scheduled Castes in Mizoram and most of them don't have any permanent residence and they are found moving from place to place both within and outside the state. The list of Scheduled Castes of Assam is applicable to Meghalaya, Arunachal Pradesh and Mizoram.

The overall literacy rate of the state is 88.8 per cent in 2001 Census. This is significantly higher if compared to 82.3 per cent recorded in 1991. Next to Kerala, the state holds the second highest position in literacy among the states and union territories of the country. The male female literacy gap is very low. The male literacy rate is 90.7 per cent, occupying the third position and female literacy rate is 86.7 per cent, the second position in the country in 2001 Census. Among the districts, Aizawl district has the highest literacy rate of 96.5 per cent while Lawngtlai is the least literate with 64.7 per cent.

The total working population in Mizoram was 467,159 persons in 2001, showing 52.6 per cent of the work participation rate. There has been a decline of the main workers from 86.1 per cent of the total workers in 1991 to 77.6 per cent in 2001. Meanwhile, there has been a substantial increase in the marginal workers from 13.9 per cent in 1991 to 22.4 per cent in 2001 Census. Among the total workers, 54.9 per cent are cultivators in the state, significantly higher than the national average of 31.7 per cent in 2001 Census. On the other hand, agricultural labourers in the state are only 5.7 per cent against 26.5 per cent at the national level. Household industry workers constitute merely 1.5 per cent of the total workers in the state. Other workers constitute 37.9 per cent of the total workers in the state.

The elderly population is growing

People aged 60 years and over have increasingly a larger share in the total population. From 4.42 per cent in 1981, the share of old age population has increased to 5.52 per cent in 2001. The elderly population (aged 60 and above) grew much faster than the total population over the last three decades. Between 1981 and 2001, the total population grew by 80 per cent from 493,757 persons in 1981 to 888,573 persons in 2001 while the elderly population increased from 21832 persons to 49023 persons, showing an increase of 124 per cent. During 1981-1991, the population of 60 years and over increased by 52 per cent, from 21832 persons to 33185 persons. In contrast, the total population increased by about 40 per cent from 493,757 persons to 689,756 persons. In 2001, people of 60 years of age and over numbered 49,023 in Mizoram, showing a decadal growth rate of 48 per cent during 1991-2001. The total population has shown a growth rate of only 29 per cent during the same period. (Table1).

The percentage share of elderly male as well as female population in the total population has been rising. Between 1981 and 2001, the number of elderly male increased from 11,270 to 24,800 persons. In 1981, the elderly males accounted for 4.38 per cent of the total male population and the share rose to 5.40 per cent in 2001. The elderly female grew from 10,562 to 24,223 persons, showing an increase in their share from 4.47 per cent to 5.64 during the same period. The share of elderly population in rural and urban areas is also increasing steadily. In rural areas, the share increased from 4.60 per cent to 5.74 per cent. The share of elderly population recorded an increase from 3.89 per cent in 1981 to 5.29 per cent in 2001 (Table 2).

TABLE 1

Growth of old age population (persons 60 years and above) and total population (all ages), Mizoram, India, 1981-2001

Year	Total Population	Old Age Population		Decadal Growth Rate (%)	
		Total	Per cent	All Age	60 years and over
1981	493,757	21832	4.42	-	-
1991	689,756	33185	4.81	39.7	52.01
2001	888,573	49023	5.52	28.8	42.7

Sources:

1. Census of India 1991. *Ageing Population of India - An Analysis of the 1991 Census Data*, Registrar General, India, New Delhi.
2. Census of India, 2001, *Mizoram Primary Census Abstract* Directorate of Census Operation, Mizoram.

During 1981-1991, the population of 60 to 69 years showed the highest growth rate of nearly 70 per cent as against the growth rate of 52 per cent recorded for 60 years and over population and another 40 per cent for total population (all ages). The number of persons in the age group 70-79 grew by 28 per cent and 80 years and over population by 30 per cent during the same period. In contrast, those aged 70 to 79 showed the highest growth rate among the older population between 1991 and 2001. While the number of persons in the age group 60-69 increased by only 36.36 per cent, the age group 70-79 increased by nearly 80 per

TABLE 2

Persons aged 60 + and their percentage share in total population by sex and residence, Mizoram

Year	Total			Rural			Urban		
	Total	Male	Female	Total	Male	Female	Total	Male	Female
1981	21832	11270	10562	17091	9072	8019	4741	2198	2543
1991	33186	17013	16173	18948	9876	9072	14238	7134	7101
2001	49023	24800	24223	25683	13322	12361	23340	11478	11862
Percentage share in total (all ages) population									
1981	4.42	4.38	4.47	4.6	4.7	4.48	3.89	3.41	4.43
1991	4.81	4.74	4.89	5.1	5.08	5.11	4.48	4.34	4.63
2001	5.52	5.4	5.64	5.74	5.72	5.75	5.29	5.07	5.53

Sources:

1. Census of India 1991. *Ageing Population of India - An Analysis of the 1991 Census Data*, Registrar General, India, New Delhi.

2. Census of India, 2001, *Mizoram Primary Census Abstract*, Directorate of Census Operation, Mizoram.

cent. For persons aged 80 years and over, the growth rate was 42.11 per cent. For the elderly males as well as the females, the age group 60-69 showed the highest growth rate during 1981-1991. However, both elderly men and women in the age group of 70-79, recorded the highest growth rate during 1991-2001 (Table-3).

TABLE 3
Percentage of decadal growth rate of population aged 60+ and total population (all ages) by age and sex, Mizoram 1981-2001

Age group	Period	Percentage decadal growth rate		
		Total	Male	Female
60-69	1981-91	69.56	59.36	82.38
	1991-01	36.36	33.69	51.22
70-79	1981-91	27.82	39.66	17.44
	1991-01	79.59	79.02	80.14
80 +	1981-91	29.82	31.94	28.09
	1991-01	42.11	42.42	41.91
60+	1981-91	52.01	50.96	53.12
	1991-01	47.72	45.77	49.77
All ages	1981-91	39.7	39.55	39.85
	1991-01	28.8	27.88	29.84

Sources:

1. Census of India 1991. *Ageing Population of India - An Analysis of the 1991 Census Data,* Registrar General, India, New Delhi.
2. Census of India, 2001, *Mizoram Primary Census Abstract* Directorate of Census Operation, Mizoram.

Age structure of the elderly

The number of elderly persons declines with increase in the age. In 1981, about 57 per cent belonged to 60 to 69 years, nearly 30 per cent in 70 to 79 years and 13 per cent in 80 years and over. In 1991, the proportion of the population 60 to 69 years has increased, constituting 74 per cent of the elderly persons. The share of 70 to 79 years and 80 years and over in contrast declined to 25 per cent and 13 per cent respectively.

In 2001 Census, there were 28932 persons (59 per cent) in the age group 60-69, 14783 persons (30 per cent) in the age group 70-79. Population 80 years or over numbered 5308 persons (11 per cent) (Table 4).

TABLE 4
Persons aged 60 years and above and their percentage share by age during 1981-2001 in Mizoram

Age/Year	1981		1991		2001	
	Total	Per cent	Total	Per cent	Total	Per cent
60 to 69 years	12513	57.31	21217	63.93	28932	59.02
Males	6969	61.84	11106	65.28	14851	59.88
Females	5544	52.49	10111	62.52	14081	58.13
70 to 79 years	6442	29.51	8234	24.81	14783	30.15
Males	3008	26.69	4201	24.69	7519	30.32
Females	3434	32.51	4033	24.94	7264	30.00
80 years and over	2877	13.18	3735	11.25	5308	10.82
Males	1293	11.47	1706	10.03	2430	9.80
Females	1584	6.54	2029	12.54	2819	11.64
Total	21832	100	33186	100	49023	100.00

Sources:
1. Census of India 1991. *Ageing Population of India - An Analysis of the 1991 Census Data,* Registrar General, India, New Delhi.
2. Census of India, 2001, *Mizoram Primary Census Abstract* Directorate of Census Operation, Mizoram.

Number of elderly women per elderly men is rising.

The sex ratio (the number of females times 1000 divided by the number of males) has increased over the years. In 1981, there were 11270 men and 10562 women aged 60 and over, yielding a female-male ratio of 937. In 1991, the ratio increased to 950 and in 2001, it had further grown to 976. The elderly sex ratio i.e., the number of elderly female per elderly male increases steadily with age group. In 2000, there were 14851 men and 14081 women in the age group 60-69, giving a sex ratio of 948. In the 70-to-79 age group, the female-male ratio was 966 and in the 80 years and over group, the ratio was 1160. The sex ratio in each age group did not show any consistent growth pattern. In 1981, the sex ratio in the age group 60-69 was 795; this rose to 1074 in 1991. In 2001, the ratio slides back to 948. In the 70-to-79 age group, the sex ratio fell from 1142 in 1981 to 960 in 1991 and then increased again to 966. In the 80 years and over, the ratio fell down rather steadily (Table 5).

TABLE 5
Number of Females per 1000 Males by Age, for the 60 years and Over Population 1981, 1991, and 2001

Age	1981	1991	2001
60 years and over	937	950	976
60 to 69 years	795	1074	948
70 to 79 years	1142	960	966
80 years and over	1225	1189	1160

Sources:

1. Census of India 1991. *Ageing Population of India - An Analysis of the 1991 Census Data,* Registrar General, India, New Delhi.
2. Census of India, 2001, *Mizoram Primary Census Abstract* Directorate of Census Operation, Mizoram.

Centenarians are increasing

The number of centenarians increased during 1981-1991. There were 67 centenarians in 1981 Census consisting of 29 males and 38 females. The number had increased to 215 persons in 1991 Census with 162 males and 53 females. The number of centenarians increased by 283 per cent over the decade 1981-1991 while male centenarians showing an increase of 459 per cent grew faster than female centenarians which were increasing approximately at 39 per cent.

Dependency ratio of the elderly is increasing

The elderly persons aged 60 years and above are considered to be dependants on the younger persons belonging to the working age group of 15-59 years. The dependency ratio for the elderly is the number of persons aged 60 years and above per 100 persons of the age group 15-59 years. The dependency ratio among the elderly persons has increased from 7.95 per cent in 1981 to 9.33 per cent in 2001. The dependency ratio is higher in the rural areas as compared to that of urban areas. In 2001, the dependency ratio was 10 per cent in rural areas in contrast to 8 per cent in urban areas (Table 6). A refined dependency ratio for the elderly may be taken as the ratio of non-workers aged 60 years and over to workers in the age group 15-59 years. In 1991, for the elderly population, the number of non-workers per 100 economically active persons was 5 in Mizoram.

Elderly persons at the district level

Serchhip district, with 53,861 elderly population and accounting for 6.47 per cent of the total population, got the highest proportion of the population 60 years and over while Lawngtlai district had the lowest proportions. With 3417 elderly population, Lawngtlai district's elderly population was 4.64 per cent. Out of the eight administrative districts, five districts exceeded the state's average value of 5.52 per cent. These districts are Mamit (5.90 per cent), Aizawl (5.53 per cent), Champhai (5.90 per cent), Serchhip (6.47 per cent) and Lunglei (5.58). Three districts, viz., Kolasib (5.50 per cent), Lawngtlai (4.64 per cent) and Saiha (4.79 per cent) fell below the state's average (Table 7).

Socio-economic profile of the aged population

The socio-economic characteristics of the elderly persons such as work status, literacy, level of education, marital status, etc are important indicators of their general wellbeing, happiness and contentment. Table 8 gives some of the selected indicators of the socio-economic status of the elderly population in Mizoram,

TABLE 6
Old age dependency ratio by sex and residence

Year	Total			Rural			Urban		
	Total	Male	Female	Total	Male	Female	Total	Male	Female
1981	7.95	7.66	8.29	8.42	8.43	8.41	6.63	5.57	7.93
1991	8.66	8.33	9.04	9.52	9.24	9.85	7.73	7.33	8.18
2001	9.33	9.04	9.66	10.27	10.11	10.44	8.49	8.05	8.96

Sources:

1. Census of India 1991. *Ageing Population of India - An Analysis of the 1991 Census Data,* Registrar General, India, New Delhi.
2. Census of India, 2001, *Mizoram Primary Census Abstract* Directorate of Census Operation, Mizoram.

based on 1991 census. A good number of the elderly persons continued to remain economically active even after retiring from regular employment. This has been possible with the improvement of the health conditions of the aged persons. The 1991 census figures show that the proportion of workers was 53.22 per cent for the elderly as against 48.91 per cent for the total population. This percentage was 66.93 for elderly males and 38.81 per cent for elderly females. The female's work participation rate is seen to be quite much lower as compared with the elderly males. The work participation rate in the rural and urban areas was 55.58 per cent and 50.08 per cent respectively. About 75 per cent of the economically active elder population are cultivators.

TABLE 7
District-wise number of persons aged 60 years and over, 2001, Mizoram

State/ District	Total Population	60 years and over	
		Number	Per cent
Mizoram	888573	49023	5.52
Mamit	62785	3692	5.9
Kolasib	65960	3625	5.5
Aizawl	325676	18019	5.53
Champhai	108392	6398	5.9
Serchhip	53861	3488	6.47
Lunglei	137223	7656	5.58
Lawngtlai	73620	3417	4.64
Saiha	61056	2928	4.79

Source: Census of India, 2001, *Mizoram Primary Census Abstract* Directorate of Census Operation, Mizoram.

The proportion of married persons among the elderly was 66 per cent in 1991 while the widowed elderly constituted 27 per cent. Unmarried (never married) and divorced elderly persons came to about 3 per cent and 4 per cent respectively of the total elderly persons. Literacy level for the elderly population in Mizoram was 60 per cent in 1991 as against 82.27 per cent. Elderly women had a low literacy rate of only 43 per cent as against 77 per cent of elderly men. The majority of the elderly literate had below primary education. About 15 per cent of elderly persons had primary education and about 1 per cent are graduates and above (Table 8).

TABLE 8
Socio-economic Status of the Elderly Population 1991

Sl. No.	Items	Unit	Total
1.	**Work Participation Rate**	Per cent	53.22
	Male	-do-	66.93
	Female	-do-	38.81
	Rural	-do-	55.58
	Urban	-do-	50.08
2.	**Marital Status**		
	Never married	-do-	3.32
	Married	-do-	65.72
	Widowed	-do-	27.31
	Divorced	-do-	3.64
3.	**Literacy rate**	-do-	60.28
	Males	-do-	77.06
	Females	-do-	42.62
4.	**Level of Education**		
	Literate below primary	-do-	72.28
	Primary	-do-	14.94
	Graduate and above	-do-	0.97

Source: Census of India 1991. *Ageing Population of India-An Analysis of the 1991 Census Data,* Registrar General, India, New Delhi.

REFERENCES

1. Census of India 1991, *Ageing Population of India - An Analysis of the 1991 Census Data,* Registrar General, India, New Delhi.

2. Census of India, 2001, *Mizoram Primary Census Abstract* Directorate of Census Operation,Mizoram.

3. *World Population Ageing 1950-2050* Population Division, DESA, UN Secretariat www.un.org/esa/sovdev.

CHAPTER 2

Social and Economic Status of Elderly Persons in Mizo Society

Thangchungnunga

Introduction

This paper attempts to study the role of elderly persons in social and economic aspects. Since old age is a stage in the life of an individual it would be relevant to look into its major characteristics across cultures or tribes. Not all individuals age in the same way, and the ageing of each individual (cohorts of individual born at the same time) is affected by the unique situation of time in history such as the prevailing norms, mores or attitudes. Moreover, the time span of being old by no means constant. In the early twentieth century, when the Mizo society was yet largely illiterate, a person considered himself as old in his early forties. If he were blessed with children who could work in the field, he would abstain from doing harsh manual work. For instance, among the mountain tribes of IKS in Uganda, the ageing process started in their late twenties and senility ensued immediately on account of ill-treatment of the aged. Now, the public consider those as old people who are anywhere from less than 50 to over 75, and most of the people who are in their 60's or older do not look upon themselves as old.

In the past, to a great extent even now, in Mizo community, old age (at least up to senility) has been associated with some special characteristics as an asset in its culture, such as usefulness in the performance of chores, skill in certain arts and storytelling, control of property rights, power in the family, useful experience or extensive knowledge. It is a matter of few decades for the society to experience demographic change and this later aspect which has a semblance of developed economy may not be given much importance. Economic development has changed the nature of employment and the proportion of older men has declined in the labour force posing problems of income maintenance for those no longer economically active. Levels of educational attainment have been rising. Urbanization has transformed the residential setting with the accompanying change in family structure. Thus the social content of the aged today differs markedly from the earlier situation.

The demographic base

In the developed nations, there has been a marked rise in the number of older people, almost in the same proportion of population expansion. Over the first half of the 20th century the annual rate of increase in the age category of 65 and over was from about 1 per cent in France or Sweden to nearly 3 per cent in Canada or U.S. But in Mizoram the increase in older people aged 60 and above to the total population was a little over 1 per cent in 20 years from 4.42% in 1981 to 5.52 per cent in 2001. The same figure for the whole country stood at 7.7 per cent in 2001. The percentage of population older than 60 in 2000 in Philippines was 5.5%, Thailand 8.4%, China 10.1%, Hong Kong 14.4% and Japan 23.3%. It is also projected that the number of Asians older than 60 is set to explode over the next four decades and by 2050 Japan will have 42.4 per cent of its population living beyond 60 years. The decadal growth rate of people aged 60 and above in Mizoram has been recorded as 52.01 per cent from 1981-1991 and 42.70 per cent from 1991-2001 respectively.

A peculiar demographic feature of aged people in Mizoram is of the longevity for male and female population that stands almost in equal number. According to the census records, the total number of persons aged 60+ is as shown in the following table:

Year	Total	Male	Female
1981	21832	11270	10562
1991	33186	17013	16173
2001	49023	24800	24223

Source: Census of India 1991. *Ageing population of India. Mizoram Primary census Abstract.*

In higher age bracket also, the proportion is found to be nearly constant whereas in the west the proportion of females has been rising among older people. It has been found that male mortality rates are generally higher at all ages than corresponding rates for females. Hence there is typically an excess of females over males among the aged. In the category of people age 75 and over in the United States, there are only about 73 men for every 100 women, a discrepancy that has been widening.

For an individual within a society, the secular declines in mortality have greatly improved the chance of surviving into old age. That does not mean that the length of life attainable by human species has changed, but the proportion of people enduring into the higher ages has risen. In a random survey from the records of tombstones at Serkawn, Mr. Zuia found that the average age at death was 22 years. Serkawn is one of the oldest villages in terms of permanent dwelling location. What can be inferred from this finding is that the average life time of the Mizo till the third quarter of the 20th century might well have been 20 to 30 years. But today a man or a woman can look forward to living well into his or her 60s.

Age may confer wisdom, but it may also have profound societal implication. Its direct implication in the physical toll that time wreaks on our bodies - sapping our strength, eroding our vision and hearing, raising the odds that we will be ambushed by everything from tooth decay to heart disease. Common health problems arise such as incontinence, sleeplessness and a weakened immune system. A decline in cognitive abilities, loss of coordination, dexterity and increase in mental confusion has become more pronounced. The prevalence of Alzheimer's doubles every five year after 65. Eventually incidence of disease of the mind and body snowball. Almost half of all 90- years-olds suffer from some form of dementia.

Social status

We have mentioned that in traditional and agrarian society of the Mizo, old age has been associated with some special characteristic regarded as an asset in our culture. Their authority on moral questions is highly respected and they are looked upon as preserver of tribal values and chivalry. In early communities older men were always in close circle of friendship pursuing common interest such as hunting or fighting. It could be argued that friendships of long enduring nature are of practical value to the community. Every civilized religion began in a small group of friends. Mathematics effectively began when a few Greek friends got together to talk about numbers and lines and angles. However, the older the individual is, the fewer social roles he plays on the average and the fewer and less varied are his contacts with other people and with the environment. Fortunately, we have a well-knit society which offers varied and abundant opportunities of social contact even for the older people and, therefore social activity is especially great among those aged who are in good health or who come from higher rather than lower socio-economic background. It may be convenient to discuss briefly the social roles of older persons under various activities.

Work and retirement

Retirement is not at all a familiar term in the age of our parents though it has now been widely institutionalized. It is now common that the ageing individual faces the culmination of his occupational role and a final period of retirement. Even in our society, the modal role for older men today is retirement, not work. Of course, there are a good number of men and women who remain in the labour force in their later years under the compulsion of economic necessity. As far as possible, older people avoid back-breaking labour. Quite often, the older people prove to be better workers. As compared with the young, older people still in the labour force tend to be more strongly committed to the kind of work they do, to adapt better to the job, to express greater satisfaction with it. Though some lucky oldsters continue to work with higher efficiency, many of them appear to accept with contentment their new role of retired persons.

Political roles

There is perhaps no other community where partisan politics on the line of party alliance is as pervasive as in Mizo community. Even those who take neutral stance are more likely an opportunist who would with servility try to be near to the party in power. This is a legacy of Indian democracy and in such political climate, older people, even those with little education, are significantly involved in the political system. They are better represented among the political elite and in leadership positions in many types of decision making. They are more disposed to keep up with the news and with public affairs through the mass media.

In general, today's generation of older people are more conservative than younger people in their political attitude. They are not at all vocal even on the question of their own economic self-interests such as Old Age Home, Social security or Health Insurance, yet there is little indication whether future generations of old people, subjected to shifting political climates and to rising levels of education, remain passive or adopt a less conservative stance and a generally greater flexibility of attitude.

Voluntary associations

There is a plethora of associations in our society layer after layer. This is most probably a by-product of our political system which would be only goaded into action by organized voice. Associations such as clubs, lodges, auxiliaries and the many other organizations in modern society offer a potential link between older people and the larger community. Membership in such association is less widespread among older people than membership in a church or voting in a national election. When people grow older, average membership in such voluntary association shows a tendency to fall. Even the special clubs (such as Golden Age clubs or Senior Centres) established in many Western countries to provide older people with recreational, educational, health or welfare services seem to attract comparatively few participants.

The formation of a state-level Old People's Association and Pensioner's Association in the past few decades was an attempt to build a mechanism of mutual help and cooperation among the old age. There are branch associations all over the state at the level of local units and leaders of the unit organized various activities. They frequently organize seminar, dinner party, handicraft instruction and singing competition or certain kinds of fellowships for recreational purpose. This pleasure in co-operation, in talking shop, in the mutual respect and understanding of man who frequently see one another tested, is biologically valuable. Voluntary association of this sort promotes interest in companionship that gives a cushion against leading a life of loneliness or boredom.

Economic status

In the absence of extensive research on past trends and on age patterns today, it is difficult to know the work participation rates of older persons. At best, we can make intelligent guess and quote figures from the air. In the realm of economic activity, older people are, on the average, comparatively disadvantaged, although individual variations are many. In the developed nations, their low status is indexed by their comparatively low rates of participation in the labour force and by their low average income.

In Mizoram the bulk of employment is provided by service sector, and industrial activity is minimal while agriculture is still predominant. Agriculture and small enterprises which provide self-employment are the areas in which the aged are free to continue work, and under the pressing circumstances of need, many old people continue to work to eke out a living. By a rough estimate, about 50 to 60 per cent of the rural young people aged between 18 and 30 at all times stay away from home or their villages and are not available for work. Some move out of their village in pursuit of higher education and others in search of work. In this situation, the responsibility of back-breaking work mostly rests on older people.

In spite of its economic backwardness, Mizoram has been registered to be the most urbanized state in the country. In this process of modernization, there have been massive movements from villages to cities and urban centres. It is the elderly who have been left behind as age-mates die off and younger generations move away. Generally, the individual's ties to his place of residence become stronger as he grows older. And older people who own their homes, or those who have strong social connections with the neighborhood, are the least willing to leave. For the poor families, the question of economic independence does not arise at all, and they live from hand to mouth. Even in the midst of abject poverty, most old people play the enduring role of parents.

In Mizo community, the joint family system was unheard of except in a few cases, and the nuclear family system has been adopted widely. Traditionally, the youngest son lives in the parental home with his family and it is the practice for the elder brothers to live separately after having their own families. However, the ties of the elderly to their relatives and to their children in particular are by no means limited to visiting. There are also widespread exchanges of material support of various amount and kinds, ranging from financial contributions and care in illness to baby-sitting and help with housework.

Conclusion

Our society is undergoing a rapid transformation through the inroad of capitalistic development. This brings with it social changes because the competitive race of accumulating wealth has put the cohesive fabric of communal harmony asunder. In our traditional community, the aged found security in a familial social organization in which those who were in want got help from others. We are now on the way of adaptation to new situations. Old age pension scheme, though far from being adequate, has been instituted, and the first old age home constructed in Government. Complex does not attract many old people to join. To be precise, there are only four persons living in the home at the present moment. This is a clear proof that the family is still of central importance to the older person's security. However, there is a vivid trend that today's aged couple with their inclination to live separately from their children, is likely to depend primarily upon each other, turning to relatives only under conditions of special need.

CHAPTER 3

Ageing Gracefully: Role and Activities of Mizoram Upa Pawl

Thanseia

Introduction

From the historical facts one could trace that the Mizo are not a very old tribe. This is evidenced by their tools, clothes and garments, dwelling places and food habits prevalent among them after their coming down from the east to settle in these hills some time in 1600. Until the year 1900, there was no school in Mizoram. There were villages, scattered here and there, ruled by the chiefs, who often fought with one another. Shifting their jhum lands and even village locations for every six years or so was quite common in those days. And there were no inter-village paths. In those days, the life span of the Mizo seemed alarmingly short and life expectancy as a whole was also terribly short. The epitaph of most of the tombstones depicted that those hard-working jhum cultivators died at an early age of, say, around 40. Those persons who were only 40 years of age behaved like old men- smoking pipes, bearing beards, sitting in the sun naked; even the women folks were not different. In those days, males seemed to outnumber females; there were hardly any special facilities for older persons, excepting that very high respect was shown to the older persons by the younger group.

The missionaries who came to Mizoram, then known as Lushai hills, during the last decade of the nineteenth century introduced modern education to them. However, the pace of development was very fast only after Independence in 1947. One should not forget that the present older generations are the persons who had been working so hard to foster progress and development for the present day Mizoram.

As we all know today, this modern world of ours has been paying more attention to older persons focussing on their protection, support, security and all-round betterment. Because of this realization of their problems, the UNO in its special meetings in 1991, 1992 and 2001 adopted resolutions giving high priority to the security of older persons. As such, Government of India through the Social Justice and Empowerment Ministry framed National Policy on Older Persons (NPOP) in 1999 for the all-round development and betterment of the older persons the implementation of which largely rest on the States and U.T. concerned. The UNO in 2002 held a very important meeting in Spain in which it passed resolutions which are so significant for the aged of all countries. Till now, however, nothing tangible in this regard has been done in Mizoram in spite of the fact that the Central Government earmarked the year 2002 for general review of the implementation of the policy in all states of India.

Life expectancy of older persons has also increased due to advancement in modern civilization, better diets and better lifestyles, sanitation, health-care facilities etc. The population of 65 years and above has greatly increased both in urban and rural areas. While the proportion of older persons increase over the years, the fast declining of the traditional support mechanism, a sort of joint family system in Mizoram, make the older group vulnerable and feel lonely and isolated. For instance, casual study found that older persons above

80 yrs of age who have been well looked after by their sons/daughters and grand children, feel very lonely. Their loving children and grand children are not close enough to them to listen to their old stories. This problem needs urgent attention if ever possible at all.

It cannot be simply taken for granted that children will be able to look after the aged ones in the family whose needs and care not only multiplied as they become older but also costlier. Many households found very difficult to provide adequate support and care to the aged persons. It is now very pressing to see that rights of livelihood of older persons are not violated and that they get opportunities and equitable shares in benefits under different development programmes. Some of the older groups in Mizo society both in urban and rural areas are in need of adequate shelters, suitable loans under special provision as envisaged in the National Policy of Older Population.

The elderly group, especially women, must not become victims of triple neglect and of discrimination on account of gender, widowhood and age. Women in Mizo society had been deprived of their rights to some extent in the society itself, religious circles and so on. Women however qualified and deserving, they might be, could not be ordained as Pastor or Elder in the churches; and according to the customary laws, husbands could easily divorce their wives by simply saying 'I divorce you'. Even an old wife had to go empty handed. Old women, under normal situation, occupy a very important status at home in Mizo society till now. More care could be provided to this group in the form of special provisions in the state budget, making annual action plan to enrich and update their knowledge, integrating traditional with contemporary needs and transmit socio-cultural heritage to their grand children.

In Mizo society, family binding spirit has always been strong. As time goes on, things are changing so fast that people in large number have been migrating to urban areas in search of economic opportunities, better education for their children, new life styles etc. Consequently, new generations could not pay much attention to their older-olds living with them. So a living arrangement, most emotionally satisfying should be made for them and support system be made functional and activated through the services of the NGOs and Government. The wrong notion that older persons being regarded as 'discarded and useless entity' should now be done away with.

As it is well known, older persons are more vulnerable to different sickness and diseases, heart problem, stroke, cancer etc. As such they deserve special healthcare facilities and treatment under special provisions. Different services like Day Care, Multi Service, Citizens' Centre, reach-out services, seminars and workshops of various kind may be organized occasionally by the NGOs, Government and even churches for these people. The Senior Citizens Association of Mizoram strongly feels the need of such services for the older persons especially in urban area. The Association feels the imperative needs of introducing a special subject of Science of Aging, GERONTOLOGY in local Colleges and Mizoram University.

Role and Activities of Mizoram Upa Pawl (Mizoram Senior Citizens' Association)

In order to address several problems and issues relating to older persons in Mizo society, the Mizoram Upa Pawl (Mizoram Senior Citizens' Association) was founded as a non-government organisation in 1957. However, the constitution specifying the aims and objectives as well as various other necessary provisions pertaining to the organisation and its structure, was formally adopted in 1961 by the General Body Meeting. It was registered under Societies Registration Act XXI of 1860 in 1977.

The motto of the association is "To be a blessing to many others". The aims and objectives of the Society may be summed up in short as below:

(a) To make the Senior Citizens to be able to meet their special biological, social and emotional needs so that they could continue to enjoy healthy and happy life;

(b) To advise and assist public leaders;

(c) As far as practicable, to maintain and uphold the Mizo customary laws, cultures, traditions and practices from ancient time and if necessary to help in amending or improving those which on careful examination are found no longer suitable for the present ways of life;

(d) To offer opinions to the concerned authorities in matters concerning economic development;

(e) To be very watchful of the political, social and economic life of the Mizo and to help guide the people from wrongful and undesirable trend towards more beneficial and honourable targets;

(f) To offer advice wherever the association feels it to do so to the state government for the efficient management of any of its machineries;

(g) To be ready, when situation demands to work together with other voluntary organisations for a common good cause.

Members of the Mizoram Upa Pawl (in short MUP) in every unit and area are actually engaged in finding out destitute among their fellow members in particular and the poor and needy in general within their local limit and give them financial assistance from their own contribution and sometimes by rendering physical work. To make their life more enjoyable and occupied, they always organize meeting in which recreational items of different descriptions including cultural items, games and dancing which every member could enjoy were chalked out and included in the programme. Sometimes lectures on various subjects like health education, sanitation, care of the aged and how to rear a successful family are given by qualified resource persons including doctors, professionals and others. The MUP has instituted a MIZO MEDAL award to those who exhibit extra-ordinary bravery, scholarship, high quality of social work. In political and economic fields the organization gives awareness to the general public of the need of having good and clean administration where the rule of law could reign and where economic self-sufficiency could be achieved. The organisation declared 2006 as "Year of Anti-Corruption". Representatives of the organization often have special interactions with Ministers and high officials of the state giving them constructive advice on issues concerning public interest.

The MUP at present has more than 500 units, 67 areas and 4 Sub-Headquarters all over the state. The organisation has never been involved in party politics. Any Indian citizen who has crossed over 50 years of age residing in Mizoram could become a member. There is no discrimination on the basis of community, creed, rich and poor. The Executive Committee, one of the most important decision making bodies, used to meet at least 4 times a year and the highest body, the assembly meets once a year. The executive committee has recently resolved to constitute CHARITY FUND amounting to at least Rs. 50 lakhs to assist the needy members of the association. In this way the association has been trying its level best to be a blessing for others.

The state government has been implementing various schemes icluding Central Government schemes for the benefits of the elderly people. However, the schemes and projects of the government are still a from satisfactory. For example, the old age pension given to the deserving older persons in Mizoram since 1974 is still very small and payment irregular in comparison with the amount given by other states. For instance, Tripura government paid Rs. 120 per month per the recipient as Old Age Pension every month regularly at their own doorstep whereas Mizoram government has given, at irregular interval, only a sum of Rs. 100 per month, not at their doorstep but at Aizawl, the state capital. The total recipients in Mizoram come to 10,525 elderly persons.

National Policy on Older Persons (NPOP)

The MUP very much welcomes the new national policy on older persons of India (NPOP) announced by the Government of India in 1999. The Central Government has already instructed all the states and U.Ts to prepare State Action Plans for older persons to implement the policy. The MUP members are happy to learn that the long awaited State Action Plans have now been prepared by the Government of Mizoram. However, in connection with this State Action Plan, the MUP suggested other 20- point new schemes to be included in the State Action Plan. Of the said suggestions, only a few may be mentioned below:

(a) Setting up of a State Council for Older Persons.

(b) Introduction of income generating schemes for senior citizens.

(c) Inclusion of representatives of MUP in State Loan Boards and other state-level committees.

(d) To help solve the health problems of the elderly, a Geriatric Department/Ward in each District Civil Hospital of the state.

Mention may be made here that the state government, recognizing the vast experiences and wisdom of elderly people appointed MUP members in 36 standing developmental committees under different state government departments. In addition, the state government quite often sponsor local workshops and seminars for the aged. The State Government also run and look after Old Age Homes since 1989 where the aged people who have no relatives to look after them, are taken care of, providing them with amenities and medical facilities.

The elderly people in Mizo society from time immemorial have been occupying important status in the family; they are care takers of the family, givers of spiritual and moral guidance and inspiration, looking after minor children at home while the adults are at work in the field. However, in the new era of modern development, elderly people have become less dominant within the family circles. The idea of keeping older persons in old age home, however disabled they might be, has never been thought of in Mizo Society. In the villages as well as in urban areas, the helpless elderly people in need of help have always been taken care of by the village people. As time goes on, social environments are changing fast and the need for such homes could no longer be undermined. The MUP has been contributing its best for the smooth and efficient working of these homes.

Ageing gracefully

Older citizens all over the world including Mizoram are getting more and more attention as their number increases. There is ample evidence that older people - those over the age of 60 years or above, though their number has increased, they have become more fit, and have more to offer than any other time in the past. Today even in Mizoram many well known politicians, businessmen and professionals continue to work and contribute to society well beyond the usual age of retirement. As such, old age should be thought of as bonus and as an opportunity for individual renaissance. Looking forward to the future with enthusiasm, and seeing old age as a period for potential to grow, one could keep the vital spark that existed once within oneself alight. The challenge for aging gracefully is therefore, to keep mentally stimulated and alert as well as physically fit and active as possible as ever.

In a traditional society like the Mizo, elderly people continue to be active and important figures in their community, their skills and abilities benefiting the community while in many advanced nations like the western society, the elderly people are always considered as burden to their society. The elderly people in Mizo community have comparatively many more constructive and rewarding years in store. The wealth of knowledge, experience and wisdom they already accumulated with age has always been acknowledged by younger generation. Retirement and old age can be most satisfying as experienced by most of the MUP members, if one retains old interests as well as develop new ones. Many of them keep themselves active and alive by joining voluntary works of different descriptions.

Mizoram has recently been designated by some agencies as the most developed state among the seven states of the north east region, especially in terms of human development indicators like literacy rate and some development indicators like village connectivity, rural electrification etc. There is a joke among the MUP members: "A very bright Mizo young student once remarked to his grandparents that it was impossible for them to understand the next generation of young people as the old people grew up in a different world. Today we have television, jet planes, spaceships, nuclear energy, computers and what not?" When the student paused for breath the MUP member said, "You are right my boy, we did not have those things when we were young. But, we invented them" Yes, all achievements made in various sectors of the economy, like big and beautiful buildings in Aizawl and in other district towns, good roads crisscrossing the state, educational institutions etc are all the handiworks of their grandparents.

Research work has repeatedly shown that light work after retirement and in old age improves health, morale and life expectancy. Older people in Mizoram are also often willing and exceedingly able to do voluntary work. Their wisdom and experience is of great value to voluntary organisations, charitable organization and many other non-government organisations, in which work matches the preferences and abilities of the employees. Voluntary jobs need to provide opportunities for learning, growth and self expression. They should feel that they are of use to a community. Such services of the MUP in Mizoram enrich their own lives as well as the lives of those they serve. So to grow old graccfully, it is good to remember that continued mental and physical stimulation are the two essential keys to feeling good and staying young.

Old people must also realize that younger people are not automatically healthier, wealthier and more carefree than they are; young people too have problems, they get lonely and have health problems. Many young people appreciate being able to call on the wisdom of age in crisis. In fact, old people must know that there is no magic formula for achieving a happy and productive old age life but it is very important to prepare to meet the challenges for the coming years. It is never too late to learn something new. Some Mizo retired persons got admitted themselves in the local university and obtained Bachelor degree in Law, Master Degrees in their chosen courses, diploma and certificate of higher education courses while a few of them especially in Aizawl city even after 70 joined the local computer courses. There are some who are still strong enough even after 90 years to come to the MUP Headquarters submitting their own written articles for publication in the MUP monthly journal. It is found that these groups of older persons in Mizo society take interest in other peoples' lives, they pray for others and go to places of worship regularly. It is not strange that people are found to have longer life expectation than their uncaring counterparts.

References of some research works in brief may be worth quoting. In 1984 at Duke University School of Medicine of USA, a research team found that religious faith and prayer could certainly heal even serious illnesses of any kind and could bring about good health in the elderly people. Cases of 455 sick old persons of the same illness were taken up for study; some of them attend place of worship regularly and pray for others while some never at all. Such group of religious elders, in general, were released from the hospital within 4 days while the "never at all group" require 12 days more nursing care. At Danmouth Medical School, USA, a research team also found the same results. Old loving people who had been "blessings" for others live longer than those who never thought of the welfare of others. The Yale University Research team had 2812 old sick people with heart problems under their care found that prayer helped reduce blood pressure and improve blood circulation and brain wave significantly. During the investigation period, half of the never-pray-at-all group members died. All those who pray and take interest in the welfare of other group members have been able to lead active life. In Israel, a research team studied cases of 3900 old persons suffering from cancer and lung patients for 16 long years. It was found that all those who pray regularly and receive the loving care of other people died less and live longer by 40% than the 'never at all' group. In John Hopkins School of Medicine, "Faith and Medicines subject" was introduced as one of the compulsory subjects. It is very essential for all the elderly people of the North East to realize the benefits and the fruits of being a blessing for others by joining good local voluntary organizations, national and even international NGOs and religious bodies so as to be of, at least, some help for the general public and to commit oneself with godly devotion which is so beneficial for all things as it holds promise of the life now and that which is to come later.

CHAPTER 4

Health Conditions and Access to Health Care Services by Elderly Persons in Mizoram

Jane R. Ralte

Introduction

With improvement in preventive medicine and health care in the country, the expectation of life at birth has gone through different phases. It has increased from 32 years in the forties to 42 years in 1951-60 and to 58 years in 1986-1990. It is expected to be 67 years in 2011-2016. In other words, people have now better health and live longer, giving rise to increasing number of elderly citizens. From 12 million in 1901, their number was about 20 million in 1951 and 57 million in 1991. Population projections made by Registrar General, India indicate that this number would be 100 million by 2016. According to the 2001 Census, 7.7% of the total population are above the age of 60 years in India. Issues related to the health care needs for the elderly have not been duly addressed in the current health care delivery system. It is only in the last few years that there has been some recognition that these needs of the elderly require both special organizational arrangements and special professional skills and training.

Health Conditions of the Elderly Persons

"You do not heal old age. You protect it, you promote it, you extend it," so said Sir James Sterling Ross. Growing old should thus be considered as a natural progression of life. The various physical and psychological changes accompanying old age needs to be well understood and taken into consideration for providing optimal care to the elderly. This aspect of care to the aged is called *clinical gerontology* or *geriatric*. This is an up-coming speciality with special emphasis given to different organs/systems and the effects of ageing on them, various degenerative and other diseases of old age, treatment of these conditions which includes the preventive aspects of care. *Geriatric gynaecology* is an appropriate example where needs have given rise to a new medical field which deals with numerous gynaecological conditions associated with old age.

Health problems of the aged may be divided into three broad headings:

Problems due to the aging process

With aging changes take place in the body which are mostly deleterious resulting in various disabilities and eventually lead to the death of the organism. Some of the disabilities considered incident to the aging process are Senile cataract, Glaucoma, Nerve deafness, Bony changes affecting mobility, Emphysema, Failure of special senses, Changes in mental outlook etc.

Problems associated with long-term illness

Some of the common chronic diseases associated with aging are Degenerative diseases of the heart and blood vessels (atherosclerosis, cardio vascular diseases), Cancer, Accidents (fracture of the neck of femur due to fall), Diabetes (elderly population account for about 75% of diabetics), Diseases of loco-motor system (gout, rheumatoid arthritis, osteoarthritis), Respiratory illnesses (chronic bronchitis, asthma), Genito-urinary system diseases (prostate enlargement) etc.

Psychological problems

Aging may give rise to psychological problems like Mental changes (impaired memory, rigidity in outlook), Sexual adjustment (diminution of sexual activity), Emotional disorders (bitterness, depression, suicide) etc.

Old age may last as long as 20 or 30 years and thus it is helpful to split the elderly up into the following smaller age groups. The social and biological characteristics of people in each of these age groups are sufficiently different to make these categories meaningful. For example, the young old are recently retired, tend to be wealthier than other elderly people and have a good social network. Each age group has its special health needs. The health services appropriate for the age groups 60-69 and 70-79 would be different from those required by the higher age group of 80 years and above.

the young old : 65-74 or 60-69 years,

the old old/old : 75-84 or 70-79 years and

the oldest old/very old : 85+ or > 80 years.

Health Requirements of Elderly Persons

An ICMR study done for rural areas has highlighted the following health problems among elderly persons over the age of 60 years (Table 1).

The goal of health services to the elderly would have to be based on the general principle of providing affordable services of adequate and acceptable quality as near the beneficiary as possible. It is recommended that special rates of user charges be levied for the elderly so as lessen the burden on the household and to induce them to seek medical attention for the elderly with no hesitation It is in this context that schemes for health insurance become important.

TABLE 1

Sl. No	Ailment	Reported %
1.	Visual impairment	88
2.	Locomotive disorders, joints, muscles	40
3.	Neurological complaints	18.7
4.	Cardio vascular diseases	17.4
5.	Respiratory diseases	16.1
6.	Skin conditions	13.3
7.	Gastro intestinal disorders	9
8.	Psychiatric problems	8.5
9.	Hearing loss	8.2
10.	Genito urinary disorders	3.5

Health care services for the elderly persons will have to be delivered at three different levels, namely primary, secondary and tertiary levels. The primary health care system would have to be the main provider of such services to the elderly, because of its reach. It would have to be strengthened and oriented for this purpose because the health and medical problems of the elderly would often be accompanied with disability, loss of some faculties and psychological problems. These problems are not always manageable at home or would require special training or orientation in those who cater to the needs of such elderly persons.

Geriatric care facilities would have to be provided at the secondary and tertiary care levels. The private health institutions should be encouraged to provide such facilities, and Government could provide incentives for any initiatives undertaken by private players. This would reduce the immediate investment that would, otherwise, have to be made to provide such facilities in all public health institutions.

The management of both public and private institutions would need to be sensitized to the special needs of the elderly. Certain measures can be undertaken to improve services for the geriatric patients like provision of single point counters to avoid multiple trips to various counters, barrier free passage ways, elimination of long waits etc.

Current Scenario in Mizoram

There are on-going programmes which cater for the health of the elderly citizens like the National Programme for Control of Blindness, under which sight is restored through cataract operations. However, it will not be wrong to say that the geriatric health care services in Mizoram are still in a fledgling state. Various attempts have been made to provide special health care/package to elderly persons. One of the initiatives undertaken is implementation of a World Health Organisation programme "Community Based Health Care for the Elderly in Mizoram" with effect from first November 2005. The objectives of this programme are:

(i) Providing health care for identified diseases like hypertension, diabetes, and special sensory impairments;

(ii) Providing simple physiotherapy and fitness exercises for affected persons

(iii) Developing a medium for social interaction.

(iv) Increasing health awareness among the elderly.

The programme runs its weekly clinic at the Headquarters of MUP (Mizoram Elderly Citizens Association) which is centrally located and easily accessible. This has enabled large numbers of patients to attend the clinic. The programme also runs monthly Clinics at Agapia Social Centre, Chanmari.

Pattern of cases attending MUP Clinic (10 months duration)

An in-depth study of the health care requirements of the elderly persons in Mizoram was also undertaken covering both government and private hospitals in the capital city. Profile of patients attending the Out Patient Department (OPD) of Civil Hospital, Aizawl and Narareth Medi-Tech Hospital was studied retrospectively for a period of 4 and 12 months respectively. The age group considered in this study as elderly persons are all persons over the age group of 50 years to match the figures considered as members by MUP.

TABLE 2

Sl. No	Complaints	No. of cases
1.	Endocrinology system	181
2.	Sensory organs and peripheral nervous system	131
3.	Digestive system	125
4.	Respiratory system	99
5.	Cardio vascular system	89
6.	Bone and Joint Disease	49
7.	Excretory System	24
8.	Skin	21
9.	Central Nervous System	14
10.	Dental Disease	3
11.	Gynaecological Disease	2
12.	Others	90
	TOTAL	828

A. Findings at Civil Hospital, Aizawl

The OPD attendance in selected departments of Medicine, Surgery, Gynaecology, Orthopaedic, ENT, Eye was studied in detail for 4 months.

Total Number of patients = 25, 264

Patients ages above 50 years = 2,619 (10.36%)

I. Diagnosis-Sex distributions

Sl No	Diagnosis	Male	Female	Total	%
1.	Visual impairments	292	360	652	*24.89*
2.	ENT disease	234	305	539	*20.58*
3.	Gastroenterology	140	112	252	*9.62*
4.	Locomotors, joint and muscle disease	134	107	241	*9.2*
5.	Respiratory disease	120	93	213	*8.13*
6.	Gynaecological disease	-	185	185	*7.06*
7.	Genito-urinary disorder	81	48	129	*4.92*
8.	Cardiovascular disease	45	35	80	*3.05*
9.	Diabetes mellitus	42	29	71	*2.71*
10.	Cholelithiasis	21	40	61	2.32
11.	Neurological disorder	28	25	53	*2.02*
12.	Infection	30	13	43	*1.64*
13.	Skin disease	21	16	37	*1.41*
14.	Ano-rectal disorder	17	8	25	*0.95*
15.	Appendicitis	9	5	14	*0.53*
16.	Malignancy	6	2	8	*0.3*
17.	Goitre	1	3	4	*0.15*
18.	Others	9	3	12	*0.45*
	Total	1230	1389	2619	*100.00*

II. Diagnosis-Age group distribution

Sl No	Diagnosis	50-59	60-69	70-79	>80	Total
1	Visual impairments	329	165	128	30	652
2	ENT disease	270	159	80	30	539
3	Gastroenterology	141	68	33	10	252

(contd.)

Sl No	Diagnosis	50-59	60-69	70-79	>80	Total
4	Locomotors, joint and muscle disease	119	74	37	11	241
5	Respiratory disease	105	57	40	11	213
6	Gynaecological disease	139	35	11	-	185
7	Genito-urinary disorder	50	42	30	7	129
8	Cardiovascular disease	37	28	14	1	80
9	Diabetes mellitus	31	22	9	9	71
10	Cholelithiasis	32	24	4	1	61
11	Neurological disorder	21	23	6	3	53
12	Infection	15	25	1	2	43
13	Skin disease	15	15	7	-	37
14	Ano-rectal disorder	8	7	9	1	25
15	Appendicitis	6	8	-	-	14
16	Malignancy	4	3	-	1	8
17	Goiter	4	-	-	-	4
18	Others	-	12	-	-	12
	Total	1326	767	409	117	2619

B. Findings at Nazareth Medi-Tech Hospital, Aizawl

The profile of the total OPD attendance was studied in detail for a period of 12 months.

Total Number of patients = 903

Patients ages above 50 years = 176 (19.49%)

I. Diagnosis-Sex distribution:-

Sl No	Diagnosis	Male	Female	Total	%
1.	Malignancy	30	23	53	*30.11*
2.	Infection	26	17	43	*24.43*
3.	Gastroenterology	20	18	38	*21.59*
4.	Diabetes mellitus	6	6	12	*6.81*

(contd.)

Sl No	Diagnosis	Male	Female	Total	%
5.	Cardiovascular disease	7	4	11	*6.25*
6.	Respiratory disease	5	5	10	*5.68*
7.	Psychiatric problem	2	2	4	*2.27*
8.	Locomotor disorder, joint and muscle	2	-	2	*1.13*
9.	Neurological disorder	1	1	2	*1.13*
10.	Genito-urinary disorder	1	-	1	*0.56*
	TOTAL	100	76	176	*100*

II. Diagnosis-Age group distribution:-

Sl No	Diagnosis	50-59	60-69	70-79	>80	Total
1.	Malignancy	31	6	13	3	53
2.	Infection	19	13	10	1	43
3.	Gastroenterology	26	9	2	1	38
4.	Diabetes mellitus	7	3	1	1	12
5.	Cardiovascular disease	5	6	-	-	11
6.	Respiratory disease	1	3	3	3	10
7.	Psychiatric problem	4	-	-	-	4
8.	Locomotor disorder, joint and muscle	2	-	-	-	2
9.	Neurological disorder	2	-	-	-	2
10.	Genito-urinary disorder	-	-	1	-	1
	Total	97	40	30	9	176

Discussion

The elderly persons constitute 10.36% of total attendance in Civil Hospital, a government institution, with more number of female elderly patients (53%). The attendance of elderly patients is almost double (19.49%) in the private hospital surveyed, which may be due to the availability of easily accessible services. The number of male elderly patients is higher at 76% in the private hospital. A common trend observed is that the percentage of attendance progressively decreases with the increase in age in both hospitals. Attendance was found to be 50-55% between the age group of 50-59 years, 22-29% between the age group of 60-69, 15-17% between70-79 and 4-5% above 80 years. The most common disease conditions in the elderly are visual impairments, hearing impairments, malignancy/cancer, problems of the gastro-intestinal tract etc.

As per the statistics available from the on-going WHO sponsored geriatric programme (November 2005-August 2006, a period of ten months), the maximum number of clients attending these clinics are aged between 71-80 years. Diabetes mellitus accounts for 21% of all cases, hypertension accounts for 10%, followed by lung diseases 7%, cataract 5% and osteoarthritis 4%.

The existing health care services in the state and the on-going programmes are not adequate to meet all the health care needs of the elderly. The health care institutions in both public and private sectors of Mizoram are also not particularly geared up for the elderly citizens. There is deficiency in the infrastructure and physical facilities which adversely affects the delivery of health care to this group of population. There is also deficiency in the knowledge level, attitude and orientation of the health staff towards geriatric care. In other words, the whole system is not very conducive towards providing comprehensive health care for the elderly citizens. Some attempts have been made by the Department of Health and Family Welfare in this area. However, there is still much left to be done.

The issues relating to the elderly are complex since they include social, welfare and cultural parameters. These issues need to be dealt with in a comprehensive manner so as to ensure that the elderly lead comfortable lives with assured minimum health care, sustenance and shelter, preferably within the family system. The role of the "care-givers" who are an important component in ensuring the health of the elderly in their own families needs to be recognized and built upon. Orientation of care givers so that they can recognize presentations of the common ailments of this age group and who will be able to provide basic treatment at home is essential. This will take care of the "pre-hospital" component of care. An important aspect that needs to be recognized is that elderly women are more disadvantaged than men.

The process of aging is something which no one can ignore or escape from. However, steps can be taken to make it less traumatic while giving more dignity to this process and at the same time imposing less financial burden on the elderly themselves or their relatives. Many factors which contribute to the disease burdens associated with aging are potentially responsive to preventive interventions. For example, if tobacco consumption is stopped it can lead to a healthier life style and prevent many diseases in later years. It is therefore essential to design and implement preventive strategies which are appropriate and socially acceptable for the specific community so as to reduce various risks and also maintain functional independence. Disease prevention strategy in the elderly has great potential to improve their quality of life and increase life span.

Recommendation for Better Health Care for the Elderly

(i) Formulation of a policy for the elderly with particular safeguards for women and identification of the administrative Department responsible for implementation of this policy;

(ii) Capacity building at all levels of public health care delivery systems, namely primary, secondary and tertiary levels in terms of infrastructure as well as the technical know-how and special skills

Areas potentially amenable to preventive health care in the elderly are as follows

Primary	Secondary	Tertiary
Health Habits Smoking, Alcohol abuse, Obesity Nutrition, Sleep Coronary Heart Disease risk factors immunization influenza pneumovax tetanus Injury prevention Latrogenesis prevention Osteoporosis prevention	Screening for – hypertension, diabetes, periodental disease, dental caries, sensory impairment, medication side effect, colo-rectal cancer, breast cancer, cervical cancer, prosthetic cancer, nutritionally induced anaemias, depression, stress, urinary incontinence, podiatric problems, fall risk, tuberculosis, syphilis, stroke prevention, myocardial infarction.	Rehabilitation Physical deficits Cognitive deficits Functional deficits Caretaker support Introduction of support necessary to prevent loss of autonomy

through sensitization and training for all categories of workers;

(iii) Involvement and encouragement to private health institutions to provide geriatric care facilities;

(iv) Sensitisation of the managements of both public and private institutions to the special needs of the elderly and provision of single point counters to avoid multiple trips to various counters in an institution, elimination of long waits;

(v) Reduction of user fees for health services in the case of the elderly patients, so as to lessen the burden on the household in availing of medical assistance for the elderly;

(vi) Health insurance schemes for the elderly need to be introduced and implemented;

(vii) Non-government organisations could be actively associated and encouraged to establish geriatric health care centres/counselling centres to advise the elderly and their families.

Conclusion

The Constitution of India, in Article 41 of the Directive Principles of State Policy, specifies that the State within the limits of its economic capacity provide for the assistance to the elderly. The National Policy in Older Persons of January 1999 mandates State support for the elderly with regards to health care, shelter and welfare. It also provides for building up a strong and vigorous voluntary initiative through NGOs. The National Population Policy 2000 also refers to the needs of the elderly while the National Health Policy specifically includes concepts relating to geriatric care.

The elderly population impacts on the society in different ways. The various health problems associated with aging makes a greater demand on the health services of the community. In developed countries like England about two-third of all hospital beds are occupied by elderly citizens over 65 years. This puts on additional financial burden on the community besides the stress of taking care of the aged in ones own family. Therefore, there is need for taking pro-active steps towards providing comprehensive health care for the elderly persons in Mizoram. This will cover a whole gamut of activities like orientation of the care providers at home and in health care set-ups, construction of "geriatric-friendly" hospitals, imparting training of different categories of health care workers, system/process improvement to cater to the elderly etc.

ACKNOWLEDGEMENT

I wish to acknowledge with thanks the assistance received from all my colleagues and patients. In particular I wish to mention by name the following persons who have made this study possible with their valuable contributions and inputs:

Dr. Zairemthiama, MO, WHO-sponsored cancer control programme.

Ms. K. Lalchawimawii, Staff Nurse, WHO-sponsored cancer control programme.

Mr. C. Ramhmachhuana Hualhang, Data Entry Operator, WHO-sponsored cancer control programme.

Ms. Sailopari, M.S.W., WHO-sponsored community based health care for the elderly.

Ms. Zarzoliani Pachuau, Staff Nurse, WHO-sponsored community based health care for the elderly.

Ms. C. Zothantluangi, Clinical Psychologist, WHO-sponsored Tobacco Cessation Clinic.

Ms. Lalmuanpuii, MSW, WHO-sponsored Tobacco Cessation Clinic.

REFERENCES

German, P.S., Fried, L.P., *Annual Review of Public Health*, Vol.10, 1989,P.325

Park, K., *Parks Text book of Preventive and Social Medicine*, 18th Edition, Jan.2005

Registrar General Census Commissioner, India, Population Projections for India and the states, 1996-2016 of 1996

Registrar General Census Commissioner, India, Ageing Population of India- An analysis of the 1991 Census Data of 1999

Task Force on Health and Family Welfare, Government of Karnataka, April 2001, Towards Equity, Quality and Integrity in Health, Final Report of the Task Force on Health and Family Welfare

VAHI (1997), *Report of the Independent Commission on Health in India*, Chapter 14, Health Problems of Specialised Groups

Weir, J. H. (1967). *Royal Society Health Journal*. 87,144

CHAPTER 5

Social and Economic Security Programme for Elderly Persons in Mizoram: Role of State Government

Lalbiakkimi

Introduction

The importance given to older persons and the way they are treated and recognised differ from country to country and society to society. In developing countries such as India, the status enjoyed by older persons changed with time and place. The status given to older persons in Mizoram also underwent changes with the passing of time. In the past, the economy of Mizo was solely based on agriculture (jhum cultivation). During those times, as the young and middle aged persons had to work in the jhum everyday, looking after the household and children were the responsibility of the older persons. However, there has been a drastic change in the way of life of the Mizo which automatically changed the way older persons are treated and taken care of, although in some villages, it remained the same. The changing lifestyle has led to decrease in the role played by the older persons which becomes less and less as they grow older and older. They thus, gradually become more and more withdrawn within their own family and they tend to become emotionally restrained and feel worthless.

The State Government, recognising the importance of the older persons and their contribution to the society as a whole has taken various steps for their welfare which are as follows:

Old Age Pension

In developed countries the facilities that are available for the care of the aged are better compared to India which, due mainly to resource constraints, still lacks quality and attention. This is not to say that care of the aged is neglected. In fact, most States and Union Territories within their resource capacity offer aid to older persons who are poor. By April 1982 in India 20 States and 7 Union Territories had given old age pension for supporting older persons who are poor. The old age pension given for supporting the aged ranges from Rs 30 to Rs 60. There are some states that give Rs 100 a month as old age pension. For most states the eligible age for receiving this old age pension is 65 years old. But some states also give this pension to people who are younger than 65 years if they are widows or physically handicapped.

In Mizoram Old Age Pension was introduced soon after it achieved the status of Union Territory, and as many as 150 people were selected to receive Old Age Pension. In the beginning Rs 30 was given monthly which comes up to Rs 360 annually. As the years passed and with rising inflation Rs 30 as monthly pension was considered meagre and was increased to Rs 60 a month in 1981-82 and in 1993-94 it was again increased to Rs 100 a month.

On 15thAugust 1995, the 47th anniversary of India's Independence, the Prime Minister of India announced a new programme called 'National Social Assistance Programme'. The main purpose of this programme is to help the poor and the needy. In Mizoram this programme is implemented through the Social Welfare Department. For the implementation of this programme District Committees headed by Deputy Commissioners have been formed in the 3 districts of Mizoram – Aizawl, Lunglei and Chhimtuipui. The Committee is responsible for the effective implementation of the different schemes under the NSAP.

One of the schemes under NSAP is the 'National Old Age Pension Scheme.' The assistance for older persons is provided by this scheme in the form of Old Age Pension. According to the 'Guidelines on the implementation of National Social Assistance Programme in Mizoram' as approved by the State Government those who are eligible to receive Old Age Pension are as follows:

(i) He/she has attained the age of 65 (sixty five) and is a resident of Mizoram, provided that in case of physically and mentally handicapped person, the minimum age limit shall be 55 (fifty five)

(ii) He/She is a person living under the poverty line.

(iii) He/She has no relation who can maintain him/her and

(iv) He/She has been a resident of Mizoram for not less than 10 years on the date of making application.

Mode of Application

Application forms may be obtained free of charge from the Office of District Social Welfare Officer and Child Development Project Officer (CDPO) concerned. Applications for Old Age Pension shall be addressed to and submitted to the CDPO concerned.

Verification of Application

All the applicants shall be screened by the recommending body at the village level such as Village Council, Young Mizo Association, Mizoram Upa Pawl (Mizoram Senior Citizens Association) and Mizoram Hmeichhia Insuihkhawm Pawl (Mizoram Women Organsiation) under the supervision of the CDPO concerned by strictly following the criteria laid down. The CDPO concerned shall forward the list of selected applicants to the District Social Welfare Officer (DSWO) concerned.

Selection of Beneficiaries

Selection of beneficiaries of Old Age Pension shall be done by the District Level Committee.

Sanction of Pension

The Deputy Commissioner of each District who is also Chairman, District Level Committee for implementation of NSAP scheme in Mizoram, shall be the sanctioning authority.

Payment of Pension

As per Government of India Guidelines, all benefit payments should be made through the Bank Account of the beneficiary in the Post Office Savings Banks or in a commercial Bank or through Postal Money Order. However, due to non- availability of Bank/Postal Services in many remote areas of Mizoram, payment through such agencies is considered not feasible in some interior villages for timely release of assistance. Mode of payment, therefore, has been modified as follows in order to suit the local needs.

The CDPOs shall make door to door benefit payment to all the beneficiaries under NOAPS in cash through pay books issued by Social Welfare Department. In this task, the CDPOs shall utilize the services of Circle Officers and Anganwadi Workers so that the pension money is delivered to the rightful beneficiary.

Stopping or Withholding of Pension

The sanctioning authority may, after giving the pensioner an opportunity of being heard, stop or withhold pension if:

The pension has been sanctioned on mistaken grounds; or

The condition for the grant of pension no longer exists.

Information about death

The Village Council and MUP concerned shall report every case of the death of the pensioner immediately after its occurrence of the CDPO concerned. The CDPO then shall ensure that payment is stopped forthwith. The amount due to the pensioner till the date of his/ her death shall be paid to his widow or her widower, as the case may be, provided the widow of the widower, as the case may be, produces a certificate from the VC/MUP to the effect that the widow/widower was legally married to the deceased pensioner. The CDPO concerned shall report every case of the death of a pensioner to the DSWO concerned.

Commutation

Pension under NOAPs shall not be commutable.

Registers to be maintained

The CDPOs shall maintain a complete record of payment of Old Age Pension in a separate bound register with numbered pages. This register and other relevant records relating to Old Age Pension cases shall be opened to inspection by any officer of the Government as may be nominated by the Social Welfare Department for the purpose.

Production of life certificate

A pensioner may receive his/her pension after production of a life certificate signed by VCP/MUP in a prescribed form. Life certificate must be submitted to the CDPO concerned twice a year.

The CDPO shall be personally responsible for payment wrongly made.

The Central Government through NOAPS grants Rs 75 a month per person. The State Government is providing for the gap of Rs 25 per month per beneficiary to the beneficiaries of NOAPS so that they can receive Rs 100 a month.

During the year 1995-96 there were 3157 individuals receiving old age pension from the State Government while there were 980 old age pension beneficiaries under NOAPS. Every once in a while the number of individuals that are given old age pension from NOAPS is increased. In 1997-1998 it was increased to 2760 persons and again to 7368 in 2000-2001. The State Government provides for an additional Rs 25 a month to every person receiving old age pension under NOAPS.

Since the State Government is perpetually facing a monetary crisis, the people receiving Old Age Pension under the State Government have all been transferred to NOAPS. The total number of people receiving Old Age Pension comes up to 10525. As we have mentioned earlier the Central Government. grants only Rs 75 a month per person and the State Government has to bear for Rs 25 in order to bring the monthly disbursement per individual to Rs 100. Therefore, the annual expenditure of State Government for this sponsorship amounts to Rupees thirty-one lakhs fifty seven thousand and five hundred (Rs 3,157,500) a year.

For both the Central and State Government combined the amount spent for the 10525 old age pensioners in a year totals to Rs 12,630,000 (Rupees one hundred and twenty six lakhs thirty thousand) a year.

Old Age Home

Old Age Home was started on March 1, 1989 by the Social Welfare Department. This is the only Home for the Aged (60+) in Mizoram. The aims and objectives are to provide care and protection, both physical and mental, to the aged (60+) both men and women, having no relatives/supporters to look after him/her. Application for admission should be submitted to the Director, Social Welfare Department. The applicant must be a permanent resident of Mizoram. Applicants having communicable diseases may be denied admission to the Home. Admission is done only after spot verification and interview by Departmental Officer. The Home has a capacity of 10 (ten) seats. All the basic needs (shelter, food, clothing, recreation) and services (washing, cooking, bathing etc.) are provided free to the inmates. Balanced and nutritious diet, as per approved diet scale and rate for various Homes under Social Welfare Department are provided to the inmates. Special diet is provided on National Days and Festivals.

Recreational facilities such as Television (cable connection), Tape Recorder, Radio, Carrom Board, Books etc. are provided. They are also allowed to keep kitchen garden near the Home for their recreation/enjoyment. Inmates are allowed to attend the Local Church Meeting. As most inmates are physically weak, devotion programmes are conducted in the Home regularly.

The physical health of the inmates are regularly checked by Medical Officer working in Social Welfare Department. All prescribed medicines are provided free. If necessary, the inmates are also taken/admitted to the Hospitals. All necessary expenditures for their treatments/Hospital bills are borne by the Department. Inmates who are not able to take bath by themselves are helped by the staff. The inmates are not allowed to go outside the locality of Government. Complex, Luangmual without the permission of Care Taker/ Warden. When the inmates die in the Home, they are buried in the cemetery of the local area where the Home is located, with the help of the local people and church if there is no claimant of the dead bodies. All necessary funeral expenses are borne by the Department.

All expenditures (including salary of staff) for maintenance of the Home is borne by Mizoram State Fund. This Old Age Home is located at Government. Complex, Luangmual, Aizawl. Old Age Home can be visited at any time with the permission of the Care Taker/Warden/any other staff. Staff Position of the Old Age Home as on November, 2006 are as follows:

Care Taker	1 (one)
Warden	1 (one)
Driver	1 (one)
IV Grade	5 (five)

Apart from the Old Age Pension and Home provided for the Aged the Government of Mizoram also often assist and aid the Mizoram Upa Pawl, an organisation working for the welfare of older persons in many areas of the state,. Besides Mizoram Upa Pawl, there are also other NGOs working for older persons, some of them are running Day Care Centres for Older Persons and the State Government gives its full support to the various NGOs working for the older persons.

State Policy for Older Persons (SPOP)

Following the state level workshop held on 9 and 10th October, 2003 at I and PR Auditorium by the Social Welfare Department under the sponsorship of the

Ministry of Social Justice and Empowerment, Government of India, the State Policy for Older Persons (SPOP) has been prepared (See Annexure).

To conclude, it may be stated that the assistance and facilities given to the aged in our state is still inadequate. We all know that the aged have given all their productive days to raising children and family, and worked for the betterment of the society as well as the government. We should think twice about the reason why the aged who had made immeasurable sacrifices to the community during their time are subjected to having to live in old age homes and why they have to be given old age pensions. Our society in the past have always looked after the aged but with changing times as mentioned earlier, our values have changed. During the time of our ancestors widows and the destitute were often looked after by the community as a whole and provided them with homes or help them in building one. The sense of duty in helping the poor and the needy is one of the remarkable traits that Mizo society possesses and even with the arrival of Christianity it continues to persist. It is now time to plan innovative welfare programmes for the aged keeping in view the changed and changing environment and lifestyles.

CHAPTER 6

Social Work Intervention with the Elderly

Kalpana N Desai and Lalmuanpuii

Nomenclature in ageing

As human service professionals Social Workers are sensitive to the nomenclature and terminology used to refer to older persons. The current choice "Older persons" is reflective of this sensitivity since it provides a place for this population within an age spectrum. The earlier terms of 'Aged', 'Elderly' and 'Old aged' tend to stereotype this population into a compartment and seem to focus on their decline in abilities. The terminology of 'Older persons' however departs from this stereotyping and locates this group as being 'Older' to others. It is based on a capability and strengths orientation and hence is a preferred term.

Ageing as a process has been recognized from time immemorial. Folklore, tradition and wisdom in all cultures have been known to reflect people who lived unto a 'ripe old age". Old age is mostly fixed at any age over 60 years or so in most nations around the world. Increasing life spans and longevity of population would however mean that there is a substantial population of persons living in a category that is often referred to as the "aged". However to place the entire population of persons of 60 years-100 years (or more) in one compartment of 'the Elderly' would be erroneous if we intend to plan interventions or programmes for them since a 30-40 year life span is a huge range in years.

Schaie K.W. and Sherry L. Willis (2002) states that placing the entire old population in one category and viewing them as undergoing a single stage of life is erroneous. In any life stage people differ radically and so it is with this stage of life. Suzman and Riley (in Schaie K.W. and Sherry L. Willis) categorise the persons over 65 years into three stages; **the young old** (65 to 75 years); **the old-old** (75-85 years) and the **very old or oldest-old** (85 years and abovc).

It is evident that both capabilities in the older population as well as a decline in abilities would be different for persons in the extremes of the age range. Hence there is need for researcher, scholars, practitioners to view this stage in a non-totalitarian manner and recognize the range in abilities of the older persons.

Social Work is a profession that addresses a range of challenges faced by a range of persons. It attempts to help persons overcome these challenges in their life through systematic interventions that are planned to bring about change. The profession of social work is based on the scientific study of human beings and uses a knowledge base that recognizes diversity in populations. The value base of Social Work is empowering and protecting the dignity of the individuals it wishes to serve. Professional Social Work is differentiated from voluntary social service in that the former uses a scientific knowledge of human behaviour, delineates specific skills and techniques in dealing with people and rests on value base that places emphasis on non-judgemental attitudes, recognition of the inherent worth and dignity of persons, acceptancc and recognition of the right to self determination by all persons.

It further stipulates a controlled emotional involvement with client populations and assures confidentiality to them in information made available to social workers. Traditionally social work began to address specific needs of populations in certain areas and specializations within the subject were built around these areas. Therefore it was common to hear of Family and Child Welfare, Medical and Psychiatric Social Work, Community Development etc as specializations of the academic discipline of Social work. Today, there is an attempt to follow an integrated method in Social Work and there is a concerted effort to practise a generalist method. However, social workers who work exclusively with older persons are referred to as Gerontological Social Workers or Gero-Psychiatric Social Workers (particularly in clinical settings).

Gerontological social work is concerned with maintaining and enhancing the quality of life of older adults and their families. It is particularly concerned with ameliorating those physical, psychosocial, familial, cultural, ethnic and racial, organizational, and societal factors which serve as barriers to physical and emotional well-being in later life. Gerontological social work interventions are directed at enhancing dignity, self-determination, personal fulfilment, quality of life, optimal functioning, and ensuring the least restrictive living environment possible. Interventions that enhance older adults' coping and problem-solving capabilities are perhaps the most basic and crucial aspect of gerontological social work. Because services are typically sought at times of crisis, gerontological social workers give special attention to the psychosocial meanings of change and loss, as well as to underlying biological, psychological, cognitive and social factors experienced by the older adult and family (in Dobrof R/GITT). Social Work works within the framework of a **bio-psychosocial** perspective and sees all problems or challenges from this angle.

Ageing – A Bio-Psycho-Social Perspective

Ageing of populations (Population ageing) and individual ageing are very different phenomena. Population ageing is a process by which older individuals come to form a proportionately larger share of the total population and is an important demographic trend and indicator for development issues (Chakraborti R.D., 2004).

Individual ageing connotes the process by which individuals age and this process is often characterized by physical and mental decline. It is a phase wherein atrophy sets in and is comprised of biological, social and psychological aspects.

Biological ageing (Physiological ageing) involves inter alia, tissue desiccation, retardation of cell division, degeneration, decreased speed, strength and endurance and a general gradual impairment.

Psychological ageing refers to the process of mental decline normally accompanying old age and this stage may not be synchronous with physical changes and/or deterioration. It is often heralded by tragic events in ones life, loss of spouse or intimate ones and/or due to leading a highly stressed life. People who have aged psychologically may exhibit greater despair, less interest in surroundings and a greater feeling of having grown *'old'*.

Erik Erikson describes this stage of life as one in which individuals seek balance between 'Search for Ego Integrity and Sense of 'despair'. This continuous need to find balance between the former and latter in this stage is described by Erikson as imperative and necessary. Therefore this stage is characterized by a person reviewing his/her past, searching for meaning, accounting for failures and ultimately trying to avoid or succumbing to despair. The successful resolution of tasks in this stage in an individual who has led his/her life meaningfully would lead to an integrated personality.

Robert Havighurst outlines developmental tasks in later life that includes adjusting to decreasing physical strength and health; adjusting to retirement and reduced income adjusting to the death of a spouse, establishing an explicit association with ones age group, adopting and adapting societal roles in a flexible way and establishing satisfactory physical living arrangements (in Schaie K.W. and Sherry L.Willis, 2002)

Social ageing

This concept is viewed in the context of roles and how society perceives persons and their contributions. Thus, social ageing occurs in the life span of the individual when others perceive his/her role as being that of an old person. These are heralded by social developments such as becoming grandparents, taking retirement, assignment of social responsibilities, etc. (Bhatia H.S., 1983).

It is therefore evident that the Bio-Psycho-Social perspective takes into account the various aspects of ageing. Social Work takes into account this perspective while planning interventions for the older populations.

According to The Social Work Leadership Institute (SWLI), ageing is a *quality of life challenge, a poverty challenge, an intergenerational family support challenge and a long-term care challenge.*

Demographic Profile – India/Mizoram

The greying of India or 'Population ageing' as it has been referred to has been largely a result of both the decline in mortality as in the decline in the overall death rate. Morbidity figures too indicate that there is better control of disease that has impacted on the quality of life. Further decline in fertility has a role to play in the overall ageing of populations.

Improvements in quality of life and development in general have resulted in dramatic increase in ageing populations across the world. In the 1950s there were around 200 million older persons (over age 60 years) in the world and this number has tripled in a fifty year span. Even more dramatic is the rise in people over 80 years of age. Demographers are agreed that the ageing trends are sharpest in developing countries.

In India, the average years people were expected to live following 60+ years in 1951 was just 10.9 years for men and 11.4 years for women. Today it has doubled and women can hope to live for another 20 years at least following 60 years while men may live another 17.3 years. (Desai, M. and Siva Raju, 2000). The percentage of persons living beyond 60years of age to total population has also steadily been rising and today approximately 7.5% of the population in India are of older persons.

In Mizoram the age at which a person may join the Mizoram Upa Pawl (MUP) which is a state wide NGO for older persons, is fifty years of age and above. A majority however are pensioners and retired persons over the age of sixty years (Lalmuanpuii 2004). The census figures of age wise data in Mizoram indicates that there are approximately over a lakh in population of persons over the age of *50 years* (Census of India 2001). If 50 years and above include older populations, this means that approximately over ten per cent of the total population in Mizoram would require care and protection as older populations.

The John Hartford Foundation (SWLI) suggests that these rapid demographic changes globally are forcing our planners to reshape their policies and improve the health care delivery needs of the older persons. It compels also the expansion of ageing competent professionals to deal with the range of issues thrown up in the wake of a 'Next Generation"

Bio-Psychosocial Issues of Older Populations and Social Work Interventions

Social Work addresses issues faced by populations using specific, scientific and systematized methods of intervention. The predominant issues that are a focus of Social Work Management include:

Physical

Access to Health Care, Nutrition Care, Illness management, Neuro-Psychiatric Care, Physical fitness and referral and management of chronic illness.

Psychological

Counselling and support services to handle issues related to loneliness, anxieties and depression, Referral services for improved psychological care, Death and Bereavement Counselling and care, facilitation in Leisure time pursuits, raising of self-esteem, motivation building, etc.

Social

Specific Social Work concerns include increase in access to social resources, improving facilities for constructive use of leisure time, organizing and running Day Care centers, initiation of self-help group and support group for older persons, widowed, bereaved, childless, etc; help in social network building, initiation of advocacy efforts to secure rights, organizing of awareness programmes, training of care-givers for chronically ill older persons, care-giver support, pre-retirement programme planning, mediation between government resources and marginalized older persons, prevention of Elder Abuse and Neglect, support in securing employment for older persons.

Health care and services

Health care and health problems among older persons are a priority area of concern for social workers since it is the prime area in which older persons seek assistance to alleviate suffering and address health needs. Studies done by Siva Raju and SC Anand (Desai M and Siva Raju, 2000) on health status of the elderly seem to suggest that both health problems as well as medical care and services are a prime area of concern in this population. A majority of the elderly (61-64%) in their study of over 300 persons showed that they considered their health status as 'fair". In a pioneering study by T Krishnan Nair in the early eighties on the rural aged in Tamil Nadu, a sample of 1598 subjects were interviewed from 200 villages. The elderly were rated on mobility status, sensory impairment, physician utilization etc and 4 out of 5 persons failed to rate themselves as being in 'good health". Bela Shah (in Ramamurti PV and D Jamuna 2004) states that *health pessimism* seems more common in this age range of population.

Medical Social Workers working in clinical and community settings (NGOs) respond in a variety of ways to address the health needs of older populations. Identification of chronic illnesses that require referrals and treatment at the community level is the first among several tasks performed by alert and sensitive social workers. Arrangement of funds, aids to treatment such as procurement for blood etc are done by a hospital based social worker. Counselling of persons prior to admission and following discharge particularly in the case of older persons undergoing surgery is considered important and crucial in recovery process. Further, arrangement and assistance of patients in need of financial support is also performed by the social worker. Micro level interventions such as these are possible in settings that are restrictive in their scope (such as a hospital).

In **Macro-practice**, social scientists in general and social workers specifically increasingly impact the policies of the government or NGOs in health care delivery system. They add to the body of research by studying the psychosocial aspects of health care, common health problems and health care utilization.

In Mizoram too, students of the Department of Social Work, Mizoram University have submitted dissertations (in partial fulfilment of their MSW degree) on subjects that are concerned with the older populations. Studies that have been conducted here on local populations include, "Self –Perceived Life satisfaction and Problems of the Rural Aged". In this small study by Lalmuanpuii in 2004, on a sample of 25 persons, it was observed that a little less than half (48%) reported various problems such as kidney problems, chronic cough and high blood pressure. While such studies may not be generalised, it is still useful to note that research in areas (where data is lacking for want of large scale studies or projects) serve to direct service providers and policy makers.

Mental Health

Gero-Psychiatry is a sub discipline that encompasses the mental health needs of the older persons. Loneliness, dependency, despair, anxiety, somatisation of problems, sleep disturbances and isolation are just some of the issues facing the therapist who works with older persons. In addition, the gero-psychiatrist or ger-psychiatric social worker works with common mental health problems like affective disorders (including depression) and dementias. Senile Dementia Alzheimers Type (SDAT) is observed to be fairly high in developing countries according to A Venkoba Rao (in Ramamurti PV and D Jamuna, 2004) and constitutes nearly 20% of psychiatric morbidity among the older persons. It is characterized by cognitive impairment and deterioration while consciousness remains intact. In the study by

Lalmuanpuii (2004) one out of 25 respondents was observed to be suffering from dementia.

Micro level intervention involves counselling of not only the elderly to cope better with issues of old age but also is directed to address care givers and family members of the older persons. It has been increasingly realized that a lot of mental health burden is faced and shared by the care givers of the elderly.

Home based training and on-site counselling to help them cope with the stresses of care giving are also necessary. Care giving for extended periods of time, particularly when the person cared for is suffering from chronic conditions like dementia (Alzheimer in particular) place a huge psychological burden on the family members. They go through the trauma of seeing a loved family member getting disoriented, regress and deteriorate while having to cater to excessive demands on their time and energy and resources. Social work intervention therefore is also geared to offer support by way of handling burn-out issues among care-givers.

Mezzo-level interventions work towards restoring the dignity of older persons and and include all those efforts that work towards involving groups by way of advocacy or awareness. Macro interventions address mental health needs of community at large and initiation of support groups for families of older persons as well as groups for the older persons themselves. It further includes all influence on policies by way of lobbying, advocacy and pressure that social workers use to mobilize people to fight for their causes.

Coping with Losses

The period of old age is a period in which many have to cope with the loss of a spouse or an intimate partner. It is a period therefore that is accentuated by the feeling of loneliness and withdrawal from active social life due to death of a partner. In some cases the loss is heralded by that of losing a job, a position, a social status etc. In this stage therefore, a person has to prepare for new life roles and learn to give up roles that she/he had assumed earlier.

Social work intervention among the widowed and/ or single elderly population has to help towards increasing social support systems. Coping with losses is better when social support is stable and sound. Scrutton states that coping with losses in older populations is more profound since people don't have time to build significant relationships again at this age. In her study K Lalhlupuii (2005) studied "Coping with Spousal loss due to cancer death in Mizoram" and included thirty persons who had lost a spouse to cancer. The sample used non-probability sampling due to the limitations of time and drew a sample each from North, East, west and South of Aizawl city. It was found that a majority of the persons interviewed belonged to the age range of over fifty years. A majority (80%) stated that they received good social support from family members during the illness and a majority (76%) reported good tertiary support as well.

K.C. Lalparmawii (2005) in her study conducted in partial fulfilment of her MSW degree studied "Menopause, mental health and social support of Mizo women". In her study of a sample of 60 women from Durtlang area women between the ages of 35-58 were included using convenience sampling to include all women who have attained menopause. Although this may not include many older persons, the study is significant as it addresses mental health issues faced by women who lose their reproductive capacity through menopause. Menopause is usually considered to be a major life event for older women. Over two-thirds (68.3%) stated that there is no primary social support to help them undergo the stage of menopause. It is therefore evident that social support is high in the case of loss of spouse but low in the case of loss of function. Menopause in women is known to lead to various psychological changes and therefore these are newer areas of challenges facing social workers. According to Rosamma Veedon Social Work intervention for new retirees or for older persons approaching retirement have to address issues related to imparting information on schemes for older persons, coping with reduced incomes, help persons explore newer sources or avenues of income and confidence building exercises to boost morale (in Desai M and Siva Raju 2000)and help people dissociate income earning capacity from morale and self-esteem.

Financial Insecurities

It is a most pressing area of concern among the elderly since they are usually in a life stage wherein they have given up active employment or remunerative work and coupled with that is the cessation of a stable income. In developing countries, the assistance given to the older persons by way of insurance and/or pension is a paltry onc and is hardly able to allow people to live in dignity for the remaining years of their life. They usually see a sharp downward shift in their ability to maintain the lifestyle they used to while in remunerative work. To compound the problems, there are often added expenditures in this stage of their life, a contingency they have mostly been ill –prepared for. Irudaya Rajan (In Desai M and Siva Raju2000) states that not all elderly persons require financial assistance. Social work intervention focuses attention on the most marginalized among the older populations. Persons below the poverty line, a large majority of the rural aged, elderly widows, elderly non-workers, elderly dependants are among the marginalized elderly who would require financial assistance.

Social workers must determine eligibility of the elderly in receiving pensions, schemes of the government and plan for implementation, welfare schemes as well as development schemes to help persons cope with the contingencies of old age. Intervention may start prior to retirement itself and help older persons in planning for constructive use of leisure time, possible re-employment, part-time employment. Social workers may keep lists of agencies or individual employers who are in need of personnel and help people find such employment opportunities that suit their abilities and circumstances. Similarly they advise the older persons in how to apply for financial assistance, where to apply for the same and what determines eligibility.

Other Issues affecting older persons

Several other issues affect older persons and require concerted effort by social workers and other professionals. **Elder abuse and neglect** is one such area of concern. Both Overt and Covert abuse have been known to occur among the older persons and it is of increasing concern that older persons are becoming unsafe within the confines of their homes. Economic abuse and exploitation, physical and mental abuse as well as socio-religious abuse (ostracism within society in relation to participation in functions after widowhood etc) are beginning to gain attention by researchers etc. Added to this are the harsh realities of urban metropolises in particular where in older persons are victims of violence and exploitation. Even where economic security is assured, older persons are often exposed to other forms of violence and a spate of newspaper reports in the nineties and thereafter are testimony to this. Mugging, burglaries, murders and homicides are a reality that stare the urban elderly even in a developing country like India.

Other issues **like nutrition of the elderly** in particular the rural elderly is an emerging area of interest. Assessment of nutritional requirements of the elderly is an important pre-requisite for designing meaningful interventions for the elderly. Quoting a study done in the late nineties by Natrajan, it was observed that Anaemia among the rural aged was found to be a common complaint in over 80% of the population as compared to the urban aged (62.7%) (Ramamurti S in Ramamurti PV and Jamuna D 2004).

Similarly malnutrition was found to be much higher in the institutionalized elderly as compared to the non-institutional ones.

Social workers based in institutions such as Old Age Homes work in teams of human service professionals to offer good care and nutrition to older persons. Institutionalised older persons often comprise of the destitute, childless, single, widowed, unmarried and houseless elderly and they require greater attention on all issues related to health and nutrition.

Social workers encourage the setting up of **non-institutional services** so that older persons remain in the confines of their family but receive some support from non-institutional services. Such services may include setting up of Day Care Centres, library and recreational services and other spaces for older persons to attend to leisure time pursuits in a meaningful manner. In addition, programmes and schemes that impart relevant information to older people on welfare measures etc are efficient ways of dealing with older persons. Training programmes, initiation of self-help groups, building support structures etc aim at fulfilling objectives of the profession of Social Work. Further, mobile schemes taking services to the doorstep such as the," Meals on Wheels" or Mobile Health Check-ups etc may be initiated in areas that see a need for such interventions. Social work professionals also may train volunteers or personnel in home-based care and in running errands for the elderly etc so that they may live their life with dignity. It has also been suggested that for gerontological social workers, the expertise has to extend to families of the older persons to help them cope with the changes occurring in the elderly.Such programmes may be designed for either the adult children of the elderly or for the youth in order to sensitise them to the challenges and needs of the older populations.

Quoting from the article by the GITT (Geriatric Interdisciplinary Team Training programme of the John A Hartford Foundation) "Social workers with their training in interpersonal relationships, group work and (often) interdisciplinary team skills play a vital role in the development and functioning of the interdisciplinary team unit and in all major phases of its work, including assessment, goal setting and care planning, and monitoring/evaluation. The social worker provides key leadership in identifying psychosocial issues.

The social worker's roles within teams include convener, facilitator, and expert in group work skills which contributes to their ability to foster team collaboration. Interdisciplinary teamwork recognizes that the complexities of older people's problems necessitate a comprehensive and planned approach to their resolution.

As with other members of the interdisciplinary team, the social work interventions benefits the older persons in terms of providing coordinated service, information, skilled services, avoidance of duplication of services, and the introduction of preventive services. The social worker acts as liaison as needed between client and family and the health care system. The social work profession's emphasis on advocacy, and its knowledge about service delivery systems in both public and private sectors, enables social workers to take a lead role in promoting interdisciplinary practice and facilitating the coordination of services, reducing duplication and potentially providing preventive approaches (CSWE in GITT).

Social work intervention faces several challenges. They work with older persons offering support to them and their care-givers. They also offer training programmes for care givers thus contributing to capacity building. They are trained in Case Management and also offer help in effectively monitoring health care services (SWLI).

They work with the disabled elderly and the institutionalized elderly in NGOS, Old –age or Senior Citizens Homes. They impact on policy initiatives and work with the government. They work at the community level and offer insights into schemes and welfare measures for the older persons. At the grass-root level they are key functionaries in implementing the national policy for older persons as also in disbursing the assistance to the older persons. As members of the National Council of Older Persons or in other capacities, they influence the planners in directions that are ageing friendly. They work in a manner that is anti-ageist and does not recognize stereotypes and further, social workers do not look at all aged as if they belong to a homogenous category but instead they recognize the uniqueness and individuality of persons and accord them the dignity that each individual requires and deserves. Research and Development initiatives are a key area for the social workers . Social workers must constantly enrich their understanding and contribute to societal understanding by adding to the research base on issues concerning older populations. In conclusion it may be said that the roles played by a social worker in this area of concern include those of counsellor, advocate, planner, administrator, resource mobiliser, change agent and trainer/educator.

REFERENCES

Bose, A.B. and Gangrade, K.D. (Eds) 1988: *The Ageing in India Problems and Potentialities* Citizenship Development Society and Friedrich Newman, New Delhi, Abhinav Publications.

Census of India 2001: *Census of India-Aged data in 2001Census,* Mizoram Directorate of Census Operation, Aizawl, Mizoram.

Chakraborti, R.D. 2004: *The Ageing of India,* New Delhi, Sage Publications.

Desai, M. and Siva Raju (Eds)1999: *Gerontological Social Work in India, Some Issues and Perspectives,* Delhi, B.K. Publishing Corporation.

GITT: The distinctive role of Gerontological, Social Work, *Journal of Gerontological Social Work,* Dobrof, R.(Ed), Vol.13(3/4) 1998, access from internet source.

Government of India 1999: *National Policy on Older Persons,* Ministry of Social Justice and Empowerment, (accessed through internet sources of Helpage India).

Khanna, S.: *Problem of Aged magnitude- National policy of Older Persons,* paper a presented at National Symposium cum exhibition on Innovation in design for elder care. http://dignity foundation.com/docs/DRKHANNA.ppt.:

Lalhlupuii, K. 2005: *Coping with Spousal Loss due to Cancer Death in Mizoram,* Dissertation submitted in partial fulfilment of the requirements of MSW Degree, Department of Social Work, Mizoram University.

Lalmuanpuii, 2005: *Self-Perceived Life Satisfaction and problems of the Rural Aged,* Dissertation submitted in partial fulfilment of the requirements of MSW Degree, Department of Social Work, Mizoram University.

Lalparmawii, K.C. 2005 : *Menopause, Mental Health and Social Support of Mizo Women,* Dissertation submitted in partial fulfilment of the requirements of MSW Degree, Department of Social Work, Mizoram University.

MUP Gen. Hq. Mizoram. *MUP Constitution:* Mizoram Upa Pawl (Senior Citizens Association of Mizoram) Aizawl.

NISD 2005: *National Initiatives on Care for the Elderly,* National Institute of Social Defence, Ministry of Social Justice and Empowerment, GOI.

Rajan, Irudaya S. 2006: *Population Ageing and Health in India,* Centre for Enquiry intoHealth and Allied themes (http://*www.cehat.org/humanrights/rajan.pdf.*

Ramamurti, P.V. and Jamuna D (Eds) 2004: *Handbook of India Gerontology* New Delhi Serials Publications.

Schaie, K.W. and Sherry L.Willis 2002: *Adult development and Aging,* 5th Edition New Jersey, Prentice-Hall

Sharma, M.L. and Dak T.M. (Eds) 1987: Aging in India-Challenge for the Society, Delhi, Ajanta Publications.

Srinivasan, Sheilu 1998: *Productive Ageing,* The Hindu Folio, October 18th . Chennai

SWLI 2005: *Population Ageing.*

ANNEXURE I

Rapporteurs Report

Lalhriatpuii and James L.T. Thanga

Inaugural Session

The seminar began with a welcome speech from the Chairman of the inaugural session Professor A.K. Agarwal, which was followed by presentation of bouquet to the chief guest, Professor A.N. Rai, Vice Chancellor, Mizoram University. Professor Lianzela, coordinator of the seminar delivered the keynote address. Then, Dr. C.J. Thomas, Director, ICSSR-NERC, Shillong delivered a speech where he stressed upon the importance and the need to study the magnitude of the problems of the elderly not only in Mizoram but the entire North East as well. The inaugural session ended with a speech from the chief guest. In his speech as a chief guest Professor.A.N.Rai mentioned that the elderly people were being neglected not because of globalization but because the young and the elderly were growing apart and living an independent life. He also talked about his personal experiences and stressed upon the need of ageing gracefully.

Technical Session I

Professor Tlanglawma, chairman of the technical session, gave an introductory speech which was followed by presentation of seminar paper by Professor T.C. Nunga entitled *"Social and Economic Status of Elderly Persons in Mizo Society: Past Present and Future Perspective"*. Mr.Thanseia, Editor of MUP journal, presented the second seminar paper on "Ageing *Gracefully: Role and Activities of Mizoram Elderly Association"*. Since Dr. Jane R. Ralte was out of station, her paper *"Health Condition and Access to Health Care Services by Elderly"* was presented by Dr. Zairemthiama.

Discussion Points:

1. A question was raised in Professor .T.C.Nunga's paper, why there is a difference in the growth rate of increased in older people aged 60 and above of Mizoram which is 5.52% from all India figure of 7.7% in 2001. The paper presenter clarified this point by saying that this could be due to the low span of life in Mizoram as compared to the rest of the country.
2. The participants sought clarification on whether funds of MUP came from the state government, SHGs or fund was raised by the members themselves.
3. In the paper presented by Dr Jane R. Ralte (read by Dr. Zairemthiama) it is written that females go to civil hospital for treatment whereas males visit private clinics, a question was raised as to whether this was the mental attitudes of both the males and females or could this be due to monetary problem or women are economically compelled to go to civil hospital. Clear clarification was not made even though the paper presenter stated that this was due to easy availability of gynaecology doctors in civil hospital.
4. Since there is no comprehensive study of the life expectancy of the elderly in Mizoram, the question was much debated over and the chairman of the

technical session proposed that the organizing authority could take this up for follow-up action.

5. The young people should be made aware of the importance of the elderly in the family and in our social life; the elderly people are facing problem due to failure of the family institution.

6. The pastors, church elders and those who preach in the church should also preach the importance of the elderly and the young generation should also spare time or make themselves available for the old people.

7. The Mizoram Synod, the biggest church organisation, observe many special days; a proposal was made also to observe Old Age Day in the church. It was mentioned in this regard that the issue has been discussed in one Presbytery meetings of the Synod though it was not passed. In some churches, Old Age day has been observed at a time convenient to them.

8. It is quite imperative to teach the younger generation how to respect the elderly; we should start from our own family institution.

9. Having an elderly association is good for the society though the state government could not meet all their demand. It was suggested that the association should try not to involve in many things that are out of their ways.

10. As elderly abuse is gradually intruding into our society, the young generation should be encouraged to be polite to the elderly people; positive comments should be passed to the elderly so as to make them comfortable.

11. Much was discussed on the economic security of the elderly. Government employees have pension fund but those who are not employed

do not have security, except their children and grandchildren. Therefore, the young generations and the government should be made aware of this issue.

12. It seemed that life expectation of the age group 60 years and over is more in rural areas than in the urban areas, this could be due to their diets that contain low intake of red meat and also due to regular physical work of the elderly.

13. Young people could not spare their time for the elderly since they are working in offices, shops etc. The elderly who are at home the whole day do not have anyone to entertain them or to chat with him or her. Therefore it is necessary to create a Day Care Centre for the elderly either at state level or local level. Funds for the Centre can be collected from the relatives of the elder people who are to be kept in the centre.

14. Having social interactions is good for the health of the elderly. It is said that computers create a gap between the young and the old people, but computers can be used as an entertainment facility for the elders as well. Being old and staying in the rural areas is quite saddening; therefore the Senior Citizens Association should take up the matter of providing a better living condition for the elder living in the rural areas.

15. Lots of investment opportunities are available these days which could generate income in the future. It would be a wise decision to avail these opportunities while we are still young. The income so generated could serve as one of the economic securities when one becomes old.

16. An important suggestion was made regarding the opening up of a new Gerontology/Geriatric department in the Mizoram University.

Technical Session II

The second technical session was presided over by Pu H. Raltawna, Vice President MUP. Lalbiakkimi presented a seminar paper on "*Social and Economic Security Programme for the Elderly Persons: Role of State Government.*" Then Dr. Vanlalchhawna presented his paper on "*Growth and Magnitude of Elderly Population in Mizoram*". Lastly, Dr. Kalpana N Desai presented a paper titled" *Social Work Intervention with the Elderly*". After these papers were presented there was a lively discussion.

Discussion Points:

1. The elderly persons themselves should try to make use of their leisure at its maximum.
2. Social Security Schemes should be made for the elderly who are non-government employees.
3. There was a long discussion on the secret for living a long life, reason cited being- non-use of intoxicants, self discipline, taking a bath in the early morning, jogging, swimming, no red meat, eating sea food as much as possible, good heart, positive outlook etc.
4. In Mizoram, there is a bus fare concession for the elderly, seats are also vacated by other passengers for the elderly persons in the bus and there is also doctor consultation fees concession, these are good practices which should be continued by the young generations.

ANNEXURE II

STATE POLICY FOR OLDER PERSONS

(Formulated by Social Welfare Department, Government of Mizoram)

With a wealth of ideas and suggestions contributed in the state level workshop held on 9th and 10th October, 2003 at I and PR Auditorium by the Social Welfare Department under the sponsorship of the Ministry of Social Justice and Empowerment, Government of India, the State Policy for Older Persons (SPOP) has been prepared.

I. State Council for Older Persons (SCOP)

Instituting the State Council for Older Persons with the Chief Minister as the Chairperson of the Council assumes the first important policy.

II. The State Policy for Older Persons (SPOP) has been formulated thus:-

III. Psycho-Social:

(a) The Social Defence Branch of the Social Welfare Department is entrusted and specially assigned to deal with matters concerning the needs and welfare of older persons.

(b) Making uniform age of 60 for extending concessions.

(c) To enumerate the aged of 60 years old and above from the electoral list and to acknowledge the EPIC cards as confide proof for senior citizens identification.

(d) Taking every possible step for the security of older persons by government and especially the community based organisations.

(e) To teach the younger generation to acknowledge and celebrate the value of old age.

(f) To propagate and encourage the family as the primary caregivers for the aged.

(g) Suitable projects should be formulated for older persons whereby they would be in a position to utilize their knowledge, wisdom and talent and to encourage them to work where they can.

(h) To set up old age home and recreational complexes in every district from available resources of the state and central government.

(i) A scheme for excursion for senior citizens to be formulated to enable them to see places of importance within the state and the country.

(j) To allow for concessional rates in Mizoram Houses and Government Accommodation for older persons.

(k) To encourage and assist the elders- especially of the age group of 60-70 years to organize their pool of human resources discipline wise, with a view of utilize their knowledge and experience for the advancement and benefit of the younger generation (example: Tutorial Institutions by the education discipline resources groups would go a long way in up-gradation of merit of students with potential for meritorious performance especially for the poorer sections of the society).

(l) To introduce a subject in the college and university curriculum regarding "Ageing" with a view to understand the perspective of aging academically and built up a wealth of data and studies which would serve to be a valuable resource for the planning process of the state government.

IV. Health Sector

1 Transit accommodation for the older persons who come to Aizawl and Lunglei for medical treatment;

2 Setting up a hospice for terminally ill and cancer patients. This is to be taken up by the nodal department on a project mode;

3 Organize free mobile clinic for the elderly in every district of Mizoram. Geriatric Ward to be opened in Civil Hospitals;

4 Seminar and awareness programs should be organized to acquaint the elderly of the common ailments and diseases that befall them and they are prone to.

5 Concessions to be extended to older persons in respect of medical consultation fees. This should however be determined by their income bracket.

V. Economic Empowerment:

1. The state government to take initiative for full coverage of old age pension in the state and raising the amount of old age pension from the existing rate.

2. Introduction of income generating schemes for senior citizens sourced from both state and central funding.

3 To impress upon the nationalized Banks to offer assistance in fostering savings with a special focus on the welfare of the senior citizens as well as for the citizens at large with a view to inculcate the need to save for the evening of their lives.

4 Steps to be taken with the active participation of the Financial Institutions and Bank not only to encourage savings but to educate the elders on the scope of availing loans.

5 To seek the active participation of the various Insurance Companies to educate the elders on the merits of availing suitable policies for the aged.

6 Special dispensation for the deprived aged in availing of Housing Loans and Residential House site allotment by the government.

7 The nodal department should facilitate the convergence of various state and centrally funded schemes for the benefit of the elder citizens. Special reservation should be made with proportionate percentage reservation of the budget against various developmental schemes, e.g SGRY, Housing, Welfare, other development department, etc. for the elderly.

VI. Transportation (Mobility):

1. Concessions to be made for the older persons in MST Buses, City Buses and Town Buses.

To utilize the voter ID card for concessions in MST Buses, Town buses and City Buses.

VII. Legal Provisions

The foundation of legal protection for older person is inherent in the Fundamental Rights of the Constitution. With special reference to the older persons there are a number of statutory provisions that affirm the protection of their rights. For instance, there is the Code of Criminal Procedures, 1973 Section 125 which inter alia, guarantees the safeguard for the older persons whereby if the children are not willing to take care of their aged parents, they can be taken to court.

The state government should set up special cells to cater to the legal needs and advice of the elderly especially in upholding their rights – e.g. property matters, inheritance issues, and other financial related issues and disputes, legal education on writing of Will and other documentation.

VIII. Other Self-Actualisation Measures

Media exposures and special programs: Special forums e.g. discussions in TV programs, and topical talks on various categories of events and issues which may be cultural, social, political, historical etc. These may be facilitated in AIR, DD and other local channels and media.

IX. Multi Sectoral Intervention:

1. All departments must be impressed to be prompt in settling the terminal claims of their retiring functionaries.
2. All Departments to be advised to set aside a special welfare fund from out of their budget for the aged. The rationale behind this being that the welfare of the aged is a multi-sectoral responsibility and that each department should contribute in the welfare activity of the elderly persons in society.

3. Non-developmental departments also have equally important part to play in the welfare of the elderly. For instance, the Accounts and Treasury Department may organize Pension (Adalats) Court as is practised in some larger states of the country. These adalats are highly laudable intervention, which are basically meant to be a fast track redressal camp/programme for pensioners.

ACTION ARISING OUT OF THE SPOP:

The state government through the nodal department i.e. Social Welfare Department shall draw up a comprehensive State Action Plan. The Action Plan which will emerge from the above stated policy for older pensions will set out clear goals both long and short term. The affirmative centres, which will unequivocally spell out the various roles assigned to the various wings and departments of the state government and also to the banks, insurance agencies, other financial institutions, NGOs and community based organisations etc., as well.

(LALRAMTHANGA TOCHHAWNG)
Secretary
Social Welfare Department
Government of Mizoram

BIBLIOGRAPHY

Bose, A.B. and Gangrade K.D. (Eds) 1988: *The Ageing in India Problems and Potentialities* Citizenship Development Society and Friedrich Newman, New Delhi, Abhinav Publications.

Census of India 2001: *Census of India-Aged data in 2001Census,* Mizoram Directorate of Census Operation, Aizawl, Mizoram.

Census of India 1991, *Ageing Population of India - An Analysis of the 1991 Census Data, Registrar* General, India, New Delhi.

Census of India, 2001, *Mizoram Primary Census Abstract,* Directorate of Census Operation, Mizoram.

Chakraborti, R.D.2004 : *The Ageing of India,* New Delhi, Sage Publications

Desai, M. and Siva Raju (Eds)1999: *Gerontological Social Work in India, Some Issues and Perspectives,* Delhi, B.K. Publishing Corporation.

German, P.S., Fried, L.P., 1989: *Annual Review of Public Health,* Vol. 10.

GITT : The distinctive role of Gerontological, Social Work, Journal of Gerontological Social Work, Dobrof R.(Ed), Vol.13(3/4) 1998, access from internet source.

Government of India 1999: *National Policy on Older Persons,* Ministry of Social Justice and Empowerment, (accessed through internet sources of Helpage India).

Government of Karnataka, *Towards Equity, Quality and Integrity in Health, Final Report of the Task Force on Health and Family Welfare.* Task Force on Health and Family Welfare, April 2001.

Khanna, S : *'Problem of Aged magnitude- National policy of Older persons'*, paper presented at National Symposium cum exhibition on Innovation in design for elder care. http://dignity foundation.com/docs/DRKHANNA.ppt.

Lalhlupuii, K. 2005: *"Coping with Spousal Loss due to cancer death in Mizoram"*, Dissertation submitted in partial fulfilment of the requirements of MSW Degree, Department of Social Work, Mizoram University.

Lalmuanpuii, 2005: *'Self-Perceived Life Satisfaction and problems of the Rural Aged'*, Dissertation submitted in partial fulfilment of the requirements of MSW Degree, Department of Social Work, Mizoram University.

Lalparmawii, KC 2005 : "Menopause, Mental Health and Social Support of Mizo Women", Dissertation submitted in partial fulfilment of the requirements of MSW Degree, Department of Social Work, Mizoram University.

MUP Gen. Hq. Mizoram. *MUP Constitution*: Mizoram Upa Pawl (Senior Citizens Association of Mizoram) Aizawl.

NISD 2005: *National Initiatives on Care for the Elderly*, National Institute of Social Defence, Ministry of Social Justice and Empowerment, GOI.

Park, K., 2005 *Parks Text book of Preventive and Social Medicine*, 18th Edition, Jan.

Rajan, Irudaya S. 2006: *Population Ageing and Health in India*, Centre for Enquiry intoHealth and Allied themes (http://www.cehat.org/humanrights/rajan.pdf

Ramamurti, P.V. and Jamuna, D. (Eds) 2004: *Handbook of India Gerontology,* New Delhi, Serials Publications.

Registrar General Census Commissioner, *India, Population Projections for India and the states, 1996-* 2016 of 1996.

Registrar General Census Commissioner, *India, Ageing Population of India- An analysis of the 1991* Census Data of 1999.

Schaie, K.W. and Sherry, L. Willis 2002: *Adult Development and Aging,* 5th Edition New Jersey, Prentice-Hall.

Sharma, M.L. and Dak, T.M. (Eds) 1987: Aging in India-Challenge for the Society, Delhi, Ajanta Publications.

Srinivasan, Sheilu 1998: "Productive Ageing", *The Hindu,* October 18th, Chennai.

SWLI 2005 : *Population Ageing*

UN Secretariat *World Population Ageing 1950-2050* Population Division, DESA, www.un.org/esa/sovdev

VAHI (1997), *Report of the Independent Commission on Health in India, Chapter 14, Health* Problems of Specialised Groups.

Weir, J. H. (1967). *Royal Society of Health Journal, 87,* 144.

INDEX

H

I

J

L

M

N